More of Him, Less of Me

A Doctor's Devotional for Spiritual Health

Jason David Eubanks, MD

DAWN TREADER

Jason David Eubanks, MD

ISBN-13: 978-1-7325322-0-5
ISBN-10:1732532206

Unless otherwise noted, Scripture quotations are from the NIV translation.

DEDICATION

To every heart that prays, "Teach me your way, Lord, that I may rely on your faithfulness; give me an undivided heart, that I may fear your name"(Ps 86:11).

To every friend and family member whose prayers have helped sustain and encourage me in life's hardest moments.

To every writer, past and present, whose words have been the Spirit's instrument in helping me find my way.

Jason David Eubanks, MD

CONTENTS

Acknowledgments i

Foreword iii

Preface v

1 January 1

2 February 35

3 March 65

4 April 99

5 May 131

6 June 165

7 July 197

8 August 231

9 September 265

10 October 297

11 November 331

12 December 363

Jason David Eubanks, MD

ACKNOWLEDGMENTS

My deepest thanks to my Editor, Gail Eubanks, PhD, and
Assistant Editor, William Eubanks, MA. Your support and contributions
to this book (and the work of my life) have been priceless. I love you both.

Thank you *Abba*, my Father, for loving me; thank you Jesus for saving me;
thank you Spirit for living in me. This work is your work.

Foreword

Folk wisdom says you don't really know someone until you "walk a mile in their shoes." Since that can never really be done—the same mile in the same shoes—the next best option is to walk side by side. Miles later when you've worn the soles off your shoes, you get a pretty good glimpse of the soul of the one you walk beside.

Over the years, I have walked hundreds of miles beside Dr. Jason David Eubanks. We've worn the soles off our hiking boots clambering over boulders in the Rockies; meandering through museums in Europe; and treading muddy goat paths, glaciers, volcanic rock beds, and the African bush. Curiosity and awe were our daily compass. Joy came in unexpected bursts of light: The morning sun infusing color in the stained-glass windows of Paris' St. Chapelle. A full rainbow arching through the Icelandic mist. A sunset blazing an amber halo on lions' manes. I saw nature's wonders and the artistry of human hands write songs of praise in Jason's soul. And, because he was an English major at the university where I teach, I heard great writers stretch his mind as he read through centuries of ideas and shared with me authors, poems and passages he loved.

Amazing as these family trips were, the best journey we have shared can't be plotted on a map. GPS won't get you there. It can't be photographed. It's the daily walk of faith. We've been walking side by side on that shared path since Jason as a child heard the power and love of God in bedtime stories and songs: Aslan's roar in Narnia and the lyrics, "My God is so big, so strong and so mighty, there is nothing my God cannot do." In the years since, the best places he has visited are where God visited him. The titles of some readings in this book mark spots on that map of his heart: "Abounding Grace," "Transforming Tears," "Binding Love," "For the Joy of Obeying," and "Gentlest of Ways."

More of Him, Less of Me is filled with postcards from these places God took Jason to learn His majesty, mercy, relentless love and uncompromising holiness. The life stories behind some entries involve both rugged terrain and moments of exquisite beauty. But, the destination —to know "Christ is All"—has been worth it. It's been a joy to share his journey as traveling friend, professor, editor, and best of all, mom.

The "spiritual postcards" in this book are powerful for me on two different levels. The first is the sheer example they set of discipline and focus. These daily meditations are the work of a working man reading his way through the Bible in a year. That alone, from my perspective, is a reason to read them. By 7:30AM most mornings, Jason's penetrating blue eyes are peering over a surgical mask into the interior network of someone's spine, but they have already studied a Bible passage. His gloved fingers, which will walk with grace along spinal discs and nerves, have already scripted the day's reflection. This "just do it" discipline inspires me.

Besides this power of leading by example, I love the way Jason captures the sharp contrast between the soft mercy of God and His tough commands. His reflections call us to a high bar of holiness. God's voice comes as Coach as well as Comforter. The promises that sustained Jason's faith in tough years radiate hope. He does not, however, sugarcoat or hide the life Christ calls His disciples to live. Written the year following a season of genuine wrestling with God, Jason's tone exudes the "all in" spirit of one who has decided to follow Jesus whatever the cost. It reveals the faith of a youth becoming the conviction of a man. As such, his reflections take a hard look at the hard costs of shaping a heart that is soft enough to reveal "More of Him, Less of Me." He models how this can come to be.

Some of Jason's entries reveal that God's Word acts as a "fountain of life," washing over us with refreshment and gentle healing. They are like the smooth stones he loved finding as a boy on the shores of Lake Erie. Before skipping the paper-thin ones on the skin of the water—shattering sun rays as they danced on the lake—he would marvel how smooth they were. Unable to see the churning and abrasion below the surface, he wondered how rough and ragged edges could be rubbed so round and smooth. Many of his entries reveal this slow soul-work of grace.

Others entries show how the Word of God is more like the chisel that shaped sculptures Jason loves: Rodin's "The Hand of God" and Michelangelo's "Pieta." At times, God's Word can be "sharp" and "penetrating," as it hacks off chunks of whatever blocks His glory in us. It may also cut through the comfortable lies of our culture. Some of the toughest entries in the book signal places where Jason felt the hard chisel of God's grace at work on him. As the stone submits to a sculptor, he came to see God's hand doing what Michelangelo did when he said, "I saw the angel in the marble and carved until I set him free."

Are we willing to let God see the angel in us and work to set it free? When Jesus walked and talked with His disciples, He began that work in them. This book continues that conversation. As you read these reflections on God's Word, you will be in the company of a pilgrim wearing out the soles of his hiking boots on the path towards home. Your soul may be smoothed to skip like a stone on water or some stony parts chiseled to free "the angel" in you. Either way, the joy of the journey will be walking beside a man reading the Word and committed to, "Do justice, to love mercy, and to walk humbly with [his] God"(Micah 6:8).

Gail Kepler Eubanks, PhD

Editor, *More of Him, Less of Me*

Preface

*Every Christian would agree that a man's spiritual health
is exactly proportional to his love for God.[1]*
—C.S. Lewis

The physician and evangelist Luke wrote his gospel "so that you may know the certainty of the things you have been taught"(Luke 1:4). In a similar spirit, *More of Him, Less of Me* is my attempt as a doctor to strengthen our spiritual health by reminding us of God's essential truths and inspiring us to love Him more. This effort is the product of obedience. While called to perform complex spine surgery during the daylight hours, when God's Spirit called my mornings and evenings to write reflections on His Word, in grace I obeyed. *More of Him, Less of Me* emerged.

As the "midnight" work of a surgeon, this book is not, as C.S. Lewis says of his *Reflections on the Psalms,* primarily "a work of scholarship." Like Lewis, I am "no higher critic, no ancient historian, no archeologist. I write for the unlearned about things in which I am unlearned myself." [2]

But precisely because this book is not a "work of scholarship," because I am a spiritually "unlearned" person daily rubbing shoulders with the world's pain and brokenness, this devotional may relate to many. The perspectives contained in this book are hard-earned: Full of the spiritual sweat, tears, and shouts of joy of a child of God. They are the lessons learned by a pilgrim of faith stumbling forward on his homeward journey.

As such, in some ways this devotional is a spiritual autobiography of that journey. It is a one year walk through the Bible, narrated by a man's over thirty year pilgrimage of faith. All along my way has been encouraged and informed not only by family and friends, but also the voices of many saints who have gone before us. This devotional also intends to honor these disciples who have so profoundly contributed to my spiritual life. As "friends" of my soul, their influences are woven into the pages that follow.

From C.S. Lewis and J.R.R. Tolkien I have learned the reality and complexity of spiritual warfare. G.K. Chesterton has reminded me to live a life of spiritual wonder. Henri Nouwen taught me that I am a beloved child of God. Dietrich Bonhoeffer put a price tag on spiritual discipleship. Andrew Murray impressed upon me the primacy of humility and the power of prayer. A.W. Tozer led me to the personhood of the Spirit, while Thomas Watson and Soren Kierkegaard reminded me what it means to love God. Oswald Chambers, who I read daily for years, instructed me in the nuanced voice of God's Spirit. The list goes on.

---

[1] C.S. Lewis, *The Four Loves* (New York: Houghton Mifflin Harcourt, 1988), 217.
[2] C.S. Lewis, *Reflections on the Psalms* (New York: HarperCollins, 1986), 1.

From the influence of these voices, *More of Him, Less of Me* strives to inspire spiritually healthy living. Jesus said, "It is not the healthy who need a doctor, but the sick. I have not come to call the righteous, but sinners"(Mark 2:17). Christ reminds us: We are spiritually sick, sick unto death apart from His transformative work in our lives.

But once transformed, we have a part to play in staying spiritually healthy. A.W. Tozer says, "Our error today is that we do not *expect* a converted man to be a transformed man...."[3] Perhaps this is because we recognize the daily challenge before us. While the transformed life is always fulfilling and continually bathed in God's amazing love, it is rigorous and sometimes costly. It invites us to be disciples committed to the disciplines of spiritual health. And, as Oswald Chambers reminds us, "It takes a tremendous amount of discipline to live the worthy and excellent life of a disciple of Jesus in the realities of life."[4]

Discipline is the key word here. Just as a doctor's surgery or prescription for healthier living is only as good as our compliance to the treatment recommendations, so also our spiritual lives will only remain healthy if we commit to keep them so. We decide to make our lives *more of Him and less of us*. God's grace enables us to do it.

This daily devotional is my answer to helping us achieve this goal. Like an effective doctor's visit, I hope this book will encourage, but also challenge. I intend to affirm the steps we've already taken, and push us to better things. My aim is honesty about what is broken, and clarity about how best to heal it. Some of the truths exposed, like a new medical diagnosis, may surprise us. They may even spiritually "shock" us as they seek to convert the irregular beat of our spiritual hearts to God's intended rhythm. Admittedly, not every perspective will be universally agreed upon. But then, neither is every physician's medical judgement. We do our best, whether in the office, home or on the spiritual battlefield, to interpret what we think is good and right. We are works in progress, led by the Spirit.

May God's Spirit lead you to a deeper understanding and love of Him as you spend this year making your life *more of Him and less of you*.

Jason David Eubanks, MD
Chief of Spine Surgery, University Hospitals Ahuja Medical Center
Associate Professor, Department of Orthopaedic Surgery
Case Western Reserve University School of Medicine
Cleveland, OH

---

[3] A.W. Tozer, *Man, The Dwelling Place of God* (Public Domain), 126.
[4] Oswald Chambers, *My Utmost for His Highest* (Grand Rapids: Discovery House Publishers, 1992), July 7.

In the deep nights I dig for you, O Treasure!
To seek you over the wide world I roam.
For all abundance is but meager measure
Of your bright beauty which is yet to come.

—Rainer Rilke
The Book of Hours (Public Domain)

JANUARY

January 1

This is the Day

Psalm 118:24—This is the day the Lord has made; let us rejoice and be glad in it.

When you decide that today is God's day, that He made it and He owns it, everything changes! There is no longer room for dwelling in doubt or fear. Worry suddenly seems silly and unnecessary, and the insecurities that fettered you yesterday are lost in the arms of your loving Father.

The primary reason so many of us struggle with the various plagues of inner turmoil is that we have not declared the day as God's. We still live under the illusion that we are in control. We consider ourselves the absolute masters of our daily destiny. When the days begin to unfold before us, and we start to see that this fixed belief may not be true, panic sets in. Joy is stolen from us because we have allowed ourselves to be victimized by our own faulty paradigm.

The fault in this is ours. God wants us to approach today, and every day, with the full and resolute understanding that the day belongs to Him—*this is the day the Lord has made!* The Creator who set the sun and moon in the sky, who littered the heavens with stars, and made the intricacies of your body and mine, is the very God who controls the details of the day. The Lord dresses the lilies of the field and feeds the sparrows of the air (Matt 6: 26-29). This same God knows our needs and vulnerabilities this day and the next.

Are you being tempted? Jesus was also tempted and emerged victorious (Matt 4:1-11). Do you have enemies attacking you? Christ was betrayed, beaten, and killed only to rise again in eternal triumph. Thirsty? Jesus hung on the cross and said, "I am thirsty"(John 19:28). There is nothing in this day that our Lord has not either created or personally experienced and conquered.

The God who says to you, "Do not let your hearts be troubled," "Do not fret," and "Do not be terrified; do not be discouraged," speaks as the God who owns today and all that it holds for you (John 14:1; Ps 37:1; Josh 1:9). He wants you to rejoice and be glad in everything that lies before you today—sun or rain, love or hate, hunger or feasting—knowing that they all belong to Him, and He will use them for His glory and your good (Rom 8:28).

You can be a prisoner of today or you can reign over it with the King who owns it. The choice is yours. Joy and freedom come when you decide to declare, *"This is the day the Lord has made!"*

January 2

Delighted in Me

2 Samuel 22:20—He brought me out into a spacious place; He rescued me because He delighted in me.

We must get rid of any notion that salvation in Jesus Christ has anything to do with merit or pity. Rather, I am saved as a "gift of God"(Eph 2:8). But this gift is not given as some sentimental act of pity. To the contrary, His gift is the ultimate act of a love that *delights in me*! As C.S. Lewis reminds us, "To please God…to be a real ingredient in the divine happiness…to be loved by God, not merely pitied, but *delighted* in as an artist delights in his work or a father in a son—it seems impossible, a weight or burden of glory which our thoughts can hardly sustain. But it is so."[5]

At the end of his life, David understood this truth better than most. David knew God had rescued him from "the hand of all his enemies"(2 Sam 22:1) simply because He *delighted in him*. David's life, like yours and mine, was full of sin—his was adultery, polygamy with foreign wives, pre-meditated murder, and a pride that cost the lives of thousands. He was not brought into *a spacious place* because he deserved God's favor. He was rescued because the Lord *delighted in him*.

Are you convinced today that the Lord *delights in you*? Do you understand that you are saved not because of your merit, but because of a love that rejoices over you? Have you considered that this love runs so deep and so true that it was willing to die for you? If you are in Christ, you must be filled with the knowledge that "The Lord your God is with you, He is mighty to save. He will take great *delight in you*, He will quiet you with His love, He will rejoice over you with singing"(Zeph 3:17).

To be this object of God's *delight* is the highest gift we can be given. It is same way God refers to His only Son—"Here is my servant, whom I uphold, my chosen one in whom I *delight*…"(Is 42:1). As the recipients of God's *delight*, we are given the place of sons and daughters —"You are all sons of the Most High"(Ps 82:6).

Rejoice today that though we are undeserving, we are children of God! Let us celebrate, that though sin makes us pitiful, we are not pitied, but loved with an unimaginable *delight!* We have a Father who longs to bring us into a spacious place, simply because…He *delights in us!*

---

[5] C.S. Lewis, *The Weight of Glory* (New York: HarperCollins, 2001), 39.

4

Love One Another

John 13:35—By this all men will know that you are my disciples, if you love one another.

The litmus test of our discipleship commitment to Christ is our *love for one another.* It is not pious living or perfectly crafted sermons that tell the world we belong to Jesus: it is our *love for one another.* Piety and charismatic language can be self-serving; but love that is true, love that is Christ-like, is the exact opposite. John says, "This is how we know what love is: Jesus Christ laid down His life for us"(1 John 3:16). To love as Christ loves comes at a great cost: We must lay down our lives for our brothers and sisters as He did for us.

To be fair, loving others needn't be a painful experience. Often, it can be the most meaningful and rewarding experience life can offer us. It can be argued that the life that has not truly loved has not been lived. But love is always hard work, and it is invariably costly. It requires us to do what we sometimes do not want to do, to give up what we would rather hold on to, and to go where we have no desire to be. The true disciple of Christ understands: "Love in [Jesus] was pure action. There was no moment, not a single one in His life, when love in Him was merely the inaction of feeling, which hunts for words while it lets time slip by, or a mood which is self-satisfying, dwelling on itself with no task to perform— no, His love was pure action."[6] As Jesus moved in love, so must we: "let us not love with words or tongue but with actions and truth"(1 John 3:18).

When the world looks at your life, do they see the motive force of Christ's love? Do they observe the "pure action" of Jesus? As disciples of Christ, we must not succumb to the warm and fuzzy notion of love that is so prevalent in contemporary society. Our love must be the love that tells the world we are disciples of Christ. This kind of love is *pure action.* It lays down its life and goes against the grain of every natural inclination.

Ask the Lord today to give you the grace to love as Christ loved— with *pure action.* This will only happen as you decide your life will become *more of Him and less of you.*

---

[6] Soren Kierkegaard, *Works of Love* (New York: HarperPerennial, 2009), 106.

January 4

The Weeping Necessity

1 Samuel 30:4—So David and his men wept aloud until they had no strength left to weep.

The capacity to weep is a prerequisite for intimacy with the Lord. Until I have, like David and his men, *wept aloud until [I have] no strength left to weep*, I will never get to the place of knowing the heart of God and my sufficiency in Him alone. At first, our capacity to weep is on the line of ourselves—and it must be so. The frontier of my heart must be conquered before I can go to new places beyond self.

We see this in the tears of David and his men. They were robbed of everything they had cherished. The Amalekites destroyed the lives David's men lived in Ziklag and David found himself "distressed because the men were talking of stoning him…"(1 Sam 30:6). David wept until he had no strength to weep, and only in this moment of total destitution, this nadir of weakness and vulnerability, was he able to find "strength in the Lord his God"(1 Sam 30:6). Until David was broken, reduced to poverty and robbed of all he loved, he was unable to be filled with the strength he needed to rally his men and go forth in the power of God. Unless I too have *wept until my strength is gone*, I cannot hope to be filled with the strength of God—too much of me still remains. I must be emptied to be filled.

But as I grow in my relationship with the Lord, my capacity to weep will change its object and its tenor. I will begin to mature into Christ-like sensitivity, to be "more deeply moved"(John 11:38) by the lives of those around me. "Jesus wept"(John 11:35), not over His life, His own sinfulness or His destitution at the hands of men, but because of the pain He saw in the lives of all those around Him. The more the Spirit of God lives in us, the more readily we will weep with the suffering of the lost. And it is these tears of the heart that will mobilize our intercessory prayer and service. It is the weeping that will cause us to do God's work.

Have you wept over the tragedy of your own life, its brokenness apart from God and the glorious victory He gave you in Christ? Have you walked with Jesus closely enough to know the tears that move you to do His work in the lives of others? God's people are called to be a joyful people, not weeping willows. But it is only possible to live with the joy of Christ when we have wept deeply and completely, first for ourselves, and then for the world around us.

Have you wept?

January 5

Every Day Manna

Exodus 16:35—The Israelites ate manna for forty years…until they reached the border of Canaan.

Perhaps the most remarkable thing about the manna of God was not the bread itself, or the fact that it fell from the sky, but rather the faithfulness of its provision over forty years of wandering in the desert. The manna God rained down on His people was not a one-time miracle. It lacked the splendor of the parting Red Sea, but had the consistency of the rising sun. It came without fail, six days a week, for forty years. Only the cloud and the pillar of fire that led the people were more constant in their presence.

And yet, despite this daily bread, the Israelites grumbled. Instead of praising God for the consistency of His provision, they bemoaned the sameness. They failed to see each day of manna as a new instance of grace, a miracle every morning. How like you and me!

Are not some of the greatest gifts in our lives those we take for granted, like the manna at the feet of the Israelites? Many of us go decades of our lives without a single health problem. Our bodies carry on complex processes, flawlessly, without our ever thinking about it. Or perhaps we have been blessed with parents who have prayed over our lives since birth, a spouse who has faithfully loved us for years, or a steady job that pays the bills even if it does not bring the personal fulfillment we long for. Each of our lives have some manna, some daily grace of God that helps sustain us over the years. Too often it goes largely unnoticed and unappreciated amidst the daily grumbling.

The secret to a full life in the Spirit is to find in the same mercies, however small, new mercy every morning (Lam 3:23). If we do not recognize and give thanks for God's grace in the persistent mercies of our lives, then we miss the opportunity to be filled with joy and to prepare the way for even more blessing—"Whoever has will be given more, and they will have an abundance"(Matt 13:12).

What is the neglected manna in your life? The Israelites took a portion of their manna and placed it in a jar before the Lord so that they would never forget God's faithful provision (Ex 16:33). Is there a token you can keep to always remember God's daily goodness in your life? Declare before God and others your gratefulness for the faithfulness of the Lord, the *everyday manna* in your life. Find in the same mercies the new mercy of a God who is sustaining you day by day on the way to the Promised Land.

7

January 6

Own Your Pain

Proverbs 14:10—Each heart knows its own bitterness….

There is a divine personalization to pain. Each heart knows it own unique sorrow. The loss that you have sustained, the hatred that you have endured, and the hunger pangs that you have felt are yours, and yours alone. Even those who have shared these pains with you will not know them the same way. God never intended them to.

Too often we glibly categorize pain. Perhaps this is an effort to tame or heal it, as if it were some well-defined disease that could be universally cured. But no one manifestation of pain is the same. This uniqueness gives it incredible power for good or evil. God intends it for good—the instrument of our perfecting. But so long as our pain is not our own, so long as it is a category or a collective experience, it is powerless to refine us. And more often than not, it can be the devil's tool in undoing us through a wicked cynicism and despair. Therefore, "The main question is, 'Do you *own your pain*?'" and have you come to "integrate your pain into your way of being in the world…?"[7]

When you have the courage to *own your pain*, to claim and value it as from God, you stop being a victim of a seemingly chaotic and senseless universe. You start becoming the child of God that you were intended to be. The unique pain in your life has been allowed by the direct providence of a Father who loves you more than you can imagine! Everything you have suffered up till now, every pain that is yet to come, has been woven into the intricate design of who God wants you to be.

When you begin to see the uniqueness of your pain, you begin to understand the amazing love and wisdom of a Father who is raising you up to be the child that He desires. Chastised here, corrected there, you are not a victim. You are a chosen child disciplined in a love that often involves sorrow. But this pain is your gift. When unwrapped and treasured, it will reveal your Father's love in a unique way.

If you choose to understand the uniqueness of your own pain, you will never again make assumptions or judge the anguish of another. You cannot know their pain—only Jesus does. But your pain can be a "concrete way in which you participate in the pain of humanity,"[8] as it softens your heart more into the heart of Jesus. In this way, you will be ready for God's service. And ultimately, your own sorrow will lead you to the joy that "no one else can share"(Prov 14:10).

---

[7] Henri Nouwen, *The Inner Voice of Love* (New York: Image Books, 1998), 72
[8] Ibid, 103.

Abounding Grace

2 Corinthians 9:8—And God is able to make all grace abound to you, so that in all things at all times, having all that you need, you will abound in every good work.

We regularly forget that *God is able.* Though our Bibles may be open to revealed truth and countless examples of His *abounding grace*, when it comes to the details of our lives, suddenly God becomes impotent. We don't see how He could possibly care about our daily minutiae. So instead of trusting in God's grace and provision and taking Him at His word, we worry and waste our efforts. And yet, Jesus said, "do not worry about your life, what you will eat or drink, or about your body, what you will wear. Is not life more important…?"(Matt 6:25).

But while worry and anxious efforts are the antithetical signs to a Spirit-filled life, neither are we called to live lives of care-free indolence that waits around for God to do what we should do ourselves. It is sinful to worry. But it is equally sinful to slothfully cease from work. We are not called to be sluggards or to lack initiative. Solomon reminds us, "The sluggard craves and gets nothing, but the desires of the diligent are fully satisfied"(Prov 13:4). Elsewhere, he reminds us, "All hard work brings a profit…"(Prov 14:23). Indeed, God Himself is always working: "My Father is always at His work to this very day, and I [Jesus] too am working"(John 5:17).

If the Master is working, so must the servant. Whatever work God has given me to do, I am to "work at it with all [my] heart, as working for the Lord…"(Col 3:23). When I dedicate my work to the Lord and trust His grace in the details of that "ministry," I can have assurance that He WILL provide all that I need. I am to work, but not to worry. I trust in His *abounding grace!*

Do you doubt that God is able to meet your needs? Do you believe His grace "is sufficient for you"(2 Cor 12:9)? Are you convinced that He is preparing "a place for you"(John 14:3) in your eternal home as well as providing for the details of today and tomorrow?

If you are doubting God's provision, then you are saying, "God is not able." You are putting reins on the *abounding grace* of the Lord in your life. God knows what you need better than you do: "your Father knows what you need before you ask Him"(Matt 6:8). Therefore, as you work, "seek first the Kingdom of God and His righteousness, and all these things will be given to you as well"(Matt 6:33). The richness of Christ will be yours. He will give you all you need so that His work in you may abound for the glory of His name. Release the reins and let His *abounding grace* run free in your life!

January 8

Only After

John 12:16—At first His disciples did not understand all this. Only after...did they realize....

It is more the rule than the exception that our spiritual understanding is marked by the "only after." We, like the disciples, are often slow to see God's purposes in our lives (Matt 15:16). The disciples had read the prophets. They knew the Scripture and the words which predicted the works Christ fulfilled. And yet, when Jesus rode into Jerusalem on the back of a young donkey, *at first His disciples did not understand.* They forgot the words of Zechariah—"Rejoice greatly, Daughter of Zion! Shout, Daughter of Jerusalem! See, your King comes to you, righteous and victorious, lowly and riding on a donkey..."(Zech 9:9). Perhaps distracted by the energy of the moment or blinded by their preconceived expectations, it is *only after* Jesus is glorified that the full realization of Christ's fulfillment of the Scriptures becomes known to His followers.

If this was true for the disciples, what is true for you and me? What has the Holy Spirit been whispering into our inattentive ears? Perhaps He is speaking as plainly as the prophets and yet, wrapped up in your busy life and its many concerns, you cannot hear Him. Maybe there is some pressing concern to which you have reached a forgone conclusion and you are missing the meaning of the Christ who is riding before you on a young donkey.

Too often we forfeit the true joy God intends for us because we have not listened to what He has been clearly telling us all along. Sadly, it is *only after* we have gone through some crisis or run down some unnecessary road that we finally see the full meaning of what the Lord has been saying from the beginning. Had we been listening, we might have enjoyed the full measure of the moment—the triumphal entry, past, present and future. We might have spared ourselves years of wandering.

The disciples' experience teaches us to listen carefully to all that the Lord is speaking to us in the present. Let us make it our goal to listen so well that we catch the full meaning of every moment and live less of our lives in the spiritual retrospect of *only after*. Just think where we might go with God by reclaiming all the time we have spent on needless fretting and wasted efforts in the perspective of the *only after*!

Jesus Came Down

2 Samuel 22:36—…you stoop down to make me great.

He parted the heavens and *came down*….(Ps 18:9)

To understand the person of Jesus Christ, both in His humanity and His divinity, we cannot miss the importance of His *stooping down*. Indeed, God's entire story depends upon this movement. Jesus, "being in very nature God, did not consider equality with God something to be grasped, but made Himself nothing, taking the very nature of a servant, being made in human likeness"(Phil 2:6-7).

In His sermon on the bread of life, Jesus is quoted as saying seven times that He "*came down* out of heaven"(John 6:51). He says, "For I have *come down* from heaven, not to do my own will but the will of Him who sent me"(John 6:38). In another moment, the adulterous woman is brought before Jesus by an angry mob of Jews. What does Jesus do? He *stooped down* and "wrote in the dust with His finger"(John 8:6), before forgiving the guilty woman and setting her free. In yet another example, some of the final moments of His earthly existence were marked by Jesus *stooping down* to wash His disciples' feet (John 13:1-7).

At the end of his life, David understood this essential truth: his God was the God who *stooped down*. David had felt God's power on the battlefield. The Lord had *stooped down* to enter David's battles and enabled him to "bend a bow of bronze"(2 Sam 22:35). Without this kind of *stooping down*, there is no virgin birth, no sermon on the mount, and no forgiveness on the cross. *Stooping down* means everything!

Perhaps the most difficult part of accepting Christ's stooping is the implications it has for each of us. After washing His disciples' feet, Jesus says, "Do you understand what I have done for you?"(John 13:12). When we acknowledge a God who has *stooped down* to make us great, we must then also acknowledge a Lord who tells us, "I have set you an example that you should do as I have done for you"(John 13:15).

Have I s*tooped down* for my Lord? Can I say with Paul, "I consider everything a loss compared to the surpassing greatness of knowing Christ Jesus my Lord, for whose sake I have lost all things"(Phil 3:7)? Do I find myself *stooping* for my family, my brothers and sisters in Christ, even those I do not love or particularly like? Am I "poured out like a drink offering on the sacrifice and service coming from…faith…?"(Phil 2:17).

To belong to Jesus is to know that He *stooped down* to lift me up and that to lift up others I too must stoop (Matt 23:11-12). Are you following the example of our Lord? Are you *stooping down*?

January 10

The Ministry of the Ordinary

Acts 4:13—When they saw the courage of Peter and John and realized that they were unschooled, ordinary men, they were astonished and they took note that these men had been with Jesus.

In our ordinary, everyday lives, how we respond in the face of persecution and pain, and the words we utter when no one else knows what to say, matters immensely to how the world sees Jesus. We can magnetize or repel others. We can transmit the light of Christ or obstruct it. Irrespective of our "significance" in the world, we can be immensely significant for the cause of Christ in the life of another.

The Apostles were a perfect example of this *ministry of the ordinary.* Many of them were fisherman who, when brought before the Jewish leaders were asked, "By what power or what name did you do this [healing]?"(Acts 4:7). Peter answered by saying, "by the name of Jesus Christ of Nazareth....[for]...Salvation is found in no one else, for there is no other name under heaven or earth by which we must be saved"(Acts 4: 8, 10,12). Because of their ordinariness, the courage of Peter and John in the face of opposition and persecution caused the Jews astonishment and "they took note that these men had been with Jesus"(Acts 4:13).

You may not feel as if you have the gift of language. Your place at work might not be an overtly influential one. Your role as a single parent is probably overwhelming, but sadly, not entirely unique. And yet, it is in the very ordinary details of our lives, in the plainness of who we are in the midst of difficulty and tedium alike, that Jesus has the opportunity to shine most brightly. The commonality of our everyday lives allows Christ to shine through us as He reaches out to the multitudes.

When we have personal strengths, they often get in the way of Jesus. But John and Peter were "unschooled, ordinary men," handpicked by Jesus as the vessels of His infant Church. In these jars of clay, Christ breathed a courage that demonstrated an "all-surpassing power...from God and not from [the disciples]"(2 Cor 4:7).

If you are feeling ordinary, you are the perfect vessel for the work of Christ in the world. It is in the simple jars of clay like you and me that Christ so often pours out His ministry into the world. We will know that the Spirit has commandeered us for this work when the world looks at us and takes note that we have "been with Jesus." In our ordinary lives, we are honored to be unremarkable vessels filled with the all-surpassing power of a most remarkable God!

January 11

Listening Carefully

Luke 10:39—Mary…sat at the Lord's feet listening to what He said.

Have you sat at the feet of Jesus and listened to what He is telling you? Or, are you constantly bustling about with the preparations of Martha, too busy to listen well? While there is certainly a time for doing the labors of the every day, the primary work of the Lord is "to believe in the One He has sent"(John 6:29). And the only way we can truly understand Jesus well enough to believe in Him with all our hearts and souls is to sit at His feet and listen to what He is saying.

Our Lord said to His disciples, "consider carefully how you listen"(Luke 8:18). We all know what it is to listen or have others not listen to us. When we perceive others not focusing on what we are saying, we are often hurt. We might feel insignificant and neglected. Should we expect Jesus to feel any different?

When we apply our contemporary tendency for multi-tasking to our relationship with Christ, we are not capable of listening well. We miss the nuances in His voice, the subtle expressions on His face, and the tender love in His eyes. In our bustling about, it is difficult for us to concentrate on what we hear. As a result, the message of Jesus often has no place to root and it becomes like an unfruitful seed sown along the path in rocky or thorny places. We may hear some part of the Word, but because we miss the fullness of it revealed, "the worries of this life and the deceitfulness of wealth choke it, making it unfruitful"(Matt 13:22).

We must, therefore, consider how we are listening to Jesus. If we are not sitting in the stillness of His presence, humbly at His feet, we are not listening well. We may be "worried and upset about many things"(Luke 10:41) which keep us from sitting at His feet and listening. But when we choose, like Mary, "what is better"(Luke 10:42), then the seed falls on good soil—the brokenness of our receptive spirits. It will produce in us a "crop, yielded a hundred, sixty, or thirty times what was sown"(Matt 13:23).

Are you listening with the ears of Mary or Martha? Don't miss your moment at the feet of Jesus. Pray, "O God within me, give me grace today to recognize the stirrings of your Spirit within my soul and to listen most attentively to all that you have to say to me. Do not let the noises of this world so confuse me that I cannot hear you speak."[9] Help me, Jesus, to *listen carefully*!

---

[9] John Baillie, *A Diary of Private Prayer* (New York: Scribner, 2014), 67.

January 12

From There

Deuteronomy 4:29—But if from there you seek the Lord your God, you will find Him if you look for Him with all your heart and with all your soul.

"*But if from there….*" The "there" of your heart may feel like the remotest place imaginable, unreachable by anyone you know, much less a God you have never seen. But where men fail to venture, God will not hesitate to go. His very invisibility means He can find a way to where you are: "He is there as He is here and everywhere…near to everything, next to everyone, and through Jesus Christ immediately accessible to every loving heart."[10] There is no unreachable shore of the soul for God. As the Psalmist says, "Where can I go from your Spirit? Where can I flee your presence?(Ps 139:7). Whether in the heavens or the depths or the "far side of the sea," we can know that His hand will guide us and hold us fast—*if* we seek the Lord (Ps 139:9).

And there is the rub—we must seek Him and *look for Him with all our heart and with all our soul.* We cannot expect to find Him if we refuse to look. Jesus says, "seek and you will find; knock and the door will be opened to you"(Matt 7:7). No half-hearted effort will suffice.

The people of Israel were repeatedly guilty of this sin. Under the reign of Jeroboam II, they turned away from the Lord. Their best spiritual efforts were not directed at God, but toward the more tangible calf worship of Bethel and Gilgal. *Even from there,* however, God was willing to redeem the Israelites. The Lord says, "Seek me and live…"(Amos 5:4)!

Like the Israelites, we may be tempted to think we are too far from God. We may have lived a long time in places like Bethel and Gilgal. We may not feel we have the spiritual strength we need to seek God; we may be utterly exhausted, driving our lives on fumes. But those very fumes must be entirely engaged in seeking the Lord. When we choose to do this, however, we will find Him. He will make Himself known to us. We will see quite clearly that He has always been there, right beside us, even when we felt most alone and most estranged. The reason we didn't see Him is that we weren't looking with our everything.

Do not let the "there" or the "here" of your past or present keep you estranged from the love of our Father. There is no distance too great, no place too remote, to keep Him from you *if* you decide to seek Him with *all your heart and with all your soul.* But you must take the step. And it must be a full step, with everything that you are and all that you have. Then, even from the untouchable, unreachable "there," you will find Him.

---

[10] A.W. Tozer, *The Knowledge of the Holy* (New York: HarperCollins, 1961), 76.

January 13

Thief of the Heart

2 Samuel 15:6—…he stole the hearts of the men of Israel.

In the person of Absalom we see the embodiment of the thief and robber described by Jesus. Our Lord said, "I tell you the truth, I am the gate for the sheep. All who ever came before me were thieves and robbers…"(John 10:7). It is, perhaps, no small coincidence that Absalom, the conspiring and aspiring son of King David, "would get up early and stand by the side of the road leading to the city gate"(2 Sam 15:2). Poised by the gate, Absalom *stole the hearts of the men of Israel,* for the "thief comes only to steal and kill and destroy"(John 10:10).

We should not be surprised by Absalom's proximity to the gate. As the "sheep" gather to pass through the gate, "the wolf attacks the flock and scatters it"(John 10:13), isolating the weak and unhealthy and devouring them. It is when we are close to the gate that we are most vulnerable to be stolen away by the lies of the scheming enemy who whispers amidst his ranks, "Be subtle! Be subtle! You can make yourself invisible. Be secretive! Be secretive! You can move without a sound. Thus you hold the enemy's fate in your hand."[11] Satan's subterfuge takes us unaware while we ask, *"Haven't we arrived? What could possibly happen here?"*

Are you finding your heart stolen away? If your spirit's allegiance is drawn to any person, be they a pastor, leader, or anyone other than Jesus Christ, examine your loyalties. Be suspicious of anyone whose charisma parades itself near the gate of our Lord. Absalom's good looks and flattering tongue diverted the attentions of men and women away from the true king (2 Sam 15:3-4).

Be aware that the voice of the true Son will ring differently. Unlike Absalom, Christ will not seek to steal the hearts of His brothers and sisters away from the King. Rather, He will gladly direct them through the gate into the presence of the reigning Lord. Conversely, anyone standing near the gate who does not recognize the King is not a true son or daughter—he is a thief and a robber.

Finally, let us never forget that we are not immune from Absalom's sin. If the execution of our gifts in the body of Christ gets in the way of Jesus in the lives of others, we become thieves and robbers. We must seek never to be spiritually robbed but also to never steal, consciously or unwittingly, the hearts of others away from Christ. If we are living for Jesus, our goal will always be to point to the Son and never eclipse Him in the lives of others. Our commitment must be—*more of Him and less of me.*

---

[11] Sun Tzu, *The Art of War* (New York: Chartwell Books, 2012), 35.

15

January 14

Fighting Against God

Acts 5:38-39—For if their purpose or activity is of human origin, it will fail. But if it is from God, you will not be able to stop these men; you will only find yourself fighting against God.

Sometimes the very war we think we are fighting for the Lord is actually a battle against Him. We have insidiously allowed ourselves to confuse our own purposes with those of God, and we have hijacked the name of the Lord for our own agendas.

Peter and the Apostles found themselves confronted by a Sanhedrin afflicted with this spiritual confusion: "We gave you strict orders not to teach in this name [Christ]"(Acts 5:28). If we give the Jewish authorities the benefit of the doubt, we will see this command to the Apostles as an effort to obey the Lord by keeping His commands and the Jewish tradition pure of "heretical" teachings. But was it truly in God's best interest or their own? The wise teacher Gamaliel rises and addresses this question when he says, *"if their [the Apostle's] purpose or activity is of human origin it will fail. But if it is of God, you will not be able to stop these men...."* History has overwhelmingly borne out this truth and the verdict is clear: God's purposes never fail.

Is there something in your life that you are passionately pursuing in the name of God? Are you certain that it is God's fight or are you possibly warring against Him and His purposes as the Sanhedrin did? The more passionately and vocally we pursue things in the name of God, the more careful we must be to keep our hearts continually bowed before the Lord. Our spirits must be faithfully in step with His Spirit. The constant tendency is for our personal agendas to infiltrate even the best of intentions. What once started as a godly effort may become corrupted and injurious to the purposes of the Lord.

How do we prevent this pharisaical tendency in our lives? On a regular basis we must join David in saying, "Search me, O God, and know my heart; test me and know my anxious thoughts. See if there is any offensive way in me, and lead me in the way everlasting"(Ps 139:23-24). We must pray that the Spirit will keep our activities and our intentions true to His purposes and protect us from becoming "Pharisees" full of a misdirected zeal that finds itself *fighting against God.*

The Simple Things

2 Kings 5:13—Naaman's servants went to him and said, "My Father, if the prophet had told you to do some great thing, would you not have done it? How much more, then, when he tells you, 'Wash and be cleansed'!"

So often our spiritual lives are marked by an appetite and expectation for the spectacular. Our culture has taught us to anticipate the fantastic, the exceptional or the extraordinary: the next new and amazing thing. Jesus said of this thinking, "'Unless you people see signs and wonders...you will never believe'"(John 4:48).

Naaman, the leper commander from Aram, was one of these men. When he went to Elisha to be healed of his disease, he is told to "Go, wash...seven times in the Jordan, and your flesh will be restored and you will be cleansed"(2 Kings 5:10). But Naaman "turned and went off in a rage," because he was expecting something spectacular: "I thought that he [Elisha] would surely come out to me and stand and call on the name of the Lord his God, wave his hand over the spot and cure me of my leprosy"(2 Kings 5:12,11).

Initially, Naaman would not accept the *simple thing*; he demanded the extraordinary. Perhaps it was his cultural conditioning or, perhaps, his pride. In either case, he would not have been healed were it not for the intervention of his servants who counseled him to do the commonplace thing: wash in the Jordan.

Are you expecting God to do the exceptional or miraculous in your life? God can, and sometimes does, perform His miracles with the fireworks of heaven to announce them. But, more often than not, the healing work of God is done in the ordinary, *simple things* of life. If God asks you to *go and wash in the Jordan*, do it. Don't stand around looking for the extraordinary. The reason so many of us are not healed is that we, like Naaman, refuse to do the daily and mundane tasks through which God's healing so often flows.

If you are wanting to be healed, *go and wash yourself in the Jordan*. When you stoop to do the *simple thing*, God will show you the exalted power and majesty of heaven.

January 16

Cut to the Heart

Acts 2:37—When the people heard this, they were cut to the heart....

When was the last time you were *"cut to the heart"?* Perhaps you were rebuked by someone you love. Maybe it was a sermon that touched you or a passage of Scripture that convicted your conscience. After the Spirit of God descended upon Peter and the Apostles, the people in the crowd listening to them were *"cut to the heart* and said to Peter and the other Apostles, 'Brothers, what shall we do?'"(Acts 2:37).

If the Spirit of the Lord is living in us, we too will be frequently *cut to the heart.* We will bleed often and sometimes profusely. When we meet with God in prayer, we will feel the tip of His blade. Every time we read the Word of God, it will slice us in a new way, for the "Word of God is living and active. Sharper than any double-edged sword, it penetrates even to dividing soul and spirit, joints and marrow; it judges the thoughts and attitudes of the heart"(Heb 4:12).

While these may seem like brutal moments, the results are positive. Where we have been cut we will heal with the scars of holy remembrance. These scars remain to remind us both of God's love and our own vulnerability. The heart that does not bear these scars is either spiritually infantile or dangerously stone-like. To have a heart that is cut means that it is alive and freed to live and love, first for God and then for others. C.S. Lewis speaks to the importance of this vulnerability in love when he says,

> Love anything and your heart will be wrung [cut!] and possibly broken. If you want to...[keep] it intact you must give it to no one [certainly not God!]....[and] lock it up safe in the casket...of your selfishness. But in that casket...it will change. It will not be broken; it will become unbreakable [uncuttable!], impenetrable, irredeemable. [12]

Beware of the heart, especially your own, that is not marked with the scars of God's blade. To know God and to walk with Him is to be cut. Do not be a spiritual masochist who seeks self-injury of the soul, but neither live shut up in your "coffin," hardened to God and people alike, living for yourself alone. Choose to live in a way that makes you vulnerable to bleed for the things of God, knowing that Jesus bled from a love that gave us life. Be *cut to the heart* by the God who loves you.

---

[12] C.S. Lewis, *The Four Loves* (New York: Houghton Mifflin Harcourt, 2011), 316.

I Will Celebrate

2 Samuel 6:21-22—I will celebrate before the Lord. I will become even more undignified than this, and I will be humiliated in my own eyes.

How far will you go to glorify the Lord? Will you, like David, praise the Lord even at the cost of humiliation in your own eyes? As the Israelites brought the Ark of the Lord into Jerusalem, celebratory dancing and singing accompanied it. David decided that he would *celebrate before the Lord* at all costs, even if it brought displeasure to his wife Michal. It was "before the Lord"(2 Sam 6:21) that David celebrated, and whether or not it pleased men or even himself, did not matter. While we may sympathize with the opinions of Michal, her pleasure, as well as that of everyone else, was subordinate to God's. What mattered most to David was that God was glorified and honored.

As the Ark of the Lord is honored with "burnt offerings and fellowship offerings before the Lord"(2 Sam 6:17), David knows God does "not delight in sacrifice...[or] take pleasure in burnt offerings"(Ps 51:16). Rather, He desires "a broken spirit; a broken and contrite heart..."(Ps 51:17). Therefore, David is willing to be broken. He momentarily strips himself of his royal dignity—as he says, *"more undignified than this... humiliated in [his] own eyes"*—that the name of the Lord might be glorified.

So long as we are constrained by the borders of our own fragile egos and the opinions of others, we cannot fully celebrate before the Lord. To truly glorify God we must, like the dancing David, first divest ourselves of every opinion (particularly our own!) save the opinion of the Lord Jesus Christ. If we are still unwilling to be criticized, rejected, humiliated, and debased, we are not serving the Lord, but the fickle opinions of others.

Are you still living your spiritual life within the confines of public or private opinion? Do you find that you are taking yourself so seriously that the "undignified" and effusive praise of the Spirit within you is being stifled? If so, remember that "solemnity flows out of men naturally; but laughter is a leap. It is easy to be heavy: hard to be light. Satan fell by the force of gravity."[13] We must rise on the wings of celebratory praise! Though we may disappoint some and offend or alienate others, it is only God's verdict that counts: "Against you and you only have I sinned and done what is evil in your sight..."(Ps 51:4). Let us choose to celebrate before the Lord and let God judge the motives of the heart.

---

[13] G.K. Chesterton, *Orthodoxy* (Peabody: Hendrickson Publishers, 2006), 117.

January 18

Presence and Absence

John 1:16—From the fullness of His grace we have all received one blessing after another.

Do you see your life as blessed? Are you convinced that you have received so much more than you deserve? The secret to contentment is the rooted understanding that *we have all received one blessing after another* from the fullness of God's grace. If we lack contentment in our lives, it is not because we have not received. Rather, we have chosen to focus on *absence* rather than *presence*. We are seeing what we don't have rather than what we do.

The grace of Jesus, like an April rain, falls softly and universally, to nourish and ripen the lives of all those He loves. Even the wicked find themselves watered in this way, for the fullness of Christ's grace "rain[s] on the righteous and the unrighteous" alike (Matt 5:45). Have you dared to honestly consider your life in the *presence* of this grace rather than the *absence* of what you don't have? When I have the courage to stop looking at the empty spaces in my life and start focusing on those that are literally brimming with blessing, I begin to see the largess of God in my life. The grace I have received in just one day is enough to silence my softest complaint.

However, when I look and see the blessings God has brought in my life, I must never succumb to the temptation to see these blessings as deserving or the natural product of my own industry. Such thinking is not only idolatrous, but sets in motion a discontent that is always needing more. In Christ, the disciple understands that it is *from the fullness of His grace [that] we have received one blessing after another*, not from anything he or she has done. The disciple is convinced that "I have what I have from the love of God, and I have it sanctified to me by God, and I have it free of cost from God by the purchase of the blood of Jesus Christ, and I have it as a forerunner of those eternal mercies that are reserved for me; and in this my soul rejoices."[14]

The next time you are asked, "How are you doing?" can you reply with heartfelt sincerity, "Better than I deserve!"?

---

[14] Jeremiah Burroughs, *The Rare Jewel of Christian Contentment* (Public Domain), 29.

January 19

But Why?

Exodus 5:23—Ever since I went to Pharaoh to speak in your name, he has brought trouble upon this people, and you have not rescued your people at all.

Do you find yourself in the midst of some work God has called you to, questioning the efficacy of your efforts or the wisdom of the Lord's leading? Perhaps you are doubting His faithfulness to carry you through to its promised end. If you are saying, "Why have you…?" or "Is this why…?"(Ex 5:22), then you know the birth pains that rattled Moses on the eve of Israel's exodus.

God may have already come to you with absolute clarity, speaking to you in a "burning bush," with definite direction and clear instructions. And though you obeyed, putting your shoulder to the work and your heart to the cause, you may have found nothing but the hardness of Pharaoh's heart or the grumbling of those you have come to serve. You may, for a time, find no progress at all.

But when your reality bumps up against the seemingly unfulfilled promises of God, remember that "I the Lord will speak what I will, and it shall be fulfilled….For…I will fulfill whatever I say, declares the Lord"(Ezek 12:25). Your current frustrations, the troubles all around you and the incessant roadblocks you see before you, are only the pains of your spiritual "pregnancy's" final moments. God is working in ways you do not even see to prepare for the miracle He is about to perform.

If, therefore, you face trouble or resistance, it may be that someone's heart needs to be hardened to stone like Pharaoh's so that God's glory can burst through in all its amazing majesty. In your life this resistance may be a domineering boss, a wayward child, or a miserably selfish spouse—all hearts of apparent stone that God calls you to minister to. But when the time is right, God's work in and through your life will come to fruition despite these "stones," just as surely as He brings new life into the world. God's message to you will be, "Now you will see what I will do"(Ex 6:1). Then the delivery of His promise will roll out before you in unimaginable power and glory.

In the pains of your pregnant spiritual labor, be faithful. Never lose sight of the reality that God promises to be faithful to the faithful (Ps 18:25). The completion of His work in your life will come as you persist in trusting in Him.

January 20

He Must Increase, I Must Decrease

John 3:30—He must become greater; I must become less.

> Our whole destiny seems to lie…in being as little as possible ourselves…
> [and] becoming clean mirrors filled with the image of a face that is not
> ours.[15]   —C.S. Lewis

The daily challenge of my life and yours is this: *more of Him, less of me*. No one understood this better than John the Baptist. Jesus said of him, "I tell you, among those born of women, there is no one greater than John…"(Luke 7:28). This "greatness" had nothing to do with John's position in society, the way he looked or dressed, or even the eloquence with which he spoke. Jesus says, "What did you go out to the desert to see?….A man dressed in fine robes?…A prophet? Yes, I tell you, and more than a prophet"(Luke 7:24-26).

John ate locusts and dressed in camel hair clothes, but he was the messenger sent to prepare the way for the coming of the Lord (Luke 7:27). He did the work of God; but most importantly, he did not stand in the way of his coming King. John could have made his ministry about himself. The people flocked to him. Satan would have liked nothing better than a self-consumed Baptist—a perfect misdirection. But instead, John understood the joy of being the friend who "attends the bridegroom," waiting and listening for Him (John 3:29).

Have you decided, like John, to be the friend who waits in eager expectation for the coming Christ? Can you say, "That joy is mine…"(John 3:29)? We are all called to participate in the preparations for the coming of our Lord. And the only way to do this successfully is to commit, each day, to the divine arithmetic: *"He must become greater; I must become less."*

While nothing could be more antithetical to the dogma of today, John shows us that "greatness" in the eyes of Jesus depends upon this fundamental addition and subtraction. In every choice I make, in every relationship I nurture or curtail, in the work of my hands and the words of my mouth, I must decide to make it *more of Him and less of me*. If my spiritual life is a healthy one, the trajectory of my thinking and the actions of my living will increasingly lead to Christ in all things, at all times, until He comes again, and then forever.

Pray for the Spirit's help to make your life *more of Him and less of you*. Nothing could please Him more! And when this spiritual focus becomes the mission of your every day, you will know the joy of John!

---

[15] C.S. Lewis, The *Business of Heaven* (New York: HarperCollins, 1984), 267.

January 21

Whom Do You Serve?

Joshua 24:15—But if serving the Lord seems undesirable to you, then choose for yourselves this day whom you will serve....

In his song "Gotta Serve Somebody,"[16] folk singer Bob Dylan reminds us: We have a choice as to whom or what we will serve, but not a choice to abstain from serving. If we think that we serve nothing, we fool ourselves and show that we are captive to the very delusion we believe ourselves freed from. All of us serve. The question is whom or what?

Joshua challenged Israel with this very question. After wandering through the desert and then finally moving into the Promised Land, the Israelites had a choice: Serve the Lord, or serve the defeated gods of Canaan, or no god at all. When Joshua says, *"if serving the Lord seems undesirable to you,"* it appears that some of the Israelites struggled with the "undesirable" notion of living under God's covenantal law.

Like these Israelites, the contemporary world often struggles with the idea of serving God. In today's world there is little to no sense of duty —much less heartfelt desire—to serve a God who has been painted as an arcane, distant and morally restrictive Lord of Israel. Many wonder why we must serve anything at all, save our gratification of personal pleasure.

Service to God has been pejoratively portrayed because of the necessity of submission. To say, as Joshua said, "we will serve the Lord"(Josh 24:15), requires conscious surrender. Most of us abhor the idea of surrendering. We have no desire to give up control of our lives. Submission which begets service is anathema to the culture's thinking.

But the disciple of Christ must remember that the "Son of man did not come to be served, but to serve..."(Matt 20:28). We can choose to serve "the gods beyond the River"(Josh 24:15), which today might translate into physical appetites, work, or the delusion that we serve nothing at all. But unless we choose to serve the Lord, service to anything else leads to an eternal emptiness. It is only when we lose our lives in the service of Christ that we find them (Matt 16:25).

Whom or what are each of us serving? Will we choose today to serve the Lord, and find the life and meaning we were created to take?

---

[16]Bob Dylan, 1979, "Gotta Serve Somebody," *Slow Train Coming.*

January 22

Open Wide

Psalm 81:10—Open wide your mouth and I will fill it.

It is a great deception to believe that Jehovah is a God who delights in withholding. Nothing could be further from the truth. While the culture spreads the lie that God wants to starve you of all that tastes good in this life, the truth is your Father wants to "feed you with the finest of wheat; with honey from the rock..."(Ps 81:16). He longs to fill "the hungry with good things"(Ps 107:9).

We may fix our eyes and our hearts on something; we may even ask God directly for it in our prayers. But when it doesn't come when we expect it, we may turn away and pout like little children. Instead of keeping our arms raised in praise, our hearts filled with hope, and our mouths *open wide* to be filled, we give up and close down. Instead of waiting patiently and walking obediently, we turn to our own ways. In response, God says in exasperation, "If my people would but listen to me, if Israel would follow my ways..."(Ps 81:13)!

The reason we sometimes do not receive the bounty of the Lord is that we have allowed ourselves to become incapable of reception. We have shut the mouths that God so wants to fill. Jesus says, "Which of you, if your son asks for bread, will give him a stone?...If you, then, though you are evil, know how to give good gifts to your children, how much more will your Father in heaven give good gifts to those who ask of Him!"(Matt 7:9,11).

God knows what we want and what we need. And whether "we like it or not, God intends to give us what we need, not what we now think we want."[17] But because He loves us deeply, He desires to fill our lives with good things—to stuff our mouths with both sustenance and sweetness. So when things don't come when we expect them or in the manner we imagined, we must not close our mouths or keep them so busy with complaining that they are incapable of receiving. We must keep listening and obeying. We must remember that our Father is a God who, like the prodigal's father, delights in a banquet.

Let us remember today that the "Lord longs to be gracious to you..."(Is 30:18). He desires to "satisfy your needs...and...strengthen your frame"(Is 58:11). He has promised that "those who seek the Lord will lack no good thing"(Ps 34:10). *Open your mouth wide* and trust Him to fill it!

---

[17] C.S. Lewis, *The Problem of Pain* (New York: HarperCollins, 2001), 47.

January 23

Only Still

Exodus 14:14—The Lord will fight for you; you need only to be still.

When was the last time you were *still*? Not sleeping or resting, but *still*—motionless in striving, hushed in worrying, and peaceful in trusting? The sad reality is that our lives are not celebrated for stillness. We are applauded for our actions, honored for our ambitions, and sympathized with in our anxiety. But God thinks differently. He says, "Be still, and know that I am God"(Ps 46:10). He commands us to cease our efforts to outrun the advancing enemies of our lives and to surrender to His providential care: "Do not be afraid....you will see the deliverance [I] will bring you today....The Lord will fight for you..."(Ex 14:13-14).

When we refuse to be still, we forfeit the grace and power that could be ours in Christ. He who calmed the wind and the waves with a simple—"Be still"(Mk 4:39)—is the same Lord who parted the Red Sea and destroyed the advancing Egyptian army. He is the very God who wants to abate the storms and defeat the armies waged against your life and mine—if we will only be *still*.

But to be *still*, "only" *still*, requires the greatest of strength and the deepest of courage. We think wrongly about stillness if we imagine it as a position of weakness. It is not an act of doing nothing. To "only...be *still*," not peppered with personal effort or anxious striving, requires the greatest of will and the hardest of actions. It requires complete surrender and the total subjugation of the personal will into the hands of God. The strongest position is what we often consider the weakest—humbly, quietly, completely surrendered, *still* in the hands of God.

Believers who have surrendered to this "only" stillness will find the Lord fighting the battle for them in unimaginable ways. They will be empowered to step forward into God's unfolding plan—to walk through the walls of water and journey onward toward the Promised Land. Stillness brings power, peace, and Kingdom-guided action. Ironically, it is stillness of heart that keeps the journey going; stillness that shatters the enemy (Ex 15:6); and stillness that will "bring them in and plant them on the mountain of [His] inheritance"(Ex 15:17).

To be *still* before God is not to do nothing. It is to do everything. When you are *only still*, and let God be God in your life, you spiritually thrive. Do you have the courage to be *still—only still*?

January 24

Identity in Christ

1 Corinthians 4:3-4—I care very little if I am judged by you or by any human court; indeed, I do not even judge myself. My conscience is clear, but that does not make me innocent. It is the Lord who judges me.

Most of us do not have to reach very far into the past to find the last time we allowed the comments of others to influence our assessment of ourselves. Judgement is something we do all the time, every day, almost unconsciously, and in a variety of capacities. It is not, however, something we are called to level against others, or even against ourselves. Too often identities are based on human judgements. One woman finds her identity crushed by criticism, while another lives for the adulation of others. One man becomes self-satisfied in his lenient and misguided self-assessment, while another despairs in his overly scrupulous, false humility. Each of these responses is sinful.

But there is good news! In Christ, we are freed from the power of all human judgements, external and internal alike. For the disciple of Jesus, *identity is in Christ and Christ alone.* The disciple knows "The freedom of self-forgetfulness. The blessed rest that only self-forgetfulness brings."[18] It is *more of Him and less of me.*

As I begin to forget myself, I begin to move away from the power of judgement at the hands of others. Jesus is my only judge, the only opinion that matters. In this reality, we are, like Paul, increasingly impervious to the pettiness of human opinion. We are not innocent, as Paul says; but, we are freed by the blood of Jesus. We are judged only by the One who created us, who knows our hearts, and delights in us still. With the Psalmist we say, "The Lord is with me, I will not be afraid. What can man do to me?"(Ps 118:6).

Do you find yourself overly affected by the comments and opinions of others? Are you still getting bent out of shape emotionally by the court of human opinion? If so, your identity is not yet fully rooted in Christ. You are still holding on to some fabricated opinion of yourself that God never intended for you. The insecurity you feel, the despair you may struggle with, or the inflated sense of self-importance that you have deluded yourself with, stems from the fact that Jesus is still not the root of who you are. When Christ is your center, the opinions of others can come and go. It does not matter. Jesus is your judge, just as He is the lover of your soul. You are a beloved child of God!

Root your identity in Christ and let opinions fall where they may.

---

[18] Timothy Keller, *The Freedom of Self-Forgetfulness* (Leyland: 10Publishing, 2015), 32.

Shrewd

Luke 16:8—For the people of this world are more shrewd in dealing with their own kind than are the people of the light.

> ...the highest form of warfare is to out-think the enemy....[19]
> —Sun Tzu

Shrewdness has often been unfairly maligned. We think of the salesperson who hides the fine print, the lawyer who appears to bend the law, or the politician who weasels out of a diplomatic quagmire. Unfortunately, these *shrewd* maneuvers can often be costly, both fiscally and interpersonally. Shrewdness can result in carnage. But it needn't always. In fact, as Christians, we are called to be *shrewd,* piercingly astute.

Jesus says, "be as *shrewd* as snakes and as innocent as doves"(Matt 10:16). If we are not as *shrewd or shrewder* than the world around us, we will not be effective as we go "out like sheep among wolves"(Matt 10:16). We must be able to think like the enemy, anticipating every attack and counterattack, so that we do not become victims. We must engage shrewdness, but not succumb to its carnal appetites. A dove without the shrewdness of the snake is more likely to be dead than singing God's praises. And while there is a time and a place for martyrdom, we "must never choose the place of our martyrdom."[20] If it is God's will for my life to be given for His glory, it will happen. But for the great majority of us, we are called to live and work, to go out among the wolves. To spiritually survive as we do this, we must be *shrewd.*

We must determine to be sheep endowed with heavenly wisdom and savvy, a shrewdness that sees the world for what it is, and keeps the Kingdom's purposes always in mind. The *shrewd* believer studies the enemy and the battleground. To be *shrewd* in a Christ-like fashion may require more diplomacy, perhaps a bit more creativity. Consider Christ's response to the trapping question of paying taxes to Caesar. Our Lord said, "'Give to Caesar what is Caesar's, and to God what is God's'"(Matt 22:21). Could Christ have been any more *shrewd?* Without Christ's shrewdness, we are spiritually naive and ineffective. God desires neither for our lives.

We must stop relegating shrewdness to the darkness and begin seeing it as a tool for God's glory. Christ's light must shine, even if it takes some ingenuity to make that happen. Strive to model Christ's *shrewdness.*

---

[19] Sun Tzu, *The Art of War* (New York: Chartwell Books, 2012),19.

[20] Oswald Chambers, *My Utmost For His Highest* (Grand Rapids: Discovery House Publishers, 2012), Sept 30.

January 26

Laughing at Tomorrow

Proverbs 31:25—...she can laugh at the days to come.

    Your ability to laugh at the days to come is one of the simplest measures by which you will know if your life is truly "hidden with Christ in God"(Col 3:3). When we die to ourselves spiritually, we die. The old is gone. Death of self is a finality or it is not death at all. The reason so many struggle with worry, fear, and anxiety is that this kind of death has not occurred. The heart is *not* liberated to *laugh at the days to come* when it so tenaciously clings to the past.

    But when my "old self [is] crucified with Him [Christ]"(Rom 6:6), then I find the freedom and power to look not only today, but even tomorrow, straight in the face, and laugh the laugh of heaven. Hidden with Christ in God, I understand that "The Lord is my light and my salvation... the stronghold of my life—of whom shall I be afraid?"(Ps 27:1). Though I am surrounded by the complexities of life, though an army of pain and suffering may "besiege me, my heart will not fear; though war break out against me, even then will I be confident"(Ps 27:3).

    This confidence follows only on the heels of complete surrender, when I place my life in His hands and say, "I love you, O Lord, my strength....[you are] my rock, my fortress and my deliverer"(Ps 18:1-2). If I truly believe this, then there is an invincibility about today and tomorrow: "I will not be afraid. What can man do to me?"(Ps 118:6). Surely, "If God is for us, who [or what] can be against us?"(Rom 8:31).

    When you find yourself struggling to *laugh at the days to come*, take a moment to step back and examine the degree of your surrender to Jesus. Have you completely entrusted your life and its details to the One who created and saved you? God promises to "keep him in perfect peace whose mind is stayed on [Him]..."(Is 26:3 ESV). You cannot *laugh at tomorrow* without the peace of Christ. You cannot have the peace of Christ unless your mind is steadfast and your heart is trusting unwaveringly in the God who resurrected your life.

    If you, like Lazarus, have spiritually walked forth from the tomb into this new and resurrected life, then you cannot help but laugh at the days to come because Jesus, your salvation, is standing right beside you. Take the grave clothes off and laugh in the arms of the One who loved you enough to conquer the grave and bring you home. Tomorrow has nothing Jesus has not already defeated! If He is your deliverer, *laugh at the days to come!*

Out of the Storehouses

Matthew 13:52—He said to them, "Therefore every teacher of the law who has been instructed about the kingdom of heaven is like the owner of a house who brings out of his storeroom new treasures as well as old."

There is no follower of Jesus who will not, at one time or another, be called upon to teach. You may not be a pastor, priest or elder. Unless the Spirit has led you to these positions, be grateful that you are not. These dedicated teachers "will be judged more strictly"(James 3:1). But, we all teach. If you are privileged to be a mother, you teach as you mold a child's heart and mind. If you are the friend of a neighbor or colleague who does not know Jesus, you are challenged to be a teacher in their lives as well, like it or not. When unbelievers ask you why you do what you do or why you believe what you believe, you must "Always be prepared to give an answer for the hope that you have"(1 Peter 3:15).

The wonderful reality about our teaching responsibility is, however, that we are never alone. We have been given the lesson plan in God's Word. And we have the constant companionship and assistance of the Spirit within us who promises to "give you the right words at the right time"(Matt 10:19).

With the Word and the Spirit, you will bring *"out of [your] storeroom new treasures as well as old."* The timeless truths of the gospel, those you embraced at first, will be seasoned with the new treasures the Spirit reveals to you in your current and personal walk of faith. Your teaching will be unlike anyone else's, flavored with the particular life experiences and perspectives that God has so carefully woven into you. It won't, therefore, be my story or anyone else's, but it will be God's story played out in you. He will be manifest in the details. Each time you interact with the Word, something new will be revealed to you to build upon the old and to further prepare you for those teachable moments in the lives of others. Your life is God's teaching instrument, a tool for Him to further His Kingdom's cause.

Though you may not consider yourself a teacher, if Christ is in you, He is teaching through you. Be ready for God to require you to empty your storehouse of the old and the new treasures, the wisdom, experience and failures He has so carefully allowed into your life. In this sharing, the Spirit's manifestation will teach Jesus to a world that does not know Him.

January 28

Gentlest of Ways

Hosea 12:3-4—…as a man he struggled with God. He struggled with the angel and overcame him; he wept and begged for his favor.

> I love you, gentlest of Ways,
> who ripened us as we wrestled with you.[21]
> —Rainer Rilke

Have you wrestled with God? Are you grappling with Him even now in some area of your life? You will know when you have struggled with God when you find yourself forever changed. Jacob wrestled with the Lord and found himself changed: Physically, his hip was dislocated. Spiritually, he received the transformative blessing of God. And even his name changed, from Jacob to Israel—*the one who struggled with God* (Gen 32). Jacob's life, and the life of the nation he would birth, would never be the same.

For some, there is no way to be transformed—to spiritually mature and ripen into the men and women God desires them to be—without wrestling mightily with the Lord. Many of us avoid the idea, perhaps for obvious reasons. We know it will hurt and will require a tremendous effort. We also must know it will change us, sometimes beyond recognition, and some part of us doesn't really want to change.

But if we decide to engage with the Lord when He comes down to meet us, alone, in the darkness of night, we will find in Him a strength so strong that it can only be "the gentlest of ways." Omnipotence knows no fear. The greatest strength is gentle. God could have destroyed Jacob with a flick of His finger. And yet, like a loving father, there was no need for Him to flex His muscles. He allowed Jacob to "overcome" in their match. The Lord then "blessed him there" at the scene of their struggle (Gen 32:29). This act of mercy was not lost on Jacob and he named the place Peniel—"because I saw God face to face, and yet my life was spared"(Gen 32:30). Jacob was changed by his encounter with God.

When you are engaged by God in the spiritual wrestling match that will define your life, rejoice! It will cause you pain, perhaps even great personal loss. But in the end, you will be forever changed—and that for the better. You will see afresh, in the God you once saw as far away, a Lord who came near. You will know an omnipotent opponent whose love and mercy are so great, and so specific to who you are, that you will cry out, *I love you, gentlest of Ways!*

---

[21] Rainer Rilke, *Book of Hours: Love Poems to God* (New York: Riverhead Books, 2005), 89.

January 29

Always Working

John 5:17—Jesus said to them, "My Father is always at His work to this very day, and I too, am working."

Work is love made visible.[22]
—Kahlil Gibran

Our Father is a tireless worker. He is *always at His work to this very day*. The sun never sets on His vocation. When my day is closing, His work in the life of another is dawning. He does His work in and through His people, scattered in every corner of the globe. His work never ceases.

Soberingly, if the Lord had only my life or yours to contend with, this would be full-time work enough. But the reality is that He dwells in millions upon millions, and the multiplicity of His work in their lives is unfathomable. He is at once always loving (Lam 3:22-23) and always blessing, "so that in all things at all times, having all you need, you will abound in every good work"(2 Cor 9:8). He is with one hand forgiving (1 John 1:9) and with the other fighting for us—"The Lord will fight for you..."(Ex 14:14). He is providing for our daily needs (Matt 6:30), listening to our prayers (1 John 5:14) and healing our wounds—"I will restore you to health and heal your wounds..."(Jer 30:17). He is doing all things at all times—He is always at His work!

The disciple's challenge is to become more a conduit of this work and less a dead end recipient. With increasing measure, we must let His work flow through us rather than remain in us. As we love our children, treat our patients, provide for our spouses, and forgive our neighbors, we must be instruments of God's unceasing work, not obstacles to it.

The more you begin to see your daily labors as the fingers of God's work in the world, the more you will begin to stand in awe of who He is and what He does. As you allow His work to flow through you, the electric charge of His power will begin to energize you in ways you never imagined. Your love for Him will grow, an affinity that becomes a magnetism to be with Him and to partner in His work: "And when you work with love you bind yourself to yourself, and to one another, and to God."[23] You will, like Christ, hunger to do God's work because it draws you to God (John 4:34).

The Lord is always working—and praise God that He is! His work sustains everything. Pray today that the Lord increasingly guides you in becoming a holy conduit of His unceasing work in the world.

---

[22] Khalil Gibran, *The Prophet* (New York: Vintage Books, 2015), 31.
[23] Ibid, 29.

The Jonah Within

Jonah 4:9—But God said to Jonah, "Do you have any right to be angry about the vine?" "I do," said Jonah, "I am angry enough to die."

Whether we like to admit it or not, all of us have, at one time or another, been a pouting Jonah before an omnipotent God. After being chased by a storm, swallowed by a great fish, and sustained across desert plains on the journey to Ninevah, Jonah still does not understand, or perhaps accept, God's will in regards to the Ninevites. Jonah had decided that God should exact vengeance, not mercy, upon the city of Ninevah. When Jonah came to realize that God might not act in accordance with Jonah's expectations, and that he himself would have to serve as the messenger, he fled. He was so consumed with his version of reality, that he could not tolerate the idea of God acting contrarily.

When God grants mercy to Ninevah, Jonah's sense of justice is challenged. Jonah cannot, or perhaps, chooses not, to see beyond his narrow view—he is *angry enough to die* over the withering of a vine he neither planted nor cared for. In this anger he fails to see the purpose and pleasure of saving 120,000 souls for the Kingdom of God.

While the stakes in my life and yours may never be the eternal destiny of an entire city, I cannot see Jonah as a selfish child unless I am willing to admit that I have never been angry at God for acting in a way divergent from my expectations. The Christian who has clenched fists at God or stomped his feet in frustration at the humiliation of being broken will understand Jonah's cry: "take away my life, for it is better for me to die than to live"(Jonah 4:3). Without these "Jonah" moments, we cannot truly know our fellow man or our Father God. Because we are sinners and prone to fabricate our world views, all of us are capable of being as spiritually blind, stubborn and selfish as Jonah.

But fortunately, God pursues us. He loves us so much that He chases us in the storm, hides us in the belly of a fish, and sustains us in our long journeys. He patiently bears with us and employs us, despite our worst efforts, to enact His glorious purposes for His Kingdom on earth.

We must be careful to acknowledge our inner Jonah. Seeing him in us, we can be humbly moved to love the plans of God for the Ninevites, even when we do not understand or agree with them. When we make this choice, the love of God for the Ninevites becomes wonderfully ours as well.

January 31

Mercy Triumphs

James 2:12-13—Speak and act as those who are going to be judged by the law that gives freedom because judgment without mercy will be shown to anyone who has not been merciful. Mercy triumphs over judgment!

When people speak about you, do they describe a person of mercy and grace? Do the words of your conversations and the actions of your life demonstrate the lovingkindness of Jesus? Or do they reveal the principled judgments of your personal opinions? The danger for the disciple is the propensity to impose a personal, spiritual plumb line upon the world. Though Christians may be well-intentioned, far too often they become people characterized by a spirit of self-righteous judgment rather than mercy. Whether this stems from pride, a deep sense of insecurity, or a fundamental failure to recognize their own sinfulness, the result is the same: a noxious spiritual odor that drives others away from Christ.

Not surprisingly, therefore, unbelievers often appear more merciful than the body of Christ. And yet, Jesus says to us, "go and learn what this means: 'I desire mercy...'"(Matt 9:13). God wants us to extend mercy to others, just as we have been the recipients of His lavish mercy. After telling the parable where the Samaritan shows mercy, Jesus says, "'Go and do likewise'"(Luke 10:37). Is this mercy permeating your life?

As Christ's disciple, I must speak and act with an acute awareness of Jesus's mercy and grace in me. If the Spirit alerts me to an imbalance between less of God's wellspring of mercy and grace and more of my personal opinions and judgments, then my life's calling has been inverted. I am not living *more of Him and less of me*. Instead, I must allow Christ to pour out His mercy from me rather than elect to play the part of a miniature providence, choosing when and where to love and forgive.

While there is a definite purpose and place for judgment, that place is in the hands of God—"It is mine to avenge..."(Deut 32:35). The Lord may use us in the administration of His judgments. But God alone is the Judge. We are merely the instruments He sometimes employs to carry those judgments out. When we forget this paradigm, we become roadblocks to God's love, because "Judging others makes us blind, whereas love is illuminating."[24] We can be sure that, sooner or later, God Himself will move us out of the way—perhaps not gently.

The next time you are given the choice between judgment and mercy, choose mercy. Say, "*No,*" to your self-righteous principles and, "*Yes,*" to God's love that longs to pour out mercy on a desperate world.

---

[24] Dietrich Bonhoeffer, *The Cost of Discipleship* (New York: Touchstone, 1995), 185.

FEBRUARY

February 1

Remain

John 15:4—Remain in me, and I will remain in you.

The only way to spiritually survive, much less thrive and bear fruit, is to *remain*. Jesus says, "I am the vine; you are the branches. If a man *remains* in me and I in him, he will bear much fruit…"(John 15:5). The reason so many of our lives are unproductive spiritually is that we have decided not to *remain*. Jesus has not left us, for He says, "I am with you always…"(Matt 28:20). Rather, it is we who have grown restless and allowed ourselves to wander.

This restlessness is the child of Satan. It is the discontent that drove him from heaven and the plague that he sent among the sons of men. Satan still sows dissatisfaction, the lie that wandering is superior to the grace of *remaining*. But nothing could be further from the truth.

When we decide to *remain* in Christ, He remains in us. As we determine not to wander and chase after the lies Satan has woven into the world, the blessings of being in the vine become ours. We are nourished, supported, loved and enabled to bear fruit. Whatever it is we ask in His name, we shall receive as we *remain* in Him (John 15:7).

This choice to *remain* is an active one. It requires a strict resolution and a strong determination. No one drives me away. I allow myself to wander. When my life withers spiritually, I am to blame. I have not *remained*.

Have you determined that you will *remain* in Christ? As Andrew Murray says, "Abiding in Jesus is nothing but the giving up of oneself to be ruled and taught and led, and so resting in the arms of Everlasting Love."[25] Have you decided to abide in this Love? This commitment must be made anew every day. No matter what life serves up, what pain we experience or success we bathe in, will we *remain* in the vine? We can wander if we like, but we should not at the same time expect the blessings of the vine. Our wandering will wither us. Sadly, however, this wandering is sometimes the very thing we must do to help us realize the importance of *remaining*.

Christ is rooted in the Father. Are you? It is only in *remaining* that your spiritual life will burst into blossom.

---

[25] Andrew Murray, *Abide in Christ* in *Collected Works on Prayer* (New Kensington: Whitaker House, 2013), 25.

Perfect Peace

Isaiah 26:3—You will keep in perfect peace him whose mind is steadfast, because he trusts in you.

"There can be no peace without hope…."[26] But, Christians also know there is no lasting hope apart from Christ. Everything else that advertises as "peace" is transient, if not illusory. *Perfect peace* can only come from the One who exists outside our finite and flawed realities.

When it comes to the struggle to find this peace, our world today is little different than the world of the prophets. It is filled with false doctrines and deceptive teachers. Jeremiah says, "prophets and priests alike, all practice deceit. They dress the wound of my people as though it were not serious. 'Peace, peace,' they say, when there is no peace"(Jer 6:3-4). In the absence of the saving grace of Jesus in our lives, the wound is more than serious. It is fatal (Nah 3:19).

This "wound" may be dressed with whatever poultice, or cultural lie, my conscience allows. But it will bring no healing or peace. It will be nothing more than a flimsy wall. In the storms, it will be exposed for what it is—"the wall is gone and so are those who whitewashed it, those prophets…who…saw visions of peace…when there was no peace"(Ezek 13:15-16). We may spend our entire lives building walls and fortifications of finance, relationship, or vocation in an effort to obtain "peace." But if our foundation is not in Jesus, *perfect peace* will elude us.

In the end, our consciences betray us. Rather than choosing to find peace in Jesus, we worry over our own efforts, often retreating into fictional, inner worlds or taking pills. But, on some level we were designed to know that nothing we build can withstand the storms—"it is going to fall"(Ezek 13:11).

Have you found yourself exhausted in your search for peace? Do you fear the inescapable reality that everything you have constructed is destined for destruction? Until you reach the spiritual epiphany that true peace cannot be found apart from the blood of Jesus, you will continue to live a life on the run, trying to obtain the unobtainable and outpace the inevitable.

If, however, you trust in Jesus, "the peace of God, which transcends all understanding, will guard your hearts and minds in Christ Jesus"(Phil 4:7). *Perfect peace* can be yours when Christ lives in you. Will you choose to trust in the One who offers that peace to you?

---

[26] Albert Camus, *The Plague* (New York: Vintage International, 1991), 292.

The Power of a Question

Daniel 1:8—But Daniel resolved not to defile himself with the royal food and wine and he asked the chief official for permission not to defile himself in this way.

> You can tell whether a man is clever by his answers. You can tell whether a man is wise by his questions.
> —Naguib Mahfouz

The last time you were faced with a choice which promised to compromise your convictions, did you acquiesce and go with the flow? Did you make a scene of refusal or disobedience? Or did you simply ask a question?

Sometimes a simple question is all it takes for God to open the door of an otherwise closed heart or mind to allow for the Spirit's purposes to proceed unobstructed. Not following the crowd or disobeying orders will often meet an angry resistance. But a question, winsomely given in humility and grace, can sometimes disarm even the most ironclad opponents.

Daniel did not refuse to become a student of the Babylonian king. He did not resist regarding learning the ways of the Chaldeans. But he also did not compromise his beliefs or his purity before his holy God. So he asks a question. And in this simple resolution, his superior's defenses are lowered, and a compromise is obtained. Daniel is able to proceed forward with a clean and holy conscience before God and the Babylonians alike. Daniel found the middle way. And, most importantly, God is glorified in the process.

In the end, Daniel and his Jewish brothers are blessed by the Lord. Their obedience amidst adversity becomes the vehicle for God's glory in the heart of Babylon. And it all began with a question, wisely birthed in spiritual resolve.

If you find yourself in a moment of potential compromise, choose to stay true to your convictions. Should the Spirit lead, have the courage to ask a question. Sometimes, the inquisitive one, asking a question in humility, is the very one who opens the door for God and His purposes to unfold in the lives of others.

February 4

The Good Shepherd

John 10:14—I am the good shepherd; I know my sheep and my sheep know me....

> Be our shepherd, but never call us—
> we can't bear to know what is ahead.[27]
> —Rainer Rilke

When the poet Rilke says to God, *"Be our shepherd, but never call us— we can't bear to know what is ahead,"* he articulates the push and pull of Christ in the hearts of many believers. On one hand, we want what the shepherd has to offer us: safety, security, and guidance. On the other, however, we have no interest in embracing what it means to be a part of the flock.

In our spiritual lives, Jesus is the Shepherd, whether we accept it or not. Most of us like the idea of a "shepherd" watching over us from some distant hill, ready to race over and protect us from the attacking wolves. We like it, so long as He stays over there, statuesque and silent, requiring nothing of us yet allowing us to wander where we want to wander and consume what we want to consume. But like the poet, very few of us want the Shepherd to call us. Very few of us want to be pulled away from our autonomy and personal choices.

When the Shepherd calls, we are faced with the choice of listening to and following Him or going our own way. We are forced to look ahead, to leave the green pastures of the present and move into the unknown. Has this ever caused you to say, *I can't bear to know what is ahead?*

Do you find yourself today fearing the future? If so, you have forgotten what it means to be a part of Christ's flock. Jesus reminds us that, "When he [the shepherd] has brought out all his own, he goes on ahead of them, and his sheep follow him because they know his voice"(John 10:4). With Jesus as our Shepherd, we need not fear what lies ahead. It may appear terrifying. It may seem like a departure from everything good and secure. But if you remain in the flock, His voice will go on ahead of you. He will guide you to green pastures and lead you beside quiet waters (Ps 23:2). He will "lay down His life for the sheep" and "go after the lost sheep until He finds it"(John 10:15; Luke 15:4).

If you desire to face today and tomorrow with the confidence that the *Good Shepherd* is always with you, then you must be ready to listen to His voice and follow wherever He leads you. You will learn to "know Him" and rejoice that He knows you!

---

[27] Rainer Rilke, *Book of Hours: Love Poems to God* (New York: Riverhead Books, 2005), 103.

February 5

Chink in Your Armor

1 Kings 22:34—But someone drew his bow at random and hit the king of Israel between the sections of his armor.

Some of us spend our entire lives changing in and out of various "suits of armor." There may be one suit for the pursuit of love to protect us from the joust that nearly toppled us. Perhaps another, crested in money, to ward off the memory of a poverty so severe that it made the body ache with hunger. Maybe still another for the spirit, to protect it from a "silent" God who allowed us to suffer that now unspeakable pain.

In keeping our armory full of suits, we might imagine ourselves invulnerable and immune to hurt. And if there is one suit we still do not have to protect a known weakness, even then, might we like King Ahab before the Arameans, use a bit of artifice to ward off the enemy? Why not disguise ourselves and assume another identity?

That is exactly what King Ahab did when he advanced against the King of Aram in spite of the Lord's explicit counsel. Like many of us, he trusted in his suit of armor and in his cleverness. He said to King Jehoshophat, his ally, "'I will enter the battle in disguise, but you wear your royal robes'"(2 Kings 22:30). In assuming the role of a common soldier, Ahab convinced himself he could skirt the death sentence prophesied. He trusted in his own protective schemes.

Are we living like Ahab, fixed in the belief that we have thought it all out and are prepared to come unscathed through the battle that lies before us? Unless we can say in our unarmored "nakedness," "The Lord is my rock, my fortress and my deliverer"(Ps 18:2), we are as duped as the marked man Ahab. Achilles had his heel; we have our chink in every suit of armor we put on other than Jesus Christ our Lord.

Although Ahab thought he had it all figured out, *someone drew his bow at random and hit the king...between the sections of his armor.* When the Lord is on the battlefield, there are no random arrows. If we, like Ahab, are trusting in our armor, "The Lord's arrow of victory"(2 Kings 13:17) will find us out, and the chink in our armor will be our demise. But if we choose to trust in the Lord, in our unarmored nakedness, we will find all the protection we need.

41

February 6

Sabbath Rest

Exodus 20:8—Remember the Sabbath day by keeping it holy.

Some commandments are gifts to us even when we fail to recognize them as such. Perhaps the most widely disregarded command is also the most underappreciated gift: keeping the Sabbath. Jesus tells us the "Sabbath was made for man…"(Mark 2:27). But all too often it is seen as an irrelevant relic of the past or an impossible request in our busy and overcommitted lives. Nothing, however, could be further from the truth.

God intended the Sabbath as a day to rest from the work of the week and a time to connect with Him in a focused and restorative way. When God created the world He "rested from all His work…and blessed the day and made it holy"(Gen 2:2-3). He did not need rest. But He knew we would. So the Sabbath was given as an opportunity to know the blessing of God—"Blessed is the man who…keeps the Sabbath without desecrating it…"(Is 56:2). Just as there is a difference in the restorative rest of a nap versus a full night's sleep, so also in the spiritual realm. Our daily devotional times must be complimented by a concentrated Sabbath rest.

Ironically, as much as we all yearn for rest, we rarely take the kind of rest God desires for us. For this reason, the Lord made the gift of *Sabbath rest* a command: "For six days, work is to be done, but the seventh day shall be your holy day, a *Sabbath rest* to the Lord. Whoever does any work on it must be put to death"(Ex 35:2). Even a death sentence, however, was not enough to curb the desecration of God's day. In breaking the Sabbath, the Israelites fell away from God. They found themselves in the hands of "an unquenchable fire…"(Jer 17:27).

Honoring the Sabbath no longer carries a death sentence. But its desecration in our lives is no less an affront to God. It signals spiritual death in us. And it is the greatest of missed blessings in our lives. As Isaiah warns, if you find your "feet…breaking the Sabbath" as you do as "you please on [His] holy day"(Is 58:13), recognize that you are grieving God. Like the Israelites, instead of calling "the Sabbath a delight and the Lord's day honorable," we often go "our own way"(Is 58:13), and rob ourselves. When we think we are using our time wisely, we are missing the chance to "find…joy in the Lord…"(Is 58:14).

If you are finding your spiritual life tired, lifeless and dry, come back to God's blessing. Honor God by honoring His Sabbath. Find your life restored with the fullness of His Spirit. The Sabbath was made for us: We must stop throwing it away and start enjoying the fullness of joy and peace that come from time with our Father.

Likable

Luke 21:17—All men will hate you because of me.

So long as we concern ourselves with our "likability," we are probably not walking closely in the footsteps of Christ. Jesus was liked by some who witnessed what He did; but, He was also hated by others, like the Pharisees, who saw the darkness within themselves by the light of His presence.

But liked or disliked, Jesus walked on to Calvary. We do not see a flustered Jesus saying to Himself, "I wonder if they will like me?" or "Did I say the right thing, the politically correct thing? Will they take offense?" Christ did not concern Himself with *likability* among men. Rather, His concern was pleasing His Father and doing His will.

In the Apostle Paul we see a similar spirit. In his letter to the Corinthians, Paul is a man whose "self-worth, his self-regard, his identity is not tied in any way to their verdict and their evaluation of him."[28] Paul doesn't care about being *likable*. He wants to glorify the Lord!

Are you "trying to win the approval of men, or of God? Or [are you] trying to please men?"(Gal 1:10). If so, you "would not be a servant of Christ"(1:10). To please God we must follow Jesus's example. We must have a mind focused on the Father's will, irrespective of what the world thinks—even to the point of being hated. The more fully Christ unfolded His ministry, the more brightly He shone in His teaching and miracles. Conversely, the closer He came to fulfilling His ultimate purpose, the more violently He was hated. As His truth illuminated the world more distinctly, it required men and women to see themselves for the first time in a new light. Many hated what they saw. Instead of seeking forgiveness and changing, they transferred their hate to Him—the divine scapegoat.

Should we expect any different? Christ said, "If the world hates you, keep in mind that it hated me first"(John 15:18). As the world grows darker, the light of Christ within you will likely induce a growing hatred for the darkness it exposes. The time will come when *all men will hate you* because of Jesus.

When we are walking with Jesus, we should not be surprised when we are unfairly treated and viciously attacked. While we should not seek to behave in ways that become a stumbling block to others, we should not worry about being *likable*. Pursing *likability* is a sure way to become spiritually ineffectual. Instead, we must determine that we will seek to please God and let the affections of others fall where He wills.

---

[28] Timothy Keller, *The Freedom of Self-Forgetfulness* (Leyland: 10Publishing, 2015), 25.

February 8

Lonely Places, I.

Mark 1:45—As a result, Jesus…stayed outside in the lonely places.

Without solitude it is virtually impossible to live a spiritual life.[29]
—Henri Nouwen

There may be a season in your life, perhaps multiple, where you find yourself feeling as if you are *outside in lonely places*. Depending upon our personal constitutions, such times of loneliness and isolation can be difficult or delightful. But in every life, these solitary places are essential to our spiritual development. We do not know God without them.

No one demonstrated this reality better than Jesus Himself. Christ was a man who not infrequently, and quite intentionally, "went off to a solitary place"(Mark 1:35) where He spent time with the Father in prayer. Although Christ walked among the crowds, broke bread with the thousands, packed Himself into houses filled with bodies wanting to touch His cloak and hear the timbre in His voice, Jesus also deliberately spent time in *lonely places*. Such moments were defining times in His spiritual ministry. They were essential places of connection with His Father and His will. In a *lonely place* in the desert, Jesus resists the devil's temptation and claims His Father's power over darkness (Matt 4:1-11). At another time Jesus takes Peter, James and John and leads "them up a high mountain by themselves" where Christ is visited by Elijah and Moses (Matt 17:1,3). And, in perhaps the most climatic *lonely place*, Gethsemane, Christ decides in His ultimate isolation to change the world forever (Matt 26:36-45).

When God brings you to *lonely places* in your life, don't be afraid. Rather, remember Jesus, and rejoice in knowing that God is giving you a special opportunity to connect with Him and define your faith. If our lives lack these "solitary places," then we must, like Jesus, intentionally create them. If we are constantly amidst the crowd, we will not easily hear God's voice. And, without these *lonely places*, we will not likely appreciate the company God brings. If our lives do not know the depravation, starvation, persecution, and silence that *lonely places* sometime bring, we will never know the full sweetness of God's companionship, faithfulness, and love.

In the *solitary places* of our lives, we find it possible to recharge, reflect, and refocus—to sharpen our Christ-like vision of the world. Then we are able to return to the crowds and the valleys, ready to do the work of our Lord. Rejoice in the *lonely places!*

---

[29] Henri Nouwen, *Making All Things New* in *The Only Necessary Thing,* ed. Wendy Wilson Greer (New York: The Crossroad Publishing Company, 2015), 42.

February 9

Angels

Matthew 18:10—For I tell you that their angels in heaven always see the face of my Father in heaven.

One day we shall stand amazed at how the angels of heaven have worked in the details of our lives, often without our even noticing. Who knows how many of the near misses, the accidents suddenly averted or the kindnesses unnaturally and unexpectedly given were the work of the legions of heaven?

The Lord's angels are His messengers and ministers. Consider their many roles. They bring "good news of great joy…"(Luke 2:10). They bear the sword of God's wrath against the enemy (2 Chron 32:21). They watch over the innocence of childhood (Matt 18:10). They are the hands and feet, the eyes and mouth of God reaching into our world. They are His "ministering spirits sent to serve those who will inherit salvation"(Heb 1:14). His angels encamp "around those who fear Him," and deliver the righteous as God so directs (Ps 34:7). The Father's angels "guard you in all your ways," and "lift you up in their hands so that you will not strike your foot against a stone"(Ps 91:11-12).

In all their radiant glory, full of God's power, it is the Lord's grace that keeps us from seeing them. For if we saw the working of the angels in our lives, we might be prone to fall "down to worship at the feet of the angel who had been" ministering to us (Rev 22:8). Instead, they most often move silently in and out of our lives, working God's wonders unnoticed, imitating the very unaffected humility of Christ Himself. They recognize themselves as "fellow servant[s]…of all who keep the words" of truth (Rev 22:9).

Have you paused to consider how those who *always see the face of [our] Father in heaven* have been charged with the care and protection of your life? Like Elisha's servant, open your eyes and see the "hills full of horses and chariots of fire all around…"(2 Kings 6:17). Know that in the midst of the darkness, God's heavenly servants are surrounding you at His command. Their eyes are fixed on the Father, their ears attentive to His slightest word, and their hands ready to do His will in your life and mine. Rejoice in the angels who teach us the importance of always seeking the face of our Father!

February 10

Leaving the Past, in the Past

Isaiah 43:18—Forget the former things; do not dwell on the past.

One of the surest ways to halt our spiritual growth is to pitch our tents in the past. No one, save Jesus Christ, has lived a perfect life: "for all have sinned and fall short of the glory of God..."(Rom 3:23). But the miracle of salvation in Jesus is that the past does not enslave us anymore. We are commanded to *forget the former things* and *not dwell on the past.*

This biblical forgetting does not mean, however, that we cease to remember the past. It is not a call to global amnesia of all former things. Indeed, our past is an integral part of who we are, and it was designed by God for our sanctification and His glorification. We remember the past to learn from it, but we do not dwell in the past. We are called to leave the past behind us and pilgrimage onward. Failure to do this is a determination on our part to pitch our spiritual tents in the past, and it is sinful. Christ died to free us from the chains of the past. To hold on to it is to deny the work of Jesus in our lives.

Have you left the past behind in your life to "press on and take hold of that for which Christ Jesus took hold of [you]"(Phil 3:12)? We are called to "Forgetting what is behind and straining toward what is ahead..."(Phil 3:13). Are you ready to move forward into the future God has prepared for you?

When Jesus leads you out of the strongholds of the past, breaking your chains (Ps 107:14), and guiding you towards the "Kingdom of the Son"(Col 1:13), be careful that you do not longingly look back. Jesus says, "No one who puts his hand to the plow and looks back is fit for service in the Kingdom of God"(Luke 9:62). Once saved from destruction, to look back is an insult to the Savior's work of grace in our lives. It is to fall into the dead end traps of regret, anger, bitterness and revenge—the fruits of sin. Jesus says, "Remember Lot's wife!"(Luke 17:32). Don't be turned into a pillar of salt by clinging to the former things.

Let us remember what God has taught us in the past, but not fix our anchors there. May we press on toward what is ahead. Let us refuse to look back, and "fix our eyes on Jesus" instead (Heb 12:2). Through the strength of the Spirit, may the past propel us in God's direction, rather than prohibit us. Let us *leave the past in the past* and decide to move towards God's glorious future!

February 11

Absolute Surrender

Hebrews 10:9—Then He said, "Here I am, I have come to do your will."

> The condition for obtaining God's full blessing is *absolute surrender....*[30]
>
> —Andrew Murray

One sentence changed the course of history: *Here I am, I have come to do your will.* When Jesus uttered these words, He conquered the power of sin and set in motion the reclamation of the world. But just imagine if Christ had been as willful and selfish as we often are. Suppose He had clung to His rightful throne as the Son of God and refused to bow down in obedience to the Father's will. He could have refused to humble Himself unto death. It would have been very reasonable to resist the tortures of the men He created. And yet, He did not. He chose to present Himself as an offering to the Father. He said, *"Here I am, I have come to do your will."*

In this statement, we see an *absolute surrender.* There are no strings attached. Jesus chose to make "Himself nothing, taking the very nature of a servant"(Phil 2:7). Have you surrendered to the Father in this way? Too often we try to broker a deal with God. We come congratulating ourselves for our willingness to serve, but wanting to do so without divesting our personal thrones. Jesus shows us that this kind of service is no service at all. Christ, the King of kings and the Lord of lords, clung to nothing and sacrificed everything. He was ready to do the will of God, no matter what.

Have you placed your life on the altar as Jesus did? Have you said to God, *"Here I am, I have come to do your will"*? Do you desire to see God's blessings? Then you must surrender to the Father as Christ did, for "the condition of God's blessing is *absolute surrender* of *all* into His hands."[31] The prophet Isaiah recognized this when he said with enthusiasm, "Here am I. Send me!"(Is 6:8). God went on to employ this enthusiastic submission by enabling Isaiah to prophesy about the coming King.

The One who said to God, *"Here I am, I have come to do your will,"* is the very One who says to you and me, "If anyone would come after me, he must deny himself and take up his cross and follow me. For whoever wants to save his life will lose it, but whoever loses his life for me will find it"(Matt 16:24-25). You will never find your life and the reason for your existence until you have reached the point of *absolute surrender*—*"Here I am, ready to do your will."* Will you begin to make a discipline of surrendering your will?

---

[30] Andrew Murray, *Absolute Surrender* (Peabody: Hendrickson Publishers, 2005), 68.
[31] Ibid, 67.

February 12

One Hand for the Labor, One for the Sword

Nehemiah 4:17, 23—Those who carried materials did their work with one hand and held a weapon in their other, and each of the builders wore his sword at his side as he worked....Neither I nor my brothers nor my men nor the guards with me took off our clothes....

In this gun-crazy world, when was the last time you woke up in the morning and dressed yourself with a sword at your side? Did you go to the work of your day with one hand to the labor and the other steadying the weapon of your defense? The Israel of the post-captivity reconstruction was acutely aware of the enemy's capacity to strike at any time. They never changed their clothes, always had a weapon ready at their sides, and continually listened for "the sound of the trumpet"(Neh 4:20) to call them to arms against the advancing foe.

This sense of the urgency of attack has been largely lost, save for the pockets of persistent persecution still scattered across the globe. Too many of us have been lulled into the complacency of Satan's lullaby of comfort and prosperity. Do we wake up every day remembering that "our struggle is not against flesh and blood, but against...the powers of this dark world and the spiritual forces of evil..."(Eph 6:12)?

Satan and his forces never rest. He is a hungry lion, incessantly prowling, "looking for someone to devour"(1 Peter 5:8). With this in mind, we must approach every day with a keen awareness that the battle for our inner temple is always on. As disciples of Christ, we should never live in fear, for our Lord has "overcome the world"(John 16:33). But neither should we neglect the constant vigilance and preparedness of the men who were rebuilding the walls of Jerusalem. The disciple who sleeps on the job, who leaves his or her spiritual sword at home, will be devoured, sooner or later.

Are you aware that the enemy is all around you? As you go about God's work, can you feel him prowling in the shadows? It is not spiritual paranoia to be aware of the powers of darkness stalking God's work—it is reality. If Satan can get you to think you're safe or that the enemy is a figment of your imagination, he has already won the battle.

Approach each day ready to labor with one hand and defend with the other. This duality never ceases for the disciple. Do you have the sword of Christ's power in your hand?

February 13

Remembering Our Way Out of the Pit

Psalm 42:6—My soul is downcast within me, therefore I will remember you….

> …if one has only one good memory left in one's heart,
> even that may sometimes be the means of saving us.[32]
> —Fyodor Dostoevsky

When we are downcast or even depressed, remembrance can drown us or save us. This difference in fate is not dependent on perspective, for both can follow from looking back. Rather, what we fix our eyes on when we remember is what matters.

In the downcast moments, it is quite natural for our focus to be a negative one. We may say with the Psalmist, "My tears have been my food day and night…"(Ps 42:3). We remember those moments of our persecution, humiliation, rejection, failure, or loss as David did: "These things I remember as I pour out my soul: how I used to…"(Ps 42:4). The downcast soul that looks back only to the failures of self, the follies of others, or the egress of blessing, will find it hard to move from depression into the light of today and the brilliance of tomorrow.

But when we fix our eyes on Jesus, we find the strength for today and the hope for tomorrow. Can we dare to focus on His past provision in the times of "famine"? Do we recall His comfort amidst great loss? When we remember in this way, we slowly place the present difficulties in perspective. We find that God is "able to do immeasurably more than all we ask or imagine"(Eph 3:20).

King David's struggles should be a great comfort to all of us who find ourselves downcast in spirit. David knew many dark moments. But amidst depression, David chose to remember God. He clung to the good memories. He looked back to see the hand that created and sustained him. His soul resonated with Asaph's determination: "I will remember the deeds of the Lord….I will remember your miracles….I will meditate on all your works and consider all your mighty deeds"(Ps 77:11-12).

Perhaps the best encouragement to look to God is to remember He never forgets you (Matt 6:26). When you do, God will lift you out of "the slimy pit"(Ps 40:2) of your depression. You may "suffer mortal agony"(Ps 42:10) as you are freed from pain. But in remembering, He will lead you to saving truth: "I will yet praise Him, my Savior and my God"(Ps 42:5).

---

[32] Fyodor Dostoevsky, *The Brothers Karamazov* (New York: Barnes & Noble Books, 1995), 727.

February 14

Looking for the Living

Luke 24:5—Why do you look for the living among the dead?

Spiritually speaking, we are often like the women approaching the tomb of Jesus—looking for the risen Christ among the dead. This misguided search has led the contemporary world to a deep discontent. Instead of seeking the living Jesus, many have determined to pack their lives with experiences, possessions, people, and places as if to draw life from all those things which, like themselves, are also fading away. These people are looking for *the living among the dead*, or that which is nearly so. Is there any wonder that it so often ends in a lack of fulfillment?

The women who approached the tomb of Jesus found themselves in a similar, fruitless search. God's angels said to them, "Why do you look for the living among the dead?" These women were loving and well-intentioned. They were coming to care for Christ's body according to their cultural customs. But they had, like so many of us, forgotten the words of Jesus: "On the third day He will rise again"(Luke 18:33). They were looking for the *living among the dead*. They were expecting to find their Lord in a place that could not contain Him.

One of the reasons so many "seekers" have missed Jesus is that they too are looking in the wrong places. If we saw a man kneeling in a graveyard, crying next to a tomb, we might have empathy for him. We might understand him to be a victim of a great loss or heartache. But if that man then told us he was looking for his loved one, expecting to find her sitting there on the stone, we might become concerned for him.

But is our world really any different? Countless lives are wandering aimlessly about looking for meaning and purpose in a world of decaying things. They have succumbed to Satan's formula for destruction: "An ever increasing craving for an ever diminishing pleasure...."[33] As long as they persist in looking among the dead and dying, they will never find the life they seek, for "In Him was life," and "through Him all things were made; without Him nothing was made that has been made"(John 1:4,3).

Not until we see Jesus as the source of all life and living will we find what we so desperately desire. So long as we keep looking among the dead and dying, we will find only fleeting pleasures, elusive dreams, and unfulfilled lives. Let us pray today for those who are currently looking for the life of Jesus in all the wrong places. Let us ask the Lord to help us make known to them the truth of the angel: Jesus is alive!—"Seek the Lord while He may be found"(Is 55:6).

---

[33] C.S. Lewis, *The Screwtape Letters* (New York: HarperCollins, 2013), 53.

February 15

Spiritual Accounting

2 Kings 12:15—They did not require an accounting from those to whom they gave money to pay the workers, because they acted with complete honesty.

Does your life invite the need for a constant public accounting? Or do you live differently, inspiring in others the confidence of Christ who lives in you? Increasingly, our world is one which requires external accounting because personal integrity and honesty can no longer be expected. There are now legal injunctions to force people to do what once was the instinctual, right thing to do. The increase in rules and regulations in our work places, social relationships and governmental agencies is proportional to the decrease in moral virtue and personal ethic in our culture. As God is pushed out of hearts, the accounting increases.

Just the opposite was true among the Israelites in the days of King Joash. While the king spearheaded the renovation work on the Temple of the Lord, funds were collected from the people. The monies were allocated to the appropriate craftsmen and workers. The leaders *did not require an accounting from those to whom they gave the money to pay the workers, because they acted with complete honesty.* These men lived in a manner which dispelled fear and mistrust. Their honesty and integrity of conduct mitigated the need for petty public accounting.

Has your life been marked by this kind of personal integrity? Do you possess an honesty that inspires confidence? If I am a disciple of Jesus, I must live with an inner personal accounting so scrupulous in its self-examination and so rooted in the grace of Christ, that there is no need for others to waste their time worrying about how I conduct myself. They will cease to see me, but Christ in me. I must determine, through the grace of Jesus, to "strive diligently for perfect interior freedom and self-mastery in every place, in every action and occupation, so that [I am] not the slave of anything,"[34] and that Christ in me will dispel all fear and doubt in others.

The saint lives a life that shines with an honesty that drives away fear and speculation. It is the honesty of Jesus. While this purity may induce hatred from our enemies, it will discourage the need for a constant accounting from others. If the world is still keeping a ledger on all we do, we are not living a life filled with Christ.

Pray that the Spirit empowers you to live in a manner that requires accounting from no one but God—*more of Him and less of you.*

---

[34] Thomas A Kempis, *The Imitation of Christ* (New York: Catholic Book Publishing Corp, 1993), 178.

February 16

No Man But Jesus

Daniel 2:27-28—No wise man, enchanter, magician or diviner can explain to the king the mystery he has asked about, but there is a God in heaven who reveals mysteries.

There are few things easier or more natural to do than to take credit for the work that God does through us. While the Lord is the generative force behind all that we do, His work is manifested through our hands. And because our tendency is to live by sight, and not by faith, we love to praise men and, in return, to receive their praises. None of us are immune.

Daniel, however, reminds us how we are to respond to a world that wants to deify the man, rather than the Maker. He says, *"No...man... can explain...the mystery...but there is a God in heaven who reveals mysteries."* Daniel refuses to take credit for God's work. Instead, he raises his arms to the "great God...[who has] shown...what will take place..."(Dan 2:45).

Does my life point to Jesus, or does it point to me? I might gladly take credit for the successes and the good works God does through me, but then find it necessary to blame God or others when things go poorly. Do the actions of my every day cause the world around me to say, "'Surely your God is the God of gods and the Lord of kings...'"(Dan 2:47)?

The world does not need more of me or you. It needs more of Jesus in us. The next time you are asked if you are "able," may the response you give and the action you carry out lead all eyes to heaven. Let the credit be given where the credit is due—Christ in you, your hands, your feet, your eyes—all of you!

> Christ has no body now but yours,
> No hands, no feet on earth but yours,
> Yours are the eyes through which He looks
> Compassion on this world.
> Yours are the feet, with which He walks to do good
> Yours are the hands, with which He blesses all the world.
> ...Christ has no body now on earth but yours.[35]
> —St. Teresa of Avila (1515-1582)

---

[35] St. Teresa of Avila, "Christ Has No Body"

February 17

Praising in Imperfection

1 Corinthians 13:10-12—...but when perfection comes, the imperfect disappears....Now we see but a poor reflection as in a mirror, then we shall see face to face.

When we pause to consider that the best of what this world has to offer is only a poor reflection of what is to come, our collective response should be, "Praise the Lord. Praise the Lord from the heavens, praise Him in the heights above"(Ps 148:1). We are right to glory in the beauty God has woven into our world. The poet says, "Glory be to God for dappled things—/ For skies of couple-colour as a brinded cow;/ For rose-moles all in stipple upon trout that swim...."[36] And if we can see the beauty of God in these imperfect things, speckled and blotched as they are, a poor reflection, just imagine what it will be like *when perfection comes!*

The ability to mentally and spiritually climb the "ladder" of praise from the imperfect present to the coming perfection is an essential component of our spiritual maturation. I will never be able to appreciate the full beauty of God's perfection if I have not learned to see His beauty all around me now, woven into the imperfection of my present world.

We can begin this spiritual journey of praise by celebrating the beauty and goodness we see in creation. For, "since the creation of the world God's invisible qualities—His eternal power and divine nature—have been clearly seen, being understood from what has been made, so that men are without excuse"(Rom 1:20). If we cannot be brought to see the Lord in His creation and praise Him for His qualities in the world around us, we will unlikely be moved to praise Him for what He has done for us (Ps 8:3-4)—the second stage of praise. Understanding Christ's work on the cross requires a foundational recognition of God's invisible qualities (His power, goodness, wisdom, love, etc.), as demonstrated in the created world.

From praise of creation to praise for redemption, we move to the finale of praise—the praise we must bring before Him when *we shall see Him face to face.* In this final stage, the believer learns to praise God simply for who He is: *Yahweh,* the great *I AM.*

The next time the brilliant colors of the sunset bring you to praise, rejoice in knowing that even this beauty is only a *poor reflection* of what is to come. Let the setting sun set the stage for your heart to hear the message of the redeeming love of the One who will make all things new. He is the God who is both the Perfecter and the Perfection to come!

---

[36] Gerard Manley Hopkins, "Pied Beauty," in *The Poems of Gerard Manley Hopkins*, ed. W.H. Gardner and MacKenzie (Oxford: Oxford University Press, 1970), 69.

February 18

The Way of the Heart

Zechariah 7:10—In your hearts do not think evil of each other.

Even the casual student of the Psalms cannot escape the almost consuming presence of enemies in the thoughts of David. He says, "See how my enemies have increased and how fiercely they hate me!"(Ps 25:19). He was constantly aware that his enemies gloated over him, whispered against him, persecuted him, and despised him without apparent cause (Ps 35:19; 41:7; 9:13; 69:4). It would seem only natural that David himself would be prone to despise the very men who hated him and the God David served. Not surprisingly, David says, "I have nothing but hatred for them, I count them as my enemies"(Ps 139:22). Have I not felt this way too?

But the prophet Zechariah challenges this thinking by telling the people to *not think evil of each other* in their hearts. His command intimates the words of the coming Christ and so bridges the Old Testament Hebraic Law with the teachings of Jesus and the New Covenant that go straight down to the thoughts of the heart.

Christ gives us a good example of this scrutiny of the heart in His Sermon on the Mount. Speaking on the topic of adultery, Christ says it is no longer necessary for a man to actually sleep with another man's wife to sin. Simply looking "at a woman lustfully has already committed [him to] adultery with her in his heart"(Matt 5:28). You no longer had to kill someone to be in danger of judgment. Just being angry at your brother would subject you to judgment (Matt 5:21-22). Therefore, rather than despising the enemies who surround you, Christ now calls you to "Love your enemies and pray for those who persecute you"(Matt 5:44). Is there any challenge that requires so much *more of Christ, and so much less of me?* Apart from Christ in me, I cannot hope to pray for my enemies, much less love them.

When we truly know Jesus, we live in the confirmation that He is greater than any enemy who attacks us. In the power of this truth, we are freed to *not think evil of each other.* We are then empowered to love and pray for those who persecute us. It will not be easy or, in the beginning, particularly pleasurable. But it is *the way of the heart*—God's heart.

If you find it impossible to pray for your enemies, then you do not know Jesus and the victory He offers you. For in Christ, all things are possible (Phil 4:13). Reach out and take the grace Christ gives—let your heart be *more of Him and less of you.*

Failure to Pray

1 Samuel 12:23—As for me, far be it from me that I should sin against the Lord by failing to pray for you.

Sin and prayer are diametrically opposed to one another when it comes to their effect on our lives. Sin separates us from God. Prayer draws us close to Him. So when we choose not to pray, we move further away from God. We fall into sin.

The prophet Samuel understood that a *failure to pray* was a sin against the Lord. When he found himself rejected by the people of Israel in favor of a king, Samuel could easily have become bitter towards the ungrateful Israelites. He could have walked away into "retirement." But in grace, Samuel chooses to stay and comfort the people. He says, "Do not be afraid....For the sake of His great name the Lord will not reject His people"(1 Sam 12:20,22). Instead of calling down curses or abandoning the ungrateful Israelites, Samuel chooses to remain faithful in prayer.

Is your life sinning against God through a failure to pray? Do you realize that "Our limited prayers, with the excuses we make for them, are a greater sin than we know"?[37] Are you aware that our failure to pray "shows that we have little taste...for fellowship with God; that our faith rests more on our own work and efforts than on the power of God"?[38] Do you recognize that our silence shows that "the spirituality of our life—our abiding in Christ—is altogether too weak to make us prevail in prayer"?[39]

When it comes to our prayer lives, most of us are often overly generous in our self-evaluations. We make excuses for our lack of prayer, citing insufficient time, lack of inspiration, or incertitude on the efficacy of our efforts. We are likely to admit we do not pray enough, but unlikely to admit that our *failure to pray* is a sin against God.

But the Lord has designed prayer as the vehicle by which we are able to draw near to Him. When I fail to pray, it sends a loud and clear message to God—*I don't need you; I don't want to be near you; I don't love you enough to spend time with you.* Such a message comes from a heart that has grown cold. It has separated itself from the Father. If I am to remain connected with the Lord, kept as "the apple of [His] eye," and hid "in the shadow of [His] wings"(Ps 17:8), I must not fail to pray. I must decide, as Samuel did, that I will not sin and distance myself from God by failing to pray to Him.

---

[37] Andrew Murray, *The Ministry of Intercession* in *Collected Works on Prayer* (New Kensington: Whitaker House, 2013), 706.
[38] Ibid.
[39] Ibid.

February 20

Binding Love

John 3:16—For God so loved the world that He gave His one and only Son, that whoever believes in Him shall not perish but have eternal life.

> Love is not blind; that is the last thing that it is. Love is *bound*; and the more it is bound, the less it is blind.[40]
>
> —G.K. Chesterton

I should never suppose for one instant that God's love for me is one of pity. Equally, I must never imagine that in giving us Jesus, God was somehow forced to do so. Could He not have withheld His hand by keeping Christ by His side in heaven and letting us perish in the flames of our own choices?

In sending His Son, did God have to somehow blind Himself to the wretchedness of who we are? For who can give what he cherishes most to him that deserves it least? And yet, that is exactly what God did for me and you. *God so loved the world*, so loved you and me, that H*e gave His one and only Son.* God did this with His eyes wide open, staring openly and honestly into the very core of who we are. In so doing, God showed that love, in its purest form, *"is not blind....love is bound; and the more it is bound, the less it is blind."* It chooses to love, irrespective of what it sees.

In loving us this way, by sending us His Son, God bound Himself to us. He did not reject us, although He might very well have done so. He embraced us; He made a way for us to come to Him, to *not perish but have eternal life.* In this conscious and purposeful decision, God showed us that "The point is...when you love a thing, its gladness is a reason for loving it, and its sadness a reason for loving it more."[41] In the sadness of the human condition, God loved us enough to send us His Son. For Love loves no matter what. It gives what it treasures most to those who deserve it least. God loves us in this way.

Never forget that the gift of Jesus was not a blind or coerced one. He was given as the ultimate gift of love to a motley crew of spiritual rebels like me and you. He is the gift that binds us to the Father and loves us no matter what. Praise the Lord today for the *binding love* that gave us Jesus Christ our Lord and Savior!

---

[40] G.K. Chesterton, *Orthodoxy* (Peabody: Hendrickson Publishers, 2006), 66.
[41] Ibid, 62.

After All

2 Chronicles 32:1—After all that Hezekiah had so faithfully done, Sennacherib King of Assyria came and invaded Judah.

The tendency in the life of the faithful is to see faithfulness as deserving, earning a buffer against harm. When the faithful King Hezekiah endeavored to lead the heart of his people back to Jehovah, it might have been easy for him to expect God's blessing upon his efforts. He might have thought, "Haven't I been good God, doing the work you desire?"

Hezekiah had made a renewed covenant with the Lord, reestablished the service of the Temple, celebrated the "Passover of the Lord," and "sought his God and worked wholeheartedly"(2 Chron 29:10, 36; 30:5; 31:21). Surely such devotion to God should not go unrecognized? And it didn't. God, in His goodness, "prospered" Hezekiah (2 Chron 31:21).

But *after all* this faithfulness on the part of Hezekiah and *after all* the blessing he received from God, destruction knocks at the door in the form of King Sennacherib. Hezekiah might have been angry at God. He might have shaken his fists at heaven demanding to know why he was being attacked on the heels of his persistent fidelity. Shouldn't I have peace?

Perhaps you find yourself in a similar position, committed to God heart and soul, and faithful in the work He has called you to do. And yet, destruction comes knocking at your door. How will you respond?

Faced with this very dilemma, Hezekiah did not retreat in fear or assume a moral high ground and blame God for an apparent injustice or an undeserving evil. Hezekiah chose, instead, to persist in faithfulness and trust in God: "'With [Sennacherib] is only the arm of flesh, but with us is the Lord our God to help us and to fight our battles'"(2 Chron 32:8).

When the enemy attacks you on the heels of your faithfulness or in the midst of your richest blessings, do not be surprised. Indeed, expect it and be ready for it. *After all* you have done and all that God has done for you, know that your enemy sees it as clearly as the Lord does and wants to bring you down in the midst of it. Be ready to parry this attack by not pouting over an apparent inequity or quivering in the face of impending disaster. Trust that the God you serve is with you always. And *after all*, He will reign victorious!

February 22

Captive for Christ

2 Corinthians 10:5—...we take captive every thought to make it obedient to Christ.

If we come to believe that our salvation in Christ ensures a life without conflict, we are sorrowfully deluded. While we can rejoice in the final outcome—"He gives us victory through our Lord Jesus Christ"(1 Cor 15:57)—we must never forget that the war is on. The battle rages every day, until that day, when He comes again.

There is, perhaps, no greater battlefront in our lives than the unchartered territories of the mind. Satan infiltrates the ranks of our thoughts every day. For this reason, Paul tells us to "wage war" with weapons of "divine power to demolish strongholds"(2 Cor 10:4). Through consistent prayer, the power of the Spirit within us, and the cutting blade of the Word of God (Heb 4:12), we "Fight the good fight..."(1 Tim 6:12).

Are you fighting this daily battle? Are you acting upon your thoughts before they act upon you? We must intentionally take our thoughts *captive for Christ,* or be captivated by them. As A.W. Tozer says, "if you would cultivate the Spirit's acquaintance, you must get hold of your thoughts and not allow your mind to be a wilderness in which every kind of unclean beast roams and bird flies. You must have a clean heart."[42]

To counteract this spiritual readiness, Satan suggests that the mind doesn't matter. He wants us to think the mind is a place hidden from God and immune from His judgement. But are we so naive as to believe our thoughts are hidden from the eyes of God? The Psalmist says, "The Lord knows the thoughts of man"(Ps 94:11); He has "searched me" and perceived "my thoughts from afar"(Ps 139:1-2).

Rather than fear this reality, we ought to rejoice in it. Knowing God knows the worst of who we are and loves us still, ought to encourage and free us in the power of His love. Knowing that there is final victory in Christ ought to urge us on in our battle against our inner darkness, as we take captive our thoughts for Christ. Illuminated by the Spirit, we must make it our goal to think about "whatever is true, whatever is noble, whatever is right, whatever is pure, whatever is lovely, whatever is admirable...excellent or praiseworthy..."(Phil 4:8).

If we do not actively subjugate our thoughts to Christ by the power of the Holy Spirit within us, we will become the spiritual prisoners of those thoughts. Are you a captor or a captive of your thoughts? The battleground for your mind is your battle. But victory comes to those whose strength is in the Lord!

---

[42] A.W. Tozer, *Life in the Spirit* (Peabody: Hendrickson Publishers, 2009), 35.

February 23

Everlasting Hope

Romans 4:18—Against all hope, Abraham in hope believed....

The mark of a saint is the determination to hope when others cannot—to see promise when others see only the dismal and present reality. Are you in the midst of great pain? Have you been waiting years to see your prayer answered? Is your body, like Abraham's, "as good as dead"(Roman 4:19) in the face of a promise, as yet unfulfilled?

Abraham was promised to become the father of many nations. But as the years passed and he had no son through Sarah, he might have doubted God's word, or perhaps, the interpretation of it. Instead, he chose *against all hope* to believe. "Without weakening his faith....he did not waver through unbelief regarding the promise of God..."(Rom 4:19-20).

Are there categories in your life where you have given up on hope in God? Maybe you, like Abraham, have been waiting years for the fulfillment of God's "promise" in your life. In the face of such waiting, these possibilities exist: Either the fulfillment of the promise is not what you're expecting, and what God is giving you is more of Himself. Or, your waiting is simply pregnant with expectation for God's timing to birth it into your life with the joy of hope fulfilled. Perhaps it is a bit of both.

Solzhenitsyn, the Russian Nobel laureate, said, "A human being is all hope and impatience."[43] Too often, however, we give up on hope in favor of impatience when we should be doing the exact opposite. But when we, like Abraham, couple persistent hope with tireless patience, we find "hope does not disappoint us, because God has poured out His love into our hearts by the Holy Spirit, whom He has given us"(Rom 5:5).

Yet, "I'm no Abraham," you say. And you are right—you're not. You are you, however, faced with the same choice, in a different time: the "hope choice." God will not decide to hope for you—you must make that choice, just as Abraham did. But when you choose to hope when there appears to be no hope, you will find on the boundary of this decision the Holy Spirit waiting to comfort you with the Father's love. He will sustain you in faith until the time of God's fulfillment.

The moment you decide to hope against all hope, God will meet you in your weakness. You do not need to muster the strength for the rest of the journey—God will provide it. You need only decide to hold on to hope, regardless of the "facts." Irrational? At times, it may seem so in the moment. But that is faith, and that is the power of God in hope.

Have you determined to hold on to this *everlasting hope*?

---

[43] Aleksander Solzhenitsyn, *The Gulag Archipelago* (New York: Harper & Row, 1973), 574.

February 24

One Man

John 11:50—You do not realize that it is better for you that one man die for the people than that the whole nation perish.

Caiaphas, the high priest of Israel in the time of Christ, could not have been more wrong about the person of Jesus. But one thing Caiaphas did ironically understand that the Jewish Sanhedrin did not—*it is better... that one man die...than that the whole nation perish.* And not just "one man," but "the *one man*, Jesus Christ," who allowed "God's grace and the gift of that grace...to overflow to many!"(Rom 5:15). Caiaphas, hoping to stop heresy, protect his hold on religious authority in Israel, and squash any budding insurrection, endorsed and initiated Jesus's road to Calvary. To his surprise, however, Caiaphas did anything but squash the Christian movement: he participated in breathing life into it.

God often works this way, inverting or transforming the intentions of men for His own purposes and the glorification of His name. He did it in the life of Joseph when the sons of Jacob sold their brother into the slavery of Egypt (Gen 50:20). Why couldn't God do a similar transformation in your life? Perhaps God has a Caiaphas in your life right now, an enemy who appears to have it out for you. Trust in the Lord and His purposes for your life and watch how God will use even the most malevolent intentions for your good. Have we not been told, "we know that in all things God works for the good of those who love Him and have been called according to His purpose"(Rom 8:28)? Jesus loved His Father and knew His purpose. Can you say the same?

As we begin to understand the providential purposes of God in our lives, we will begin to smile at the subtle, and sometimes not so subtle, ironies that God weaves in and out of our lives. The wicked intentions of others will be turned into instruments of God's grace and mercy. Those who would try to stop the purposes of Christ may suddenly find themselves unwittingly used in the very advance of His gospel. God transformed the persecuting Saul into the evangelizing Paul. Why would he not transform us and the "enemies" who surround us?

Truly it was better, infinitely better, that *the one man* die, than that all of us should perish. Praise God for the misdirected motives of Caiaphas and the timidity of Pontius Pilate! The failings of both men participated in giving to us the *one man* who changed the world. Thank God today that "those who receive God's abundant provision of grace and the gift of righteousness reign in life through the *one man*, Jesus Christ"(Rom 5:17).

February 25

The Spirit of Sonship

Romans 8:15—…you received the Spirit of sonship. And by Him we cry, "Abba, Father."

Is the Spirit of God living in you today? One of the truest tests to determine His presence within you is your capacity to cry out to Him, *"Abba, Father."* When we are able to call the Lord, *Abba, Father,* "The Spirit Himself testifies within our spirit that we are God's children (Rom 8:16). If I cannot say with my mouth and believe in my heart that God is my Father and I am a son or daughter of the Lord, brother or sister of Christ Himself, then the Spirit of God does not *live* in me.

The *Spirit of sonship* is the seal of salvation, the proof of a life reclaimed. No one who has been truly transformed by the blood of Christ can escape the irrepressible sense of God's paternity. As Henri Nouwen says, "Calling God '*Abba*' is entering into the same intimate, fearless, trusting and empowering relationship with God that Jesus had."[44] When we are able to call God *Abba*, we are "claiming God as the source of who we are….It is the claim of love."[45]

Is your time with God a stiff and distant one, or does your spirit cry out to Him with the intimacy of *"Abba"* as it rests peacefully in the arms of its Father? Do you recognize that you are a "co-heir with Christ"(Rom 8:17), a son or daughter of eternity? Has the immensity of this privilege brought you to tears of love?

If you are still struggling with the ability to call God your Father, it is because you have not allowed the Spirit to dwell within you. When you open the door and He enters in, nothing will be more natural than to cry out to God, *"Abba, Father,"* every day, every waking moment.

Your Father in heaven loves you more than you can imagine! If you know Him today as *Abba*, give thanks for His amazing, paternal love. But if you are still struggling to call Him *Father*, let the Spirit in—the *claim of love* wants to claim you, that you might claim Him in return. Choose today to embrace the Father whose arms are reaching out for you in love!

---

[44] Henri Nouwen, *Bread for the Journey* in *The Only Necessary Thing,* ed. Wendy Wilson Greer (New York: The Crossroad Publishing Company, 1999), 59.
[45] Ibid, 59.

Hands Full

Exodus 23:15—No one is to appear before me empty handed.

In the Church of today, the idea that we must enter the house of God with an offering in our hands has largely been lost. While the offering may be given in church or online, there is no requirement to give. Because the work of Christ has freed us of the need for physical sacrifice, our approach to God is not dependent on sacrificial "pigeons or a lamb." Christ became the sacrifice by entering "the Most Holy Place once for all, by His own blood, having obtained eternal redemption"(Heb 9:12). Christ became the "mediator of a new covenant..."(Heb 9:15).

In setting us free from the ritualistic slavery to the "blood of goats and calves"(Heb 9:12), Christ did not intend, however, that we approach the Lord with empty hands. Unfortunately, we often do just that. We abuse our liberty and take our freedom for granted. Whether we are sitting in our place of worship or praying within the quiet of our homes, our approach to the Father must bring with it the same holy reverence that the Old Covenant instilled. We must not come empty-handed! Our offering might be a tithe, the first fruits of our labors. It might be a broken heart and a bucket of tears. It might be a song we would like to sing, or a commitment we have determined to do.

But whatever our offering is, it must always include our reverent praise. God desires hands heavy-laden with worship—the open, upraised hands of praise. Though life has moments when praise is a struggle, it is, nonetheless, imperative to offer it. There is no life so difficult, no pocket so penniless, no heart too broken, that it cannot approach the throne of God with something of praise in its hands. Are your *hands full* of reverent praise to the Lord?

If we dare approach God empty-handed, we prove that we do not know what it cost Jesus to set us free. We trivialize the work of Christ and dishonor the majesty of our God. Let us pray that the Spirit helps us approach our Father with *hands full* of praise even when our souls are downcast within us, when our enemies surround us, and our minds and bodies grow weak (Ps 43:5; Ps 27:3; Ps 73:26). Even then, especially then, let us decide that God is worthy of our *hands full* of praise!

Open Doors

2 Corinthians 2:12-13—Now when I went to Troas to preach the gospel of Christ and found that the Lord had opened a door for me, I still had no peace....So I said goodbye...and went on....

There are times when we spend years of our lives praying over someone or something, only to find all doors closed. Then suddenly, when we least expect it, a door opens. Is it of God? Or is it a false passage? We might be too tired and disillusioned to walk through the door. Or we may, in excitement, run through without pausing to consider what lies on the other side.

How do the prayerful and cautious advance in the face of an open door? Do they walk through it in the absence of God's peace simply because it opened? Or do they wait, or walk on, looking for a door that gives them God's peace?

Blindly refusing to walk through an *open door* may destroy the possibility that God has opened the door and prepared an opportunity for us. An obstructive response may be selfish and sinful. The alternative, however, which races forward without prayerfully considering what follows, is foolish. We must recognize that not every open door has a beneficial conclusion. Although God can redeem our choices, some doors are not meant to be walked through. And sometimes, in spite of our choices, or because of them, God allows one *open door* to lead to another.

Such was the case for the Apostle Paul. God opened a door for him and, in obedience, he walked through it. But when Paul, through prayer, did not have God's peace as a confirmation that he was where he should be, he *went on*, led by God's Spirit to another place.

Sometimes God's open door may not lead to your anticipated destination. When God, for example, opened a door for His people through the Red Sea, they spent forty years wandering in the wilderness before the door to the Promised Land opened. At other times, like the Apostle John, God may open a door just to show us a glimpse of His glory, before He places us back where we were. We were meant to have the vision, but not the passage (Rev 4:1).

An *open door* is just that—an *open door*. We must always approach the possibilities it presents with the guidance of the Spirit. If God leads, walk through it. Be confident that His providential hand will guide you, even if other doors lie beyond. If the Spirit, however, does not give you peace, then, like Paul, move on. Pass the door, or wait where you are, trusting God will open another where the peace of His Spirit reigns.

February 28

On Bended Knee

Hebrews 5:7—...and He was heard because of His reverent submission.

Do you doubt that God hears your prayers? If you do, it is likely because you have forgotten the example Jesus set for us in reverent submission. When Christ taught His disciples to pray He said, "Our Father in heaven, hallowed be your name, your Kingdom come, your will be done on earth as it is in heaven"(Matt 6:9). In the very first words of this prayer, Jesus reminds us of our subordinate position below our exalted heavenly Father. Jesus emphasizes reverence saying, "hallowed be thy name...." And finally, in perhaps the greatest example of submission, Christ says with His mouth, and lives with His life, "Thy will be done...."

In this position of reverent submission, Jesus never doubts that the Father hears His prayers. He says, "Father, I thank you that you have heard me. I knew that you always hear me...."(John 11:41-42). This prayer is all the more remarkable because Jesus was "in very nature God," but "did not consider equality with God something to be grasped, but made Himself nothing, taking the very nature of a servant..."(Phil 2:6-7). Rather than pray in reverent submission, Jesus very well could have commanded and dictated His will upon the world. But He did the exact opposite—"He humbled Himself and became obedient to death—even death on a cross!"(Phil 2:8). Rather than rallying the legions of heaven to His defense on the night of His betrayal, Jesus bows in reverent submission to the will of the Father and says, "not my will, but yours be done"(Luke 22:42).

Too often we do the exact opposite of Jesus. We approach prayer as the lords of our own lives, burdened with personal agendas. We forget that God is God, and we are not. We fail to revere the power and majesty of His holy name. When we pray we often hesitate to bow down in submission to the Father. We protest like Satan: "Is there no place/ Left for repentance, none left for pardon?/ None left but by submission."[46] Even Jesus, God incarnate, "knelt down and prayed"(Luke 22:41). Why do so many of us refuse to physically and spiritually bow?

As disciples of Jesus, we ought to pray with full confidence that God hears our prayers, not because they are beautiful, sincere, or uttered from the lips of clean living. Rather, He hears them because our hearts are bowed down in the *reverent submission* of Christ that says *not my will, but yours be done.*

Are you praying *on bended knee*?

---

[46] John Milton, *Paradise Lost* (London: Arcturus, 2014),105.

MARCH

March 1

I Will

Psalm 101:1—I will....

What have you determined in your heart that *you will* do today? Although God is the King of your life, He will not make you do anything. If your life is filled with spiritual garbage, He will not require you to throw it out. If your relationships are a mess, He will not clean them up for you. The Lord forgives the chaos we create in our lives through sin, but we must *will* to put our spiritual houses in order. The moment, however, we say, *I will*, He is faithful to help us make it happen: "He will do it"(1 Thes 5:24).

David "willed" his life into glorifying God. In Psalm 101, he says, *I will* to seven things: *worship, purity of heart, disciplining the flesh, abjuring wickedness, keeping good company, loving humility,* and *living with integrity.*

He begins by focusing completely on God through *worship.* He says, "I *will* sing....I *will* sing praise"(v.1). Worshiping God requires intentionality of the heart, soul, and mind.

David then moves to issues of spiritual discipline. Speaking of *purity of heart,* David says, "I *will* walk...with a blameless heart"(v.2). He decides to live a life of inner purity, pleasing to his God. Further, he commits to *disciplining the flesh*: "I *will* set before my eyes no vile thing"(v.3). Like David's life, the Spirit will not take away the filth of our physical lives. God provides the strength and grace to make it happen, but we must *will* it.

These commitments to personal discipline then shift to interactions with others. David exhorts us to *abjure wickedness*: "The deeds of faithless men I hate"(v.3). While our culture celebrates rebellion and tolerates moral corruption, as Christians we must say, "they *will* not cling to me"(v.3). Similarly, David also recognizes the importance of *keeping good company*: "Men of perverse heart will be far from me"(v.5). We cannot live holy lives when we constantly keep the company of spiritually lawless men. Eventually, they corrupt us.

Finally, David concentrates on essential values. He speaks of *loving humility*: "Whoever has haughty eyes and a proud heart, him will I not endure"(v.5). Jesus described Himself as humble (Matt 11:29). As disciples, our lives must also have the fragrance of Christ's humility. Likewise, Christians must live lives of *integrity*: "No one who practices deceit will dwell in my house"(v.7). God hates hypocrisy. As disciples, we must make integrity our highest priority.

As David demonstrates, do not wish your life to glorify God—*will* it to do so! Perhaps start with David's list of "wills." Trust God's mercy when you fall short of the mark. But remember that what you *will* determines the health of your spiritual life. What *will* you do today?

March 2

The Zealous Impediment

Matthew 16:22—Peter took him aside and began to rebuke him. "Never, Lord!" he said. "This shall never happen to you."

When Jesus stands before you and asks you what He asked His disciples—"Who do you say I am?"—how will you respond? Have you been living as if Jesus was simply a great prophet, an exemplary moral teacher, or a sectarian leader of a motley crew of ancient Jews? Or, does your heart declare with the emphasis of Peter, "You are the Christ, the Son of the living God!"(Matt 16:16)?

Peter got it right, at least initially. He understood that Jesus was the Messiah and the Savior of His people. But no sooner had Peter's enthusiastic response been blessed by Christ, than Peter quickly forgot that he stood in the presence of the King. Peter challenges the Lord—*Never, Lord!....This shall never happen to you.* Instead of humbly bowing before the will of the Lord he had just publicly proclaimed, Peter's zeal blinds him to the messianic way. While Peter's heart meant well and his intentions appear to have been noble, they were a stumbling block to Christ. His zeal became an impediment to the ways of the Lord. Peter did not "have in mind the things of God, but the things of men"(Matt 16:23).

When we, like Peter, come to an understanding that Jesus is the Lord of our lives, we must be careful not to allow our personal passions to become a stumbling block in the way of Jesus in our lives. The enemy of Christ is often the "believer" who proclaims Jesus as Lord and then goes about executing and dictating his or her own personal agenda on the ways of God. The disciple, on the other hand, is the one who says, "You are the Christ," and then, like Jesus Himself, says, "Thy will be done." The disciple recognizes the Lord as the Lord and then gets out of the way; he never forgets that it must always be *more of Him and less of me.*

In your love for the Lord, never stop proclaiming Christ as the Lord of your life. Say it loud and clear. But in the wake of this proclamation, there must then be a quiet submission. Avoid Peter's mistake by waiting for the Spirit to gently lead you in the ways of the Lord rather than allowing your zeal to become a stumbling block to the purposes of God in your life. Never forget that you stand in the presence of a King, and the only proper response is that of a will that bows down—"Yes Lord! Thy will be done."

March 3

The Devoted Things

Joshua 7:12—I will not be with you anymore unless you destroy whatever among you is devoted to destruction.

If you have come to a place in your life where you feel as if God is not with you anymore, or He is distant and disconnected, it may be that your life is harboring "devoted things." This was the case for the nation of Israel after the defeat of Jericho. A man named Achan decided to hold on to contraband that God had specifically forbidden. His personal defiance brought disfavor for the entire nation of Israel and threatened to drive the Lord out of their presence. Jehovah then said to them, *"I will not be with you anymore unless you destroy whatever among you is devoted to destruction."*

What is it in your life you are holding on to that is *devoted to destruction*? A great many seemingly beautiful and good things can be responsible for driving God out of our lives. For Achan it was a Babylonian robe, a pile of silver, and an image of gold. For you and me it might be a relationship, a job, a stock portfolio, or a family we cherish. It might even be some firm and fixed belief that stands rooted and resolute against the truth of Jesus Christ in our lives. Whatever it is, if it separates me from Christ, it is *devoted to destruction*. Even if it is a "good" thing, I can allow it to become an instrument of Satan in my life. As C.S. Lewis says, "There is but one good; that is God. Everything else is good when it looks to Him and bad when it turns from Him."[47]

God cannot and will not share the stage of our hearts with any *"devoted thing."* Therefore, we act wisely when we pray for the Spirit's help to examine our hearts and seek out any hidden, *"devoted things"* that are keeping us from God. Until we determine to destroy whatever it is in our lives that is *devoted to destruction*, we are in the clutches of the darkness. We risk driving the Lord from our lives.

Ask the Lord to give you the courage and strength you need to part from the *devoted things* in your life. If they are things, you may need to get rid of them; if they are people, you made need to reprioritize their roles in your life. But if you desire to have *more of Him and less of you,* you must determine that nothing, no matter how good and precious in your eyes, will stand between you and Jesus Christ in your life. *Destroy whatever among you is destined for destruction!*

---

[47] C.S. Lewis, *The Great Divorce* (New York: HarperCollins, 2001), 106.

March 4

No Satisfaction

Esther 5:13—But all this gives me no satisfaction....

Sometimes contemporary music and ancient literature echo the same thing: whatever we have is not enough. The Rolling Stones and the Book of Esther alike declare the absence of satisfaction in the things of this world.[48] We can, like Haman the wealthy Persian noble, have the ear of the king and incalculable riches, and still be without peace. Haman hated Mordecai the Jew. And this hatred spoiled Haman's life of wealth: *all this gives me no satisfaction.* Satan sells the lie that contentment comes in the accumulation of things, the breadth of our experiences, or the sweetness of revenge—anything other than the truth: Jesus Christ.

Jesus had an encounter with another rich man much like Haman. This man had everything the world could offer. And yet, he was unsatisfied. He asks Jesus, "Teacher, what good thing must I do to get eternal life?"(Matt 19:16). Jesus responds, "If you want to be perfect, go, sell your possessions and give to the poor, and you will have treasure in heaven. Then come, follow me"(Matt 19:21). The rich man turns and walks away sad because he cannot imagine parting with his wealth.

As the life of Haman and this inquisitive rich man demonstrate, true and lasting contentment cannot be found in riches, power or human relationship. It can only be found in Christ. We must sacrifice the other "idols" of our lives. Until we do, we are like Haman, imprisoned in the insatiable search for a satisfaction we will not find.

Christ alone is able to satisfy our deepest longings. Have you found this satisfaction? The contentment of the Spirit is your proof. If you are easily angered, often irritable, and rarely happy with what you have, it is likely because you have quenched His Spirit. The disciple, however, may still desire good things, but his contentment is not in them. He finds joy even without them. He has found Christian contentment, that "sweet, inward, quiet, gracious frame of spirit, which freely submits to and delights in God's wise and fatherly disposal in every condition."[49] He has learned "the secret of being content in any and every situation..."(Phil 4:12).

---

[48]The Rolling Stones, 1965, "Satisfaction," *Out of Our Heads.*

[49] Jeremiah Burroughs, *The Rare Jewel of Christian Contentment* (Public Domain), 3.

March 5

Holy Hatred, I.

Romans 12:9—Hate what is evil; cling to what is good.

Hatred suffers from a terrible image problem. It has become synonymous with everything negative, from crimes against humanity to the daily things that we loathe to do. Children and adults alike, flippantly and carelessly say, "I hate this," or "I hate that." And while hatred can and does fuel both inner turmoil and atrocities against God and man, in its *biblical place*, hatred is not only a good thing, it is a necessary thing.

God Himself created the capacity for hatred towards anything and anyone who stands against Him. Consider what He tells us to hate: God "hate(s) all who do wrong," and "hate(s) wickedness"(Ps 5:5; Ps 45:7). If I am to be a disciple of Christ, my heart must also hate evil—"To fear the Lord is to hate evil"(Prov 8:13). If I say that I love the Lord, I must despise wickedness—"Let those who love the Lord hate evil…"(Ps 97:10).

When you find yourself in the presence of wickedness, does your anger burn within you? Do you find yourself saying, "I hate pride and arrogance, evil behavior and perverse speech"(Prov 8:13)? Or do you simply hate things of no eternal consequence—the gray winter days, the tedium of your work, or the mundane chores of daily life? Is your hatred always pointing outward, or does it have the courage to look within and find the very object of its anger lingering there?

We can sense when the Spirit of God is living in us when we hate evil and despise wickedness, first in ourselves, and then in the world around us. We cannot love the Lord, and have the Spirit living in us, and not loathe everything and everyone that willfully sets itself up against God. We must "hate and detest falsehood," "hate those who cling to worthless idols," and "hate those who hate you, Lord, and abhor those who are in rebellion against you"(Ps 119:163; 31:6; 139:21). This is *holy hatred*.

In our spiritual lives, it is foolish to say that we must do away with hate. To do so is to deny an essential characteristic of the God who created us. As C.S. Lewis says, "the absence of anger, especially that sort of anger we call *indignation,* can…be a most alarming symptom. And the presence of indignation may be a good one."[50] *Holy hatred* is a necessity of every disciple of Christ and it must be at war with evil and wickedness. We must hate what God hates just as surely as we must love what He loves.

---

[50] C.S. Lewis, *Reflections on the Psalms* (New York: HarperCollins, 1986), 34.

March 6

Why Has All This Happened?

Judges 6:13—...if the Lord is with us, why has all this happened to us?

One of the sharpest and most enduring criticisms of the Christian faith is the question of Gideon: *"If the Lord is with us, why has all this happened to us?"* We hear this in many circumstances: the parents who walk away from faith after the death of their child; the woman whose violation leaves her bitter and full of self-loathing; the nation that abandons God in the face of a seemingly inexplicable genocide. If God is here and God is good, *why*?

Gideon is approached by the angel of the Lord and told, "The Lord is with you..."(Judg 6:12). But despite looking divinity in the face, Gideon sees only the pain around him and the oppression of his people under the hand of the Midianites. The weakness of Gideon's faith and his pride prevent him from truly seeing God's presence standing before him in the form of the angelic messenger.

Gideon's ensuing response is pregnant with the fallacious thinking common to us all—that of supposing we know what is best for us. When the events do not unfold according to our plans or desires, when loved ones die unexpectedly or warring nations brutally occupy us, instead of waiting for God to reveal the greater good behind the current oppression, we jettison God as either not good or not present. But, what if in this horrible event, God is both present and good? What if He is allowing "the hand of Midian"(6:13) to refine us and bring us to a greater, unexpected goodness we cannot yet see?

Strikingly, Gideon's *why* elicits no direct answer from God, only the command to "'Go in the strength you have and save Israel out of Midian's hand'"(6:14). Centuries later, books have been written and lives have been dissipated on waiting for an "acceptable" answer to Gideon's inquiry. Is your life one of them?

We can continue to stand around waiting on a response or come up with our own, but God has already responded. He gave the answer in His command to Gideon: "Go....I will be with you..."(6:14,16). In the midst of our oppression or pain, we must simply choose to "go in the strength [we] have," trusting that He is with us. Even if we are feeble and faltering, we must take the next step. In His time, He will reveal to us both His glorious presence and His great design for all that we do not now see.

Why has all this happened to us? We may never know in this life, but we should still "go" in faith. Once we do, we can be sure, the assurance we seek will come in God's time.

The Prayerful Pause

Nehemiah 2:4-5—Then I prayed to the God of heaven, and I answered the king....

Who among us cannot remember a time when we spoke hastily and then later regretted what we said? James reminds us, "If anyone is never at fault in what he says, he is a perfect man..."(Jam 3:2). The tongue fails us all the time. It fails, unfortunately, more than it succeeds. There is no instrument of the body more capable of life or death than the tongue. With it "we praise our Lord...and with it we curse men, who have been made in God's likeness"(Jam 3:9).

And yet, there is hope for this unwieldy weapon. As in all things, it can be redeemed by the Lord. Nehemiah demonstrates the tongue's "salvation" as he stands before the most powerful man in the known world, the King of Persia. When this king asked Nehemiah a question, Nehemiah "was very much afraid"(Neh 2:2), aware that his answer would have the potential for life or death. But, as is often the case, an ounce of fear can be helpful. Instead of offering a hasty reply, Nehemiah prays before he responds. In his fear, He takes a *prayerful pause*. He asks God to help him in his response and to temper his tongue with holy wisdom.

Nehemiah is a man who understands that "The heart of the righteous weighs its answers, but the mouth of the wicked gushes evil"(Prov 15:28). As Nehemiah demonstrates, with increasing wisdom comes a decreasing tendency to speak before seeking the Lord's counsel. Once we have prayed and placed the matter before God, we can rest assured that what we say is part of God's providential plan, be that for our benefit or detriment. The goal is God's glory.

If you are finding that your tongue leads you into trouble more often than not, start by practicing the discipline of a *prayerful pause* before you answer the question you have been given. Commit to think of Christ, what He would say and how He would want you to respond. Your *prayerful pause* will make it more probable for God's favor to fall upon the ears of your audience.

Practice the *prayerful pause*.

Restoration

Psalm 71:20—Though you have made me see troubles, many and bitter, you will restore my life again....

When it comes to troubles in this life, the primary difference between the Christian and the non-Christian is not the nature of the troubles themselves, but rather the perspective with which those troubles are met. Trouble is ubiquitous. The disciple of Christ is not immune. In fact, Jesus says to His disciples, "In this life you will have trouble"(John 16:33). But, whereas the man who serves himself, another god, or no god at all, cannot know with certainty that he will survive his trouble, and so is prone to fret and worry, the disciple of Christ can have a confident peace.

David says, *"Though you have made me see troubles, many and bitter, you will restore my life again...."* How can David, God's beloved servant, much less us, know with confidence that life will be restored on the other side of the trouble that presses in against him?

First, God's past faithfulness causes David to cling to God's promise: "I will be with him in trouble. I will rescue him and honor him"(Ps 91:15). The King of Israel believes that "God is not a man, that He should lie, nor a son of man, that He should change His mind. Does He speak and not act? Does He promise and not fulfill?"(Num 23:19).

Second, David realizes the glorification of God's name is the fundamental reason we can have confidence we will be delivered from trouble. The Lord says to David, "call upon me in trouble; I will deliver you, and you shall glorify me"(Ps 50:15 ESV). Our deliverance may not come when we think it should or in the form we think best, but it will come. And when it does, it will be in a manner that best exalts the name of God, even if it means He brings us home into His presence.

Never forget that though your troubles may be as bitter as David's, they are but the individual threads of a tapestry God is weaving. They will all "work together for the good"(Rom 8:28), not only for you, but, more importantly, for His great name. In your troubles, seek the Lord, for "The righteous cry out, and the Lord hears them; He delivers them from all their troubles"(Ps 34:17-18). Trust that the Weaver of your life tapestry "will carry you"(Is 46:4) as you trust in Him amidst your trials.

When troubles come to your life, many and bitter, pray that the Lord gives you the grace to press on in confidence. Know with absolute certainty that *restoration* will come, whether in this life or the next, not because of who you are or what you have done, but because your *restoration* is linked to His glorification—and God will be glorified! Nothing, and no one, not even the powers of darkness, will keep this from happening.

March 9

I Have Told You

Mark 13:23—So be on your guard; I have told you everything ahead of time.

When it comes to a knowledge of God in our lives, we are, as Paul says, a people "without excuse"(Rom 1:20). We might imagine a great many rational arguments for why we do not know God or why it is impossible that He exists and is moving in our world. But the truth is, "since the creation of the world God's qualities—His eternal power and divine nature—have been clearly seen, being understood from what has been made..."(Rom 1:20).

And if the created world around us is not witness enough, then God has also given us His written Word. Of this Word, He says, "let the reader understand..., I have told you everything..."(Mark 13:14, 23). To claim that I do not know who God is or how He desires me to live my life is like receiving an instruction manual for a new piece of equipment, deciding to throw that manual out, and then complaining that no one has explained to me how this new machine works or how I am to operate it. When it comes to my life of faith and my relationship with God, I must open the manual, read it, and follow the instructions. Any failure to do this on my part deserves any lack of full functionality that may follow.

This very obstinacy in the practical matters of life also pervades the heart and minds of many. They prefer to spiritually fumble on their own, ignoring the instructions, and trying to piece together a functional life that runs as smoothly and efficiently as the one designed for them by God. The root of this obstinacy is pride and the overwhelming belief that "I can figure it out on my own." And while some lives can do this for a while, in some categories and to a certain degree, there are often unnecessary sputtering starts in faith and disastrous ends that God never intended for us.

Are you trying to go at it on your own? Or have you committed to read and study God's instruction manual for your life? Can you see the warning signs posted for your safe and productive operation of your life? Jesus says, *be on your guard,* for God has told us *everything ahead of time*, save the exact day of Christ's return. No excuse can ever be made that God did not tell me what was going to happen. The Lord has repeatedly said, "It is written..."(Matt 4:4). Will you open His Word and read it?

Different Forms, Same God

1 Corinthians 12:6—There are different kinds of working, but the same God works all of them in all men.

> As kingfishers catch fire, dragonflies draw flame…
> Each mortal thing does one thing and the same:
> Deals out that being indoors dwells;
> Selves—goes itself; *myself* it speaks and spells,
> Crying, *What I do is me: for that I came.*
> …For Christ plays in ten thousand places,
> Lovely in limbs, and lovely in eyes not his
> To the Father through the features of men's faces.[51]
> —G.M. Hopkins

Nature is, perhaps, God's greatest reminder of His limitless variation. And what is true of the natural world around us is no less true of God's people—*for Christ plays in ten thousand places.* I can spend my life being frustrated by this lack of conformity, wishing everyone else did things the way I do. Or, I can choose to delight in the fact that God works in different ways in different people.

If I cling to my self-centered and narrow-minded view of how things "should" be, I will quickly find myself disillusioned and hopelessly frustrated. More importantly, I will miss the incredible beauty and power of a God who is able to work out His purposes in so many different ways.

Do you find yourself frustrated with how God appears to be working or not working in the life of another? Perhaps the actions you observe are completely inexplicable or counterintuitive to your understanding. You wonder, "What is that person thinking?" And yet, God may very well be behind it, working out His purposes in a different way, translating them into a "language" that you cannot yet understand.

In light of this reality, be quick to recognize that *Each mortal thing does one thing and the same: Deals out that being indoors each one dwells.* And in the end, though we may not at first understand or even like what we observe in others, unless it directly contradicts the words of Christ or speaks against His Spirit, it is God behind this multiplicity of selves. He is working differently in everything and everyone.

Delight in a God whose power knows no limits to its beautiful variation!

---

[51] Gerard Manley Hopkins, "As Kingfishers Catch Fire, Dragonflies Draw Flame," in *The Poems of Gerard Manley Hopkins*, ed. W.H. Gardner and MacKenzie (Oxford: Oxford University Press, 1970), 90.

March 11

Doing Your Duty

Luke 17:10—…when you have done everything you were told to do, should say, 'We are unworthy servants, we have only done our duty.'

What is our *duty* to Jesus? All too often we see it as little more than a polite acknowledgement or periodic interaction on a Sunday morning. For some, there is no apparent duty at all, and any suggestion that there should be causes a contemptuous bristling. "What do I owe to a carpenter who lived and died over 2,000 years ago in a dusty corner of Israel?" The truth—everything!

Christian or not, we must all understand that we are servants. Either we serve Jesus Christ, or we serve some other "god" we may not even recognize. Either way, we are servants. Servants, Jesus reminds us, have duties before they have privileges: "Suppose…you had a servant plowing or looking after the sheep. Would he say to the servant when he comes in from the field, 'Come along now and sit down to eat'? Would he not rather say, 'Prepare my supper, get yourself ready and wait on me while I eat and drink; after that you, you may eat and drink'?"(Luke 17:7-8).

Why then do we so frequently resist duty in our lives? Instead of being grateful to serve a Lord who has given us everything, even the privileged *duty* of service to Him, we find reason to complain. We blame God for our sense of *duty*, saying, "If you made me, you made this feeling of responsibility that I've always carried about like a sack of bricks."[52] Our pride elevates us in our own minds above the position we were created for and sows the selfish seeds of discontent and rebellion. We begin to think we deserve thanks for the little we do. But Jesus asks, "Would [the master] thank the servant because he did what he was told to do?"(Luke 17:9).

So long as we continue to see ourselves as worthy of acknowledgement and praise, we will find it almost impossible to fulfill our duties to the Lord. It is easier for the ruined life, the prodigal son convinced of his unworthiness, to understand the role of servant than it is for the son who has remained. And yet, the *duty* for both is the same—to love and serve the Father with all their heart, soul, strength and mind.

When we don't admit we have a *duty* to Christ, we fool ourselves. When we look for a pat on the back for the little we do, we are expecting a commendation for doing the *duty* we were created and expected to perform. Let us start understanding that we are servants with a *duty* to love and obey the Father who has first loved us. Then He will elevate us to the privileged positions of sons and daughters of God!

---

[52] Graham Greene, *The Heart of the Matter* (New York: Penguin Books, 1999), 230.

March 12

Thrown Overboard

Jonah 1:15-16—Then they took Jonah and threw him overboard, and the raging sea grew calm. At this the men greatly feared the Lord, and they offered a sacrifice to the Lord and made vows to Him.

It might be that your single greatest act of ministry in the lives of others is to be thrown overboard into the raging sea. We have this idea that we have to do great things for God or that it must be done in a certain way. But when God comes and tells us to go somewhere we deem hopeless or irredeemable (such as Ninevah), we turn and go the other way (Jonah 1:2). Ninevah was never part of our plan.

The fantastic reality of our Lord's love, however, is that He is able and willing to redeem even our acts of disobedience and use them to bring Him glory. God pursued Jonah, and the storms began to rage. As the waves beat against the ship, Jonah knew his sin and he told the men to throw him overboard. But what Jonah did not likely know was that God would use Jonah's disobedience to bring a crew of idolatrous men to fear the Lord God Almighty.

Like Jonah, I might be possessed of the illusion that I can go about business my own way, even when God clearly leads me in another direction. But even though I board a ship for Tarshish, I cannot escape God's providential plan. Through my disobedience, God is likely not only to teach me something about myself and my King, but also to use my disobedience to His advantage in the lives of others. My sin just might position me to glorify God in a place I never imagined.

Those who, like Jonah, have sinned and become convicted of it are often the best poised to minister to the lost—"I know that it is my fault that this great storm has come upon you"(Jonah 1:12). It should come as no surprise, however, if the Lord chooses to throw us overboard into the raging sea. Just because we have confessed, does not mean that there are not consequences to our disobedience. And these very consequences may calm the storm and change the lives of others forever.

Do not aspire to Jonah's disobedience. But if you do willfully disobey, know that God is able to redeem your life and turn even your disobedience into an instrument of His grace in the lives of others. You may get tossed into the sea so that others witness the mighty hand of God's redemption. Whether a "big fish" is there waiting for you or not, you can be sure—the name of the Lord will be praised.

March 13

Old Time is Still A-Flying

1 Corinthians 7:29, 31—...the time is short....For this world in its present form is passing away.

> Gather ye rosebuds while ye may,
> Old Time is still a-flying;
> And this same flower that smiles today,
> Tomorrow will be dying.[53]
> —Robert Herrick

There is no time like the present. What now is, soon will not be. And what comes next depends, in part, upon what I do in this very moment. I can choose to do with my spiritual life what I so often do with my physical one—put off till tomorrow what I might, and maybe should, do today. And while another day's dust on the countertop may not have any eternal significance, the same is not true of my soul. Am I living today with the conviction that *time is short...[and] this world in its present form is passing away?*

When I truly understand the ephemeral nature of my life and of everything around me, the Spirit within enthuses me with a sense of holy urgency and personal conviction. If I believe I have time, I'm likely to fritter it away on a variety of comparatively unimportant things. But when I'm vitally aware of a deadline and I hear the clock ticking, I'm much more apt to remain focused on the task before me. God's tasks all have eternal significance and, as such, ought to be given priority in our lives.

When you are tempted to think the work of God in you or the life of another can wait until tomorrow, remember that the *present form is passing away.* Your opportunity today may not exist tomorrow. The words of forgiveness or love that might have been the saving grace in the life of someone today, may be too late tomorrow or have little significance or relevance.

Make it your ambition today to "be free from concern"(1 Cor 7:32), and as unfettered from the cares of the world as possible. They will cause you to dissipate your time and energies and, perhaps, tempt you to put off till tomorrow the very task of today that has some true, eternal significance. To be "concerned about the Lord's affairs"(1 Cor 7:32) is to grab the ephemeral in the here and now. Are you ready to catch time by the tail and claim this moment for God?

---

[53] Robert Herrick, "To the Virgins, to Make Much of Time," in *The Norton Anthology of English Literature,* ed. M.H. Abrams (New York: W.W. Norton & Company, 1993), 1361.

March 14

Heads Held High

Leviticus 26:13—I broke the bars of your yoke and enabled you to walk with heads held high.

When the Israelites were enslaved by the Egyptians, they lived under a heavy yoke. But God rescued them, broke the bars of this oppression, and brought them to His Promised Land. He gave them reason to *walk with heads held high.*

Similarly, when Christ "sets you free, you will be free indeed"(John 8:36). He breaks the yoke of sin that bound you. He enables you to walk with a freeing confidence and the swagger of heavenly grace. Fully redeemed by the work of Christ on the cross, "there will be no room for vanity," as you are "free from the miserable illusion that it is [your] doing."[54] Devoid of any trace of "self-approval," you can lift your head high as you "most innocently rejoice in the thing that God has made [you] to be...."[55]

Because of this call to rejoicing, it is a wicked injustice to see the life of devotion to Jesus as simply bound by rules, regulations, and self-denial. To be sure, the redeemed life does not, and cannot, look like it once did. It is bowed to Christ and His will. But in this bowing, there is an exalting. Like the redeemed Israelites, we are called to stand with *heads held high.*

So when the world suggests that I am bound to a deluded tyranny, I must ask myself, "Do I know that I am truly free?" When I am told my faith is foolishness—an embarrassment of reason or a relic of a quaint, provincial time—can I cling to God's promise that "my head will be exalted above the enemies who surround me"(Ps 27:6)?

In Christ, we are exalted! God wants us to walk with our *heads held high,* because "Perfect humility dispenses with modesty."[56] We are clothed in Christ and we shine. We best embrace God's glory in us when we stand tall, *heads held high,* and walk with the confidence of Christ. We are called to live among the self-empowered with the exalted power of Jesus.

In the freedom this power brings, let us remember: It is no sin to "boast in the Lord"(2 Cor 10:17). He has broken our yokes and lifted our heads, that we might do just this. As Paul says, "May I never boast except in the cross of our Lord Jesus Christ..."(Gal 6:14). *Hold your head high* in light of the weight of Christ's glory in you!

---

[54] C.S. Lewis, *The Weight of Glory* (New York: HarperCollins, 2001), 37.

[55] Ibid, 38.

[56] Ibid, 38.

March 15

Grace of Giving

2 Corinthians 8:7—...see that you also excel in this grace of giving.

It is nearly impossible not to give at all. Even the most stingy and selfish of hearts is forced to give something or some part of him or herself in the most basic of human interactions. Perhaps even the total recluse might be caught giving to some animal or fictitious friend of the imagination. Giving is part of who we are because we were made in God's image, and He is the ultimate giver.

But to understand giving as an act of grace and to personally excel at doing it, is entirely different. Paul says to the Corinthians, "But just as you excel in everything—in faith, in speech, in knowledge, in complete earnestness and in your love for us—see that you also excel in this *grace of giving*"(2 Cor 8:7). As a disciple of Christ, I might demonstrate a stalwart faith among the fiercest of life's trials and exhibit wisdom in times of uncertainty. But, if I do not give of what God has given to me—my energies, my time and resources, and every other category that God has entrusted to me—I am not fully carrying out my discipleship. I am not doing as Christ has done.

To excel in the *grace of giving* is to commit to a spirit of generosity which emulates our Father and His Son. Giving began with God, who created the world and everything in it, and then reclaimed it all in the act of a Father "who did not spare His own Son, but gave Him up for us all..."(Rom 8:32). In a similar demonstration of love, Jesus "gave Himself for our sins..."(Gal 1:4). He did not spare even His life.

God the Father and Jesus the Son have shown us how to give. The only way to *excel* in this *grace of giving* is to do it with the motive force that God has used: love. When we infuse our giving, not just with duty or necessity, but with the love of God the Father and Jesus the Son, we will become generous beyond our natural tendencies. Our giving will take on a grace—the grace of God. How much one gives and what he or she gives is a matter of the Spirit's leading. What is of primary importance to the Lord is the earnest willingness to do it. When we have this enthusiasm within us, we prove that we are filled with the love of Christ, who, "though He was rich, yet for your sakes He became poor, so that you through His poverty might become rich"(2 Cor 8:9).

Are you excelling in the *grace of giving*? While we will never be able to match the generosity of God and the sacrificial love of Christ, we can decide to give in the spirit with which our Lord has given to us. Let the love of God infuse your giving.

March 16

Godly Sorrow

2 Corinthians 7: 9-10—...you became sorrowful as God intended....Godly sorrow brings repentance that leads to salvation and leaves no regret....

When Solomon said, "Sorrow is better than laughter"(Ecc 7:3), he did not intend to suggest that our lives should seek out suffering and pain. That would be the clear work of a spiritual masochist. Rather, the King of Israel intimated what the Apostle Paul later enumerated to the Corinthians —the importance of *godly sorrow*. *Godly sorrow* is that mourning in our lives that drives us back into the arms of our Lord. When Jesus said, "Blessed are those who mourn, for they will be comforted"(Matt 5:4), He meant just what He said. Only the mourning heart recognizes the depth of its sin in a way that drives it to Christ to be cleansed and comforted.

Mourning over his sin, David says, "The sacrifices of God are a broken spirit, a broken and contrite heart O God, you will not despise"(Ps 51:17). Have you been broken to the point of *godly sorrow*? If you have not, at some point in your life, said with the Psalmist, "My soul is weary with sorrow"(Ps 119:28), then question whether you have ever truly grasped the depth and the breadth of the sin within you or the miracle that heals you. For God knows "our happiness lies in Him. Yet we will not seek it in Him as long as He leaves us any other resort where it can even plausibly be looked for."[57] If there is always laughter and merriment, we will never meet Jesus face to face.

Jesus Himself was a "man of sorrows" who "took up our infirmities and carried our sorrows..."(Is 53:3-4). He was "pierced for our transgressions [and]...crushed for our iniquities; the punishment that brought us peace was upon Him, and by His wounds we are healed"(Is 53:5). If we are truly in love with this *man of sorrows*, then we ourselves will know *godly sorrow*. When the Spirit lives in us, we will weep over that which separates us from the One we love. The Spirit within us will produce in us an "earnestness...[and] eagerness to clear [ourselves]...[and an] indignation,...alarm... longing...concern...[and] readiness to see justice done"(2 Cor 7:11).

When we understand the importance of *godly sorrow* in our lives, we will be ready to receive the grace that transforms our mourning into songs of joy: "I will turn their mourning into gladness; I will give them comfort and joy instead of sorrow"(Jer 31:13). Blessed are those who mourn over what Christ mourns!

Have you been blessed with *godly sorrow* in your heart?

---

[57] C.S. Lewis, *The Problem of Pain* (New York: HarperCollins, 1996), 94.

The Unlikely Instrument

John 4:39—Many of the Samaritans from that town believed in Him because of the woman's testimony....

One thing that the story of the Samaritan woman at the well teaches us is that sometimes God uses the most unlikely people to be the instruments of His saving grace. Since Jesus clearly desired to bring the Samaritan people of Sychar to salvation, it would have made sense for Him to meet with the village elders and religious leaders of the town. He might have gathered the people, worked some miracles, and demonstrated His wisdom and power to the crowd.

Instead, Jesus never enters the village at all. He stops at the well, and it becomes His pulpit to a crowd of one. He intentionally chose to address a marginalized woman of ill repute rather than seek out the respected men of the village. When the disciples return from the town and find Jesus conversing with her, they are "surprised to find Him talking with a woman"(John 4:27). This interaction broke every social convention; but then, that is what Jesus chose to do time and time again. And praise God He did! The destiny of us all depends upon His willingness to override social norms.

When you look at your own life, do you identify with the Samaritan woman—an imperfect person going about your daily work and addressing basic needs? If so, be ready: Jesus may be poised to use you mightily in the salvation of others. While you could be tempted to think that your *ordinary* life does not have much to offer the ministry of Jesus, you could not be more wrong. The Samaritan woman was a sinner like you and me, living out her *ordinary* day, when Jesus apprehended her life to be an *unlikely instrument* in bringing many to faith. Because of the testimony of that one unexceptional woman, *many of the Samaritans from that town believed.* Imagine what your life may be able to accomplish for Christ's Kingdom!

Jesus wants the quotidian details of your life and mine to be transformed by His saving grace. Ordinariness and imperfection, wielded in the hands of our Lord, can be the most extraordinary tools for the gospel in the hearts of the men and women God wants to reach. Pray that you will never limit Christ's ability to use your imperfection to touch the lives of others.

March 18

The Danger of Proximity

Micah 7:5—Do not trust a neighbor; put no confidence in a friend. Even with her who lies in your embrace, be careful of your words.

God designed the heart to trust so that it might be able to enjoy relationship with Him. Trust allows intimate *proximity*. Those we embrace as friends or lovers are allowed to come close. In this nearness of heart they are able to both bless us and be agents of pain in our lives.

The problem is not that we trust, it is that we too often put our trust in the wrong things. Instead of completely placing our trust in God, our tendency is to put our trust in the proximal people and things in our lives. But Jeremiah says, "Beware of your friends, do not trust your brother. For every brother is a deceiver, and every friend a slanderer"(Jer 9:4). Those we choose to trust are given the access they need to bring us harm, intentional or not. David laments, "Even my close friend, whom I trusted…has lifted up his heel against me"(Ps 41:9).

Because we are sinners, we will injure others and they, in turn, will inflict deep wounds upon us. The tendency is for us to respond with a surprised hurt like David: "If an enemy were insulting me, I could endure it; if a foe were raising himself against me, I could hide from him. But it is you, a man like myself, my companion, my close friend with whom I have enjoyed sweet fellowship…"(Ps 55:12-14). We expect injury from an enemy, but not from a friend. The hurt is somehow deeper because it is close to the heart and defies our expectations. But should it?

There is no sphere of human relationship immune from the daggers of the soul. David saw it when he walked in the house of God (Ps 55:14). Micah reminds us that a "man's enemies are the members of his own household"(Micah 7:6). Whether it is in the house of God or the place we call home, we may be wounded by those we allow to draw near.

Until I understand that "I am the worst" of sinners (1 Tim 1:15), I will continue to be surprised and disillusioned by the wounds sustained at the hands of my friends. But while the pain they cause might incline me to despair, the blood of Christ covers it and brings hope and healing! Though Jesus "would not entrust Himself to them, for He knew all people"(John 2:24), He nonetheless chose to love deeply and completely.

If I am commanded to *put no confidence in a friend*, how then do I love as Jesus did? Like Christ I focus on the glimmerings of God in them. Fixed on that light, as on a star in the night sky, suddenly Christ's perspective becomes mine. I am empowered to love as He loved, not guarded or cynical, but with eyes open and arms outstretched, covered in the blood of the Lamb.

March 19

Cliff Diving Pigs

Matthew 8:34—And when they saw Him, they pleaded with Him to leave their region.

Watching Jesus exorcise demons and drive them into a herd of pigs that dove over a cliff must have been an incredible sight. It is little wonder that the people of the Gadarenes came out in force to meet the man who performed such an unusual event. And yet, instead of rejoicing over the salvation of the two demon-possessed men or celebrating the man who made it happen, we see people panicking. They plead with Jesus to leave their region. There is no jubilation, only fear.

On the one hand, we can sympathize with the town's people. Someone lost a great fortune over that cliff. Who would want his or her herd to be the next? There is a point at which the proximity of the divine in our midst becomes a bit too uncomfortable, and like the people of the Gadarenes, the natural response is to push away or run in the other direction. We would much rather have our "god" contained and controlled: there when we need him and not when we don't.

But Jesus goes where He pleases. And thank God that He does! So if He were to drop by to exorcise the remaining "demons" in your life, would you celebrate or mourn the collateral loss? Would you, like the people of the Gadarenes, be asking Jesus to leave? Are you ready to be irrevocably changed, or are you afraid of what that change will cost and how it will look? Make no mistake—there is no encounter with Jesus that does not leave us changed!

We must, therefore, beware of any pleading for Jesus to leave the region of our hearts. This sort of spiritual sentiment is the sign of an inner sickness and an indication that it is not well with our souls. More likely than not, our pleas for Christ to leave will not be overt. They might be of the subtler kind, the gentle avoidance or the graceful omission. But in the end, anything other than a welcome, even if half-hearted at first in our bowing submission, will be seen as a rejection. And despite His boundless love for us, Jesus will not hesitate to step into His boat and cross to the other side. We can be sure, someone else is waiting there to welcome Him.

When Jesus comes into your region changing the lives of everyone and everything He encounters, be careful you do not push Him away.

March 20

Christ is All

Colossians 3:11—...Christ is all....

When the Apostle Paul says, "Christ is all," we must know that "These three words are the essence and substance of Christianity. If our hearts can really go along with them, it is well with our souls; if not, we may be sure we have yet much to learn."[58]   Going further, understanding the sufficiency of Christ and the completeness we can have in Him is the only thing that truly matters in our lives: Christ and Christ alone. Have you decided that *Christ is all* in your life?

Arriving at this conviction requires that we consider who the Bible says Christ is. He is from the beginning and, "Through Him all things were made; without Him nothing was made that has been made"(John 1:3). He is the "Alpha and the Omega, the First and the Last, the Beginning and the End"(Rev 22:13).   He created the immeasurable expanse of the heavens and the depths of our hearts. No one but Jesus can measure their limits.

And because Jesus Christ knows these limits, He condescended to become our salvation: "Salvation is found in no one else, for there is no other name under heaven given to men by which we must be saved"(Acts 4:12).   Do you hear the imperative—"must be saved"?   If salvation is necessary, then sooner or later I must acquiesce to the truth that Christ is the only way. He alone is sufficient: "My grace is sufficient for you, for my power is made perfect in weakness"(2 Cor 12:9).

This sufficiency of Jesus rests on the fact that "in Christ the fullness of the Deity lives..."(Col 2:9).   God the Father has decided that Jesus is the *only* way that we can be reconciled to Him through the life that He lays down of His own accord (John 10:17-18).   Further, Christ is the singular avenue to completeness, the fullness for which we were created (Col 2:10). And this fullness will always evade us so long as we hold on to any part of ourselves.

For *Christ to be all* in you, you must be nothing—zero.   There is only one way to reach the completeness of 1.   It is not $1 + 1$, as our natural inclinations would desire, but $1 + 0$. For, "The value of each human soul considered simply in itself, out of relation to God, is zero."[59] Have you reached the understanding that in the equation of eternity, the only way to reach completeness is for *Christ to be all* in your life?   The entire Bible and 2,000 years of history can be summarized in three words—*Christ is all*.

---

[58] J.C. Ryle, *Holiness: Its Nature, Hindrances, Difficulties and Roots* (Chicago: Moody Publishers, 2007), 387.

[59] C.S. Lewis, *The Weight of Glory* (New York: HarperCollins, 2001), 170.

Reductio ad Absurdum[60]

Psalm 53:3—Everyone has turned away, they have together become corrupt; there is no one who does good, not even one.

One of the most deceptive "gods" of today is the god of goodness. In his genius, Satan has twisted the mind of men to deify the idea of goodness. Whether in our works or our treatment of others, the contemporary ideology suggests that being "good" and doing "good" is all that matters. Such a neat and tidy, personal god, is completely in our control. It can be improved upon or temporarily abandoned with no ill effect; it can be redefined or justified as necessary for the occasion; and, it always seems to find itself on the right side of the one who made it.

But the Word of God argues against this self-made god of goodness. As the Psalmist reminds us, "All have turned aside, they have together become corrupt; there is no one who does good, not even one"(Ps 14:3). When the rich young man addresses Jesus as "Good teacher," even Jesus says of goodness, "Why do you call me good?...No one is good—except God alone"(Mark 10:8). While we may be capable of good things as the Spirit enables us, we have no intrinsic goodness apart from God. For this reason, to build a life around "being good" is a *reductio ad absurdum*—a false and impossible reality.

This deluded thinking is the result of taking an exclusive attribute of God, *goodness*, and making many believe that they can embody it and define themselves by it. This is just as ridiculous as suggesting man is capable of perfect love and total knowledge! Only God is all-knowing (1 John 3:20). Only God loves perfectly (1 John 4:8). Only God is good (Mark 10:8)!

We must let go of any illusion that we are good, and that we can build a life purpose around our "goodness." Instead, let us "Give thanks to the Lord; for He is *good*; His love endures forever"(Ps 107:1). Rather than building our world around our works, may we "Taste and see that the Lord is *good*," and know in our hearts that "those who seek the Lord lack no good thing"(Ps 34:8,10). If we do not clearly understand that we are "sinful from birth"(Ps 51:3), we are paying homage to the god of goodness. And this god, Satan's god, is anything but *good*. It is an idol that mocks the very character of the God who created us.

When we give up the notion that we are *good*, the goodness of God will be ours. May we trade the "good" that is no good in us, for the only *good* that matters: God and God alone.

---

[60] A ridiculous impossibility

March 22

At His Word

John 4:50—The man took Jesus at His word and departed.

We will not see the transformative power of Christ in our lives until we choose to believe what He says to us and act upon it. The royal official of Capernaum made that choice—*the man took Jesus at His word*—and his son was healed. The official did not question Jesus, but departed. And in the simple act of departing, the man said to all posterity, *"I believe!"*

Have you taken Jesus *at His word*? Or are you still questioning and trying to satisfy your incredulity? While there is no sin in asking questions, and Jesus has no fear of our most pointed inquisitions, when we don't take Jesus *at His word*, we are the losers. Christ knows "'How foolish [we] are, and how slow to believe all that the prophets have spoken!'"(Luke 24:25). But the degree and length to which we stand around and allow our questioning to keep us from "departing," is to limit Christ's transformative power in our lives.

It is easy to accuse Jesus of not speaking and acting in our lives like He did in the life of the royal official. We can choose to see Christ as partial in this, unfair and impotent in the struggles of our lives or simply locked in the storybook of an ancient time. But if we say these things to ourselves, we must also be careful that we hold ourselves up to the standard set by the royal official. Unless we are taking Jesus *at His word* by obeying and departing as this man from Capernaum did, we have no business whining about the lack of Christ's motivity in our lives.

A reason so many may not see the power of Jesus working in their lives is simply because they have chosen not to take Jesus *at His word*. A tacit familiarity with the words of Christ is not a belief that causes me to "depart." When I depart, I declare my belief as living and active. My action says to Jesus and to the world at large that I believe Christ is who He says He is and will do what He says He will do. It is faith made visible. And because I have chosen to take Jesus *at His word*, the floodgates of heaven are now opened and every power in the universe is deployed at our Lord's service to move in my life as He sees best.

Have you determined to take Jesus *at His word*? The moment you do, Christ will unleash His holy power in your life.

Fighting the Lord's Battles

1 Samuel 25:28—...for the Lord will certainly make a lasting dynasty for my master, because he fights the Lord's battles.

Are you busy fighting the Lord's battles or your own? Is your life filled with countless petty skirmishes that trample the name of God and dissipate your energies? David's ascendency to power and favor in the nation of Israel followed on the footsteps of fighting *the Lord's battles*, God's way. Whether he was slaying Goliath and the Philistine army or sparing the life of King Saul, his warfare, or the merciful withholding of it, brought glory to the name of God.

But when David finds himself snubbed by the petulant Nabal, David decides to engage in his own war. Rather than obeying the Lord's injunction—"It is mine to avenge; I will repay"(Deut 32:35)—David sets off to take vengeance in his own hands. He says, "May God deal with David, be it ever so severely, if by morning I leave one male alive of all who belong to him!"(1 Sam 25:22). Only the wisdom of Abigail keeps David from sinning. She says, "Let no wrong doing be found in you....[so that] my master will not have on his conscience the staggering burden of needless bloodshed or of having avenged himself"(1 Sam 25:28,31).

Far too often we, like David, succumb to the desire to fight battles we have no business fighting. We allow ourselves to be consumed with our own agendas and reputations. We forget that our primary purpose is to *fight the battles of the Lord*. In fighting our own battles, we find our strength sapped and our vision increasingly blurred. Our energies are dissipated, our relationships suffer, and our intimacy with the Lord is neglected. Satan would like nothing better than to wear us out fighting a bunch of petty skirmishes of no significance so that we are rendered ineffectual for the battles that truly matter. Finally, and perhaps ironically, the very wars we make to protect our self-interests often serve to defame us, weaken our position with God and men, and burden our consciences.

How then do I know whether I am fighting for the Lord or for myself? I must ask myself two things: Is this fight bringing glory to the name of the Lord? Does this battle have eternal significance? If the answer to either question is "No," I must critically question my motives. If the Lord sends me an Abigail to stay my sword, I must be ready to listen. Pushing ahead may lead to needless "bloodshed." When I am fighting the Lord's battles, both His name and His eternal purposes in my life will be magnified.

When we commit to *fight the Lord's battles*, we can say with confidence, "If God is for us, who can be against us?"(Rom 8:31).

March 24

Condemned or Not Condemned?

John 3:18—Whoever believes in Him is not condemned, but whoever does not believe in Him stands condemned already because he has not believed in the name of God's one and only Son.

When we are listening to the words of Jesus, we must make a determination about Him. Either we believe in Him as the "one and only Son" of God, or we do not. Indecision, avoidance, or flagrant lack of choice is synonymous with disbelief. I must ask myself the following questions: Have I been candy-coating the teachings of Jesus in my life and in the lives of others? Have I been too soft and sweet with a world that Jesus tells us is condemned to eternal death?

The devil's lie is that Jesus is just another holy man, a great moral teacher, even a prophet of God. But to say that He is the only Son of God who came "to save the world through Him"(John 3:17), and that we are condemned without Him, is another thing entirely.

Today's Church is increasingly guilty of a lack of urgency and sobriety on the question of Christ. We must see the disbelieving world around us as not just misguided, apathetic and ruled by personal fancy, but as condemned to hell apart from salvation in Christ. We do God and His people a grave injustice when we water down this reality because we think it too harsh. Jesus sets it up this way, not us. It is the truth He proclaims, and we must live it and preach it. Until we see the reality of hell, we will not see the absolute necessity for Christ within us and the world around us.

Are there some in your life who have not dealt definitively with the question of Christ? If you love them, you will begin to see them as condemned people who, apart from a rebirth in Christ, are destined for destruction. This is not cruel thinking, but compassionate. Yeats' words deeply resonant with the compassionate disciple:

> Things fall apart; the centre cannot hold;
> Mere anarchy is loosed upon the world,
> The blood-dimmed tide is loosed, and everywhere
> The ceremony of innocence is drowned....[61]

In this crescendo of the Second Coming, it is the greatest act of love on our part to attempt to save the lost from condemnation. Let this love fuel our urgency for them. Let the saving words of Jesus speak through us!

---

[61] W.B. Yeats, "The Second Coming," in *Modern British Literature*, ed. Frank Kermode and Hallander (New York: Oxford University Press, 1973), 192.

March 25

Worthy of Fire

Numbers 31:23—...and anything else that can withstand fire must be put through the fire, and then it will be clean.

When James tells us to "Consider it pure joy, my brothers and sisters, when you face trials of many kinds"(James 1:2), we may find the idea of rejoicing in tribulation absurd. We may question what good could possibly come from our current difficulty. In the midst of our pain, we might struggle with the idea that trials produce perseverance and make us "mature and complete"(James 1:3).

But there is a much more fundamental reason to rejoice in the fires that test our lives. God puts to the flame not only what is unworthy, but especially that which is of great substance and significant value. If there is purifying fire in my life, it is because I am of value to the Lord.

The battles of the Israelite army made this principle powerfully clear. Having defeated the Midianites, the army of Israel returns victorious, carrying the spoils of war. But, God required that the "Gold, silver, bronze, iron, tin, lead"(Num 31:22), all the elements of substantial value, be *put through the fire* to purify them. The spoils of a weaker constitution received a soaking purification "with the water of cleansing"(Num 31:23). In both cases, cleansing was required of all that was won (Num 31:23). What remained after this cleansing was only the cleanest, purest and finest of what once was.

If your life is being purified by fire or water, "consider it pure joy." Not only is God working in you to make you "mature and complete," the full radiance of your intended self, but He is also telling you how much He values you. God purifies what He wants to use for His glory.

But in all cases remember that God promises not to allow more than "what you can bear"(1 Cor 10:13). Though you may have "had to suffer grief in all kinds of trials," know that these have come "so that your faith—of greater worth than gold, which perishes even though refined by fire—may be proved genuine and may result in praise, glory and honor when Jesus Christ is revealed"(1 Peter 1:7). When the fire comes, remember you are of great value to the purposes of God. He will bring you through the flames to claim you as His own (Zech 13:9). For, "We are God's own, to Him, therefore, let us live and die."[62]

---

[62] John Calvin, *Golden Booklet of the True Christian Life* in *Devotional Classics*, ed. Richard Foster and Smith (New York: HarperCollins, 2005), 137.

March 26

The Greatest Commandment

2 Kings 23:25—Neither before nor after Josiah was there a king like him who turned to the Lord as he did—with all his heart and with all his soul and with all his strength....

According to Jesus, the correct answer to the question, "What must I do to inherit eternal life?" is: "Love the Lord your God with all your heart and with all your soul and with all your strength and with all your mind…"(Luke 10:25,27). In another place, our Lord refers to this as the *"greatest commandment"*(Matt 22:38). Given the importance of this injunction, it ought to shock us that King Josiah is the *one* man (other than Christ Himself) who is specifically noted to have followed the "greatest commandment."

If we desire to do the will of God and to inherit eternal life, then we must learn from the life of Josiah. Though he ruled in a kingdom poised for imminent collapse and was surrounded by wickedness, Josiah chose to turn toward the Lord with all his heart, soul and strength. When the Book of the Law is found in the Temple and read before Josiah, his heart was moved for the things of the Lord. He wept and "tore his robes"(2 Kings 22:11) in anguish over his nation's disobedience.

Even though the prophetess Huldah predicts the certain destruction of Israel after his death, Josiah does not despair to the point of inaction or apathetic complacency; he does not rest, satisfied that he will be gathered to his fathers and spared the sight of this destruction (2 Kings 22:20). Rather, his soul is convicted to action and he publicly "renewed the covenant in the presence of the Lord" and the people (2 Kings 23:3).

This renewed commitment uses Josiah's physical and spiritual strength to unleash on his nation an unprecedented, holy zeal. Josiah goes throughout the Kingdom of Judah and ruthlessly roots out the endemic idolatry. He slaughters the pagan priests, destroys the high places, and smashes the altars of the foreign gods. He takes no quarter with wickedness. He offers no conciliatory peace with the darkness.

Do you desire to fulfill the *greatest commandment* in your life? Then let your life become more like the life of Josiah and you will come closer to what Jesus desires for us—"not turning aside to the right or to the left"(2 Kings 22:2). Like Josiah, weep over what saddens the Lord, and remain steadfast to His covenantal commands. But begin by being ruthless in the rooting out of evil in your life.

To love the Lord with all your heart is to live like Josiah. Will you choose to live this kind of life?

March 27

The Good and the Bad

Job 2:10—Shall we accept good from God and not trouble?

Why is it that our relationship with God is one of the few areas of our lives in which we have the expectation of one-way blessing? There is no human relationship in which we do not expect ups and downs, good days and bad days, the rough with the smooth. We can expect that from the weather and even our own physical bodies. Why then do we expect only blessing from God? This is an unrealistic expectation founded in the supposition that we necessarily know what is best for us. It forgets that "God intends to give us what we need, not what we now think we want."[63]

Job's sufferings led him to understand, better than most, that God gives us what we need, not what we deserve or want. Though Job began in a place of prosperity, Satan saw this as the reason for his devotion to God. If we are similarly living in prosperity and peace, we can be sure that Satan is aware—"Have you not put a hedge around him…and everything he has?"(Job 1:9). If the Lord then allows difficulty to come into our lives, can we say with Job, *"Shall we accept good from God and not trouble?"*

The true test of the disciple is the ability to praise God for who He is and not for what He does or does not bring into our world of expectations. Like Job, the disciple is capable of praise even in the midst of disaster: "The Lord gave and the Lord has taken away; may the name of the Lord be praised"(Job 1:21). This praise need not be beautiful. It may be half-hearted at first, stained with tears and moments when, like Job, we curse the day we were born. But in the end, we are called to a rejoicing that finds contentment "whatever the circumstances"(Phil 4:11).

The only way to rejoice in the midst of trouble is to turn our focus away from that trouble towards Jesus. It does not mean we live in denial of pain. Job could not ignore the sores that afflicted his body. But it does decide to look beyond our flesh towards the God who holds all things in His hands. So long as we fixate on what we do or do not have, we prove that our contentment is not in God, but in what He has or has not given us. When we fix our eyes on Jesus, however, we can say with Job: "My ears had heard of you…now my eyes have seen you"(Job 42:5).

Whether God has placed you in green pastures or in a barren desert, allow the landscape to fade away until all you see is the face of Jesus. Then, "Whether well fed or hungry, whether living in plenty or in want," you will be able to "do everything through Him who gives you strength"(Phil 4:12-13).

---

[63] C.S. Lewis, *The Problem of Pain* (New York: HarperCollins, 2001), 47.

March 28

Finish

2 Corinthians 8:11—Now finish the work, so that your eagerness to do it may be matched by your completion of it....

Enthusiasm for a project or a job is a wonderful thing: It helps to get the ball rolling and, in many cases, breathes life into a great many causes that might otherwise have lain neglected, dormant or lifeless. The unfortunate reality, however, is that most "start-ups" will be abandoned, as the spark to start them is not enough to fuel their continuance. The same reality is vitally true in our spiritual lives.

The Apostle Paul stresses this point in his letter to the Corinthians. He says, *"Now finish the work, so that your eagerness to do it may be matched by your completion of it...."* While the specific context here concerns giving, the principle applies to all acts of service. Positive energy matters in our work for the Lord. But, when it goes on to bear fruit, it blesses others even further. Consider the life of Jesus. Where would we be if Christ never hung on the cross and said, "It is finished"(John 19:30)?

Is there some work that God has called you to which, at first, you began with great enthusiasm and then, through the constraints of time, the pull of other responsibilities or interests, perhaps even the difficulty of the work itself, caused you to let that work flounder? Did you start with vigor only to let the work go unfinished? The life of the disciple is about the long game and, ultimately, the finished work. Enthusiasm has an initial role and can be a blessing and encouragement to many. But, how we go about the work, whether with the joy of the Lord or with a spirit of burdened drudgery, also matters. This is no less true for the final product. The finished work matters immensely!

In the end, where I finish the race and how I finish it matters more than how enthusiastically I began it. Whether I dive in or come initially kicking and screaming, if I finish the work God has called me to, if I arrive at the gates of heaven through God's grace, God's way, I will have completed the only work that really matters.

What is the work you have been called to? Whether it is a specific task or the work of your life, *finish* it for Christ and His Kingdom. Match your initial enthusiasm with a final product that brings glory to God.

March 29

Overflow

Romans 15:13—May the God of hope fill you with all joy and peace as you trust in Him, so that you may overflow with hope by the power of the Holy Spirit.

> Thus the *overflow* from things
> pours into you.
> Just as a fountain's higher basins
> spill down like strands of loosened hair...
> so streams the fullness into you,
> when things and thoughts cannot contain it.[64]
> —Rainer Rilke

The nature of the Spirit of God is that of *overflow*. There is no ocean or corner of the universe that can contain Him. Should the finite expanse of our souls be any different? When those who know us best look at our lives, do they see the Spirit overflowing from our souls? Does hope pour out from us like a constant spring pushing up, irrepressibly and inexhaustibly from the depths? Do joy and peace flow from us like a river?

If the Spirit of God lives in us, it *overflows*—it cannot help but do so. There is no vessel on earth or in all creation that can contain one characteristic of God, much less His entire Spirit. David says, "my cup *overflows*"(Ps 23:5). What is happening to your cup? Is it overflowing? Can you say with the Apostle Paul, "I *overflow* with joy..."(2 Cor 7:4)?

When the Spirit is living in us, the *overflow* of our lives will be the unbridled freedom of living in the confidence of Christ, for "where the Spirit of the Lord is, there is freedom"(2 Cor 3:17). Is that freedom bursting from the seams of our souls? And if not, why? Are we repressing it? Have we allowed ourselves to become unreceptive vessels? Do the fruit of the Spirit well up within us and pour out into the lives of all those around us (Gal 5:22)? Or, are we guilty of quenching the Spirit in our lives?

Paul tells us, "Do not quench the Spirit"(1 Thes 5:19). Every life, however, has moments when the Spirit does not overflow: days of doubt, feelings of unrighteous anger, and periods of disillusionment. Only God Himself is free of these. But when the Spirit lives in us, we do not remain in these times, for God's Spirit is irrepressible. He will always *overflow* the cup He has poured Himself into. If He hasn't, He was either never poured in or the vessel was made an unreceptive one by a calculated rejection. God's people *overflow* with God's Spirit. Are you overflowing?

---

[64] Rainer Rilke, *Book of Hours: Love Poems to God* (New York: Riverhead Books, 2005), 161.

March 30

Left Him to Test Him

2 Chronicles 32:31—...God left him to test him and to know everything that was in his heart.

What parents, who truly love their children and desire for them to move out into the world, will not, at some point, step back, release, and watch how it goes? It must be so. If a child is to walk out into the world, his parents cannot always stand at his side. And if we know this to be true of our physical parents, why then do we find it so hard to accept this of our Father in heaven? Like King David, we find ourselves crying out, "Why, O Lord, do you stand far off?"(Ps 10:1), when God must give us space to independently seek Him, serve Him and love Him.

When I feel that God is far from me, I must first ask myself: "Am I to blame? Have I wandered away? Did my feet place distance between us?" If the answer to these questions is "yes," then I have no business blaming God for His apparent remoteness. I must draw near.

But if the answer is "no," and I, like King Hezekiah, have tried to live a life of righteousness and wholehearted devotion to the Lord, then God's apparent distance is not a sign of His disapproval or rejection. Rather, it is a demonstration of His deepest love and trust. When God appears to withdraw in this way, we may persist in faithfulness or we may fail. Either way, God is in control. Hezekiah failed. He entertained the envoys from Babylon and, in his pride, showed them his riches. These riches would feed the Babylonian lust for the future conquest of Jerusalem.

Job was another man whose faithfulness to God provoked Satan's scheming, because Job was "blameless and upright, a man who fears God and shuns evil"(Job 1:8). God trusted Job enough to step back and allow him to walk on his own. God did not abandon Job anymore than He abandons us, as we sometimes feel in our own lives. The Lord simply removed His imminent presence to test Job's faithfulness, just as He left Hezekiah *to test him and to know everything that was in his heart.*

When you are living a righteous life and suddenly you feel as if God has left you, know that your moment has come: He is trusting you with something more. Your Father who loves you more than you can imagine, loves you enough to see what you are made of. Where will you turn and what will you do when He is no longer standing right beside you? Resist the temptation to moan, "God, God where are you?" Know that He is there; trust that He is with you. Walk forward in faith.

Will you be faithful when your Father steps back?

March 31

Perfect Timing

Romans 5:6—...at just the right time....

There are many categories in our lives where we appear to understand timing quite clearly. No one would argue that nine months is the appropriate time for the development of a human baby. Significantly less time and the challenges of prematurity require modern medicine to intervene in the struggle to survive. Too much longer, and the child and mother both suffer the consequences of a more painful labor or a potential cesarean section. In the everyday chemistry of the kitchen, we understand that there is a perfect time to pull the cake from the oven. Too soon and the center remains undone and the cake collapses. Too long, and the cake dries out, burns or becomes unpalatable. The seeds germinate in the spring and the leaves fall in autumn; the monarchs migrate and the bears hibernate when the angle of the sun tells them they should—*perfect timing*!

When examples of God's *perfect timing* are all around us, why then is it so difficult to accept and embrace it when it comes to the desires of our hearts and the passions of our bodies? Do you find yourself struggling with God's timing right now? Are you finding it difficult to believe that "He has made everything beautiful in its time"(Ecc 3:11)?

When you are tempted to grow frustrated with God's timing in your life, remember that "the revelation awaits an appointed time...and will not prove false. Though it linger, wait for it; it will certainly come and will not delay"(Hab 2:3). God's timing is always perfect, and *at just the right time*, in *the fullness of His time* (Gal 4:4), He will work out in your life the plans He has ordained. As the bulbs contain within them all they need to burst into blossom, yet wait patiently for the spring's perfect moment, so also God has placed within you all that you need to accomplish His design for you. But it must be, *at just the right time!*

God has filled the world around you with countless examples of His *perfect timing*. Why be surprised when your life is subjected to the same standards of patient waiting that you observe in creation? Rejoice in knowing that He knows best and *at just the right time* He will produce the blossom in you that will bring joy to you and all those around you.

APRIL

April 1

On the Brink of Battle

Joshua 1:9—Have I not commanded you? Be strong and courageous. Do not be terrified; do not be discouraged, for the Lord your God will be with you wherever you go.

When we find ourselves terrified or discouraged, we most likely are too tired to continue hoping or we have forgotten the God who is with us. Perhaps we have decided He does not exist. Whatever the cause, we have resigned ourselves to a deep and existential aloneness we were never created for. We were made to stand beside Him and know His power. For, "If God is with us, who can be against us?"(Rom 8:31). The child who knows the presence of his Father feels His strength even in the midst of darkness and the very shadow of death (Ps 23:4). This very Father wills that we, His children, be impervious to the terror that turns us from our goal and the discouragement that dims our light in the world.

So as Joshua stood at the edge of the Promised Land and on the cusp of the work he had been created for, God commands him to meditate on His Word, to do what it says, and to *be strong and courageous.* God did not request. He gave an authoritative command followed by the promise of prosperity, success, and His constant presence—*I will be with you....*

If we hear only the command, and not the ensuing promise, we are likely to despair. For who can stand on the edge of the battle and not taste fear? But when we choose to believe God's words, fear does not linger, and we take on the invincibility of heaven. As the military strategist Sun Tzu reminds us, "a great solider first places himself in an invincible position...."[65] Joshua did just this—he trusted, he obeyed, and he conquered in the invincible power of God.

Have you heard God's command and believed His promise? Are you, like Joshua, fighting your battles with the Lord at your side? Or have you forgotten His promise in the shadow of giant enemies?

The next time you are tempted to linger in discouragement, remember His promise. Feel your Father standing beside you. Refuse to be terrified by the enemy. Go forward into the work God has called you to knowing that He will never leave you nor forsake you, *for the Lord your God will be with you wherever you go.*

---

[65] Sun Tzu, *The Art of War* (New York: Chartwell Books, 2012), 25.

April 2

Choices

Matthew 24:12-13—Because of the increase of wickedness, the love of most will grow cold, but he who stands firm to the end will be saved.

Before the light of Christ's triumphal return, Scripture tells us that the current spiritual darkness will increase. We see all around us the *increase of wickedness* and the *love that grows cold.* How does our faith survive in a world where sin flourishes? How do we make good *choices* where the darkness makes it hard to see clearly? There "arises every day anew the question how here, today and in [our] present situation [we are] to remain and...be preserved in this...life...with Jesus Christ."[66] How do we stand firm in faith? What is the will of God today, for this very decision?

There is no standing against spiritual darkness unless we commit to "not conform any longer to the pattern of the world..."(Rom 12:2). Similarly, there is no ascertaining the "pleasing and perfect will of God," unless we are "transformed by the renewing of [our] mind[s]"(Rom 12:2). Only then can we "examine what is the will of God, what is rightful in a given situation, what cause is truly pleasing to God...[in this]...concrete life and action."[67] When we are spiritually transformed, we might hope to make good *choices.*

God gives us *choices* because He loves us. He gives us reasoning minds to navigate those *choices* and find Him and His will on the other side of each decision. In this process, God desires that "the whole apparatus of human powers...be set in motion when it is a matter of proving what is the will of God."[68] Seeking the Lord in prayer and bowing before Him in our hearts, we can be assured that if we ask "God humbly, God will give [us] certain knowledge of His will;" and "after all this earnest proving, there will be the freedom to make a real decision, and...the confidence that it is not [us] but God Himself who...gives effect to His will."[69]

If you desire to make *choices* that conform to the will of God so that your heart does not grow cold, begin by offering your body as a living sacrifice, a spiritual act of worship and willful submission to your Lord (Rom 12:1). Submitted in this way, God will lead you to His pleasing and perfect will, even as He gives you the freedom to choose. God's way in your life will be a unique way. One choice at a time, the Lord's name will be glorified in you as the Spirit leads you into the arms of the Father.

---

[66] Dietrich Bonhoeffer, *Ethics* (New York: Touchstone, 1995), 43.
[67] Ibid, 43.
[68] Ibid, 43-44.
[69] Ibid, 44.

April 3

Go and Tell

Mark 5:19—...Go home to your family and tell them how much the Lord has done for you, and how He has had mercy on you.

Stories connect people and cultures. They bind us together, generation after generation. From the campfire yarn to the exalted myth, stories have imparted the practical and the mystical. They have sought to explain the inexplicable, comfort the inconsolable, and give meaning and purpose to the searching soul.

Some of the greatest stories are those of the transformed lives. When God moves in a life, He imparts a story of reclamation and transformation that must be told. Such was the case when Jesus met the demon-possessed man at the tombs. Christ extricated Legion (a collection of demons) from the man who then, in the wonder of his healing, "begged to go with" Jesus (Mark 5:18). But though the healed man wished to follow his healer, Jesus gave him an assignment. Our Lord said to him, *"Go home to your family and tell them how much the Lord has done for you, and how He has had mercy on you."* Jesus told the man to go and tell his story—God's story of mercy in a man.

What is your story of mercy and grace? Have you shared it with your family, much less a larger community? Story has been written into our lives for the telling. The mercy and grace that God has shown you has little to nothing to do with you, and everything to do with God's glory in the story you are now able to tell. When we feel self-conscious about telling "our" story it is because we are missing the point. While the story involves us, it is not about us. It is "our" story only in so far as it is God's story in us. Jesus wants us to go and tell our stories to those who know us, those who know what we once were, what we now are, and what they hope us to be in Christ.

Thank God today for your story of mercy. See it as a single thread of God's greater story, the one He has been writing since the dawn of creation. Pleasure in touching the lives of all you know with what the Lord has done in you and for you, knowing that every chapter has a part to play in the glorification of God's name.

Your story can, and must, exalt the name of the One who met you at the tombs and set you free from the darkness that held you. Tell your story for the glory of God, and let it be about His work—*more of Him and less of you.*

April 4

The Necessity of Exclusivity

Jeremiah 32:39—I will give them singleness of heart and action....

In many ways, the idea of singleness of focus, or exclusivity, has become the pariah of our contemporary thinking. The voices of the crowd cheer pluralism and inclusivity, but look askance at anything which intimates "narrowness." And yet, for the disciple of Christ, it is this very *singleness of heart and action* which must define the life of faith. Followers of Jesus are born again in the Spirit. For this reason, they are "characterized by their *single* mindedness. They have only one desire: to do God's will in all things...."[70]

Does this exclusivity of purpose characterize your life? Or, is there some piece of ground you still refuse to relinquish, some way of thinking that you still cling to? Is the life you are living now one which would cause God to say—"They turned their backs to me and not their faces"(Jer 32:33)? Or, is it that which shouts, "This is a man 'after my own heart'"(Acts 13:22)?

Singleness of life purpose, as God desires it, demands both the focus of the heart and the ensuing action of the life. I am called to prayerfully approach each day asking the Spirit to "give me an undivided heart..."(Ps 86:11). When I pray this way, I can be confident God will answer my prayer, for He says, "I will give them an undivided heart and put a new spirit in them..."(Ez 11:19). Nothing could delight God more than to answer this prayer!

When you find that your heart is undivided in its devotion to the Lord, when it seeks to do His will in all things, then you will "live a life worthy of the Lord and may please Him in every way: bearing fruit in every good work..."(Col 1:10). In short, your actions will, of necessity, follow your heart. Your life will bear fruit. And though your heart will never be completely unwavering and your actions never perfectly executed, your life will be marked by a singleness of love and purpose which will bring glory to the name of God. Only an exclusive focus on Christ can empower this to happen.

Pray today that God helps you to increasingly have a *singleness of heart and action* for the things of God. Pray that Christ enables you to make your life *more of Him and less of you*!

---

[70] Henri Nouwen, "Reborn From Above," in *The Only Necessary Thing*, ed. Wendy Wilson Greer (New York: The Crossroad Publishing Company, 2015), 62.

April 5

The Closed Heart

Psalm 17:10—They close up their callous hearts....

> The closed heart does not shut out your eye, and your hand is not kept
> away by the hardness of humanity, but you melt that when you wish,
> either in mercy or in punishment, and there is "none who can hide from
> your heat"(Ps 18:7).[71]
> —Saint Augustine

There are only two ways for the heart to grow insensate to God.
Either God Himself hardens the heart, as He did to Pharaoh. Or, we
ourselves allow our hearts to close up. In the first instance, God's glory
may necessitate a heart that grows calloused before Him. We are told, "the
Lord hardened Pharaoh's heart..."(Ex 9:12). God's greater purposes
required Pharaoh's heart to close up. Such handling from God is, however,
exceedingly rare. More often than not, it is we ourselves who allow or
choose to have our hearts grow unresponsive to the Spirit's overtures.

Sometimes, this heart closure happens because of frequent and
repeated trauma. The constant friction or insults to the heart create a
"protective" callous which begins to enclose it and restrict God's entrance.
Although we may not recognize or admit it, this callosity is a choice. In the
midst of pain, we can choose to turn toward God and His healing or grow
hard and turn away—"they *made* their hearts as hard as flint and would not
listen..."(Zech 7:12).

Equally obstructive and, perhaps, more common than callosity, is
the distancing of the heart that comes from the "fat" of our lives. One
translation of the Psalmist's words says, "They [the people's hearts] are
inclosed in their own fat"(KJV). It may not be the friction of my life that
develops a callous, but rather the "fat" of my blessings that encases my
heart and keeps God out. My comfort and my prosperity may be the very
thing I allow to insulate my heart from the Spirit. Either way, whether it is
a callous that hardens, or a fat that encases and insulates, the Spirit of God
is kept at bay and we ourselves are to blame.

Have you allowed your heart to close to the Spirit of God?
Whether it is pain or comfort, or perhaps some admixture of the two, do
not allow your heart to close up before the Lord. For although God will
not be kept away by the hardness of humanity, He will not go where He has been
rejected. Remember: "he who hardens his heart falls into trouble"(Prov
28:14). Pray for the grace to keep your heart unfolded before the Lord.

---

[71] Saint Augustine, *Confessions* (Oxford: Oxford University Press, 1992),72.

April 6

Trembling Delight

Matthew 28:8—...afraid yet filled with joy....

When we truly see the risen Jesus we cannot help but be like the women leaving the tomb—*afraid yet filled with joy*. The radiance of the glory and power that conquered the grave brings us to our knees, clasping His feet and worshipping Him (Matt 28:9). We are acutely aware that there is no one like Him. And if we don't have this response, then we haven't seen Him. We are living our lives vicariously through the descriptions of others.

But just when we tremble before His resurrected power, like a leaf in a strong wind, Jesus says to us, "Do not be afraid"(Matt 28:10). The power that conquered the grave and leaves us trembling is softened by the love that drove itself to the cross and reaches out to comfort and heal us. And though we are no less in awe of His almighty power, our fear begins to give way to an overpowering, life-giving joy. Like the women, we hurry back to the disciples, trembling with an irrepressible delight.

Have you felt this quivering, irrepressible delight in your life? Do you know it today? If you are more terrified of God than comforted by His love, then you have not heard His voice saying, *"Do not be afraid."* Conversely, if you only see the love that crucified itself, then you miss the power of the resurrection, the conquering of death, and the authority that will ultimately judge your eternity.

To know Jesus is to live every day with "The fear of the Lord"(Ps 111:10) behind your every decision, fully aware of His power, and in awe of what He has done and will yet do. But it is also to live with the unveiled joy of seeing in the risen Lord the assurance of victory over death and darkness. It is to know that one day, through the grace that saves you, you will return home into the arms of your Father. For a disciple of Christ, it will not do to live without one or the other—*fear and joy*. In the presence of the Lord, the Israelites "shouted for joy and fell face down"(Lev 9:24). Shouldn't our reverence know this *trembling delight?*

The heart that walks away from the tomb *afraid but filled with joy* has seen the risen Lord. It knows, deep down inside, the love that saves and the resurrecting power that conquers. Pray that your spiritual life never forgets the essential marriage between fear and love—the *trembling delight*.

April 7

A City on a Hill

2 Corinthians 3:18—And we, who with unveiled faces reflect the Lord's glory, are being transformed into His likeness with ever increasing glory....

You know when you have been in the presence of a man or woman filled with the Spirit—the light of His presence shines from them like the light of the sun. Moses spoke to the Lord and the Israelites saw "that his face was radiant"(Ex 34:35). With the coming of Christ and the indwelling of the Spirit in all of His disciples, we are now "the light of the world. A *city on a hill*," because "The light shines in the darkness, and the darkness, cannot overcome it"(Matt 5:14; John 1:5).

Are you reflecting the light of Jesus with a radiance that no darkness can overcome? Are you being transformed, from the inside out, into a luminescent beacon for Christ? God is able to instantly transform your darkness into light—"even the darkness will not be dark to you, the night will shine like the day, for darkness is as light to you"(Ps 139:12). More often than not, however, the transformation to a divine brilliance, the radiance of the Spirit, is one God works in a slow and gradual manner—a gentle warming of light into an ever-increasing intensity. A star can take millions of years to form from its precursor gases. Should we be surprised when our spiritual transformation into bodies of brilliance often does not happen overnight?

The more we are *transformed into His likeness* the more our lives begin to bear the fruit of the Spirit: love, joy, peace, patience, kindness, goodness, faithfulness, gentleness and self-control (Gal 5:22-23). And it is this fruit, like the particles of light itself, that shower down into the darkness around us and let the world increasingly see the glory of God within us. Jesus has said, "You are the light of the world....let your light shine before men, that they may see your good deeds and praise your Father..."(Matt 5:14,16).

As disciples of Christ, we are light, not of imitation, but of transformation. God wants every one of us to be a lamp of His luminescence. Unless you are willing to be transformed into a *city on a hill*, shining with an *ever increasing glory* that cannot be hidden, you have no part in the Kingdom of God.

The Lord will shine, with or without us. Will we choose to be a light of His glory? Will we decide to be filled with the majesty of His presence?

April 8

The Endless Waver

1 Kings 18:21—Elijah…said, "How long will you waver between two opinions? If the Lord is God, follow Him; but if Baal is God, follow him." But the people said nothing.

Whether we recognize it or admit to it, many of us are still trying to live our lives in what we perceive to be the "best of both worlds." Like the Israelites Elijah addressed, we find ourselves wavering between two opinions, with God on the one side and some competing "deity" on the other. Commitment to either one seems either unpalatable or unnecessary. And sadly, many of us live our entire lives in this position of indecision until the voice of our "Elijah" queries us—*how long will you remain undecided?*

The Jews on Mount Carmel "said nothing." How will we respond? Have we truly decided that the Lord is God? Or, are we as spiritually torpid as the silent Israelites on the mountain?

When we live our lives wavering between opinions, the result is an unfulfilled existence. As long as we do not decide between God and "Baal," we cannot know either one fully. We are tugged in both directions and cannot progress. What follows is a helplessly shallow existence that misses both the true richness of relationship with the Lord and the temporary, carnal pleasures of sin.

Elijah says, "if Baal is God, follow him…." If you have decided that your personal pleasure and the will of the world is your "god," then dive in and revel in it! But do not do yourself the injustice of dipping your toes in "Baal" while still trying to hold on to the shore with some noncommittal relationship with the Lord.

Sadly, most of us are neither good at being saints nor sinners; rather, we live some muddled and confused admixture. Such a life is a tormented one, plagued by indecision, guilt and lack of fulfillment or true pleasure. The Lord says of this choice, "I know your deeds, that you are neither cold nor hot. I wish you were either one or the other!"(Rev 3:15).

Either you are for God or you are not: there is no in between! If you have decided on a life of sin, you may as well embrace it with gusto. Do it with panache! Don't skulk in the shadows and live a lie. And if you have chosen the Lord, then live in the wonderful fullness of relationship with Him! Although you will not live a perfect life, you will live a purposeful and fulfilled one.

May we step into the glorious fullness of who we are—sons and daughters of God!

April 9

Marching in the Trees

2 Samuel 5:24—As soon as you hear the sound of marching in the tops of the balsam trees, move quickly....

When we are attacked, the knee jerk response may be immediate defense or counterattack. But sometimes God speaks to us like He did to David: "Do not go straight up, but circle around behind…"(2 Sam 5:23). It may be that the timing of our parrying blow is not right. God knows that we are not prepared or perhaps He has a different plan for the glorification of His name that will catch the enemy off guard: 300 men instead of an army of 10,000 (Judg 7). If we choose to go straight up, we may meet defeat. We forget: "In all kinds of warfare, the direct approach is used for attack, but the oblique is what achieves the victory."[72]

How then do we know the when and the where of how we are to respond to the assault waged against us? In one battle against the Philistine army, David struggled with this question. He inquired of God and the Lord said,*"As soon as you hear the sound of marching in the tops of the balsam trees, move quickly...."* Like David, we must listen for God's leading. On the battlefield, we must determine to wait until we hear the Lord speak. Jesus demonstrated this. He "was always listening to the Father, always attentive to His voice, always alert for His directions. Jesus was 'all ear.'"[73] Can the same be said of us? If we are still unclear on some point, we must wait. God may not wet the fleece for us or cause the sun to go back ten steps (Judg 6:36-40; Is 38:8), but He will make His will known. And when He does, we must be ready to *move quickly.*

Too often we fail to hear the Lord's leadings in our lives because we limit the scope of His communication with us. We expect an audible voice, a visible sign, a vivid dream or a direct word from a trusted counselor. But it may be that God's plan is revealed to us, like David, in the sound of the trees, or in the quiet, persistent sense that our spirit just can't shake. We must not, like King Saul, grow impatient with the Lord when His guidance appears to tarry (1 Sam 13:7-14). Instead, we trust that He will speak at just the right time. And we must listen with attentiveness.

Are you listening for the subtle sound or sign God is preparing for you? Have you decided to "wait for the Lord"(Is 40:31 ESV)? When the battle lines are drawn up before you, God will lead you—but you must listen so well that even the sound of *marching in the trees* can be heard.

---

[72] Sun Tzu, *The Art of War* (New York: Chartwell Books, 2012), 29.
[73] Henri Nouwen, *Making All Things New* in *The Only Necessary Thing*, ed. Wendy Wilson Greer (New York: The Crossroad Publishing Company, 2015), 82.

April 10

A Better Country

Hebrews 11:16—Instead, they were longing for a better country....

> ...God wants us to long for Him with the longing that will
> become lovesickness...to keep us always moving toward Him....[74]
> —A.W. Tozer

Elections come and go. Leaders rise and fall, and the tenor and character of a nation may change overnight. If this world is all that we have, then such changes can incite worry, fear, and, at times, deep sadness. But disciples of Christ are not hostage to this tyranny. They understand, with an unswerving confidence, that their "citizenship is in heaven"(Phil 3:20). They live *longing for a better country*, not trying to find satisfaction and meaning in the changing world around them.

This longing does not mean, however, that we live disengaged and apathetic to the world around us. For although we "do not belong to the world"(John 15:19), we are in the world to glorify God in the work He has placed before us. When the nation trembles in fear, we can walk forward in courage, filled with the certainty that God is in control. Our home is in heaven and our Lord is preparing a place for us there (John 14:2).

This world has never produced a ruler, despot, or charismatic charlatan that will not one day bow before the Lord, for "He brings princes to naught and reduces the rulers of this world to nothing"(Is 40:23). God's jurisdiction is absolute. The disciple knows that the Lord "made every nation of men, that they should inhabit the whole earth; and He determined the times set for them and the exact places where they should live"(Acts 17:26). When the world cringes at a change in leadership, the disciple knows, "God did this so that men would seek Him and perhaps reach out for Him and find Him..."(Acts 17:27). The disciple reaches out horizontally with one hand to comfort others, and vertically with the other hand to praise God for opportunities for His name to be glorified.

The more the world struggles with uncertainty, the more desperately its people cling to their fragile lives. In these times, the certainty and freedom of Christ within you must shine. Is the light of Christ's confidence radiating from you in this way? When you are intimately related to the King, when your home is in heaven, nothing on earth will shake you from your hope in the Lord and His eternal purposes.

Has the hope of home and your Father's embrace filled you with inexpressible joy? Rejoice that we can long for a *better country*!

---

[74] A.W. Tozer, *Man, The Dwelling Place of God* (Public Domain), 160.

April 11

Where You Are

Numbers 1:53—The Levites, however, are to set up their tents around the tabernacle of the Testimony so that wrath will not fall on the Israelite community.

Have you ever considered that you are where you are in your life specifically for all those around you? Maybe your current place or position has little to nothing to do with you, and everything to do with your position between God and His people.

This was God's very intention for the Levites. They were instructed to pitch their tents around the Tabernacle. The remaining Israelite clans surrounded them in a concentric way. God designed the Levite's position as a space between *so that wrath will not fall on the Israelite community.*

What does this patterned encampment look like in your life? Perhaps you find yourself married to "a husband who is not a believer…"(1 Cor 7:13). You are where you are so that "the unbelieving husband [might be] sanctified through [you]"(1 Cor 7:14) and your children made "holy." Perhaps you work in a place filled with unbelievers, or at best nominal ones. Are you not, like the Levites, positioned between God and them so that you might be of use to the Lord in their lives? When we get tired and restless in the place where we have pitched our tents, we must be careful to consider why we are where we are. We must remember there is no randomness to the Lord's patterned encampment. He orders each clan to stay with "their tents by divisions, each man in his own camp under his own standard"(Num 1:52).

God has you where you are in your life for His work in the lives of all those around you. It may be that the time will come to pick up your tents and move. But until God leads otherwise, "each one should retain the place in life that the Lord assigned to him and to which God has called him"(1 Cor 7:17). Our place is a place of ministry. Joy comes when we stop seeing our lives as about "us," and start appreciating their purpose in God's eyes.

When we wonder why our tent is pitched where it is, we must remember that God has planted us in the midst of His people, to minister to them and serve Him in the work "to which God has called [us]"(1 Cor 7:17). As we begin to see our position as God's choice for us and His people, our lives become *more of Him and less of us.*

April 12

The Mind of Christ

1 Corinthians 2:16—But we have the mind of Christ.

> The continuous and unembarrassed interchange of love and
> thought between God and the soul of the redeemed man is the
> throbbing heart of New Testament religion.[75]
> —A.W. Tozer

In an intimate relationship, the better we know someone, the more clearly we can anticipate what he or she is thinking. Should it be any different in the intimacy of our relationship with Christ? While "no one knows the thoughts of God" through his or her own intuition, when the Spirit of the Lord lives in us "we may understand what God has freely given us"(1 Cor 2:11-12). How well I understand the Lord and His purposes is directly proportional to the presence of His Spirit within me.

Nonetheless, some things will always remain cloaked in mystery. For instance, Jesus says of the last days, "But about that day or hour no one knows, not even the angels in heaven, nor the Son, but only the Father"(Mark 13:32). Only the Spirit of God Himself searches these "deep things"(1 Cor 2:10). But so much of God's thinking can be known. Indeed, He wants it to be known. His Word offers us the very *mind of Christ:* His attitude towards sin, His love for the lost, His hatred of hypocrisy, His mercy for the repentant, and His will to do His Father's will. All these things can clearly be known by those who desire it.

The question is: Do I desire it? When I intimately love someone, I think about him or her, but also begin to think like him or her. The other's thoughts weave their way into my thinking. Some of this happens instinctually, without much thought. But some of it is intentional and volitional, born out of love for the beloved. This latter kind is the love God desires for our relationship with Christ.

Do you love Jesus? Then you must increasingly have *the mind of Christ.* As Tozer says, "God is a person" who can be known, but not just in one encounter.[76] We gradually grow closer to Jesus as we choose to spend time with Him, study His Word, converse with Him in prayer, learn His thoughts and know His ways. If our thinking is not becoming less ours and more His, then our love is mere lip service.

We will never be a disciple of Christ until we determine to have *the mind of Christ.* Have you decided to make Jesus's thoughts your thoughts?

---

[75] A.W. Tozer, *The Pursuit of God* in *The Classic Works of A.W. Tozer* (Public Domain), 9.
[76] Ibid, 9.

April 13

Fully Committed

2 Chronicles 15:17—…Asa's heart was fully committed to the Lord all his life.

To be *fully committed* to someone or something means we are completely devoted and singularly focused upon the object of our affection. We have determined that nothing shall separate us from that which we have bound ourselves to. The closest we come to this idea of full commitment in human relationships is within the bounds of marriage. At the altar, we pledge to remain committed "till death do us part."

But if the track record for maintaining marriage vows is any indicator of our capacity to remain *fully committed* to the Lord, our spiritual lives likely lack faithfulness. Clearly, full commitment has never been easy. For this reason, King Asa was celebrated in the Chronicles as a ruler whose *heart was fully committed to the Lord all his life*. This commitment required him to go to great lengths of obedience and even personal sacrifice. When the people of Israel were gathered before the Lord in Jerusalem, "All who would not seek the Lord…were put to death…"(2 Chron 15:13). Asa even had to raise his hand against his own family, deposing his grandmother because she had *made a repulsive Asherah pole* (2 Chron 15:16). It did not matter that she was family. Her sin stood in the way of Asa's obedience and devotion to the Lord. It had to go.

To what lengths are you willing to go in your devotion to God? In your commitment to the Lord, will you be willing and ready to stand against your own family, even those you love? Clearly, God does not call us to *jihad,* to a misdirected extremism that neglects the heart of the gospel message. This is a perversion of Satan. But He does call us to put Him first, at all times, in all things. Jesus says, "no one who has left home or brothers or sisters or mother or father or children or fields for me and the gospel will fail to receive a hundred times as much in this age…and in the age to come eternal life"(Mark 10:29-30).

The *fully committed life* is the life that does not look back. It walks forward with the confidence that Christ is enough and that all He says is true. Have you resolved that no one and nothing will separate you from the God you love (Rom 8: 38-39)? Have you decided to remain devoted to Him no matter the cost? Are you *fully committed* and ready to do all that He requires of you?

April 14

The Praise of Folly

Proverbs 19:3—A man's own folly ruins his life, yet his heart rages against the Lord.

Without the frosting of deception, reality can often be painful. Indeed, apart from the transformational work of Christ in the heart, Erasmus contends "it is truly miserable *not* to be deceived."[77] This is particularly true in matters of the soul. Only the folly of deception softens the blow of reality. For who wants to face the truth of his heart if he can blissfully live in a happy delusion of self that "costs him practically nothing, only a bit of self-persuasion"?[78]

None of us escapes this foolishness—"all men are fools, even the pious ones."[79] But while folly is universal, it does not bear the same face in every life. Worldly folly is not Christian folly. Although Christians do make silly mistakes, disciples of Christ have no trouble admitting they are fools. They know their "folly" in following Christ is the wisdom that saves them. But the man of the world clings to his delusion of self-sufficiency. His *folly ruins his life* while he helplessly *rages against the Lord.*

Spiritually, we are now living in a world that *rages against the Lord.* It appears "fortune favors the dimwits and the brash,"[80] those who are either ignorant of God's truths or have boldly rejected them. In a culture that worships success and self-actualization, the wisdom of God appears foolish. For, "Suppose you want to make a pile of money, how will wisdom help you do that? The wise man will shrink from perjury, blush if caught in a lie, and worry himself sick over the scruples thought up by moralists regarding theft and usury."[81] To thinking like this, the *wisdom* of God is folly—it makes no sense and it gets in the way. But while the world may view God's truths as folly, "the message of the cross is foolishness to those who are perishing, but to us who are being saved it is the power of God"(1 Cor 1:18).

So whose fool are you? Are you the jester of your own joke, choosing to live in a deception that will ultimately ruin your life? Will your foolishness leave you raging at a God who will refuse to rescue you because you rejected Him like the rich man calling on Lazarus (Luke 16:19-31)? Or are you a fool for Christ? Have you chosen to believe in the power of the cross to redeem every folly you have ever committed? Have you decided to live for the "foolishness" that makes sense of your folly?

---

[77]Desiderius Erasmus, *The Praise of Folly* (New York: W.W. Norton & Co., 1989),46.
[78] Ibid, 47.
[79] Ibid, 81.
[80] Ibid, 73.
[81] Ibid, 74.

April 15

Walking as Jesus Walks

1 John 2:3, 5-6—We know that we have come to know Him if we obey His commands....if anyone obeys His word, God's love is truly made complete in him. This is how we know we are in Him: whoever claims to live in Him must walk as Jesus did.

Jesus tells us, "If you love me, you will obey what I command"(John 14:15). The Apostle John goes on to emphasize that if we are in Him, we "must walk as Jesus did." Just as any child demonstrates his or her love and respect for parents through obedience, so we also, as children of God, must obey Him, if we claim to love Him. We cannot, as John reminds us, say we love the Lord and that we know Him, and then fail to go and do what He commands. The heart that loves Jesus will weep when it fails Him. The Spirit within the disciple will mourn the transgression that drives a distance between him and his Lord.

Do you wish to demonstrate your love to Jesus? Then you must obey Him. To do this, you must know His Word, the spiritual blueprint for faithful living. Obedience to Christ depends upon an intimate knowledge of what God says. If I am not daily reading and praying through God's Word and allowing the Spirit to instruct me in what I have read, I will never be able to obey, even if I want to. I must say with David, "Teach me your way, O Lord; lead me in a straight path..."(Ps 27:11). I must decide to make His "Word a lamp unto my feet..."(Ps 119:105).

Knowing the Word, we then accept the Spirit's instruction as He further teaches and uses us in the places where God has planted us. We allow Him to live in us and to walk with us in the "straight path"—the path of Christ, walking as Jesus walks. This is not a mere imitation of Jesus. Rather, through an *active passivity*,[82] we make a deliberate choice to welcome Christ and His Spirit into our lives each day, encouraging Him to permeate everything we do and say, and then getting out of the way and letting Him do it through us—*more of Him and less of me*.

When we walk as Jesus did, His light shines from us. It is like the sun shining through an ornate stained glass window—each of us a different shape, size, cut and color of glass, but subject to the very same Light. Only when He passes through the very substance of who we are, can we shine with our fullest colors to create the beauty God has intended.

Are you in Christ, and is Christ in you? Are you walking as Jesus did, letting His light shine through you to create the brilliance of His glory?

---

[82] Francis Schaeffer, *True Spirituality* (Carol Stream: Tyndale House Publishers, 2011), 47.

April 16

Forgiveness From the Heart

Matthew 18:35—This is how my heavenly Father will treat each of you unless you forgive your brother from your heart.

If your worst moments have been forgiven by another man or woman (and more graciously by God), you know that there is no greater gift than that of forgiveness. Because it is an act of love, true forgiveness can only come from the heart. There is a form of forgiveness, however, an intellectual one, which, in its dispensation, may satisfy the ledgers of the mind for a brief time. But in the end, it brings no lasting healing or rebirth. This is a cheap forgiveness, costing little to nothing and achieving even less. It is akin to Bonhoeffer's "cheap grace," which says, "Of course you have sinned, but now everything is forgiven, so you can stay as you are and enjoy the consolations of forgiveness."[83]

The obverse of cheap grace is costly grace. It is the only true grace, and requires spiritual transformation and submission to the yoke of Christ. Similar to this costly grace, the forgiveness Christ calls us to, the *forgiveness from the heart*, requires inner transformation. It is not an intellectual exercise. It is a complete rending of the heart.

You are called to "Forgive as the Lord forgave you"(Col 3:13). This means you must be ready to go to the cross, to completely surrender yourself and your heart to the Father's purposes so that the healing forgiveness of Jesus might flow from you. This is anything but a cheap, intellectual exercise, wrapped in flimsy words. If it is genuine, there must be sacrifice and change. It requires us to "Get rid of all bitterness, rage and anger, brawling and slander, along with every form of malice"(Eph 4:31). Instead, we are to "Be kind and compassionate to one another, forgiving...just as in Christ God forgave [us]"(Eph 4:32).

Do not be fooled into thinking forgiveness can be meted out without a transformation of the heart. There will be a cost, perhaps a heavy one, or it is not forgiveness at all. It took the piercing of Jesus to forgive you and me. We cannot expect to forgive others without our hearts also knowing deep pain. In the same way, to be personally forgiven is to be called to the costly ministry of *forgiveness from the heart*.

Pray today that the Spirit enables you to forgive, as you yourself have been forgiven. The only way this will happen is if your life becomes increasingly *more of Him and less of you.*

---

[83]Dietrich Bonhoeffer, *The Cost of Discipleship* (New York: Touchstone, 1995), 48.

April 17

Forfeiting Grace

Jonah 2:8—Those who cling to worthless idols forfeit the grace that could be theirs.

When we feel an absence of blessings in our lives, we are tempted to blame God. Invariably, however, we are to blame. We are likely clinging to some worthless idol which *forfeits the grace* that could be ours. The Lord "longs to be gracious to you"(Is 30:18), and to fill your life with a boundless love and compassion. But He will not share your heart with anyone or anything. He will not bring grace into your life so long as you allow the idolatrous "high places" to remain.

The godly kings of Judah understood that the Lord would not tolerate a secret idolatry. Hezekiah "removed the high places, smashed the sacred stones, and cut down the Asherah poles"(2 Kings 18:4). Josiah's zeal for the Lord "removed and defiled all the shrines at the high places that the kings of Israel had built in the towns of Samaria that had provoked the Lord to anger"(2 Kings 23:19). If we are to receive the Lord's favor, then we too must identify and destroy the "high places" and worthless "idols" in our lives. Are you clinging to an idol that is *forfeiting grace* in your life?

Idols can come in any shape, material or immaterial. They can even be something of great importance to God. One of the things Hezekiah destroyed was the bronze snake Moses held up in the wilderness. This very snake, the image that Jesus later compares Himself to, had served as God's focal point to save His people in the desert. But even this salvific symbol was capable of being a snare to the people of Israel (2 Kings 18:4). Likewise, God may use something or someone in our lives to show us His mercy. But we must remember that the "bronze snake" did not save us— God did! We must determine that we will never allow our hearts to worship anything but God and God alone.

Is there something you worship besides God? Be careful to make an idol of nothing, no matter how valuable or lovely it is. God will not tolerate anything but total destruction of the false gods in your life. While the Bible does give us examples of God toppling pagan gods, for the most part, He will not rid your life of them. You, like the godly kings of Israel, must go on the warpath. You must decide to destroy the "high places" in your life, those areas of idolatrous worship. You must smash the idols.

Ask the Spirit today to open your eyes to the idols that may be lingering in your life. Pray that God gives you the courage and strength you need to rid your life of the high places that keep you from His grace. Until you do, you *forfeit the grace* that could be yours.

April 18

God Moves in Mysterious Ways

Judges 14:4—His parents did not know that this was from the Lord....

There may come a time when someone you love deeply stands on the cusp of a great decision and you find yourself completely disagreeing with the impending choice. It may be a relationship you believe to be unhealthy or a job opportunity with great potential risk. You may think the choice unwise, potentially hurtful, perhaps even unbiblical in your understanding. In love, you give your opinion, but it appears to fall on deaf ears. What do you do?

Samson's parents faced a similar scenario when the budding hero went down to Timnah and "saw there a young Philistine woman"(Judg 14:1) he desired as his wife. His parents questioned him, and rightly so —"Isn't there an acceptable woman among your own relatives or among all our people?"(14:3). For had not God commanded, "Do not intermarry with them...or take their daughters for your sons..."(Deut 7:3)?

Although they could not see the sense in it, perhaps even God's hand in it, Samson's parents did not assert their collective will to commandeer the situation. Had they done so, despite their best intentions and desire to obey God's will, ironically, they would have been standing directly in the way of it. For they "did not know that this was from the Lord, who was seeking an occasion to confront the Philistines..."(Judg 14:4).

When we find reason to disagree with the decisions or actions of the one we love, we must be careful in the execution of our will in his or her life. "God moves in a mysterious way" and "God is His own interpretation."[84] The very thing we have learned or come to understand as God's will in our own lives may not have any relevance or transference to God's will in the life of another. When we attempt to interfere, we must be cognizant of the fact that our good intentions may be opposing the very will of God. We must always remember that God is God, and we are not. He may require the sacrifice of the one we love for a greater cause we cannot currently see. Did He not do this to His only Son?

The next time you disagree with the choice of the one you love, be careful you are not obstructing the providential will of God. Pray for humility and restraint and for an understanding you do not possess. Trust God to lead you to the appropriate response, even if that is no response at all, save prayer, and more of it! And rejoice in knowing that God will work all things for the good as He moves in His mysterious ways (Rom 8:28)!

---

[84] William Cowper, 1773, "God Moves in a Mysterious Way."

The Marriage of Mind and Spirit

1 Corinthians 14:15—I will pray with my spirit, but I will also pray with my mind; I will sing with my spirit, I will also sing with my mind.

There is a common misconception among the intellectuals of our day that the Christian faith, perhaps spirituality in general, requires a divorce of the mind from the spirit. These "thinkers" hold that no seriously thinking individual could believe what Christians believe. Blind faith, therefore, or a faith without reason, must be the prerequisite for following Christ. The reality, however, is that nothing could be further from the truth.

When Paul says, "*I will pray with my spirit, but I will also pray with my mind; I will sing with my spirit, I will also sing with my mind,*" he describes the gospel *marriage of mind and spirit*. It is the holy union necessary to become a disciple of Jesus. It is not one or the other—thinking or believing. Both are at work simultaneously, sometimes in varying measures and manifestations, as the circumstances of life dictate.

Just as any marriage or relationship is the union of two very different people for one end, so also the mind and spirit must be united to maintain a viable faith. At times, one is strong and the other is weak. At other moments, the roles reverse. But one partner never ceases to be. The absence of one or the other signals the death of the union altogether.

The spirit, therefore, that does not engage the mind will be incapable of translating into everyday living what the Lord has to say. The mind alone, however, is incapable of connecting with the divine, for "God is spirit and His worshipers must worship in spirit and truth"(John 4:24). Chambers says, "You cannot make a man see moral truth by persuading his intellect."[85] The spirit has its part to play, and the mind its own.

Do you wish to grow in your relationship with Christ? The maturing Christian is the one who understands the vital importance of maintaining the perfect *marriage of mind and spirit* in the life of faith. To hear God and then to translate His message into the action of here and now, requires both the ears of the spirit and the cognitive abilities of the mind. To be all spirit is to be an airy, ineffective, and disembodied nothing for the Kingdom's work. To be all mind is to have our feet set in concrete, reaching for the sky, but never touching the hands of God.

Pray with your spirit and your mind, and you will not only meet God, but you will know what it is He has for you to do.

---

[85] Oswald Chambers, *The Love of God* in *The Complete Works of Oswald Chambers* (Grand Rapids: Discovery House Publishers, 2000), 676.

April 20

Importunity

Genesis 18:22—The men turned away and went toward Sodom, but Abraham remained standing before the Lord.

Importunity in prayer is the state of being insistent and persistent. We must remember: "There are various elements of *importunity*. The most important are perseverance, determination, and intensity."[86] The reason that many prayers appear to go unanswered is not that God is unwilling or unable to answer them, but rather as the result of our lackluster *importunity*. Successful prayer depends upon a dogged pursuit of God.

Abraham was an importunate man who *remained standing before the Lord*. When he comes to understand that Sodom will be destroyed, he determines to boldly ask for God's mercy. Abraham does not walk away or give up; he does not admit defeat. He perseveres in his prayer to the Lord.

Abraham knows that he has "been so bold as to speak to the Lord"(Gen 18:27), but he does not desist. He says, "What if there are fifty righteous people in the city? Will you really sweep it away...?"(Gen 18:24). He perseveres: "what if the number is five less than fifty?...What if only forty....thirty....twenty....ten...?"(Gen 18: 28-32). The determination, perseverance, and intensity Abraham demonstrates in this prayer achieves the desired end—the rescue of Lot from the fires of destruction. Abraham's *importunity* shows that the "prayer of a righteous man is powerful and effective"(James 5:16).

Have you been importunate in your prayer life? Have you, like Abraham, determined to continue standing before the Lord until your prayer is answered? Jesus tells His disciples the parable of the persistent widow to "show them that they should always pray and not give up"(Luke 18:1). If nothing else, our prayers, like Abraham's or the widow's, must be so persistent that God answers them so that we "won't eventually wear [Him] out with [our] coming!"(Luke 18:5).

Importunity in prayer is a choice. You can choose to persevere and stand with willful insistence in the presence of your God, pleading Him with the deepest concerns of your heart. The question is: Will you? Decide, like Abraham, to continue standing before the Lord with the full confidence that your prayers will hear Him say, "I will"(Gen 18:32). God answers the prayers of the importunate in His providential time.

---

[86] Andrew Murray, *The Ministry of Intercession* in *Collected Works on Prayer* (New Kensington: Whitaker House, 2013), 690.

April 21

Sons and Daughters of Encouragement

Acts 28:15—At the sight of these men, Paul thanked God and was encouraged.

Having survived a shipwreck at sea, the venomous bite of a viper, and countless months on the road, Paul ultimately arrives safely in Rome. He is greeted there by the Christians who traveled far to meet him. *At the sight of these men, Paul thanked God and was encouraged.*

Are you, like these men in Rome, a reason for thanks and a source of encouragement in the lives of others? Do others in your world—employees, colleagues, family, friends—find your life to be a source of spiritual heartening or disheartening? Do others anticipate your presence with a smile or an inner cringe? Are you a source of spiritual negativity and demands on others, or a giver of the Christ within you?

We are often so self-consumed with our own lives and personal agendas that we spend little time considering how we affect the hearts and souls of those around us. But as disciples of Christ, we must pay particular attention to the effect of our lives upon others. We are the face of Jesus to the world. And while we are not called to live for the approval of the men and women around us, we ought to be cognizant of how the Spirit within us is portrayed.

When the Spirit of Jesus lives within us, we will be able to encourage others with the encouragement we have received. For, "God... comforts us in all our troubles, so that we can comfort those in any trouble with the comfort we ourselves have received from God"(2 Cor 1:4). Similarly, as we have been loved by God, we encourage others with His love, for "in loving your neighbor you cling to God...."[87]

If Jesus Christ is living in us, we will love others with Christ's love. We will, more often than not, be a source of thanks and encouragement in the lives of everyone we interact with, even our enemies! Admittedly, there will be times when, in obedience to the Spirit, we will have to stand for something that may bring offense. We may have to fight an unpopular battle. Christ offended not uncommonly when it came to matters of sin. But, at the same time, His love, and the light of His presence, won out in the hearts of many—men and women were drawn towards Him. Those who knew Him best, loved Him most. Can the same be said of you?

Seek to be a life so filled with Christ that others cannot help but thank God for you and your presence in their lives. In this way, your words and actions will drive others straight into the arms of the Savior who loves them.

---

[87] Soren Kierkegaard, *Works of Love* (New York: HarperPerennial, 2009), 76.

April 22

Integrity

1 Chronicles 29:17—I know, my God, that you…are pleased with integrity.

Integrity holds us together. It is the state of being spiritually whole that is marked by a moral rectitude and probity before God and men. When we lose our *integrity* in the presence of the Lord, we fall apart. We crumble individually, and then, eventually, collectively as a society, a nation and a world at large.

The nation of Israel repeatedly lost their spiritual *integrity* before Jehovah. And each time they did, God punished them, often at the hands of foreign conquerors. King David knew this history well. He also knew the depth of his own failures of *integrity* before God—"Against you, you only, have I sinned and done what is evil in your sight"(Ps 51:4). So in some of his parting words to his people, David stresses that God is *pleased with integrity.*

The personal *integrity* that caused David to say, "I will be careful to lead a blameless life"(Ps 101:2), has become a rarity in contemporary society. Like the devaluation of any currency in a market flooded with counterfeit bills, true spiritual *integrity* before God has lost much of its face value. In its place we see the counterfeits of moral relativism and absolute personal autonomy. While the culture teaches individual standards, the universal standards of God are increasingly seen as archaic, irrelevant and discriminatory. The Ten Commandments are taken down from the walls of judicial houses because the world no longer cares what God's standards are. And if there are not divine standards, what does spiritual *integrity* matter?

Have you determined to be a man or woman of spiritual *integrity* in a world that takes the Commandments down? Will you commit to be a person of your word, living for God's Word, no matter the cost? Will the *integrity* that marks your life cause others to trust in you and the God you serve?

If we are to call ourselves disciples of Christ, we must live with *integrity*. We must commit to obey God's commands, to do what we say, say what we mean, and to live with a moral probity that declares, "I live for Christ!"

The decision to be a person of *integrity* often comes at great personal cost. It is not the easy way, but it is the only way for a disciple who intends to walk with Jesus. If you desire to please the Lord, ask the Spirit to empower you to live a life of *integrity,* in all things, at all times.

122

April 23

Gentle

Galatians 6:1—…you who are spiritual should restore him gently.

If I am to be a disciple of Christ, gentleness must pervade my heart. Jesus valued gentleness so much that He even described Himself as *gentle*. He says, "Take my yoke upon you and learn from me, for I am *gentle* and humble in heart, and you will find rest for your souls"(Matt 11:29). When I fail to exhibit this gentleness of Jesus to the world around me, whether in the intimacy of my home or the public arena of the work place, I betray the Spirit of the very Lord I say I love and follow.

For this reason, Paul commands us to "Be completely… *gentle*…"(Eph 4:2). How is this possible? We can only do this by walking "in step with the Spirit," and allowing the Spirit to fill our lives with "the fruit of…gentleness…"(Gal 5:25, 22-23). For most of us, gentleness does not come naturally or easily. It only comes through the grace of the Spirit.

One of the chief reasons we don't pursue gentleness in our lives is our tendency to equate it with weakness. We generally fear weakness. The truth is, however, that gentleness requires more strength than all of its alternatives combined. The man or woman who exhibits the gentleness of the Lord has been gifted with the power and grace to control his or her natural inclinations. Only the Spirit can do this. And when we are equipped in this way, it becomes possible to move mountains in the hearts and minds of others. Jesus did this very thing, and the world has never been the same.

Why is it then that Christians so often forget this *gentle* power of Jesus? In the face of opposition or differing opinions, why do we use a bombastic approach, full of personal opinion and will-power? Instead, we should go the way of the true disciple, to "gently instruct in the hope that God will grant…repentance leading them to a knowledge of the truth…"(2 Tim 2:25). When someone stumbles in their faith, do we chastise him or do we *restore him gently*?

The life and ministry of Jesus attests to the fact that love and gentleness win souls to the Kingdom better than any well-constructed argument. So if my Lord describes Himself as *gentle*, how can I not long to be the same? If I desire for my life to be *more of Him and less of me*, then it must take on the gentleness of Jesus. I must let my "gentleness be evident to all," even as a "mother caring for her little children"(Phil 4:5; 1 Thes 2:7). Have you decided to let this gentleness reign in your heart?

April 24

In My Hands

Ezra 10:4—Rise up; this matter is in your hands.

It goes without saying that much of our lives is out of our control. Life and death, sun and rain: the forces of nature alone remind us of our own finitude. And yet, some of us spend our entire lives trying to tame the untamable. We try to conquer diseases that keep on mutating and forecast weather that constantly changes. All the while, we neglect the things we do have control over—the attitudes of the heart, the inclination of the soul, and the focus of the mind—all those matters God puts in our hands. Either through denial or a series of excuses, we find ways to shirk spiritual responsibility. We often blame circumstances, God, or other people for our lack of discipline or action. But in reality, the matter is often *in our hands*.

In the face of Israel's sin, Ezra was found "praying and confessing, weeping and throwing himself down before the house of God…"(Ezra 10:1). When the people also recognize their sin and the wisdom of Ezra's spiritual leadership, they say, *"Rise up; this matter is in your hands."* They want Ezra to make a new covenant with God on their behalf. Ezra could have made excuses. He could have said, "It's not my problem. I didn't take a foreign woman as my wife against the command of God. You do it." Or, perhaps he said under his breath, "God will deal with these people. Why should I?" But although God could have dealt with Israel's sin, He wanted Ezra to act. God put the matter of restitution in Ezra's hands. Ezra knew the people's sin; he knew what needed to happen; but he had not yet decided to do it.

What has God placed in your hands? Is there something in your life that you know you should deal with and yet, you find yourself dragging your feet, making excuses or blaming others for your lack of initiative? Maybe it has little or nothing to do with you or your specific actions, and yet God has placed the matter *in your hands* to deal with as a test of your obedience to Him. Have you forgotten that "Keeping God's commands is what counts"(1 Cor 7:19), and that only you can make that happen?

Whatever it is that God has placed *into my hands* (whether a specific task or the daily husbandry of my soul), I must do it. If my hands remain idle, God will hold me responsible for my inaction and miserable stewardship.

Will you be the servant who buries his talent or the one who multiplies it for his master (Matt 25:14-30)? Are you ready to *rise up* and do what God wants you to do?

April 25

The Middle Way

Ecclesiastes 7:18—The man who fears God will avoid all extremes.

The way of the disciple is not often one of extremes, although it might sometimes seem to be so or fanatics and critics may portray it that way. Rather, as followers of Jesus, we are told to walk as Jesus walked (1 John 2:6). Jesus, who in His perfection might have been capable of a righteous extremism, repeatedly shunned such moral fanaticism. Because love was His motive, He often chose to bend down and do the unconventional and the unexpected. We see Him talking alone with the Samaritan woman, healing on the Sabbath, drinking wine and eating with prostitutes and sinners (John 4; Luke 13:14; Mark 3:1-6; Luke 7:34; Matt 9:11). Although He was uncompromising in regards to sin, Jesus was not bound to a rigid set of moral rules. He was not, as we sometimes allow ourselves to be, righteous for righteousness sake.

So when Solomon says to us, "Do not be overrighteous, neither be overwise"(Ecc 7:16), he is describing the righteousness of the Pharisees and every one of us who allows the practice of faith to blind us to the heart of God's purposes. Jesus never did this. He always obeyed the Spirit, even when this led Him to do some unconventional or unexplainable things. Guided by the Spirit, Christ was never guilty of being "overrighteous" like the Pharisees. Neither did He walk in the darkness of the "overwicked." He says, "Away from me, Satan!"(Matt 4:10).

Similarly, when Solomon says, "Do not be overwicked, and do not be a fool"(Ecc 7:17), he echoes Paul's command to have no truck with darkness (Eph 5:7-9). But at the same time, Jesus repeatedly shows us that when the ways of "righteousness" butt up against the ways of God, we must always choose God's way. We must follow the Spirit's leading even at the cost of being seen as morally deviant or "unrighteous" in the eyes of men.

Have you found God's way, the *middle way* between the extremes of overrighteousness and overwickedness? Rather than the Buddhist's "middle path" of self-empowered liberation through the rejection of extremes, or Aristotle's "golden mean," where virtue lies between the polarities of vice, God's way shines the love and truth of Jesus. It may, at times, be unconventional and unexpected, but it always obeys the heart of God's purposes as revealed by His Spirit. Extremism, whether of righteousness or wickedness, is of Satan. Both blind us to the way of Christ.

To go God's way is to walk as Jesus did, never in extremes and always where the Spirit leads. Walk by the Spirit (Gal 5:16). Walk as Jesus walked.

April 26

Be Thou Exalted

Psalm 57:11—Be exalted, O God, above the heavens; let your glory be over all the earth.

How will we know our faith is genuine? Will it be proved in regular church attendance or acts of service? Can it be shown in our physical purity or the stewardship of our finances?

While these actions do reflect what lies at my spiritual core, they are secondary to the central question: In my life, who is *above* and who is *below*? As A.W. Tozer says, "Let the average man be put to the proof on the question of who is *above,* and his true position will be exposed."[88] The heart that is rightly related to God in a genuine faith is the one that continually says, "*Be exalted, O God, above the heavens.*"

David uttered these words even as he was hunted like an animal by a jealous King Saul. From this lowly position of persecution, David understood the exalted nature of a God who "reached down from on high and took hold of me," and "rescued me from my powerful enemy…"(2 Sam 17-18). David's life demonstrated that "'Be thou exalted' is the language of victorious spiritual experience."[89] As Tozer says:

> "Be thou exalted"…is central in the life of God in the soul. Let the seeking man reach a place where life and lips say continually "Be thou exalted," and a thousand minor problems will be solved at once. His Christian life…becomes the very essence of simplicity. By the exercise of his will he has set his course, and….If blown off course…by some adverse wind he will surely return again by a sacred bent of the soul….He has met his life problem at its center, and everything else must follow along.[90]

The faith that is genuine returns again and again to the reality that God, and God alone, is *above*. Nothing else must take His place. The insincere believer cannot say with his lips and believe in his heart that God is, and must always be, exalted in all things, at all times.

Do I find myself raising the hands of my heart toward heaven and saying, "*Be exalted, O God, above the heavens*"? When I belong to Christ, He is *above* and I am *below*, and nothing, and no one, shall come between. *Be thou exalted, O God, in my life!*

---

[88] A.W. Tozer, *The Pursuit of God* in *The Classic Works of A. W. Tozer* (Public Domain), 60.
[89] Ibid.
[90] Ibid.

God of Peace

1 Corinthians 14:33—For God is not a God of disorder but of peace.

If I am ever in doubt as to whether or not the Spirit of the Lord is in someone or something, I need only look for the presence of God's peace. *God is not a God of disorder but of peace.* Christ is the "Prince of Peace," and where He lives, there will be peace (Is 9:6). When I bump up against confusion and disorder, whether in the heart, the head, or in the world around me, God is not in it.

Satan is the father of all moral chaos and disorder. The sin that he sowed into the hearts of men and women began with lies that produced a subtle confusion and disordered thinking. And so long as he can keep us distracted and preoccupied, confused and bewildered, we are unlikely to refocus clearly on the Lord and His purposes.

But when I am in step with the Spirit of God, there is peace. This does not mean that I am completely imperturbable—my humanity will sneak in, sooner or later. But it does imply a predominating order and clarity of spiritual purpose. There is no constant jockeying for ascendency over others, no persistent warring against God or man. There is gentleness and kindness; there is a love that looks in the face of hate and refuses to respond in kind.

Jesus says, "Peace I leave with you; my peace I give you"(John 14:27). Do you possess this peace or is the sin within you determined to ruin the tranquility of your heart? Jesus said, "Blessed are the peace-makers, for they will be called sons of God"(Matt 5:9). Are you resolved to allow His peace within you to transform you into a peacemaker? So long as I permit the rebellious spirit within me to drive my passions in a reckless, selfish, and disordered manner, I threaten to forfeit my claim as a child of God.

God's children are anointed with His peace. In the midst of moral chaos, their lives are ordered by the Spirit. They face challenges, heartaches and defeats with the peaceful confidence of Christ. Where there is anger, they choose a soft word; where there is hatred and invective, they choose love and forgiveness. Where there is moral recklessness and selfishness, they commit to discipline and humility. They often do not do it perfectly —but they do it!

Does the peace of God live in you? Is it the compass of your soul? While the life lived for "self" is a disordered one, the life lived for God is a peaceful one. It rests assured in the Captain's course and His will to deliver His children safely home.

If God's peace is not in you, God is not likely there at all.

April 28

Such a Time as This

Esther 4:14—And who knows but that you have come to royal position for such a time as this?

You are where you are in your life, right now, doing what you are doing, because God has specifically placed you there. God makes no mistakes. So if you find yourself asking why you are working where you are working, or how you have come to live in this specific place, or to be involved in this particular relationship, at this particular time, understand that the purposes of God are at work in your life.

God is always working, allowing the chessboard of our lives to play out before Him. Because He knows every move that we will make, every victory and every loss we will endure, He knows how our years of maneuvering will end. Jesus tells us our "Father is always at His work to this very day"(John 5:17). He is engaged in every move we make and every position we assume. It does not matter whether we are dressed as pawns or kings—the woman at the well or Esther the queen of Persia. God places us where we need to be, using our choices and those of others to fulfill His providential plans.

This hand of God is clearly seen in the life of Queen Esther. When Esther was made the Jewish queen of the king of Persia, she had no idea what her position would enable her to do for God's people and His purposes. At just the right time, however, *for such a time as this*, Esther was able to intervene and thwart the wicked plans of the scheming official, Haman.

Has God placed you, like Esther, in a position of influence? If He has, be prepared to be used for His purposes and glory in the lives of others: "Do not think that because you are in the king's house...you will escape" being part of God's providential plan (Esther 4:13). If, on the other hand, you are in the service of others, rather than in a position of leadership, you are no less part of the Lord's purposes right where you are. So, "use whatever gift [you have] received to serve others...with the strength God provides, so that in all things God may be praised through Jesus Christ"(1 Peter 4:10-11).

Your current position in life, high or low, bishop or knight, pawn or queen, is for God's purposes in the here and now. There are no wasted moments in God's temporal economy, no erroneous moves on the board. He knows the game will end with Him as the final champion. With this in mind, be ready to be employed in this victory, for His glory, for *such a time as this* (Esther 4:14).

April 29

Inward Renewal

2 Corinthians 4:16—Therefore do not lose heart. Though outwardly we are wasting away, yet inwardly we are being renewed day by day.

The tendency to lose heart is entirely understandable when our focus is on *outward* things. The world around us is crumbling. From the bodies we live in, to the storms that ravage coastlines and the wars that destroy our cities, there is decay, chaos, hatred and destruction all around us. Outwardly, *we are wasting away*!

But *inwardly* the disciple of Christ is *renewed day by day*! Though his body is falling apart, he knows he is not eternally bound by that body (Phil 3:21). The disciple knows discouragement and, at times, even depression. But, he does not live in despair. When the Spirit of God lives in us and we truly understand the power of Christ and His victory over sin and death, we are incapable of despair. Though *outwardly we are wasting away*, with the Spirit's perspective and encouragement as our guide, *inwardly we are being renewed day by day*!

This capacity for renewal is directly dependent upon our perspective. Where we fix our eyes determines our inner transformation. When you decide to "fix your thoughts on Jesus," to "fix [your] eyes not on what is seen, but on what is unseen"(Heb 3:1; 2 Cor 4:18), your perspective is drawn to God's eternal vision. To look simply at the brokenness and injustice within you and around you, is to virtually guarantee that you will lose heart. It is like choosing to walk with our eyes fixed on the ground, never lifting them up to see the flowers and meadows around us and the expansive blue above us. Such a life is a limited one, "looking only on the surface of things"(2 Cor 10:7). It is bound to the muddy colors of the muck of life, rather than the fullness of what God intended.

Are you in a place in your life where you feel too tired and broken to imagine tomorrow? Is your heart discouraged by the hatred you see and disheartened by the dying that surrounds you? Jesus knows your discouragement, and He wants you to be *inwardly renewed*. All He requires of you is that you lift your eyes towards Him. A simple volitional act will begin the process of renewal. Will we allow our discouragement, disbelief or pride to inhibit Christ's transforming work in our lives?

Why not look to Jesus? Choose to say, "Though He slay me, yet I will hope in Him"(Job 13:15); I will "fix my eyes on Jesus, the Author and Perfecter of our faith…"(Heb 12:2). Don't be a prisoner of despair any longer. Look to Christ, His victory on the cross and the power of His resurrection, and the Spirit within you will begin your *inward renewal*!

April 30

Garden of Goodness

Genesis 3:2-3—The woman said to the serpent, "We may eat fruit from the trees in the garden, but God did say, 'You must not eat fruit from the tree that is in the middle of the garden, and you must not touch it, or you will die.'"

Each of us stands in his or her own garden.   There are no exceptions to the rule that God has blessed us beyond imagination and given us more "fruit" than we deserve.   While we may all encounter desperate seasons, there is no life where the blessings do not outnumber the pains.   It might be a child who bears your face, work that gives you meaning and purpose, or a roof over your head.   Maybe, you have none of these, but you still have a heart that beats, lungs that breathe, a hand that grasps and eyes that see.   "But I'm an invalid," you say, "stuck in a body that is a burden."   Perhaps instead of health, you have had the privilege of being loved and cared for in ways the healthy will never know.

Our lives are *gardens of God's goodness.*   And yet, we, like Eve before us, tend to focus on the one thing we do not have.   We look through and around the trees of God's plenty in our lives to fixate on the one tree that has been forbidden.   Do you believe that Eve was singular in this propensity?   She was merely the first of us.   Instead of gratefully enjoying the gifts God had given her, Eve, like us, longed for what God forbade.

What is the tree in the middle of your garden?   Are you longing for what God has decided is either not good for you or you are not ready for?   Instead of enjoying and tasting the richness that God has lavished upon you, have you become a victim of Satan's deception of dissatisfaction?   When the Liar says to you, "Did God really say, 'You must not eat from any tree in the garden'?" and "'You will not surely die"(Gen 3:1,4), you must respond: "Taste and see that the Lord is good"(Ps 34:8).

If you are struggling today to see the goodness in your life because of some great pain or trial, you must remember the sweetness you have already enjoyed and see the fruit literally bending the boughs of the trees in your garden.   Do not be deceived into forgetting the riches of your life or thinking the one thing you are denied is what you really need.   Ask for God's grace to stop longing for the few things that have been kept from you, and start living in the goodness He has already given you.

Spiritual contentment arises in the heart of the disciple who determines to give thanks and enjoy the plenty of the garden rather than fixate on the forbidden fruit(s).   Will you decide today to rejoice in your *garden of goodness?*

MAY

Speaking Up

Leviticus 5:1—If a person sins because he does not speak up when he hears a public charge to testify regarding something he has seen or learned about, he will be held responsible.

Solomon reminds us that "There is a time for everything," including "a time to be silent and a time to speak"(Ecc 3:1,7). More often than not, however, we error in the direction of speaking, rather than that of silence. Our world is a near constant cacophony of voices, outside and within. Most of us know little of the importance of silence.

But there are times when silence is not only injurious, but plain sinful. Sin enters silence when withholding a word or action keeps us from loving as Christ would love. It may be that we have seen or heard something of potentially great value in the life of another person. The information we hold may have the power to free the innocent or condemn the guilty. And we have the choice: will we speak or will we remain silent? Perhaps speaking up will expose us to personal guilt or shame. Maybe setting someone free will mean we ourselves will become imprisoned. How do we proceed?

When we choose to withhold in silence (for fear of consequences) a truth that the Spirit leads us to share, we severely misjudge the power of God in our lives. Jesus tells us that "Greater love has no one than this: to lay down one's life for one's friends"(John 15:13). While we probably will not have to lay down our lives for our friends, we may have to sacrifice something of personal value when we break our silence to come to the defense of another. But this act of love is the very thing Christ calls us to.

Whatever may come to us as the result of speaking the truth on behalf of another, we can be confident that the Lord will never leave us. If, on the other hand, we choose to withhold justice, to hide in the silence of personal protection or best interest, we can be sure that God will hold us responsible. We will, sooner or later, be condemned by the very silence we have levied on behalf of another.

When we are placed in a position to speak or act on behalf of another, and the Spirit of God nudges us onward, we must never hide in the safety of silence. Let us speak the truth in love, sacrifice as we ourselves have been sacrificed for, and trust that God will work all things together for the good (Eph 4:15; Rom 8:28).

May 2

Be Ready

Luke 12:35—Be dressed and ready for service and keep your lamps burning.

In many categories of our lives there is a tendency to think, "There is always tomorrow." But what if tomorrow does not come? Is your soul dressed and *ready* today? If the Master comes knocking, can you answer in an instant?

Jesus enjoins us to live in a constant state of readiness—for service, for the ministry of shining in the darkness, for the simple reception of His tender love or rebuking instruction, and for the soul's preparation for the day when He comes again. When we are not living "*ready*" lives, we demonstrate that Jesus is not our primary concern. Our jobs, families, bodies, houses and a great many otherwise good and meaningful things can distract our attentions and busy our hands. It seems "We're always preparing for something—something that never comes off."[91] While we attend to all these peripheral things, the unfortunate result is often the neglect of our *readiness* for the Christ who will knock at the door.

But if He comes knocking today, what then? There will be no time to go find our clothes, pack our bags and get our lives in order. None of it will matter. When He knocks, if our spirits are not *ready* to "immediately open the door for Him"(Luke 12:36) and go where He leads, we may miss Him altogether.

The danger with "tomorrow thinking" is that tomorrow may never come. We must live each day for Christ as if it were our last. The work we do, the words we say, and the time we spend must be pregnant with the anticipation that the Master could come at any time to call His servants home.

Are you right with Jesus today? Not tomorrow or next week, but in this very moment? Do you have any broken relationships that need to be healed? Is your work filled with Kingdom purpose? Are you confident in the grace that saves you?

Prayerfully examine your life for humble "readiness." Have you recognized that you do not know what lies ahead and that in your own strength you will falter? In this place of vulnerability, have you found the joyful hope of waiting for the return of our Lord? And if you are not completely satisfied that the returning Jesus will say to you, "Well done good and faithful servant"(Matt 25:21), then with the Spirit's help, change your life! Readiness is entirely up to you. *Be ready!* He is coming!

---

[91] G.K. Chesterton, *Manalive* (Mineola: Dover Publications, 2000), 28.

Shoulder to Shoulder

Zephaniah 3:9——...that all of them may call on the name of the Lord, and serve Him shoulder to shoulder.

Any attempt to serve the Lord on your own, unyoked from the community of believers, is to risk missing the full power of Christ in your life. We were created to serve the Lord *shoulder to shoulder* with our brothers and sisters in Christ, yoked together in the ploughing of the fields, under His guidance and for His harvest. Yoked together we are able to "Carry each other's burdens, and in this way...fulfill the law of Christ"(Gal 6:2).

The ensuing beauty of serving *shoulder to shoulder* is twofold. First, on a horizontal plane, it binds us to our brothers and sisters in the camaraderie of co-laboring. Second, on a transcendent, vertical plane, once we accept the yoke of Christian service, the power of Christ becomes ours. He bears the load for us. Jesus says, "Take my yoke upon you and learn from me...for my yoke is easy and my burden is light"(Matt 11:29).

You may say, "My burden is heavy enough, how can you expect me to shoulder the burden of that man as well?" But the moment you submit to the yoke of Jesus and fulfill the law of Christ, serving *shoulder to shoulder,* you find that those burdens of yours are somehow made lighter. They may not disappear. They may even temporarily seem to increase. And yet, yoked to your brother, submitted to Christ, your perspective will be transformed. Christ has lightened your load. Yoked in the work of Jesus, you become increasingly "like-minded, having the same love, being one in spirit and purpose"(Phil 2:2). Your attitude becomes the "same as that of Christ Jesus"(Phil 2:5).

God will not stop you from trying to plough the field in your own strength and in your own way. You must come to the end of that labor yourself. But as soon as you do, as soon as you choose to submit to His yoke, you will see the essence of who Jesus is and what He came to do. Once you decide to forget "selfish ambition and vain conceit [and] in humility consider others better than [yourself]"(Phil 2:3), then the power of Christ becomes yours. Any burden you once knew is shouldered by the Savior of the world.

Choose to serve Jesus *shoulder to shoulder* and you will unleash the amazing power of God in your life. You will "run and not grow weary... walk and not be faint."(Is 40:31). There is no burden too heavy for Him to carry.

May 4

A Different Spirit

Numbers 14:24—But because my servant Caleb has a different spirit and follows me wholeheartedly, I will bring him into the land....

Can it be said that you have a *different spirit?* When others look at your life, do they notice something exceptional about you, something that just doesn't conform to the rest of the world? Does the way you move in the world, the things you say, the peace you demonstrate and the love you give others cause them to think, "What makes him *different?*"

Caleb and Joshua were *different* than their peers—they were men who followed the Lord "wholeheartedly." When the other scouts saw giants and the face of defeat in the Promised Land, Caleb and Joshua saw the Lord and His impending victory. When the people of Israel doubted and grumbled, finding themselves distraught and filled with angst, the *different* men trusted in God and said with conviction—"He will lead us into that land..."(Num 14:8). At the risk of being stoned to death for seeing differently, Caleb and Joshua walked forward in faith.

Is your faith leading you to live a *different* life from the rest of the world around you? While you may be living among people plagued with doubt and fear, are you living with a hope and confidence rooted in Christ? The disciple of Jesus has been "set apart from all other people..."(Lev 20:26). Are you living this way? If your life doesn't look any *different* than anyone else's at your place of employment or in your neighborhood, you are likely not living for Christ. "He anointed us, set His seal of ownership on us, and put His Spirit in our hearts as a deposit, guaranteeing what is to come"(2 Cor 1:21). When the world looks at you, they must see the anointing of God—they must see Jesus! They must know *more of Him and less of you.*

Beware of living a life of conformity. While it may be easy to go with the flow, when that flow bumps up against the will of God, you must live differently. You are not called to be in constant rebellion to the world around you, but you have been set apart. And because the Spirit of God lives in you, your life must look *different*, or the Spirit has no place in your heart.

Pray today that God gives you the grace to follow after Him wholeheartedly, even at the cost of living differently. Ask the Spirit's help in making you a disciple whose life is marked by a *different spirit.*

Instruments of Righteousness

Romans 6:13—...and offer the parts of your body to Him as instruments of righteousness.

When was the last time you considered the parts of your body as *instruments of righteousness?* Are you a surgeon? Then use your hands to heal and relieve the suffering of God's people. Do you sing? Then let your voice declare God's praises. Has God given you the legs of a deer? Then, like Eric Liddell, run for the glory of God, saying, "I believe God made me for a purpose, but He also made me fast. And when I run, I feel His pleasure."[92]

We must recognize that the parts of our bodies have the capacity to be used as *instruments of righteousness* or wickedness. The choice is ours. The body, in and of itself, however physically attractive or plain, strong or weak, is simply a body. But how I use that body—in its whole a temple of the Spirit, or in its parts as potential *instruments of righteousness*—declares to God where the allegiance of my heart resides.

It is the sheer nonsense of contemporary society to suggest a strict division between the body and the soul—or, worse yet, to deny the soul's relevance altogether. What I do with my body directly affects my soul, both present tense and future. Similarly, what I do spiritually affects my body and its members. Paul says, "Do not offer the parts of your body to sin, as instruments of wickedness, but rather offer yourselves to God... and...the parts of your body to Him as *instruments of righteousness*"(Rom 6:13).

A soul that is spiritually healthy will care for its body. It will recognize the body as the temple of the Spirit and as a collection of parts dedicated to the work of the Lord. Obversely, the unhealthy soul will allow the body to grow deconditioned and unkempt, dissipated on the evil desires of the flesh (Rom 6:12).

Have you given your heart to Christ? Then your body is His, in its entirety and in each individual part, to be used by you as *instruments of righteousness* for His glory. When you neglect or abuse your body, or spend it out on the whims of your physical fancies, you disrespect and grieve the Lord who created it to be a holy instrument in His hands.

Dedicate your body to the Lord. Pray that the life you live, in the body He gave you, you will live to God (Rom 6:10).

---

[92] Collin Welland, *Chariots of Fire*, directed by Hugh Hudson (United Kingdom: Allied Stars Ltd. and Warner Bros., 1981).

May 6

Nothing But Fragments

Psalm 31:5—Into your hands I commit my spirit; redeem me, O Lord, the God of truth.

> I yearn to be held
> in the great hands of your heart....
>
> Into them I place these fragments, my life,
> and you, God—spend them however you want.[93]
> —Rainer Rilke

We will never be rescued by God until we surrender to Him. I may hear "many whispering, 'Terror on every side!'" and know that my enemies "conspire against me and plot to take my life"(Ps 31:13). But until I am able to see God as my *only* "rescue," "fortress," and "refuge"(Ps 31:2,3,4), I will resist His efforts to save me. Most of us, like David, have to be pushed to the point of "distress," when our "eyes grow weak with sorrow...and the soul and body with grief"(Ps 31:9), before we will admit we need help and that we cannot do it on our own. For as long as "what we call 'our own life' remains agreeable we will not surrender it to Him."[94]

Have you surrendered your life to Christ? Can you honestly say to the Lord, "Into your hands I commit my spirit," and "My times are in your hands..."(Ps 31:5,15)? Have you reached the stage of spiritual awareness that recognizes its helpless fragmentation apart from God—"I am forgotten as though I were dead; I have become like broken pottery"(Ps 31:12)?

You will know you are capable of being rescued when you *yearn to be held in the great hands of God's heart.* When you have the courage to see your life apart from God as nothing but broken fragments of pottery, then you will have what it takes to look at the loving hands of your Father and say, "*Into them I place these fragments, my life, and you God—spend them however you want.*"

When your life is shattered and all you see is fragments of what once was, commit yourself into the hands of the God who loves you more than you can imagine. He is the One who made you on His potter's wheel and the only One who can remake you into exactly what you were designed to be. Don't settle for a phony facsimile; be the real thing—the work of art God intended you to be.

---

[93] Rainer Rilke, *Book of Hours: Love Poems to God* (New York: Riverhead Books, 2005), 139.
[94] C.S. Lewis, *The Problem of Pain* (New York: HarperCollins, 2001), 94.

May 7

The Thorn

2 Corinthians 12:7—...there was given me a thorn in my flesh, a messenger from Satan, to torment me.

Has the Lord allowed a "thorn" to reside in your "flesh"— a physical, emotional, or psychological disturbance that appears to handicap your personal efforts? If so you, like Paul, have reason to rejoice! While every natural inclination desires to rip the thorn out, God has it there for your good. Paul "pleaded with the Lord to take it away..."(2 Cor 12:8). Perhaps you have done the same. And why not? It is a painful and constant reminder that you are vulnerable—you can bleed.

In this spirit of vulnerability, Paul exhorts us to rejoice, recognizing that God's "power is made perfect in weakness"(2 Cor 12:9). When God allows a thorn to reside in our flesh we must remember that the divine intention is not to hurt, maliciously so, but to bring us to a submission that blesses us.[95] Instead of seeing this thorn as an opportunity for God's power to rest on us, we might choose to kvetch or bask in self-pity. But the disciple who understands the will of God, comes to realize instead that "It was good for me to be afflicted, so that I might learn your decrees"(Ps 119:71). The disciple sees the thorn as an instrument of God's love to make him more divinely "lovable." For because God "is what He is, His love must, in the nature of things, be impeded and repelled by certain stains in our present character, and because He already loves us He must labour to make us lovable."[96] The thorn pierces to transform.

Perhaps you have a thorn in your flesh today to help you learn obedience: "Before I was afflicted I went astray, but now I obey your Word"(Ps 119:67). Perhaps your affliction has more to do with someone else and your weakness is God's instrument of grace in bringing that person to the cross. Just as the flesh of Jesus was pierced with divine purpose, so also your flesh may be pierced for God's purposes in your life or the life of another. Your thorn, whatever it is, will demonstrate that God's "grace is sufficient..."(2 Cor 12:9). Your weakness sets the stage for the demonstration of God's power.

Let the Spirit give you the grace to see your thorn as God's instrument of blessing and love. Commit to "delight in weakness, in insults, in hardships, in persecutions, in difficulties. For when [you] are weak, then [you] are strong"(2 Cor 12:10). The blood your thorn bleeds brings with it God's grace, power and love. Rejoice in your thorn!

---

[95] C.S. Lewis, *The Problem of Pain* (New York: HarperCollins, 1996), 110.
[96] Ibid, 41.

May 8

Oaks of Righteousness

Isaiah 61:3—They will be called oaks of righteousness, a planting of the Lord, for the display of His splendor.

When Isaiah refers to the redeemed of Israel as *oaks of righteousness*, he speaks to the resurrecting power of Jesus, the Messiah. For what tree stands more resolutely rooted in the earth than the oak? And yet, in Christ, this is exactly what God wants to do with all our broken and flimsy lives— He wants us to be "rooted and built up in Him…"(Col 2:7).

Is your life a fragmented mess? Do you feel adrift, spiritually unrooted or, perhaps, "imprisoned"? Then know that Christ came for you —to turn the tiny acorn of your spirit into an *oak of righteousness*. Christ came to "bind up the broken hearted, to proclaim freedom for the captives and release of darkness for the prisoners….to comfort all who mourn and provide for those who grieve…"(Is 61:1-3). Jesus is able to take the ashes of our lives and turn them into "a crown of beauty," placing upon us a "garment of praise instead of a spirit of despair"(Is 61:3).

God desires that our branches reach for the sky, to soak in the light of His presence and display His work in our lives. He wants the birds of the air to rest in our stable boughs, and for men and women to find respite in our shade—"Each man will be like a shelter from the wind and a refuge from the storm…"(Is 32:2)—all that *His* name may be glorified, as the One who has planted us, sustained us and given us strength.

But when the Lord resurrects your life, taking your seedling "nothingness" to an *oak of righteousness*, be careful to not rebel against your Maker, or grow overly confident in the strength He has built into you. For, "rebels and sinners shall be broken together, and those who forsake the Lord shall be consumed"(Is 1:28). Though He has made you one of the strongest of trees, the glory of His handiwork, yet, in your rebellion, you will become tinder, and return to your fragmented life. "You shall be an oak whose leaf withers…and the strong shall become tinder, and His work a spark; both will burn together, with no one to quench the fire"(Is 1:31).

God is willing and able to make you an *oak of righteousness*, strong enough to withstand the fiercest winds of spiritual opposition. But in the strength He gives you, never forget that you are a tree dependent on His rain, and one lightning strike away from the fire of His wrath.

With your mind rooted in these truths, let your arms, like the boughs of an oak, reach for heaven to praise the God who has made you, resurrected you, sustained you, and given you strength. Let your righteousness, the work of God in you, stand for all the world to see, that the name of the Lord may be praised!

May 9

Angel of Light

2 Corinthians 11:14-15—...for Satan himself masquerades as an angel of light. It is not surprising, then, if his servants masquerade as servants of righteousness.

If our view of spiritual darkness is that it is always dark, then we have no true conception of the darkness at all. From the beginning, Satan has masqueraded as *an angel of light*. He knew the Light personally and intimately. He stood in the Lord's presence and the radiance of His glory. Satan knew this radiance so well that he desired it as his own: "I will ascend to heaven; I will raise my throne above the stars of God; I will sit enthroned....I will make myself like the Most High"(Is 14:13-14). And so, when Satan rebelled, he fell from heaven as a "morning star, son of the dawn"(Is 14:12), an enemy of God well informed in God's radiant glory.

For this reason, Satan's repertoire of tactics is not limited to the obviously sordid, vile, repulsive and unspeakable things. Those already in the darkness are subject to these. Rather, more frequently than not, and particularly in his attacks against God's people, Satan's scheming is more nuanced—cloak and dagger. It is almost always a movement in our lives that is cast in a glow which does not appear dark. For, "To be greatly and effectively wicked a man needs some virtue."[97] We might admit, on a certain level, that it does not have the radiance of God in it; but the dim light we do see makes us question whether it could be all that bad. And this questioning is all it takes—"Did God really say, 'You must not eat from any tree in the garden?'"(Gen 3:1). If Satan's masquerading can get us to question God's authority in our lives, the darkness has a foothold. Conversely, "Where there is no ambivalence, Satan is powerless...."[98]

Do you find yourself questioning the legitimacy of God's commands in your life? The masquerading of light that induces this ambivalence may even come through those you think you know and love well. Satan is unlikely to come to you himself, as he did to Eve. More often than not, it will be *his servants [who] masquerade as servants of righteousness.* In your hearts, therefore, you must commit to "test the spirits to see whether they are from God..."(1 John 4:1).

The Light of the world is an unmistakable light. Be on your guard against the *angel of light* who specializes in having "a form of godliness"(2 Tim 3:5), which has no God in it at all.

---

[97] C.S. Lewis, *The Screwtape Letters* (New York: HarperCollins, 2013), 171.
[98] Soren Kierkegaard, *The Lily of the Field and the Bird of the Air* (Princeton: Princeton University Press, 2016), 65.

May 10

Amidst the Weeds

Matthew 13:29—...while you are pulling up the weeds, you may root up the wheat with them.

Perhaps you have found yourself, like King David before you, asking, "How long, Lord, will the wicked, how long will the wicked be jubilant?"(Ps 94:3). All around you what you see are men and women who appear to "have no struggles; their bodies...healthy and strong"(Ps 73:4). It may gall your spiritual sensitivity to see that "pride is their necklace," as "They scoff, and speak with malice"(Ps 73:6,8). Your heart yearns for justice and a pulling of the "weeds." But the weeds remain. Why?

Jesus's parable tells us that one of the reasons the weeds remain is for the benefit of His followers. When the servants offer to pull the weeds for the master, he responds, *"No...because while you are pulling the weeds, you may root up the wheat with them."* To pull the weeds prematurely is to risk minimizing the upcoming harvest. The rooted proximity of our lives would cause the disciples to be pulled up along with the "weeds." Impatient piety now curtails the final Kingdom abundance.

The harvest will come. And those who "are far from [God] will perish; [God will] destroy all who are unfaithful to [Him]"(Ps 73:27). God will "tell the harvesters: first collect the weeds and tie them in bundles to be burned..."(Matt 13:30). The wicked will be uprooted and thrown into the fire. Then, and only then, will the wheat, His harvest, be brought into His barn.

Rather than mourn the apparent delay of the Master in reaping His harvest, give thanks for the persistence of weeds in your life. Do not be "grieved...embittered...senseless and ignorant"(Ps 73: 21-22) before your God. Choose instead to give thanks for the mercy and patience that sustains you and also gives more time for the wicked to turn back to Him. Never forget that "The Lord is not slow in keeping His promise....Instead, He is patient with you, not wanting anyone to perish, but everyone to come to repentance"(2 Peter 3:9). While the weeds remain, there is still hope that the unbelievers will come to Christ.

Decide that you will grow *amidst the weeds* and in despite of their choking efforts, confident in the coming harvest and determined that the Master will bring you into His barn with the fullness of time. Pray today that the Spirit gives you the sensitivity and the grace to see the "weeds" in your life as an opportunity for intercession in the lives of others. Consider seeing the "weeds" as a gift for learning the loving patience of our Father. God is giving us time—the persistence of weeds attests to His amazing grace. Rejoice *amidst the weeds*!

May 11

Have You Ever Seen the Rain?

Acts 14:17—Yet He has not left Himself without testimony: He has shown kindness by giving you rain from heaven and crops in their seasons; He provides you with plenty of food and fills your hearts with joy.

Have you considered the rain? For many in the modern world, the rain has become little more than a superfluous nuisance. It is a commuter's hazard in excess and the cause of brown lawns or meaningless small talk in its dearth. Most today are so far removed from the agrarian lifestyle, we often don't know where our drinking water comes from, much less how dependent the preindustrial world was, and still is, upon rain for its daily existence. Appreciation of the rain has been largely lost in industrialized countries.

But rain holds the testimony of God. It heralds the very presence and nearness of our Lord, for "the heavens poured down rain, before God…"(Ps 68:8). Without rain, like the God who created it, nothing exists and nothing grows (1 Cor 3:6). It is God who "bestows rain on the earth; He sends water upon the countryside"(Job 5:10). God holds the rain in His hands just as He holds each one of us in His hands. In a single droplet of rain, clinging to a blade of grass, I can see my face and the world surrounding me. Just imagine the billions upon billions of droplets in a single storm. Each one might hold the image of a different person. And God, in His immensity, holds them all in His hands!

Perhaps you have decided that the rain is simply a meteorological phenomenon of condensing vapor. It is certainly that, but so much more, for "Do any of the worthless idols of the nations bring rain? Do the skies themselves send down showers? No, it is you, O Lord our God. Therefore our hope is in you, for you are the one who does all this"(Jer 14:22). God alone can shut up the heavens, holding the rain in the clouds, sometimes for years, only to unleash His showers at the prayerful request of His servants like Elijah (1 Kings 18:41-46). He can make it rain in one place, and dry in another (Amos 4:7). Are you living your life in a dry and barren place? If so, "Ask the Lord for rain…; it is the Lord who makes the storm clouds. He gives showers of rain to men…"(Zech 10:1).

As one lyricist asks, "Have you ever seen the rain?"[99] To see the rain is to see the very testimony of God. It is the rain alone, forgetting every other proof, that leaves us without excuse: Jehovah is God.

---

[99] John Fogerty, Creedence Clearwater Revival, 1971, "Have You Ever Seen the Rain?" *Pendulum.*

May 12

The Dying Gift

Proverbs 10:7—The memory of the righteous will be a blessing....

The giving we are called to as disciples of Christ extends even into death. Legacies matter immensely to God and the memories we leave behind us are meant to be gifts that point to Jesus. Is your life headed in that direction? Are you living in such a way that "life is preparation for death as a final act of giving"?[100] When death calls for you, will your dying, like the living that preceded it, infuse the world around you with the hope and love of Jesus Christ?

Too many so-called Christians live their lives in fear of death. Instead of seeing death as a doorway home into the Father's embrace, it is seen as some kind of defeat. Many of us forget that "We ourselves are responsible for the way we die. We have to choose between clinging to life in such a way that death becomes nothing but a failure, or letting go of life in freedom so that we can be given to others as a source of hope."[101]

In dying, as in living, my death must be a gift to others of "love, joy, peace, patience, kindness, goodness, faithfulness, gentleness and self-control"(Gal 5:22). And above all else, my passing must inspire hope. I must decide that "Christ will be exalted in my body, whether by life or by death"(Phil 1:20). We must live today with the determination that our deaths will impart a memory of blessing to all those who know us. We must decide that the hope of Christ living in us will have an even greater splendor in our dying, even after our deaths, because of His climatic radiance in our living. Like senescent stars, no longer burning but shining brightly in the night sky, we are called to fill the hearts of men and women with the hope of Christ as we continue to illuminate the darkness of the world we leave behind us.

Do you fear death or do you embrace its coming with the expectant hope of your final gift of love to God and His people? The Psalmist reminds us: "Precious in the sight of the Lord is the death of His saints"(Ps 116:15). May the death you die be the culmination of a life lived for Christ, a lasting memory of hope and a blessing to all those who will follow after you. Let your dying, like Christ's before you, be your final act of giving.

---

[100] Henri Nouwen, *Life of the Beloved* (New York: The Crossroad Publishing Company, 2016),116.
[101] Ibid, 118.

May 13

Weeping and Dancing

Ezra 3:12—But many of the older priests and Levites and family heads, who had seen the former Temple, wept aloud when they saw the foundation of this Temple being laid, while many others shouted for joy.

Sometimes the transformation God brings about in our lives causes some to weep and others to shout for joy. If they weep it is either because they are holding on to something or someone who no longer is, or their joy is so profound that it overwhelms them to the point of inexpressible tears. Those who shout for joy, however, are those who see the glorious transformation, but are not influenced or fettered by the weight of the past's comparison. Theirs is the simple joy.

When the Temple was rebuilt in the days of Ezra, this same array of human emotions played out in the hearts and souls of the people of Israel. The older priests, Levites and leaders remembered the former things. Perhaps in the fondness of memory, they wept over what, in comparison, now seemed a poor copy of the original. Or maybe the sight of the resurrected Temple made them overcome with emotion, a kind of elated disbelief at the healing of God. Either way, the roots of memory affected the present response. The younger generation, unfamiliar with the past, had the simple pleasure of exultation.

When God brings about a transformation or resurrection in your life or the life of someone you know, expect a spectrum of responses from the crowd. Perhaps well-intentioned, these responses and associated comments will be less a reflection on you and God's work in your life than upon the history of the soul from where they emerge. Give the giver of these responses the benefit of the doubt. Move forward in the confidence of what God has done in you, irrespective of the crowd.

But if you are one of the crowd witnessing a resurrection work in the life of another, rejoice when you are given the privilege and pleasure of simple exultation. And if you are the one who brings a historical perspective to the moment, know that your agenda will necessarily be more complex—perhaps richer and fuller, more meaningful and layered, but certainly more complicated. Trust that God knows best. Know that in the end, it is *His* purposes that matter in your life and the lives of others.

Give Christ your heart and its history, and He will carry you through every transformation and resurrection to His Kingdom perspective. Whether it is in *weeping or dancing,* the name of the Lord will be glorified.

May 14

Eyes of Faith

Luke 24:31—Then their eyes were opened and they recognized Him, and He disappeared from their sight.

For those who have sought after Jesus, a time comes for us all when, like the disciples on their journey to Emmaus, *their eyes were opened and they recognized Him....* It is an epiphany, a coming home. In this moment of clarity, this mountaintop view, the person of Jesus is seen as distinctly as if He were sitting before us. But just as Christ quickly *disappeared from their sight* on the road to Emmaus, so also He will not tarry in our enlightened presence either. And while our hearts may long to see Him, the clouds and thick darkness descend on the mountain, and we are left to see with the *eyes of faith*. But just because we do not see Him, does not mean that He is not near.

Jesus said to His disciples, "'Because you have seen me, you have believed; blessed are those who have not seen me and yet have believed'"(John 20:29). Are you wondering why so much of your life seems to be lived in a cloudy uncertainty? Why do the clear glimpses of His presence appear to be so few and far between?

We are, like the disciples, "slow of heart to believe all that the prophets have spoken!"(Luke 24:25). So Jesus walks up beside us and periodically shows us His presence. But the reason He does not stay there, where we can touch His nail-pierced hands and see His gentle smile, is the matter of faith. It takes comparatively little faith to believe in a Christ we see right before us. The God who multiples fish, casts out demons, heals the leper and walks on water, is a God we can more easily follow. However, to believe in the midst of darkness, to know that He is beside us, even when we see nothing at all—that is a faith that allows us to move mountains (Matt 17:20).

If Jesus has favored you with a moment of clarity in His presence, perhaps more than one, but then leaves you to the clouds and darkness again, alone on the road to Emmaus—rejoice! He is trusting you with the power of faith. He is counting you as one of the blessed, who believes even in the absence of sight. Never stop seeing Him with the *eyes of faith* until you see Him again, this time face-to-face and forever.

Saved in Rest, Strengthened in Quietness

Isaiah 30:15—In repentance and rest is your salvation, in quietness and trust is your strength.

It goes against the very grain of our natural inclinations to suggest that we need to be saved, much less that this salvation is independent of our effort. And yet, this is the very message that Scripture so resolutely declares—"It is by grace that you have been saved through faith, and this not of yourselves, it is a gift of God; not by works, so that no man may boast"(Eph 2:8-9). Jesus "saved us, not because of righteous things we had done, but because of His mercy"(Titus 3:5).

Salvation in Jesus follows on the heels of *repentance and rest,* not on personal striving for perfection. *Repentance* comes first because the heart that has not humbled itself before the Lord and recognized its need for grace, cannot be saved—"Humble yourselves before the Lord, and He will lift you up"(James 4:10). Elsewhere Peter says, "Repent then, and turn to God, so that your sins may be wiped out, that times of refreshing may come from the Lord…"(Acts 3:19).

Having repented of sin, the next step towards salvation is to *rest* in the arms of Christ. I am commanded to cease from my efforts at self-sufficiency and allow the grace of Jesus to work in me. Christ says, "Come to me all you who are weary and heavy laden and I will give you *rest*"(Matt 11:28). Instead of working to obtain the unobtainable, I am told to *rest* in Him and to remain in His love (John 15). When my soul chooses to stop its personal striving and dwell instead "in the shelter of the Most High, [I] will *rest* in the shadow of the Almighty"(Ps 91:1). Under the wings of His love, I will find the quietness and trust that bring strength. As I choose to *rest,* I will stop striving and start trusting—to "Be still before the Lord and wait patiently for Him"(Ps 37:7).

Have you chosen to *rest* in Jesus, or are you troubled in your spirit? Have your efforts for personal perfection left you in despair ("Despair is the price one pays for setting oneself an impossible aim.")?[102] Or, have you found the quietness of Christ that comes to those who abide in Him?

God is able to save us. He is able "to do immeasurably more than all we ask or imagine…"(Eph 3:20). But we must beat back the pride that demands we play some part in it. We must desire His immutable peace. We must invite the Spirit to fill us with His imperturbable quietness. We must remember that we are saved in *repentance and rest* and strengthened in *quietness and trust.*

---

[102] Graham Greene, *The Heart of the Matter* (New York: Penguin Books, 1999), 48.

May 16

The Power of Forgiveness

2 Corinthians 2:10-11—...I have forgiven in the sight of Christ for your sake, in order that Satan might not outwit us. For we are not unaware of his schemes.

Forgiveness does not come easily. When we are hurt, deep down to the core of who we are, the last thing we want to do is to forgive. And yet, it is the very thing we must do. In fact, "To be a Christian means to forgive the inexcusable, because God has forgiven the inexcusable in [us]."[103] Forgiveness, based in the blood and power of Jesus Christ, is a prerequisite for spiritual health. Without it, Satan has a beachhead in our lives and will begin his slow, steady and unrelenting advance against us—*for we are not unaware of his schemes.*

In the absence of forgiveness, the cornerstone of the gospel has been removed from our lives. Spiritually we begin and end with forgiveness, and if Satan can outwit us into giving up on forgiveness, choosing revenge, anger or hate instead, then he has succeeded in removing the power of the gospel from our lives. The gospel message is clear—we are forgiven and, therefore, called to forgive others—"forgiving each other, just as in Christ God forgave you"(Eph 4:32). We are called to forgive not once, but time and time again, "not seven times, but seventy-seven times"(Matt 18:21).

When it comes to our inability or our refusal to forgive, God is not fooled by our holy pageantry. We may decorate our lives with good works and bring offerings to His house, but the heart that fails to forgive is a fraudulent one. Jesus says, "leave your gift there in front of the altar. First go and be reconciled to your brother; then come and offer your gift"(Matt 5:24).

Perhaps you are able to forgive others, but you find it difficult to forgive yourself. The necessity of forgiveness to our spiritual health extends even to ourselves. To grow spiritually, we must be able to forgive ourselves as well. When God says, "I will forgive their wickedness and will remember their sins no more"(Jer 31:34), it is sinful on my part to not forgive myself and attempt to cling to that which God has expunged.

Forgive as you have been forgiven, and your life as a disciple will bear fruit. Cling to revenge against others or fail to extend to yourself the grace that God has freely given you, and Satan's hold over your life will only increase. The way of Jesus is the way of forgiveness. Ask Him for the grace and strength you need to forgive.

---

[103] C.S. Lewis, *The Weight of Glory* (New York: HarperCollins, 2001),182.

May 17

Indirect Intercession

Psalm 35:27—May those who delight in my vindication shout for joy and gladness; may they always say, "The Lord be exalted, who delights in the well-being of His servant."

It is one thing to intentionally pray for others—direct intercession. But it is quite another thing when, in our prayers for ourselves, we pray with the best interest of others in mind—an *indirect intercession*. From our infancy, we know how to ask for things for ourselves. It takes no faith at all to pray for our best interests. Even unbelievers do this.

But the more a disciple prays, the more time he or she spends with the Spirit, the more convinced he becomes that his life does not exist for his own interests, but for God's glory in the lives of others. While it is not wrong to pray for something specific in our lives—a godly spouse, meaningful work, a healed relationship—we ought to pray that God's answer to this prayer, whatever it may be, will cause others to *shout for joy and gladness* and to proclaim God's goodness as He *delights in the well-being of His servant.*

The disciple understands that the specific answer to his or her prayer is subordinate to the purposes of God, whether that manifests in the life of the disciple, or the life of another. It is not so important that God brings a specific answer to our prayers so much as it is that His name be glorified in the answer He does provide. No one understood this better than Jesus himself. He promised to answer the prayers of His disciples "so that the Father might be glorified in the Son"(John 14:13).

When you pray for yourself, pray as Christ did—"'not my will, but yours be done'"(Luke 22:42). As you spend time with the Spirit of God in prayer, pray that God's answers to the needs in your life will ultimately cause God's people to rejoice and praise His name. Determine that you will hold lightly to the specifics and tightly to the reality that God loves you deeply and desires that your life will cause others to *shout for joy and gladness,* that the Father may be glorified in you, just as He was in Christ.

The next time you are tempted to ask for the Lord's blessing in your life, ask God's grace in helping you think of His glory and His best in the lives of others.

May 18

Rejoicing in Pain

Romans 5:3-4—Not only so, but we also rejoice in our sufferings, because we know that suffering produces perseverance; perseverance, character; character, hope.

Perhaps the only scriptural command more difficult to live out than rejoicing amidst our sufferings is the injunction to love our enemies. And yet, this *rejoicing in pain* is the very thing that the Apostle Paul exhorts us to do. How is it possible to rejoice in the midst of tribulations and suffering?

The only way exultation of heart arises from the ashes of pain and suffering in our lives is when our focus is fixed on Jesus. Peter says, "do not be surprised at the painful trial you are suffering…But rejoice that you participate in the sufferings of Christ, so that you may be overjoyed when His glory is revealed"(1 Peter 4:12-13).

Left to our own devices, the natural response to suffering is often a withdrawal. There is an inward focus and a "present tense" mentality. In the face of persecution or pain, we retreat into the perceptual security of our outer shells and block out the larger perspective. And while there may be wisdom in a momentary retreat to collect our spiritual wits and refocus on Christ and His eternal purposes, we must not remain in that defensive position. We must determine to emerge. We must decide to stretch out our arms and legs and walk forward in the strength and grace that God provides.

Suffering can only do two things in our lives—destroy us or cause us to persevere. The degree to which we focus on Jesus and His eternal perspective will determine our ability to persevere with rejoicing, knowing that the suffering we find ourselves in now is building in us the character of Christ. And it is this character that will bring us to hope because Christ owns the future. To persevere in the midst of suffering, and to do so with a heart that rejoices, requires that I believe what Jesus said—"And this is the will of Him who sent me, that I shall lose none of all those He has given me…"(John 6:39).

When I am convinced that Jesus will never lose me, then no suffering, great or small, will be able to discourage me or destroy me. In the confidence of Christ, I will find the strength to rejoice in the midst of great pain, knowing that the eternal work of God is happening in me. It is this gift of eternal perspective that makes us conquerors in pain.

If you are in the midst of pain today, pray for the strength to say with your mouth, and believe in your heart, "I can do all things through Christ Jesus who strengthens me"(Phil 4:13)—even rejoice in the midst of pain!

May 19

The Predatory Time

Luke 4:13—…he left Him until an opportune time.

The danger in a victory against Satan in our lives is the spiritual smugness and false security that may follow. We may have just emerged victorious from a great spiritual skirmish in which we had to beat back the powers of darkness. Perhaps we fought with the strength of the Spirit. Maybe we stood steadfastly against repeated temptations. Our defense might have been textbook. And as Satan retreats, we wonder how he could possibly recover from the parrying blows we mustered. But we must be careful—he will. He is a Hydra with many heads. And though we defeat one, more will arise to attack us when the time is right.

Having suffered defeat at the hands of Jesus in the desert, Satan left Christ *until an opportune time.* Like a predatory cat, Satan understands the importance of timing. He is a "roaring lion looking for someone to devour"(1 Peter 5:8). Once rebuffed, he will not retire forever. For like the king of beasts, he has an appetite that must be satisfied. When we defeat him at one advance, he learns something about us that he can exploit in the next attack. He now knows the way we think, the methods we use to ward off His attacks, the limits of our resources and the degree to which we depend upon the Spirit. His predatory instincts bring him back to strike again, this time in a more educated fashion and at a more *opportune time.*

If you have defeated Satan once in your life, rejoice in God's victory. But do not think the war is won. Satan returned for Jesus, and he will return for you and me. The skirmish may go to you, but the battles continue. With each victory won in Christ, resolve that you will entrench more deeply in the Lord and heighten your spiritual awareness. Expect that Satan will come again, from a new angle, at just the right time. Do not be afraid of him, but neither be so naive as to consider him a harmless enemy.

Spiritual smugness is the very thing Satan wants most in your life. It creates the blindest of vulnerabilities. Therefore, be alert in victory and defeat alike. Give thanks for your wounds that remind you of the reality of war and never stop leaning upon the power of the Spirit within you. This Spirit will one day claim final victory over Satan in the person of Jesus Christ our Lord!

May 20

The Plain Truth and Nothing But the Truth

2 Corinthians 4:2—...by setting forth the truth plainly, we commend ourselves to everyman's conscience in the sight of God.

When it comes to presenting the gospel with our lives, the difficulty for many Christians is the tendency to take the beautiful, but naked Truth and dress it up in a needless and injurious complexity. Too often, we "use deception" and "we distort the Word of God"(2 Cor 4:2). Perhaps we do this unknowingly because we ourselves are confused. Maybe we have an ulterior motive. But, we might have good intentions.

The trouble is that "evil...comes of ignorance, and good intentions may do as much harm as malevolence, if they lack understanding."[104] For instance, we might be convinced that the truth of God's Word needs to be "adapted" to the times and sensitivities of today's world. In subtle ways, we trim it or add to it to make it seem more palatable to ourselves and to all those skeptics and critics we want so desperately to please.

But Jesus never compromised His message. He never adapted Himself to the expectations of men and women. Have I done the same? Does my life set forth God's Truth plainly, in a way that commends itself to the conscience of every man and woman I meet by the sheer force of what it is? Do the things I say and the way I live present the gospel and the person of Jesus Christ plainly, or do I find myself giving a personal version that has more of "me" and less of Jesus?

The Truth of the Gospels needs no decoration or human artifice. It does not need more of me, it needs only Jesus. He is the Truth (John 14:6). For this reason, the gospel transcends time and place just as its author, Jesus Christ, transcends all things. My duty as a disciple of Jesus, as one who "preaches" the gospel with my life, is to set it forth plainly. I am to let the gospel speak for itself in the conscience of every man and woman who sees it and hears it preached in my life. When I apologize for it, hide it or alter it, I prove that I do not know or trust the power of the Author I claim as God.

Are you committed to setting forth the truth plainly in your life, even when it offends, seems ridiculous or terribly anachronistic? Remember, you didn't write the Gospels and you never defined Jesus as the Truth—Jesus did. Let Jesus speak for Himself in the conscience of all who would listen as you make your life *more of Him and less of you!*

---

[104] Albert Camus, *The Plague* (New York: Vintage International, 1991), 131.

May 21

Greater than my Legacy

2 Samuel 19:28—All my grandfather's descendants deserved nothing but death from my lord the King, but you gave your servant a place among those who sat at your table. So what right do I have to make any more appeals to the king?

Until I see myself as the helpless Mephibosheth at the feet of the returning King David, I miss the meaning of God's story. As Saul's grandson, Mephibosheth was the descendant of a man who had hated David with an envious fervor. Saul had sinned against David time and time again and hunted him down like an animal. And yet, though generationally linked to this sin, Mephibosheth found favor in the eyes of David. The crippled grandson of Saul was given back his land and provided a place at the king's table all because of a promise spoken in love. Sound familiar?

As sons and daughters of Adam, we too are linked to a generational sin (Rom 5:12). But despite this legacy, Christ, like David, has prepared a table before us in the presence of our enemies (Ps 23:5). He has gone ahead of us to "prepare a place for you"(John 14:3), me, and all those who call upon His name.

In Mephibosheth's crippled feet and decimated family line, we see a helplessness and resulting dependence that mirrors our spiritual lives. Mephibosheth had not "trimmed his mustache or washed his clothes…"(2 Sam 19:24). Separated from his king, he had fallen into disrepair.

Apart from our true King, Jesus Christ, are our spiritual lives any different? Do we understand that we are spiritually "lame" apart from the King whose healing touch and mercy give us a place at His table?

When Jesus returns, like King David returning across the Jordan, will I still be whining about what I do not possess, complaining about what I cannot do, and expecting things I was never meant to have? Or will I, like Mephibosheth, have the spiritual humility and clarity to say, *"So what right do I have to make any more appeals to the king?"* I must never forget that apart from Christ I am a helpless, spiritual cripple who has received grace I do not deserve and mercy I have not earned. In Jesus I am no longer an enemy—I have been saved from the legacy of sin that bound me and given a place at the King's table.

May 22

Silence

Job 30:20—I cry out to you, O God, but you do not answer....

> Have you [God] just remained silent like the darkness that
> surrounds me? Why? At least tell me why. We are not
> strong men like Job who was afflicted with leprosy as a
> trial. There is a limit to our endurance. Give us no more
> suffering.[105]
>
> —Shusaku Endo

If we have not known the *silence* of God, it is unlikely we have
truly known God at all. The Lord speaks through His Spirit, sometimes
openly and plainly. At other times, it is soft and subtle, in a language we do
not at first recognize or in a manner somewhat unexpected and mysterious.
But sometimes, He is *silent,* or at least seems so. And in these times of
quiet and stillness, we must never presume that we are unloved or, more
dramatically, that God ceases to exist. In our intimate human relationships,
we know that communication does not always require audible words. We
can understand one another in and through the *silence.* Why should we
have different expectations in our relationship with the Lord?

Silence is both one of God's greatest teachers and the sign of His
deepest love. As Mother Teresa reminds us, "God is the friend of
silence."[106] When God is *silent,* He is so for a reason. There is, in this time
of quiet, something He wants us to learn about ourselves and about Him
that cannot be translated into any other form of communication. *Silence*
affords us the time to process what we have already been told and to
anticipate what might come next. It permits us to purposefully and actively
climb inside the mind and heart of the One we say we love to find out
what it is we need to know, rather than to have it handed to us. It is the
immature believer who needs constant communication. It is the seasoned
disciple, like Christ Himself, who is blessed with the challenge of God's
silence.

Do you find yourself saying with the Psalmist, "O God, do not
keep *silent*; be not quiet, O God, be not still "(Ps 83:1)? Instead of wishing
the *silence* away, dare to believe that God's *silence* in your life is giving you the
space you need to reach deeper into who He has made you to be. At the
end of this reach, you will find a fuller understanding of who He is and
just how much He loves you. Embrace the *silence!*

---

105 Shusaku Endo, *Silence* (New York: Picador Modern Classics, 2016),103.
106 Malcolm Muggeridge, *Something Beautiful for God* (New York: HarperCollins, 1971), 66.

Faith on Earth?

Luke 18:8—...when the Son of Man comes, will He find faith on earth?

The time will come, and is now fast approaching, when "Because of the increase in wickedness, the love of most will grow cold..."(Matt 24:12). Jesus knew that despite His death and resurrection, despite a ministry that would span the globe and alter the course of history, in the end, only a select few would find Him and cling to Him. With sadness of heart He asks, *"when the Son of Man comes, will He find faith on earth?"*

Now, more than ever it seems, is the time of increased endangerment of faith. We live in a world saturated with books and blogs, churches on many corners and biblical resources at the tip of our digital fingers. And yet, with all this access, true knowledge of Christ is becoming more scarce. Genuine faith is becoming an increasingly endangered species. Soberingly, it appears that "Godliness is no longer valued, except for the very old or the very dead."[107] The Word of God has never been more available and accessible and yet, fewer and fewer people are choosing to read it and live in it. Will Christ find faith amidst this vanishing act?

The challenge for every disciple is to stand against the cultural dissipation of faith and choose to believe. Each of us must decide that if Christ returns tomorrow, even if the world falls away, "I will cling to faith!" In humility I must recognize that only grace will make this possible. It will not do to have the simple, self-empowered enthusiasm of Peter that says, "Even if all fall away, I will not"(Mark 14:29). Peter's heart was right, but his source of strength was not. We must determine, like Peter, to persist in faith till the very end, at all costs, whatever it takes. But we must also determine to stand in grace. We must never forget that we are just as capable of denying Christ as Peter, but confident that grace can deliver us from our weakness and enable us to stand strong until the very end.

Have you decided that you will be standing in faith when the Son of Man returns? If He comes tomorrow, will He find faith living in you? Resolve in your heart and soul that even if you are the only one, by God's grace, you will be standing in faith when He returns!

---

[107] A.W. Tozer, *Man, The Dwelling Place of God* (Public Domain), 153.

Everything Beautiful

Ecclesiastes 3:11—He has made everything beautiful in its time. He has also set eternity in the hearts of men....

Beauty, in the eyes of God, cannot be separated from holiness. The Psalmist says, "worship the Lord in the beauty of His holiness"(Ps 29:2). Sadly, none of us possess this beauty apart from the work of Christ in our lives. Our sin makes us spiritually hideous before a beautifully holy God. But because of our Father's great love, our unsightliness can be redeemed! He is willing and able to reclaim in us that lost piece of eternity that made us in the image of God Himself. Though our spiritual faces are sometimes unlovable, God loves us still. He loves us so much that He "gave His one and only Son, that whoever believes in Him shall not perish, but have eternal life"(John 3:16).

Through this Son, God makes *everything beautiful in its time*—even me; even you! For most of us, this beautification is a long process. It is a gradual polish of increasing gleam, done by "the sanctifying work of the Spirit"; for, "It is God's will that you should be sanctified," and made beautiful before Him (2 Thes 2:13; 1 Thes 4:3). When I am tempted to grow discouraged looking in the mirror and seeing a spiritual face dirtied with the transgressions of my life, I must remember God's love for me. In faith, I must allow the "eyes of [my] heart [to] be enlightened in order that [I] may know the hope to which He has called me,"(Eph 1:18) and the beauty for which He has designed me.

Saints are not born overnight. We are justified in an instant but sanctified over a lifetime. The question is: Am I more beautiful in the eyes of God today than I was yesterday? If not, then I must open the door of my heart (2 Cor 6:13) and allow the Spirit to work in me to "will and to act according to His good purpose"(Phil 2:13). Only by the work of Jesus on the cross and the sanctifying grace of the Spirit in my life, will I be made beautiful in God's time. I must be made holy before a holy God, and only God can do that work in me.

Eternity has been set in your heart. Will you allow God to make you beautiful again? Will you permit Him to fill you with the eternal radiance of heaven?

May 25

Amazed

Mark 7:37—People were overwhelmed with amazement.

When was the last time you were *overwhelmed with amazement* in the presence of Jesus? The people of Israel, watching His miracles and listening to His words, said, "'He has done everything well,'" and "they kept talking about it"(Mark 7:37, 36). They were amazed at Jesus and couldn't stop speaking about Him! Are you filled with this same kind of amazement?

Too little time and emphasis are given to spiritual wonder. If we would dare to begin each day with a focused contemplation of Christ and what He has done for us in our lives, we would be unable to keep from saying, "Amazing love! How can it be, that Thou, my God, should die for me!"[108] The unexamined life suffers from a lack of amazement. This life simply does not bother to stop and stand in Christ's presence, to listen to and observe Him. It does not pause long enough to consider the miracles Christ has done and continues to do. It is blind to the wonderful "magic" He has worked in our spiritual lives, a transformative "magic" with "meaning…and someone to mean it."[109] This life does not spend time getting to know just how deeply Christ loves us.

And if Christ is not enough to overwhelm us with amazement, how much more the addition of God the Father and the Holy Spirit. Have you considered how amazing it is that the Father loves us enough to send His only Son to "save the world through Him"(John 3:17)? Can we be anything but speechless when we remember that the Holy Spirit has condescended to dwell within each of us? How is it possible to keep from saying, "What is man that you are mindful of him, the son of man that you care for him"(Ps 8:4)?

If we are not daily amazed at the Father, the Son and the Holy Spirit, we must question our spiritual health. Our lack of awe demonstrates that either our spiritual senses have become dangerously dulled or we have not chosen to sit with our God, to listen to His words, and to watch Him work in our lives. In intimate proximity with our Lord, we cannot help but be *overwhelmed with amazement*!

Dare to come close enough to Jesus to listen to what He has to say to you and to feel the healing touch of His hands. You will be amazed!

---

[108] Charles Wesley, "And Can It Be."
[109] G.K. Chesterton, *Orthodoxy* (Peabody: Hendrickson Publishers, 2006), 59.

May 26

Highways of the Heart

Psalm 84:5—Blessed are those…who have set their hearts on pilgrimage.

I have become a pilgrim to cure myself of being an exile.[110]
—G.K. Chesterton

Are the *highways of your heart* leading you to the presence of God? All roads may once have led to Rome, the center of power, the seat of the Emperor, and the beating heart of an empire. But are the freeways and byways of your interior headed in the direction of the eternal King? We choose the roads we take. Even when life temporarily redirects us into some back alley or lonely desert road, if our hearts are set on pilgrimage, we will find a way to get back on the road that leads to Zion: *"Blessed are those…who have their hearts set on pilgrimage"* (Ps 84:5).

In this pilgrimage, you may be called to be trailblazer and forge a road that few, if any, have ever walked. But more often than not, we travel roads already trod by the faithful before us. Their footsteps can give us hope, and the monuments they leave behind encourage us. While we do not control where these roads may twist, turn, wind or wander, we do pick where we start and what destination we are headed towards.

Though our intended destination may be the heavenly Zion, the road may very well take us through the "valley of the shadow of death"(Ps 23:4). It may require us to wade through the "slough of despond," be tempted by the city of "Vanity" and survive "Doubting Castle."[111] But if our hearts are committed to the "King's Highway," we can be assured that He is with us and that His rod and staff will comfort us. We may be directed through the "Valley of Baca" (*place of mourning*)(Ps 84:5). But God is able to make it a "place of springs"(Ps 84:6). He can transform it into an oasis of refreshment. Revived in this way, we will pilgrim onward as we "go from strength to strength"(Ps 84:7).

When the *highways of our hearts* are not sign-posted with the destination of the heavenly Zion, we're not headed for the Holy Presence we were created for. We must pull off and examine the signs. Are our lives marked by faithfulness and obedience? Are we reading God's Word and gathering together with His people?

If our road is not God's road, then we must get ourselves on the right road. Let us set our hearts on pilgrimage.

---

[110] G.K. Chesterton, *Manalive* (Mineola: Dover Publications, 2000), 108.
[111] John Bunyan, *The Pilgrim's Progress* (Oxford: Oxford University Press, 1984).

May 27

Their Eyes Were Watching God

Mark 3:2—Some of them were looking for a reason to accuse Jesus....

> They sat in company with the others…their eyes straining against crude walls and their souls asking if He meant to measure their puny might against His. They seemed to be staring at the dark, but their eyes were watching God.[112]
>
> —Zora Neale Hurston

The disciple of Christ must have his or her eyes on Jesus. But how we choose to watch Him determines friend from foe. If we are not living a Spirit-filled life, we may find ourselves watching Jesus "closely to see if He would"(Mark 3:2) do something to offend us. We can focus on Christ with the Pharisee's critical gaze. Or, we can choose to watch Him with the awestruck anticipation and deep-seated love of the disciple.

Both the disciples and the Pharisees watched Jesus intently. There was no lack of interest in Him. The disciples looked for reasons to love Jesus more, even when that meant following Him into the unconventional or "unlawful," such as healing on the Sabbath (Mark 3:2). The Pharisees, however, *were looking for a reason to accuse Jesus.* Rather than choosing to live in the freedom and love Christ offered, unbound by the law, the Pharisees chose to judge and condemn Jesus by that law. Day after day, they "went out and laid plans to trap Him in His words"(Matt 22:15).

Do you find yourself looking for reasons to accuse Jesus in your life? Are you watching for some terrible Christian inconsistency to hang your hat on so you can trap Jesus in His words? Are you trying to justify living according to your "law" rather than Christ's? If you are finding yourself searching for reasons to accuse Jesus or hunting for inconsistencies in Him to satisfy your lingering doubt, then you are becoming more of a Pharisee and less of a disciple. As David's psalms demonstrate, God welcomes the sometimes beleaguered questioning of His servants (Ps 13:1-2). The Lord smiles at the inquisitive, childlike wonder of His disciples (John 1:50). Our God even tolerates the doubts that momentarily hover over me and you. But our Lord hates the pharisaical tendency for accusation and hypocrisy.

The eyes of our hearts can be like those of the disciple or the Pharisee. Whose eyes do you have? Examine your heart today to see how you are *watching Jesus.*

---

[112] Zora Neale Hurston, *Their Eyes Were Watching God* (Urbana: University of Illinois Press, 1991), 191.

May 28

Friendship

Proverbs 12:26—A righteous man is cautious in friendship....

The contemporary age of social media has cheapened the meaning of *friendship*. With the click of a button we can "friend" a person we hardly know, and perhaps, have never even met. There is little to no personal investment required.

Such ideas of *"friendship"* could not be more contrary to the biblical sense of *friendship* endorsed by Jesus. *A righteous man is cautious in friendship* because *friendship*, in the eyes of Christ, is anything but a casual acquaintance. It requires deep intimacy, personal sacrifice, and great love.

In the intimacy of *friendship* we are truly known by others. Intimacy allows for the free and unfettered exchange of the most important parts of who we are. Jesus says, "I have called you friends, for *everything* that I learned from my Father I have made known to you"(John 15:15). This is much more than a posting of our most flattering pictures. This is our sharing of *everything*, at all times, and in all places. In biblical *friendship*, we must be able to share the depths of our hearts and our spiritual struggles—the good, the bad and the ugly. How many of your "friends" have this access to you?

The *friendship* that Christ envisions also requires personal sacrifice. Jesus says, "Greater love has no man than this, that he lay down his life for his friends"(John 15:14). The ultimate litmus test of *friendship* is that of life and death. A friend is someone I am willing to die for. When I love my friend as Christ loves me, I may be compelled, as Jesus was, to go to the "cross," if necessary, for the sake of my friend. Are you ready to die for your "friends"?

Ultimately, *friendship* is based on the love of God: "Real friends find their inner correspondence where both know the love of God."[113] Christ loved us enough to give up heaven, take on flesh, and die for those He called "friends." The awesome privilege of being a "friend" of Jesus is knowing that we are loved by God! "How great is the love the Father has lavished on us..."(1 John 3:1)! Are we emulating that love in our *friendships*?

Though it may cost us much, Jesus calls us to *friendship*, both with Him and with one another. We must not enter these relationships with contemporary casualness, but with a heavenly gravity that recognizes the importance of the relationship. To be a friend is one of life's highest callings. Never forget what it cost Christ to be your friend and be ready to give of yourself to any you call "friend."

---

[113] Henri Nouwen, *The Inner Voice of Love* (New York: Image Books, 1998), 80.

May 29

The Curse

Deuteronomy 11:26—See, I am setting before you today a blessing and a curse....

We have little to no conception of God's storyline until we understand the powerful reality of *the curse* in each of us. Apart from Jesus, we are *cursed*—separated from God by the chains of sin and death. Satan was the first of the *cursed* (Gen 3:14). Since the dawn of creation, he has made it his mission to hide the reality of sin's *curse* on our lives. He has led many to believe that curses are relegated to fairytales, myths, witchcraft and dark magic, but certainly not for moral, upstanding people. And so many are deceived, not seeing the chains that bind them.

But Moses clearly understood the reality of a *cursed* separation from God. Moses said to God's people, "I am setting before you today a blessing and a *curse*—the blessing if you obey the commands of the Lord...; the *curse* if you disobey..."(Deut 11:26-28). God's chosen people, then and now, are always given a choice for life or death. For the Old Covenant people, the choice required obedience to the law; to the New Covenant people, the choice is salvation through the grace and blood of Jesus Christ. But God always offers a choice and a way to escape the *curse*.

Under the law, Satan found reason to rejoice in the chains of the *curse*. He knew the coffers of hell would be filled with the "disobedient" since no one can keep the law perfectly. In and of itself, the law was a *curse* that only God could destroy. And so He did—"Christ redeemed us from *the curse* of the law by becoming a *curse* for us, for it is written: '*Cursed* is everyone who is hung on a tree'"(Gal 3:13). Christ hung in the *cursed* place of slaves, murders and thieves so that we wouldn't have to.

The freedom this crucifixion brings to our lives lacks meaning until we understand the powerful grip of "the law" on our souls. Many today still live under the Pharisee's belief that obedience to rules and good living is enough to save. But the law was and is powerless to save. It has a different purpose. It was meant to show us that we cannot achieve salvation on our own. Apart from the cross, we are condemned—we are *cursed*. Christ says of the unredeemed souls, "'Depart from me, you who are *cursed*, into the eternal fire, prepared for the devil and his angels'"(Matt 25:41).

Have you chosen to be free of the *curse* through the gift of God's grace in Jesus Christ? Can you sing with confidence, "My hope is built on nothing less than Jesus Christ and His righteousness"?[114]

---

[114] Edward Mote, 1834, "My Hope is Built on Nothing Less," *The Lutheran Hymnal*, 370.

Sharing Joy

Luke 1:58—…and they shared her joy.

Upon hearing the news that John had been born to Elizabeth in her old age, her friends and family gathered around her to share the joy of the rejoicing mother. What is sweeter than sharing in the happiness of those we care for? For when we love someone, we desire joy for them— the "joy of the Lord"(Neh 8:10) in their lives. And we would like nothing better than to share in that joy with them and watch its glow illuminate the life we love. Through that moment, we receive glimpses of the heavenly radiance to come.

But the real test of the disciple comes when joy arrives in the life of someone we have no particular affection for, perhaps even feelings of animosity. Do we choose to share in their joy? Or do we resent it or covet it? We are called to "Rejoice with those who rejoice; mourn with those who mourn"(Rom 12:15). The Apostle Paul's command doesn't speak merely of our friends, relatives and loved ones. The command is a universal one. You are called to "Love your enemies…," for, "If you [only] love those who love you, what reward will you get?"(Matt 5:44, 46).

One of the ways we can love our enemies and glorify God is to rejoice in their joy. If we are incapable of sharing in the joy of others, it is because we love ourselves more than God and His purposes. We prove that our focus is our "self" and our need for happiness. But when we find our joy in the Lord, we don't have the rapacious desire to covet or steal the joy God brings into the lives of others. We can celebrate with them because we have found our contentment in Christ, irrespective of what is happening in the lives of others.

Jesus came to this world to share His joy—"I have told you this so that my joy may be in you and that your joy may be complete"(John 15:11). To be a disciple of Christ is to understand the importance of participating in the joy of Christ and others. To follow Jesus is to share His joy with the world around you.

Does "your heart…throb and swell with joy…"(Is 60:5) in the Lord?

May 31

Within Your Reach

Deuteronomy 30:11—Now what I am commanding you to do is not too difficult for you or beyond your reach.

> Everything Our Lord asks us to do is *naturally* frankly impossible to us.[115]
> —Oswald Chambers

As long as we are living under the illusion that our salvation results from our goodness or personal efforts, the bar of God's expectations will always feel too high. His commands will appear too difficult to keep and, at times, nonsensical. From a human perspective, God's commands may appear so. In the untransformed life, His commands are beyond the reach of our natural strengths. But when the Spirit of God enters the disciple, the commands of the Lord are *not too difficult for you or beyond your reach.*

The work of Jesus has made that reach possible for me and you. He has provided a way to stand before a righteous God. It is not because our obedience has been made perfect, but because our salvation is no longer dependent upon that obedience. Instead, obedience is the way we demonstrate our love for God.

As a disciple of Christ, you begin to understand that His "Word is very near you; it is in your mouth and in your heart so you may obey it"(Deut 30:14). In this obedience, you then proclaim your love for the Father who has provided a way for you to reach Him through Jesus Christ His Son. You don't have to "ascend into heaven" or go "beyond the sea"(Deut 30:12-13) to get your right standing before God. It has been given to you in Jesus, the Word who became flesh, to bring the Father within reach of us all (John 1:14).

When you admit that you cannot maintain perfect obedience to God on your own, and you accept that Jesus is your only power to obey, you suddenly find it well *within your reach* to obey God's commands. Will it always be easy? Will it necessarily make sense at every turn? *Resoundingly no!* There will still be challenges. You will be tempted, at times, to give up and to walk the other way, to cheat in the shadows or question what you are doing. But God's commands will no longer seem out of reach or unattainable. The bar has not been lowered, but our imperfect efforts have been covered in the blood of Christ.

The disciple understands that I can "do everything through Him who gives me strength"(Phil 4:13). The question is: will I choose to obey?

---

[115] Oswald Chambers, *The Love of God* in *The Complete Works of Oswald Chambers* (Grand Rapids: Discovery House Publishers, 2000), 666.

JUNE

June 1

Fully Persuaded

Romans 4:21—…being fully persuaded that God had power to do what He had promised.

There is a very real sense in which the gospel must be "sold" to each of us. It does not lack intrinsic value or even its own appeal. But the hearts of men and women are inherently fickle. Blinding us to the truth, sin incessantly tries to distract our attentions. So just as there is salesmanship involved in any purchase, when it comes to the ultimate decision of the heart, to follow Christ or not, we must be completely "sold." We must be *fully persuaded.*

Are you *fully persuaded* that Christ is who He says He is? Do you have conviction, like Abraham did, "that God [has] power to do what He…promised"(Rom 4:21)? Or are you like one of the sneering crowd beneath the cross still saying, "*if* He is the Christ of God"(Luke 23:35), then He should heal my marriage, fix my finances, or get me that promotion at work?

A great many of us spend our lives on the border of conviction, never willing to be *fully persuaded.* Full persuasion necessitates commitment and action. We might agree with some portion of who Jesus is and what His gospel says. It is hard to reject a God who loves and a prophet who heals the crippled and feeds the hungry. But when it comes to being "sold" on judgment for my wrongdoing, rules about what I do and do not do with my body, or exclusion of certain lifestyles, we suddenly bristle. The cost of obedience to God's will seems prohibitive. Is it worth it?

The price-point for this question differs for every soul. How much am I willing to part with for this Jesus Christ? I might have the clarity and honesty to look at the gospel message and say, "It's too much; I'm not willing to pay that price," and then walk away. Although this decision ends in death ("if you forsake Him, He will reject you forever"(1 Chron 28:9)), there is at least an authentic individuality in it.

For those who don't walk away, there is the trap of trying to bargain down to a more "reasonable" price. In this effort, we try to *persuade* ourselves that Christ and the gospel are worth the personal cost. Sadly, many of us spend our entire lives in this place, neither walking away nor moving forward, but pointlessly attempting to barter for eternity.

Are you *fully persuaded?* If so, live as Abraham did, "strengthened in his faith and [giving glory] to God…"(Rom 4:20). Pay the price, your life "crucified with Christ"(Gal 2:20), or go your own way.

June 2

Praying to Your God

Jeremiah 42:3—Pray that the Lord your God will tell us where we should go and what we should do.

Too often prayer is viewed as a kind of conjuring of the genie in the lamp. We have already decided what it is that we want, where we should go or what we desire to do. We simply want some great power to help us actualize it.

The Jewish remnant left in the wake of the Babylonian destruction was guilty of this very thing. They approached the prophet Jeremiah and asked him to inquire of the Lord on their behalf—*pray that the Lord your God will tell us where we should go and what we should do.* But despite assurances to Jeremiah that they would "'act in accordance with everything the Lord your God sends you to tell us"(Jer 42:5), the Jews had already decided in their hearts what they were going to do. When God does eventually speak to them, it falls on deaf ears, for the people "'will not listen to the message...'"(Jer 44:16). They have taken their own "divine" wisdom.

When you pray, is your prayer more like that of the Jewish remnant? Is it a halfhearted utterance with a predetermined outcome? The Jews had already decided they were going to flee to Egypt before they inquired of Jeremiah. They simply wanted God to bless their decision. But God didn't. God said the exact opposite—stay!

Tellingly, the Jews also asked Jeremiah to pray to *his* God and not *their* God. Imagine if they had approached Jeremiah and asked him to pray to the Lord *our* God. How do you think they would have responded then to God's answer? Would they have persisted in fleeing to Egypt?

If you have it all figured out in your life, don't bother praying. Why seek wisdom from the Lord when you have already made a god of your own? And if the Lord is not *your* God, but someone else's, your pastor's or grandmother's, but not yours, then pray for Christ to save you, claim you, and call you His own.

God longs to communicate with you in prayer, to hear your heart and to give you the opportunity and privilege of listening to Him. Remember, "to pray is not to listen to oneself speak, but is to come to keep silent, and to continue keeping silent, to wait, until the person who prays hears God."[116] Pray that your heart will listen to all that *your* God has to say to you so that your life may become *more of Him and less of You.*

---

[116] Soren Kierkegaard, *The Lily of the Field and the Bird of the Air* (Princeton: Princeton University Press, 2016), 19-20.

Symphony of the Soul

1 Corinthians 13:1—If I speak in the tongues of men and angels, but have not love, I am only a resounding gong or a clanging cymbal.

> My soul is a hidden orchestra; I know not what instruments, what fiddle strings and harps, drums and tamboura I sound and clash inside myself. All I hear is the symphony.[117]
> —F. Pessoa

Is the music of your life, what you say and the things you do, a harmonious sound that is compelling to those who are listening? Or, is it a discordant noise that repels and causes others to turn away? When it comes to the sound of our lives, too little attention is paid to the tonal quality of the music we play from our souls. I might have the best of intentions for God and His Kingdom; I might be preaching His Word or serving His people. But if these efforts are not coupled with the love of Jesus, they are not only not helpful to the cause Christ, they are likely injurious to it.

While the Word of God does speak for itself, how I play it out in my life matters immensely to its impression on the hearts and minds of everyone who interacts with me. I must live His words. If I say all the right things, speaking in the very *tongues...of angels, but have not love, I am only a resounding gong or a clanging cymbal.* The content, the biblical score before me, is infallible, a perfect *symphony* waiting to be played out in my life. But just as the best of musicians must couple skill with a passionate love to produce a music that moves us, so I must also combine the love of the Spirit with what I do and say to make it resonate pleasingly to those who listen. Without this love, my life will only produce a cacophonous noise that will cause others to cover their ears and walk away.

The Spirit-filled soul is infused with the *symphony* of God's love. It causes those who hear it to literally weep with joy. It delights the "ears" of the heart.

How are you playing out the *symphony of your soul?* Is your life in tune with the Spirit's love? Does your heart possess a passion for the music, or are you just playing at playing? Does your playing reflect God's pathos? Be a lover of God's music and a musician who is passionate about God's *symphony of the soul.*

---

[117] Fernando Pessoa, *The Book of Disquiet* (New York: New Directions Books, 2017), 7.

Breaks in the Wall

Ezekiel 13:5—You have not gone up to the breaks in the wall to repair it…so that it will stand firm in the battle….

The wall to the ancient city served the same function as flesh to the human body. It surrounded city life, protected it from the elements and enemies alike, and allowed for the ingress and egress of vital commodities. But just as any cut exposes the body to possible infection, so breaks in the wall created holes for potential exploitation and destruction. A wall with holes does not serve its function. It is only a matter of time before it "is broken down, and its gates…burned with fire"(Neh 1:3).

Ezekiel chastises the false prophets of Israel for allowing this vulnerability in defense. But what was true of the physical wall of Jerusalem is just as true of the spiritual walls around our hearts and communities of faith. The fortifications of our spiritual defense must be kept ready for warfare.

To ensure this, it is first necessary to recognize the enemy's presence. If I do not feel the enemy surrounding me (Ps 22:16), I am not likely to feel compelled to work on my defenses. But, the question is not "if" there is an enemy or "if" they will attack. Rather, "When my enemies and foes attack"(Ps 27:2), will I be ready?

Readiness necessitates faithfulness in the work of wall maintenance. When was the last time that you set out in your quiet moments to examine "the wall…which had been broken down"(Neh 2:13) and honestly assess the vulnerabilities to your spiritual defenses? A circumferential walk around your wall may leave you, like Nehemiah, disgraced at the disrepair and motivated to "start rebuilding"(Neh 2:17-18).

As you work at this rebuilding, some days you will feel exhausted, saying, "'The strength of the laborers is giving out…'"(Neh 4:10). You may have enemies in your life, like Sanballat, who attempt to dishearten your efforts. But commit to persist, for "'The God of heaven will give… success'"(Neh 2:20). Know that God will frustrate the scheming of your enemies as you return "to the wall, each to his own work"(Neh 4:15). God will honor your faithful labor.

When you do God's work of wall repair in your spiritual life, your efforts also strengthen God's community of believers. Because you have been entrusted with one section of a wall surrounding God's people, the work you do in your own life affects the lives of others co-laboring with you in God's work. Convinced of this, pray that the Spirit helps you find the breaks in your wall and graces you to fix them today.

June 5

What to Say

Mark 13:11—...do not worry beforehand about what to say. Just say whatever is given you at the time, for it is not you speaking but the Holy Spirit.

How many opportunities for Christ have we missed or deliberately obstructed because of worry about what we might say? Whether in polite conversation on an airplane or public inquisition before governmental authorities, the tendency is to think: "What if I don't say the right thing? What if I sound foolish? What if I can't answer the question? What will they think of me?"

To these anxious thoughts and feeble excuses, Jesus says, "*do not worry beforehand about what to say. Just say whatever is given you at the time, for it is not you speaking but the Holy Spirit.*" Our Lord wants us to stop thinking so much about ourselves and start focusing on Him in the lives of others. We can choose to say alongside Moses, "O Lord, I have never been eloquent, neither in the past nor since you have spoken to your servant. I am slow of speech and tongue"(Ex 4:10). Or, we can choose to walk by faith, trusting that the Spirit who guides us into each circumstance and scenario will grace us with the right words to say.

In trusting the Spirit's provision, however, Jesus is not saying that we should be unprepared to answer our inquisitors. Rather, through scriptural study and constant prayer, we are called to "Always be prepared to give an answer to everyone who asks [us] to give the reason for the hope that [we] have"(1 Peter 3:15). And when we speak, we must decide not to be ashamed of what the Spirit inspires us to say, for, "If anyone is ashamed of me [Jesus] and my words, the Son of Man will be ashamed of him when He comes in His glory..."(Luke 9:26).

Do you find yourself living in shame of the Lord you claim to love and serve? Are you afraid of offending someone or finding yourself tongue-tied? When you choose to worry over how you will respond to your inquisitors, you prove that your focus is you, and not Christ. Your worry demonstrates your belief that God is not able to meet your need in the moment.

The next time you are being questioned in regards to the hope that you have in you, remember that God has orchestrated this conversation. Instead of worrying about what you may or may not say, trust that the Lord who allowed these questions to come into your life will provide you with the answers you need to glorify His name. Your duty is simply to avoid willfully obstructing the Spirit as you speak about the One you love. Your decision must be: *more of Him and less of me.*

Just As He Said

Acts 27:25—So keep up your courage, men, for I have faith in God that it will happen just as He told me.

To live in a fully predictable world is not to be a man.[118]
—C.S. Lewis

When was the last time you took a look at your own life or the life of another and honestly thought that it has all turned out exactly the way you said or hoped it would? Uncertainty and unpredictability is the reality of our lives. Things just don't always go the way we think or say they will.

The only exception to this rule was and is in the life of Jesus Christ. If I ever need reminding that I am NOT God, then all I have to do is look to the words and actions of Jesus to see the only One for whom it always happens, *"just as He said"*(Matt 28:6). When Peter is told to go to the lake and open the mouth of the first fish he catches to find the coin for the Temple tax, it happens—*just as Jesus said* (Matt 17:26-27). When the centurion says to Christ, "just say the word, and my servant will be healed," the commander finds it done—*just as Jesus said* (Matt 8:8). The colt that carried the Messiah into Bethany was found *"just as [Jesus] told them"*(Luke 19:32). Peter disowns Jesus before the rooster crows—*just as Jesus said* (Luke 22:61). Christ is betrayed by the chief priests, condemned to death, and raised to life on the third day—*just as He said* (Matt 20:17-19)!

Do you have the courage to see this "God of His word" as the *only* guarantor of every outcome in your life? Can you, like Paul and the crew tossed on the sea, say with faith, *"it will happen just as He told me"*(Acts 27:25)?

It will not do to say of Jesus, "He probably intended to say this," or "He must have meant that," or "There is probably a reasonable explanation behind that coincidence." We cannot take what we like, reject what we don't, and add or subtract where we see fit. Jesus said what He said and things happened exactly the way He said. Either Jesus Christ and the biblical account is a lie for which millions have lived and died over thousands of years, or Christ is who He says He is, and things have happened and will happen, *just as He said!*

Hope in the One who has already shown Himself true in everything He says. Christ is coming again, *just as He said.* To which truth will you be clinging when He arrives?

---

[118] C.S. Lewis, *The Business of Heaven* (New York: HarperCollins, 1984), 106.

Evidenced in Obedience

2 Corinthians 9:13—Because of the service by which you have proved yourselves, men will praise God for the obedience that accompanies your confession of the gospel....

> That thou are happy, owe to God.
> That thou continues such, owe to thyself,
> That is, to thy obedience. Therein stand.
> ...God made thee perfect, not immutable.
> And good He made thee, but to persevere
> He left it in thy power; ordained thy will
> By nature free, not over-ruled by fate
> ...Our voluntary service He requires,
> Not our necessitated.[119]
> —John Milton

Obedience is one of the most powerful spiritual tools. In addition to its primary purpose of demonstrating our love for God (John 14:15), it is also of vital importance in our evangelical work in the lives of others. When we obey, how we obey, and ultimately, the "who" we obey, has the potential to bring the glory of God into the hearts and minds of others.

Paul tells the Corinthians that because of their service, *men will praise God for the obedience that accompanies [the] confession of the gospel of Christ....* The Corinthians not only confessed the gospel—they lived it out in obedience. The gospel, without its transforming grace *evidenced in the obedience* of our lives, is powerless in the hearts and minds of others. I can preach the gospel until I am blue in the face, but if I do not couple it with my life's obedience, I risk becoming a worthless hypocrite. My obedience can cause others to stand amazed at what Christ is able to do in the life of a sinner, or mock the hypocrisy that is impotent to effect any true change.

Does the obedience of your life cause others to *praise God?* Have you decided to live out the gospel you have confessed? You must decide to obey—God will not do it for you. As Milton says, *"Our voluntary service He requires,/ Not our necessitated."* But when you choose to obey Jesus with your life, you not only demonstrate your love for Him—"Freely we serve,/ Because freely we love..."[120]—but you also bring Him glory in the hearts and minds of others. While God does not need your life to make His message known, He often chooses to use our lives to make His grace visible. The gospel is *evidenced in our obedience.* Let us commit to obey!

---

[119] John Milton, *Paradise Lost* (London: Arcturus, 2014),159.
[120] Ibid.

June 8

Life or Death?

Deuteronomy 30:19—Now choose life....

> For it is indeed true that the only true blessing consists in choosing
> rightly, but the power of choice is the glorious condition for that
> blessing.[121]
>
> —Soren Kierkegaard

When God created men and women, He set before them "life and death, blessings and curses"(Deut 30:19). He gave us freedom and the liberty to choose. The Lord could easily have created a Garden immune to temptation. He could have formed a robotic Adam and Eve, a you and me programmed to love and obey in a mechanical fashion. But He emphatically did not do this. He chose to let us choose. He gave us a choice of life or death, the power to pursue love, joy and peace, or the curses of hatred, envy, malice and the like.

The problem with this choice is that it doesn't often present itself so clearly. Through the craft of Satan, what constitutes "life" and "death" has been blurred, and, at times, inverted. In his subtly, Satan presents "life" as the fullness of the "garden" around us. It is the experience of every pleasure, taste and sensation we can get our hands on—even the ones explicitly forbidden by God. In this thinking, "life" is the here and now.

By contrast, Scripture tells us that when we choose the world, we choose "death." It is an election which places the desires of the self ahead of God. It dethrones the Lord from His rightful place in our hearts.

When we choose the Lord, however, we choose "life." God's Word says: "the Lord is [our] life," and He "has made known to me the path of life"(Deut 30:20; Ps 16:11). As we elect to "love the Lord...to listen to His voice, and hold fast to Him"(Deut 30:20), we escape the lies that lead to destruction. In this choice for Christ, it will no longer matter if the entire "garden" shrivels up and dies. If there is famine and persecution, loneliness or death, in Christ we have found the life that transcends it all.

A choice for God is an invincible one! It is a life choice grounded in the confidence that nothing "will be able to separate us from the love of God that is in Christ Jesus our Lord"(Rom 8:39)—not even death. What will you choose? The "garden," or the God who made it, and offers to give you it and so much more? By His grace, you are not a passive bystander or a cosmic victim in the spiritual battle between life and death. You have a choice! *Now choose life*!

---

[121] Soren Kierkegaard, *Spiritual Writings* (New York: HarperPerennial, 2010), 141.

June 9

Peace of Christ

Colossians 3:15—Let the peace of Christ rule in your hearts....

A primary reason so many people suffer the loss of peace in their lives is a refusal to let the *peace of Christ* rule in the kingdom of "self." Each of us has been given a choice: rule or be ruled. Those who choose self-governance, do so at a cost—a forfeiture of God's peace. While they may have total autonomy to make decisions in the way they desire, the weight of all those decisions will prohibit them from knowing the peace of the Spirit. To rule an earthly kingdom, much less the kingdom of the soul, is a job full of trouble. It faces invading armies of "thieves and robbers"(John 10:8), backstabbing politicians, financial crises, plagues that kill indiscriminately, and famines that cause people to go hungry. To be a ruler is to be hounded by never-ending problems that need resolution. Problems steal peace.

But the Apostle Paul exhorts us to something greater. He tells us the way out of this bondage of self-governance is by allowing the *peace of Christ* to rule in our hearts instead. Jesus is the "Prince of Peace"(Is 9:6) and the only ruler of the heart who can reign over our inner kingdoms with a peace that "transcends all understanding"(Phil 4:7). The only catch, however, is that Christ will not share His throne. If we desire the peace of Christ in our hearts, then we must abdicate the throne. We must let Jesus in and give Him authority.

When we surrender to Christ in this way and recognize that He is the "Son of the living God"(Matt 16:16), we allow His power, love, mercy, wisdom and grace to reign over our hearts and minds. We will know peace because He is in control, and we are not. His peace will begin flowing from the throne like a mighty river (Is 66:12) to reach the hinterlands of our souls. And what life this river brings! What greening of the hills. What ripening of the fruits of the Spirit—"God is ripening."[122] We will not recognize the barren land we once called our soul.

Do you desire a life beset with worry, anxiety, and endless uncertainty (of course not!)? Then hold on to the keys of your kingdom. Maintain your throne. Try your best to be in control of it all! But if you want peace that passes understanding, then let Jesus in. Give Him your keys and abdicate your throne. When you do, you will know the sudden and overwhelming peace of knowing that no matter what comes He is in control. Come what may, the *peace of Christ* will reign. He will carry you through to His Kingdom's best!

---

[122] Rainer Rilke, *Book of Hours: Love Poems to God* (New York: Riverhead Books, 2005), 75.

175

June 10

No Importa[123]

Galatians 2:6—As for those who seemed to be important—whatever they were makes no difference to me; God does not judge by external appearance....

The thirst for power and the desire for prestige have been two of the shaping hands of human history. Whether in the rise and fall of empires, the playground antics of children, or the workplace dynamics, the world of external appearances and its illusion of importance is never far from any of our lives. But what our world considers important matters little to God who *does not judge by external appearance.*

Has this world of external appearances placed you in a position of leadership and authority? If so, be careful to remember that the only importance your position has to God is how He can use it for His glory. Your "power" has nothing to do with you and everything to do with God's demonstration of who He is. This may come through building you up and sustaining you or tearing you down. Either way, His name will be glorified!

To this end, God does not place differing value on the life of anyone, rich or poor, black or white, uneducated or highly degreed—*no importa!* As C.S. Lewis reminds us, "God is no accepter of persons; His love for us is not measured by social rank or our intellectual talents."[124] Neither should such things matter to us. While the culture preaches *external appearances,* we must value the internal landscapes of the soul.

To emphasize how little *external appearances* matter, Jesus says, "So the last will be first, and the first will be last"(Matt 20:16). God reiterates this point to the prophet Samuel when he goes to anoint the future king over Israel. Seeing Eliab, David's promising older brother, Samuel thinks he has found the man. But the Lord says, "Do not look at his appearance or at his physical stature, because I have refused him. For the Lord does not see as man sees; for man looks at the outward appearance, but the Lord looks at the heart"(1 Sam 16:7).

When it comes to power and prestige, how do you see the world? Are you looking at the *external appearances* or are you looking, as God does, at the interior landscape of the heart and soul? In the end, nothing matters to God but what is going on in the core of who we are. Remember, that in eyes of the Lord, the proud are nothing more than "a mist that appears for a little while and then vanishes"(Jam 4:14). But, "The righteous will inherit the land and dwell in it forever"(Ps 37:29).

---

123 (Spanish) does not matter
124 C.S. Lewis, *The Weight of Glory* (New York: HarperCollins, 2001), 167.

June 11

The Sufficiency of Grace

2 Corinthians 12:9—My grace is sufficient for you….

Perhaps there is a hurt in your heart that hangs on. Though it was perpetrated years ago, it still clings to you. Or, maybe you choose to cling to it? Either way, it gnaws at your soul and you are not at peace. Some part of you desperately desires a sincere apology or justice in the life of another before you sense you can close the door on it all. Your heart feels it has received no consolation.

Humanly speaking, nothing could be more understandable. Because we were made in the image of God and "just is He"(Deut 32:4), we seem to be wired for justice. Yet the absence of an apology or a guilty sentence does not mean that God is not just. Who am I to question the ways of the Lord? Do I not remember that God "will pay back trouble to those who trouble you and give relief to you who are troubled….when the Lord Jesus is revealed from heaven in blazing fire with His powerful angels"(2 Thes 1:6-7)? If I cling to the notion that I deserve an apology, that the one who hurt me must ask for my forgiveness, I grieve God. I prove that I do not understand His grace and love at all. My heart says to God, "Your grace is *not* enough for me. I want something more."

Such thinking arises from a wounded pride. It is from the devil and it must be rebuked at every turn in our lives. So long as we grip tightly to the need for personal vindication, the sufficiency of Christ is not ours. We are called to give and expect nothing in return, to love those who do not love us in kind, and to forgive those who trespass against us, without expecting reciprocity (Luke 6:34; Matt 5:44).

To know that the grace of Christ is sufficient in my life is to leave everything at the altar—my pain, my fear, my need for vindication and justification, and any last bit of revenge I might be harboring. Instead of expecting an apology, my focus ought to be on the loving embrace of my Father. Rather than looking for the verdict that brings justice in the life of another, I should be focusing on the hope of heaven.

If you are still finding yourself plagued by the hurts of the past, question your understanding of the sufficiency of God's grace in your life. While you look for a paltry apology from another sinner, you miss the abundant love your Father is waiting to shower down upon you. He knows your pain. And His *grace is sufficient for you.*

An Accurate Sense of Self

Judges 6:14—Go in the strength you have….

When it comes to self-estimation, overestimating is just as deleterious as "under." An elevated sense of self can lead us headlong into a place we should not go at a time when we are not prepared to be there. Conversely, an unhealthy humility may leave us standing in concrete shoes, unable to go out and fight the battles God intends us to engage in.

God approached Gideon with this very call to arms. The Lord said to Gideon, "Go in the strength you have…." At first, Gideon hesitates: "How can I save Israel? My clan is the weakest in Manasseh, and I am the last in my family"(Judg 6:15). Gideon's error is to interpret God's command in light of his personal abilities and resources. Instead of listening to the voice that said, "I will be with you"(Judg 6:16), Gideon considers God's command in light of his limited human strength. He forgets who God is.

Have you found yourself guilty of a similar error in your perspective or vision of self? Has the Lord asked you, like Gideon, to do something that you cannot fathom doing in the strength you have? Perhaps it is not a specific request, but simply the injunction to live a life of faith. Even this sometimes seems like an impossible battle. So long as you interpret God's commands in light of your own abilities, you will likely not see the point in pressing forward.

But when God commands you to *go in the strength you have*, He does so with the absolute understanding that *He* is your strength. He doesn't need any of your abilities to do His work. He could accomplish His purposes with a pile of dry bones if He wanted to (Ezek 37). Instead, God wants you to realize, as David did, that "The Lord is my strength and my shield"(Ps 28:7). The Lord wants you to demonstrate enough faith to obey, irrespective of perceived or actual human strengths and weaknesses. He wants you to take the first step in the direction He is calling you in.

When we evaluate God's commands in light of our own abilities or lack thereof, we confuse ourselves unnecessarily and become a roadblock to God's intentions. He never intends us to consider His commands apart from His helping hand. Rather, when it comes to our spiritual lives, all that is being demanded of us is "a general and preliminary resolution…to do [our] best—or rather, to go on doing [our] best,"[125] and let God, working through us, do the rest. Instead of focusing on who we are, let us focus on who God is! Let our thinking be *more of Him and less of me.*

---

[125] C.S. Lewis, *Perelandra* in *The Space Trilogy* (London: HarperCollins, 2013), 270.

Honoring Honor

John 12:26—My Father will honor the one who serves me.

Some of the greatest scriptural promises are the very ones we tend to so easily misconstrue. We sometimes misapply them to the point of spiritual disillusionment and even apostasy. But just because we do not see the promises unfold as we imagined, does not mean they are untrue. Rather, like an awkward child playing at adulthood, we have attempted to see these promises through a pair of adult lenses. The images appear blurred and the distances altered because our eyes don't fit the prescription. The same holds true for biblical truths: It is not the fault of the promises, but the lenses through which we have chosen to view these promises.

This perspective is particularly true when it comes to *honoring honor* in our spiritual lives. When Jesus says, "My Father will honor the one who serves me," this is not some empty promise. He is reiterating what His Father spoke to Eli hundreds of years before—"Those who honor me I will honor…"(1 Sam 2:30). Later, to His servant David, God says, "I will deliver him and honor him"(Ps 91:15). The promise is clear—God *will* honor those who serve and honor Him. How that promise is fulfilled, however, is sometimes complex.

The ripening believer is prone to enthusiastically embrace the promise of God's honoring those who honor Him. But this believer sees it in his own way. A dangerous entitlement thinking can follow. Like the older brother of the prodigal son, the young believer may only see as far as his faithful service and loyalty to the Father (Luke 15:11-32). When his life doesn't appear to be honored in the way he believes he deserves or within the time frame he expects, the result can be bitterness, resentment, and disillusionment. His entitlement thinking blinds him to his Father's unconditional love. He doesn't recognize that God knows what is best for him and when to give it. He doesn't understand that the Father's richness has always been His son's as well.

Are you feeling frustrated by scriptural promises you perceive to be unfulfilled in your life? Have you allowed your entitlement thinking to graft them into your preconceived expectations? Remember that God *will* honor the faithful! But He will do it in His own way and in His perfect time (Ecc 3:11). The better we know our Father, the more readily we understand that though we deserve nothing, He has given us everything (2 Pet 1:3). Though life may not unfold the way we envision it, His promises are still true. He is working them out in unseen ways that will honor us and glorify Him. Pray for the grace to smile as God unfolds His glorious plan for your life.

June 14

The Sin That Finds You Out

Numbers 32:23—...and you may be sure that your sin will find you out.

Once we have committed before the Lord to do something He calls us to, we must be careful to carry it through to completion. Failure to do so is not some meaningless omission to an unseen God. Rather, it is a sin against a holy, omnipotent Lord. And that sin, we can be sure, will catch up with us—*it will find us out.*

Moses gave this warning to the Israelite clans of Reuben and Gad. Having navigated the wilderness for forty years, these clans desired to settle in the lands east of the Jordan River. But aware of God's plan for the remaining tribes of Israel, they promised to cross over the river with their brothers to conquer the Promised Land before returning to their families. Moses warns that any failure to do this "will be sinning against the Lord"(Num 32:23). It would be sin, not because their spears were necessarily needed to drive out the Canaanites, but because the clansmen made an oath before the Lord to do this specific thing. And Jehovah is the God of promises kept.

Reiterating this, Jesus says, "you have heard that it was said to the people long ago, 'Do not break your oath, but keep the oaths you have made to the Lord'"(Matt 5:33). Christ knows how seriously God takes oaths and the consequences of breaking them, so He goes on to say, "Do not swear at all....Simply let your 'Yes' be 'Yes' and your 'No' be 'No'..."(Matt 5:34, 37). It is better, Christ says, to make no oath at all than to make an oath and break it before the Lord.

Promises made before God must be promises kept. Just as God is a holy God and cannot permit unholiness in His presence, so God is a promise keeper and cannot allow broken oaths. If you are finding yourself wanting to make an oath before the Lord out of some spirit of enthusiasm or desperate need, take pause. Do you really know what you are asking of yourself? The costs of obedience to your oath may be higher than you ever anticipated. Don't be a Jephthah who loses his only daughter in an impulsive oath to God (Judg 11:34-37). But at the same time, do not willfully neglect your oath or it will lead to greater consequences still. This is a sin against God—a sin that *will find you out.*

In humility, let your "Yes" be a simple "Yes" to seek the Lord with all your heart, and all your soul, and all your mind, and let the specifics fall where the Lord desires.

June 15

Edifying

Romans 14:19—Let us therefore make every effort to do what leads to peace and to mutual edification.

When the Psalmist says, "May the words of my mouth and the mediations of my heart be pleasing in your sight, O Lord, my rock and redeemer"(Ps 19:14), we can be sure that what pleases the Lord is all that *leads to peace and to mutual edification.* Sadly, much of what we think and say is neither edifying to God and His purposes nor to the hearts and souls of all those we interact with in our daily lives.

If we were brave enough to keep a meticulous record of all that we think and say in just one day of our lives, we would likely stand aghast at how little has, as its intent, the building of God's Kingdom or the spiritual improvement of the heart. Though the Lord's people are "God's building"(1 Cor 3:9), are we dedicated to the building up of their lives? Where we might be sowing the seeds of peace and love in the life of another, too often we are littering the ground around us with malcontent and spiritually injurious comments. As disciples, however, we are called to love. For, "Love is the ground; love is the building; love builds up. To build up is to build up love, and it is love which builds up."[126]

Will you resolve to speak in love only those words which build for God's Kingdom purposes in the lives of others? Will you determine to be a person who makes *every effort* to demonstrate the peace and love of Christ in your interactions with others? The next time you find yourself in conversation and feel tempted to speak negatively towards something or someone, pause. Ask yourself, "Is this edifying?" Will this comment serve to help build them up? Will it demonstrate Christ's love and further the constructive efforts of His Kingdom? If not, then alter your comments, or say nothing at all.

Remember that your "tongue also is a fire, a world of evil among the parts of the body"(James 3:6). It has the power to build up and, sadly, the incredible power to destroy. As disciples of Christ, we must determine to make *every effort* to do and say only those things which lead to *peace and to mutual edification.* Though "no man can tame the tongue"(James 3:8), the disciple of Christ can, and must, make *every effort* to do so.

Let us pray today for the Spirit's grace to be builders and not destroyers in the lives of others. Let us choose to *edify.*

---

[126] Soren Kierkegaard, *Works of Love* (New York: HarperPerennial, 2009), 205.

June 16

The Redeemed Stumbler

James 3:2—We all stumble in many ways.

All great Christians have been wounded souls.[127]
—A.W. Tozer

Stumbling is part of walking. If you never spiritually stumble you are either going nowhere or you are a "perfect man"(James 3:2), both of which are incompatible with living. Scripture tells us we are all "under sin"—"There is no one righteous, not even one…"(Rom 3:9-10). As a consequence, we, like the Israelites, "stumble in [our] iniquity"(Hosea 5:5). Sometimes we stumble more than we should because we have forgotten God (Jer 18:15). But, even the faithful take a false step sooner or later.

For this reason, the disciple recognizes that he is always one step away from falling (1 Tim 1:15). He knows there is no sin he himself is not either guilty of or capable of committing. He is a *stumbler* saved by grace. He is a wounded person who has deeply wounded others and, at times, even been a stumbling block before God's purposes in the lives of others.

But for this imperfect disciple, there is hope. Both the wounded and those who wound alike can be healed by the wounds of Christ (Is 53:5). Redeemed sinners walk forward in confidence knowing that God will keep them from falling, even when they stumble (Ps 37:4). Consider some of the Bible's stumblers: David was an adulterer who was redeemed to the role of God's dynastic king (2 Sam 11). Jacob was a liar who founded Israel (Gen 32:28). Peter was a traitor who started the Church (Luke 22:54-62).

Like these *redeemed stumblers,* we too are capable of becoming "wounded healers"[128] in the lives of others. Because Christ healed us, He can now use us to help heal others. Therefore, like Jesus, we are called to make our "wounds into a major source of healing power."[129]

As Christ works through us in this way, remember: we have stumbled and we will stumble again. Life is about walking despite stumbling and determining to misstep less with time. When we do stumble, however, we fall into the arms of Jesus. In His loving arms we find a Savior who redeems our false steps for His glory. The way of the cross is that of the *redeemed stumbler* who knows the grace of God and decides to stumble onward in the love of Jesus.

---

[127] A.W. Tozer, *Man, The Dwelling Place of God* (Pubic Domain), 156.
[128] Henri Nouwen, *The Wounded Healer* (New York: Image Doubleday, 2010), 88.
[129] Ibid, 88-89.

The Banquet of God

John 4:34—"My food," said Jesus, "is to do the will of Him who sent me and to finish His work."

What is the food that you feed your soul? Perhaps we think we can avoid this question by playing the contemporary jester who says, "There is no such thing as the soul or eternity." Therefore, there is no need to do anything other than feed my physical body and its appetites. But this position makes a liar out of Jesus and a deluded clod out of every man and woman since the dawn of creation who has lived and died for God.

Conversely, Jesus illustrates the importance of feeding our souls by saying, *"My food…is the do the will of Him who sent me and to finish His work."* We can look at the life of Christ and just see a man who never married, never fathered children, ate many of his meals at the tables of others, and ended His life covered in the spit of Roman soldiers as He hung on a cross alongside criminals. If this is all we see, then we might be tempted to see an unfulfilled, unsatisfied man, hungry for something more. But nothing could be further from the truth.

The world has never known, and never will, a life more completely contented than that of Jesus Christ. His hunger was satisfied by doing the will of His Father and carrying out the Kingdom work. In Jesus, we see that nothing satiates the hunger of the soul and empowers it for faithful living more than doing the will of God. We can spend our entire lives ingesting one thing after the next, one experience on top of another, but always end up hungering for more, till we decide to make our soul's sustenance God and God alone.

Are you still running from one "spiritual" meal to the next? Jesus said, "He who comes to me will never go hungry…"(John 6:35). You have been invited to the *banquet of God*, to "feast on the abundance of [His] house…[and] drink from…[the] river of delights"(Ps 36:8). Will you come and eat?

Pray for the strength to stop running after the whims of your spiritual appetites and choose instead to come to Christ and enjoy the banquet of doing God's will.

June 18

The Silence of Submission

Genesis 24:50—Laban and Bethuel answered, "This is from the Lord; we can say nothing to you one way or the other."

When Abraham's servant stands before Laban and tells of his providential mission to find Isaac a wife from among Sarah's people, Laban is left speechless—*this is from the Lord; we can say nothing....* The hand of God was evident to Laban in the very details of the story. He did not question or refute. He acquiesced and he obeyed.

The ability to be silent before the providential will of God marks the seasoned believer. Our silence "expresses respect for God, for the fact that it is He who rules and He alone to whom wisdom and understanding belong."[130] But it takes practice and discipline to achieve this. In our early years of faith, the challenge is to see God in the details of our everyday lives. Our eyes must be opened and our senses alerted. We cannot hope to yield to the will of God in our lives if we fail to see His providential hand manifest in the details of the day.

When our senses have become attuned to the movings of the Spirit, the ensuing challenge is to give thanks and then obey. It is not wrong to say, "Who am I that I should go...?" or "What if they do not believe me...?"(Ex 3:11, 4:1) as Moses did. Asking such questions only reveals that God still has much work to do in our hearts' understanding of who He is and how He works out His providential will in the world. Ultimately, instead of questioning, our aim is to respond to God's voice with a humble acquiescence and a pleased obedience—*this is from the Lord.*

Do you find yourself still resisting or refuting the messengers God brings into your life? Or are you silently surveying for the presence or absence of God's will in the message itself? The longer you walk with the Spirit, the less you will question and the more you will quietly step forward in confidence, knowing that the God of every detail is directing your way. You will begin to see His fingerprint in the every day: His smile or His gentle rebuke in your every choice and His overarching love covering every corner of your life. Like Laban, you will not fear the unknown traveler who comes from Canaan to ask of you a great thing. When you see God in his journey, you will know how to respond.

Ask the Spirit to continue to instruct you in how you can increasingly become the disciple who needs to "say nothing" because you so clearly see the hand of God in each and every thing.

---

[130] Soren Kierkegaard, *The Lilly of the Field and the Bird of the Air* (Princeton: Princeton University Press, 2016), 29.

Grace and Grit

2 Corinthians 5:10—For we must all appear before the judgement seat of Christ, that each one may receive what is due to him for the things done while in the body, whether good or bad.

The interplay between *grace* and *good works* is an ongoing one in the heart of the disciple. No sooner has Paul reminded us that "it is by *grace* you have been saved, through faith—and this not from yourselves, it is a gift of God—not by works," then he emphatically declares that we were "created in Christ to do *good works...*"(Eph 2:8-10). By these works we will *receive what is due...for the things done while in the body, whether good or bad.*

If it is simply *grace* and not *works*, then why does the way I live matter at all? "Shall we go on sinning so that *grace* may increase? By no means!"(Rom 6:1). Conversely, should we trust in our *good works* to achieve our salvation? By no means!

The often misconstrued subtlety in the relationship between *grace* and *good works* is this: salvation is by *grace* alone, not by *works*. But *good works* —how I live out my resurrected life and the *spiritual grit* with which I do it —demonstrate the genuineness of my salvation. *Good works* have at least three vital purposes in the life of the disciple: they demonstrate our love of Christ; they represent Christ's person, work and glory to others; and they build Kingdom capital for the *judgement seat of Christ.*

First, do you love Jesus? Jesus said, "If you love me, keep my commandments"(John 14:15). It is nonsense to say I love Jesus and then keep on living the way I want to live. My obedience demonstrates to Jesus and others that I love Christ. My *good works* embody my love for Him.

Second, how I live and what I do, reflects on the person and attributes of the Lord I say I love and serve. I am God's representative to the world around me. We are "Christ's ambassadors, as though God were making His appeal through us"(2 Cor 5:20). To go on willfully sinning, living a life of spiritual rebellion, is to make a mockery of the very God I claim to love and serve. "Do not be deceived: God cannot be mocked. A man reaps what he sows"(Gal 6:7).

Finally, my *works* matter as they will be revealed before the *judgement seat of Christ.* What I have done will determine what I receive in the Kingdom. How I live today decides what I lay up for eternity (Matt 6:20).

While we must not forget that salvation is by *grace* alone, we must never assume that *grace* will do our part in demonstrating the genuineness of our resurrected lives. *Grace* must be followed by *works* worked out in grit, and His amazing, ongoing *grace*!

June 20

Wait, Wait, Wait...Go

Acts 22:16—And now what are you waiting for? Get up....

Much of the life of the disciple is spent learning when and how to wait and then when to get up and go. We are told to "wait for your God always"(Hosea 12:6). We are instructed to be like the virgin, prepared and ready for the bridegroom, no matter when He comes (Matt 25:1-13). But waiting in a constant state of expectation and anticipation is no easy thing! To this end the Psalmist exhorts us, "Wait on the Lord; Be strong and take heart..."(Ps 27:14).

Have you struggled to find the strength to wait on the Lord? Have you grown impatient, waiting for God to answer your prayer and move in your life in some particular way? David had to wait to see God deliver him from the hands of Saul. But in this time, David learned to, "Be still before the Lord and wait patiently for Him..."(Ps 37:7). In another instance, we are instructed to, "Be patient....See how the farmer waits for the land to yield its valuable crop and how patient he is for the autumn and spring rains. You too, be patient and stand firm..."(James 5:7-8).

But in our waiting upon God, it would be incorrect to interpret our patient stillness as a passive, spiritually torpid time. God's desire for my waiting on Him couldn't be more different! As the farmer waits for the crop to yield, he is all the time tending to it, nurturing its growth. He prunes it here and there, fertilizes it, and constantly watches over it. Likewise, when the Psalmist says we are to be "still before the Lord," this does not imply a state of spiritual paralysis. It would be more accurate to see our spiritual stillness in this time as akin to a mime impersonating a statue—every muscle of his body is tensed, engaged, and focused as he maintains his stillness. Waiting, here, is not passive; it is quite "active."

This is the very stillness required of the person who waits upon the Lord. The disciple is spiritually conditioning himself in each waiting moment. He does not allow himself the deluded luxury of growing spiritually lazy and dependent, thinking, "Waiting means I don't have to do anything until God shows up and says it's time to go." To live life in this manner is to be one of the virgins who was unprepared for the arrival of the bridegroom.

When God shows up and says, *"What are you waiting for? Get up...,"* will you be ready to spring into action with the vigor of the spiritually fit? Let your waiting on God be filled with the patience and stillness that chooses to be fully engaged.

June 21

Eyes on You

2 Chronicles 20:12—We do not know what to do, but our eyes are upon you.

Where do you turn when you don't know what to do? In the midst of our confusion and bewilderment, do we try to reason it out ourselves or seek the counsel of others at the expense of looking primarily to the Lord? When distress comes, is our primary response to keep our eyes fixed upon God, or do we look everywhere else first?

King Jehoshaphat was faced with this very dilemma when the vast army of Sennacherib attacked him. He did not know what to do, how to lead his people or defend the holy city of Jerusalem. He was, in short, "Alarmed"(2 Chron 20:3)! But in this distress, he "resolved to inquire of the Lord…"(2 Chron 20:3). And because the king and his people chose to fix their eyes upon Jehovah, the Lord showed them exactly what to do. He showed them His victory.

When you find yourself in a place where you do not know what to do, what you must do is keep your eyes fixed upon Jesus. I go astray when I allow the convolutions of my thinking and the multiplicity of others' opinions to distract my gaze upon Jesus. However, if I choose, in my moment of indecision and vulnerability, to seek God first, what I must do next will become clear. God will see to it—"seek first the Kingdom of God…and all these things will be given to you…"(Matt 6:33). As long as I look everywhere else first, I am likely to make one of two mistakes: Either, I will commit to an unwise and hasty decision in a moment of fear. Or, I may find myself spinning in the circles of indecision until I no longer have the equilibrium necessary to walk forward and do the next thing.

Is this decision to keep my eyes fixed on the Lord in my moments of vulnerability an easy one? No, and in fact, often, it is very difficult; it may, frankly, seem impractical. Isn't the problem here and now? Greater still is the challenge to keep my eyes upon the Lord when I think I *do* know what to do. When things are going well, will I choose to keep my eyes upon the Lord then?

In indecision and in apparent clarity, in hard times and in good times, in weakness and strength, the disciple of Christ is the man or woman who resolves to look upon the Lord. Determine that circumstances will not dictate the focus of your soul.

June 22

The Work of the Lord

1 Corinthians 16:10—...he is carrying on the work of the Lord....

Beware of letting a day slip by without asking yourself, "Am I carrying out the *work of the Lord?*" All too easily, our lives ease into the routines and demands of the work of the self rather than *the work of the Lord*. But what is the work of God? After feeding the 5,000, Jesus is asked this very question. He responds: "The work of God is this: to believe in the One He has sent"(John 6:29). Seems simple enough. But the reality is, many people spend their entire lives saying they believe in Jesus and then dedicating each day to a doctrine of good works and clean living, thoroughly convinced that *this* is the work of the Lord.

To be clear, the disciple of Jesus will live a life of spiritual fruitfulness and faithfulness. But, at the same time, the disciple under-stands that salvation lies in Christ alone, irrespective of works—"It is by grace that you have been saved through faith... not by works, so that no one can boast"(Eph 2:8-9). To do the *work of the Lord* is to live each day with the absolute conviction that the work of Jesus is sufficient, in and of itself, for the absolution of all our sins. And then, in this conviction, to go forth and share this gospel with the world—"make disciples of all the nations..."(Matt 28:19).

Just because I am not a pastor or missionary, a spiritual giant or a biblical scholar, does not mean that I cannot do the work of believing in the One God has sent and sharing that belief with others. Children can believe and enter the Kingdom (Matt 18:3) and I do not need a pulpit or an exotic corner of the earth harboring an unreached people to share what Christ has done. Right outside my door the fields are ready for harvest.

Are you doing the *work of the Lord* by believing in Christ and what He has done for you without the addition or subtraction of good works or holy living? God is not asking you to do something outside your capa-bilities. He is simply asking you to accept His terms—Christ and Christ alone. Will you do it? And if so, will you choose to tell about it? Will you decide to be a missionary in the mundane? Will you preach Christ in the everyday soil where He has planted you?

Believe and you will do the *work of the Lord*.

June 23

First Love

Revelation 2:4—Yet I hold this against you: You have forsaken your first love.

What is the surest evidence that you are obeying the Lord's command to "Love the Lord your God with all your heart and with all your soul and with all your mind"(Matt 22:37)? It is the absolute horror it would be to hear the words Christ speaks to the Church of Ephesus directed toward you and your life—*I hold this against you: You have forsaken your first love.* To forsake, we must abandon, desert, turn our backs and leave something behind. When we are in love with Jesus, the thought of this rejection should bring us to horrific tears. If it does not, then we must examine our hearts, for "it is because of the increase of wickedness, [that] the love of most will grow cold…"(Matt 24:12).

The reality is, that for most deserters, this process of forsaking is not a single definitive action. Rather, there is a gradual growing cold, a subtle recanting and stepwise retreat. Like the Church of Ephesus, it is quite possible to be capable of good "deeds…hard work and… perseverance…."(Rev 2:2)—even enduring hardships in the name of God (Rev 2:3)—and yet, to be guilty of forsaking our first love.

Because the act of forsaking is so often insidious, it requires constant self-examination to prevent it from rooting itself in our lives. I must ask myself, "Do I love the Lord my God with *all* my heart and soul and mind?" If the answer is anything but "Yes," then I must do what Christ commands— 'Repent and do the things you did at first"(Rev 2:5)— seek after Him with everything I am.

When we notice the slightest inklings of forsaking in our lives, we must humbly seek the Lord's forgiveness for our subtle retreats, the dimness of our spiritual fires, and the lackluster love of our hearts. Having repented, we must return to our foremost spiritual priorities. We must practice the disciplines of faith that demonstrate our love—obedience, worship, prayer, the reading of His Word, meeting with other believers, and all other Spirit-inspired activities of faith.

Are you finding these things difficult? Is it persistently hard for you to articulate praise to the Lord? Is it difficult to spend time with Him in prayer, or impossible to imagine reading His Word on a daily basis? If so, question whether you have begun to forsake your first love.

When we love someone, nothing and no one can keep us from thinking about him or her and wanting to spend time together. Similarly, if Christ is our first love, nothing will be able to keep us from Him. No good thing on earth will suffice to draw us away or cause us to forsake Him. Let us repent and return to our first love anew each morning.

June 24

Kept by the Spirit

Acts 16:6—...having been kept by the Holy Spirit from preaching the Word in the province of Asia.

To our common sense thinking, nothing could seem more in keeping with the will of God than preaching the Word. And yet, Paul and his companions were *kept by the Holy Spirit from preaching the Word in the province of Asia.* Though they thought it best to extend the ministry to this area, God had different plans. When they came to the border of Mysia, God redirected them. The "Spirit of Jesus would not allow them" to preach the Word in Asia (Acts 16:7).

Have you ever begun with an intention that you firmly believed was in keeping with God's will, only to find it thwarted or redirected? Paul and his companions were doing the very work of God; but when their ideas for how and where that work should be done differed from the Lord's, the Lord stopped them. God led them in a completely new direction for His purposes and His greater glory.

When we are doing the work of the Kingdom, we will likely make plans and set goals. But we must be ready, at all times and in all things, to have those plans and goals redirected, re-envisioned, or downright thwarted. We must never forget that our work is only part of God's greater work and that His plans always have a reach well beyond any that we can ever imagine. Though we can choose to resist God's guidance and push on with our own agendas, we will do so to our own peril.

Paul and his companions did not go into Asia. They chose to obey the Spirit's leading, and God soon favored this obedience with a vision of His new plans. In a dream, Paul was told to go to Macedonia, to begin his westward evangelical push into Europe—"we got ready at once to leave for Macedonia, concluding that God had called us to preach the gospel to them"(Acts 16:10).

When we are *kept by the Spirit* from going in some predetermined direction, let us give thanks and rejoice in what is to come. God is likely opening up a whole new frontier for His work in our lives. May the Spirit give us the grace to always do God's work God's way and never persist in going our own direction when the Lord redirects.

June 25

The Sovereign

Daniel 4:37—...everything He does is right and all His ways are just.

The lamentable truth in so many of our lives is that it often requires our complete ruination before we admit that everything God *does is right and all His ways are just.* King Nebuchadnezzar was a perfect example of this reality. He literally had the world at his fingertips. All he had to do was acknowledge that God was sovereign. Nebuchadnezzar might have kept his kingdom and saved himself from destruction. And yet, like so many of us, he attributed his position and power to himself—"Is not this the great Babylon I have built...?"(Dan 4:30).

In response to this hubris, God decided that more glory would come to His name through the chastisement of Nebuchadnezzar than through continued blessing to him. So the king was driven into the wild, stripped of his humanity and divested of his riches and glory, all that the name of God might be glorified. It was only after this complete dethroning that the Babylonian king was able to say, "the King of heaven...is right and all His ways are just"(4:37).

When it comes to this reluctance to concede power to God in our lives, are we really any different than Nebuchadnezzar? Not until our "royal authority has been taken from [us] "(Dan 4:31), or we decide to voluntarily give it up at the foot of the cross, will we escape living on the edge of ruination. We have, like the king, been given countless warnings. And though the kingdom of our hearts might not fall tomorrow, it will come—a year later as it did for Nebuchadnezzar, or a lifetime hence.

Greater is the man or woman who recognizes, amidst the plentitude of God's goodness, that God *is right and all His ways are just,* than the one who requires a forceful dethroning or chastisement. Unfortunately, more often than not, we become lost in our fictitious worlds, subject to the illusions we will not let go of short of God's total takeover in our lives.

Are you, like Nebuchadnezzar, standing on the rooftop and praising what your life has accomplished? Be careful to remember in your place of blessing that your "throne" belongs to God. Never fail "in all your ways [to] acknowledge Him, and He will make straight your paths"(Prov 3:6). Rest in the wonderful reality that your life, the "kingdom" you have been given in stewardship, along with all its responsibilities and problems, are under the control of the Lord. Acknowledge Him as the sovereign power in your life and there will be no need to make you, like Nebuchadnezzar, a man among beasts.

June 26

Strengthen My Hands

Nehemiah 6:9—But I prayed, "Now strengthen my hands."

When we are engaged in the work of God, there will be moments when our hands will feel tired and weakened for the labor. If they do not, we are likely not doing God's work at all. Sometimes this enervation will come at the hands of the enemies who surround us. Satan knows well that one of the best ways to frustrate the progress of the Lord's work is to discourage His workers. In such times, it is crucial to recognize our fatigue, be it mental, physical and/or spiritual, and pray to the Lord—*now strengthen my hands!*

Nehemiah and the people of Israel were tirelessly working on the rebuilding of the wall of Jerusalem. The enemies of Israel were concerned about the progress the Jews were making and decided to make a concerted effort to discourage and frustrate that progress. So they invented lies. They tried to frighten the Israelites so that their hands and hearts would grow too weak to do the work. But, Nehemiah recognized both the nature of this assault and the Israelites' vulnerability. He didn't live in denial, give up in despair, or bluster ahead in his own self-confidence. Rather, in wisdom, he asked God for strength.

Are you feeling weary in your labors for the Kingdom? If so, ask God to *strengthen your hands*. The unfortunate reality is that all too often we either do not ask God for strength or we have to become utterly discouraged and exhausted before we consider seeking the Lord's strength. Whether this arises from a deep-seated pride or ignorance (perhaps a bit of both), this behavior creates a needless sense of breaking-point desperation.

Instead of backing ourselves into these corners, why not start each day requesting God's strength to complete our labors and to resist the enemies surrounding us? Why not begin each day by praying, *"Now strengthen my hands"*?

In and of themselves, the hands God has given you will never be able to complete the work they have been assigned. Rather than allowing yourself to reach a point of frustrated failure, ask God for strength. The more you admit your weakness and seek God's strength, the less traction your enemies will have on you and your conscience. Your confidence will grow in the assurance that your work is God's work and He will provide all the strength you need. Has God not reminded us: "my power is made perfect in weakness"(2 Cor 12:9)?

Let us begin each day praying, *"For your glory, by your grace, through your strength, O God—now strengthen my hands to do your work today."*

Pillar of Faith

2 Chronicles 24:15-16—Now Jehoiada was old and full of years, and he died at the age of a hundred and thirty. He was buried with the kings in the City of David, because of the good he had done in Israel for God and His Temple.

Has your life been blessed with a man or woman who has become for you a *pillar of faith* and righteousness? Perhaps you are that *pillar of faith* in the life of another. King Joash of Judah had such a man in the priest Jehoiada. He was a godly priest who was *buried with the kings...because of the good he had done in Israel for God....*

When Joash was just a boy, it was Jehoiada who rescued Joash from the murdering hands of his power-hungry grandmother. And it was Jehoiada who hid and protected Joash for years until he was ready to become king. Under the careful instruction and counsel of Jehoiada, Joash "did what was right in the eyes of the Lord all the years of Jehoiada the priest"(2 Chron 24:2).

But when Jehoiada died, King Joash's *pillar of faith* no longer remained to hold him up. Joash crumbled. What had been a blessing in his life became a stumbling block. Jehoiada was a man who "showed his strength"(2 Chron 23:1) in the Lord so well that King Joash never acquired the eyes to see God on his own because Jehoiada was always there to do it for him. Jehoiada's constant shepherding and counsel kept the young king on the straight and narrow. But when this presence was no longer there, Joash's spiritual life fell apart. He listened to the counsel of sycophantic men who ignored Jehoiada's God. In the end, Joash even went so far as to murder the son of the deceased priest.

If my life, like that of King Joash, has been blessed with a *pillar of faith*, I must determine that this person does not stand in the way of my knowing God for myself. I must be grateful for, but never dependent on, him or her. For when he or she disappears, I will need to be prepared and able to stand on my own two feet, finding the strength of God without an intermediary.

Similarly, if I am the parent or friend, family member or counselor who is fulfilling the role of Jehoiada in the life of someone else, I must ask God: Do I stand in the way? If I love that person, I must not permit my shepherding and counseling to block his or her access to the Lord.

In the end, we must each claim Christ as our own. Anything or anyone, however godly or righteous, that stands in the way, is a stumbling block that will make us fall. While we should be grateful for the earthly pillars in our lives, we must never rely on them. It must be God and God alone!

June 28

Those That Trail Behind

1 Timothy 5:24—The sins of some men are obvious....the sins of others trail behind them.

There are sins in our lives that present like forest fires—full of power and burning fury, leaving a swathe of destruction in their path that no one can miss. These sins are *obvious*: "sexual immorality, impurity and debauchery, idolatry and witchcraft; hatred, discord, jealousy, fits of rage, self-ambition, dissensions, factions and envy; drunkenness, orgies and the like"(Gal 5:19-21). But there are also the more subtle sins. They are the "secret sins"(Ps 90:8): the sins of the heart. They *trail behind* us and often hide in the shadows of our self-congratulatory personal opinions. We believe they are unseen. But they are the silent killers: the sins that grow in the darkness, but destroy us nonetheless.

Whether our sins blaze like a forest fire or grow quietly in the recesses of the heart and mind, God sees them all, for "Nothing in all creation is hidden from God's sight. Everything is uncovered and laid bare before the eyes of Him to whom we must give account"(Heb 4:13). He perceives our thoughts from afar and knows when we sit and rise (Ps 139:2). So, when we choose not to forgive or to cling to bitterness, we must remember that the Lord searches the heart and examines the mind (Jer 17:10).

No matter how far we drag the anchors of our silent iniquities in the depths beneath us, if Jesus doesn't release them, they still follow us. Irrespective of the fathoms we attempt to hide them in, God sees them. Isaiah says, "Woe to those who go to great depths to hide their plans from the Lord, who do their work in darkness and think, 'Who sees us? Who will know?'"(Is 29:15). The only hope for these *secret sins* is to recognize them as sin—no distance will separate them from us or absolve us from them. Our sins must be recognized, personally owned, and then placed on the altar of the Lord, where the blood of Jesus and His forgiveness can cut the anchors we have been dragging. Only Christ can set us free!

No matter how obvious or discrete your sins, whether they are with you now, or trail behind you, God sees them. He is not fooled. But never despair. There is hope in Christ for all those sins "common to man"(1 Cor 10:13). The blood of Jesus paid for it all. Come just as you are, each day, and every day, to find your forgiveness in the love of Christ.

The Burden of Leadership

Ezra 9:2—And the leaders and officials have led the way in this unfaithfulness.

Hardly anyone escapes the responsibility of leading. Whether in the home, the office, in the stadium or on the field of war, leadership falls onto our shoulders at some juncture. And when it does, a special burden comes to rest upon us—the weight of setting an example.

When God calls us to lead, He has an extremely high standard: the model is Jesus Christ. Our lives are meant to lead with the Spirit of our Lord within us. We are called to lead with *more of Him and less of us.*

As the priest of the Jews returning to Jerusalem after the Babylonian exile, Ezra understood this high bar of leadership. Therefore, when he recognizes the terrible failure of leadership in the upper ranks of Jewish society, he demonstrates a remorse that caused him to tear "tunic and cloak" and pull "hair from head and beard and [sit] down appalled"(Ezra 9:3). Although we might not grieve it in such a visible way now, the heartfelt contrition of Ezra is a prerequisite for godly leadership. Equally important is the humility which causes us to throw our failings at the foot of the cross to find the forgiveness and power we need to keep on leading for Christ and His purposes.

For who among us is perfect in his or her leadership? Who sets a flawless example for Christ and His Kingdom? As leaders, should we despair at our impossible jobs? Of course not! But it does mean that we should consider our leadership roles with a gravity of spirit that never forgets who it is we represent. It means that we faithfully commit our leadership responsibilities and all those placed beneath our care (whether family, work, or church) to the Lord's shepherding. As Jesus reminds us, "if anyone causes one of these little ones to sin, it would be better for him to have a large millstone hung around his neck and to be drowned in the depths of the sea"(Matt 18:6).

To keep from leading the way in unfaithfulness, we must study the Scripture, contemplate the will of Christ in all situations, and be in continual fellowship with the Spirit so that we can lead as Christ would lead. When we succeed, God is glorified. And when we fail, we must own our part in it, repent, and move forward in God's grace.

If God has placed you in a position of leadership, you are there for a reason—God's reason. How you lead and the degree to which that leadership is an exemplar of God's faithfulness, has eternal consequences. Never forget to commit your leadership to Christ. In His shepherding, with His Spirit in you, your leadership will accomplish His purposes.

June 30

The Place of the Heart

Isaiah 29:13—These people come near to me with their mouth and honor me with their lips, but their hearts are far from me.

The danger of spiritual routines is that the practice of them may allow the heart to get lost along the way. None of us can escape the reality that, at one point or another in our lives, we have said one thing and then done another. We have mouthed the words, but left our hearts out of it. Our spiritual lives are not immune from this. We might attend church and Bible study, stand in the pews singing hymns, even give out of our wallets, and yet, have hearts that are far from our Father.

The Israelites of Isaiah's time found themselves guilty of this very offense before God. They had forgotten that God does "not delight in sacrifice" alone, but rather in a "broken spirit, a broken and contrite heart..."(Ps 51:16-17). I might fool the entire world with my show of piety, but I will never fool God. He sees right to the core of my heart. Our Lord values the heart above all else, because He knows that my heart will be where my treasure is (Matt 6:21). God desires to be that treasure.

In the face of the penetrating vision of God, how do I ensure I remain "pure in heart"(Matt 5:8) and dedicated to Him? To begin, I must determine that I will "seek Him with all [my] heart"(Ps 119:10). The heart that seeks after God will find Him (Matt 7:7). It will be filled with the Spirit. But if I am not seeking, I will never draw near.

Second, I must determine to shelter His Word in my heart—"I have hidden your Word in my heart"(Ps 119:11). If my heart is filled with the Word of God, then out of my heart will flow the things of God. My lips will speak words of truth, because the Truth fills my heart. Jesus says, "The good man brings good things out of the good stored up in his heart..."(Luke 6:45).

Finally, with my heart I must determine to praise the Lord: "I will praise you with an upright heart"(Ps 119:7). There will be days when this praise comes easily, and others when it is a struggle. But, it is the commitment to offer it up to God, the *I Will*, that matters. The heart that pleases the Lord is the *broken spirit* and the *contrite heart* that seeks after Him with everything it has, and praises Him for all of who He is.

Are you seeking the Lord with all your heart? Have you determined to draw near to Him, or are you simply going through the motions? Since God wants your heart above all else, refuse to allow anything to come between your heart and the love of your Father.

JULY

Lukewarm

Revelation 3:16—So, because you are only lukewarm, neither hot nor cold—I am about to spit you out of my mouth.

The temperature of rejection is often just *lukewarm*. There are frigid nights in which a near scalding shower is a great comfort and sweltering days where a glass of cold water is a refreshing rejuvenation. But *lukewarm*, whether to the palate, body or the soul, rarely pleases. In our spiritual lives, *lukewarm* is especially repugnant to God. He spits it out.

Too much of the body of Christ has allowed itself to become like the Laodicean Church—an ineffectual *lukewarm*. The light of Jesus does not burn brightly enough in them to attract others. Neither does the evil of Satan appear dark enough to warn others away. These men and women attempt to live in the middle, in the no man's land of moral incertitude. They have no desire to live at a God-honoring temperature.

But because they are wise enough to recognize the deadliness of Satan's total darkness, they choose the middle ground of moral relativism. They relegate Jesus to a good moral teacher or a teddy bear god. They may show up at church and perhaps read Scripture periodically. They might even offer half-hearted prayers when the need arises. They often consider themselves "Christians."

But Jesus is not fooled. When He walked the earth, He spent much of His time among men and women who lived duplicitous lives: scheming disciples, cheating tax collectors and hypocritical Pharisees. He knows the unpalatable taste of the *lukewarm*, the sinners who think of themselves as "good." He would rather the nominal were either hot or cold, not a muddled in between. For not only are these *lukewarm* personally lost, but they become a confusion and danger to others. They are spiritual wanderers capable of leading others astray. Perhaps you have seen how they possess a sometimes contagious confusion. It is so dangerous because it is a "comfortable" that attracts. It costs almost nothing and promises the best of both worlds. For this reason, Jesus abhors the Laodicean spirit.

In the midst of our own *lukewarm* society, our imperative is to "choose for [ourselves] this day whom [we] will serve…"(Josh 24:15). We must decide to burn hot with the fire of the Holy Spirit or have the courage to reject Him and live in the darkness. But we must not deceive ourselves into thinking we can somehow adroitly walk a fine line in between.

Lukewarm is the temperature of choosing not to choose for or against Christ. But Jesus came to force this choice. Let us choose to burn brightly for Jesus!

July 2

God's Gold

Job 23:10—But He knows the way I take; when He has tested me, I will come forth as gold.

Does your life feel as if it is in the fire? Is the heat of your affliction changing the very substance of who you are? Though it may be painful, agonizingly so, make every effort to rejoice! Jesus is making you His own. No life that belongs to Christ escapes the process of refinement —"See I have refined you, though not as silver; I have tested you in the furnace of affliction"(Is 48:10). If we are not refined, we are not fit to be in His presence, much less to be used in His service.

In the midst of his fiery furnace, Job was empowered to see God's bigger picture for his life. Job came to understand that the only way to make gold out of his spiritual life was to refine it in the fires of affliction. There was no other way for Job and there is no other way for us. Because God loves us, "Love, in its own nature, demands the perfecting of the beloved."[131] So the dross that keeps us from God, the impurities that weigh us down, must be driven from us. As long as they remain, our intimacy with the Father will know a distance.

But when the fire burns off our impurities, we emerge a purified people. The Lord then says, "They will call on my name and I will answer them; I will say, 'They are my people,' and they will say, 'The Lord is our God'"(Zech 13:9). There can be no true intimacy with the Father without the "refiner's fire"(Mal 3:2) making us His own. It is the fires of affliction, whether in our temporal relationships or our relationship with the Lord, that either destroy us or ennoble us to another level of intimacy.

When the fire comes to your life, though the pain be excruciating, rejoice in the fact that God has counted you worthy of purification. He has chosen you for His purposes, to be an instrument of His glory—"For my sake, for my own sake, I do this"(Is 48:11). When He has delivered you through the fire in your glorified self, you will be of inestimable worth to Him and His Kingdom's work. You will know Him in a way you never thought possible.

Through the fires He will bring you forth as gold—*God's gold*!

---

[131] C.S. Lewis, *The Problem of Pain* (New York: HarperCollins, 2001), 38.

July 3

Finding Truth

John 18:38—"What is truth?" Pilate asked.

When it comes to our search for meaning and truth, the way home is often a long and tortuous one. While the object of our hearts' deepest longings and the answer to our most painful questions is standing directly before us, we insist on wandering through a lifetime of lies before we are capable of noticing the Truth that was there all along. Sometimes at great costs, we learn that "What we call basic truths are simply the ones we discover after all the others."[132] Nowhere is this reduction more profound than in the question of the one and only Truth—Jesus Christ.

Jesus said, "I am the way and the truth..."(John 14:6). In this cataclysmic statement, there is an exclusivity and singularity which changes the world. There is no room for multiples: not this truth for me, and that for you. And yet, many of us live our lives refusing to believe this. Indeed, the isolation of the "Truth" has become one of the contemporary world's primary roadblocks to relationship with God.

Maybe you find yourself asking, "How can it be that there is only one truth? What of the others—is there no value in them?" If so, you are much like the Athenians standing before the Apostle Paul. You may be "very religious," surrounded on all sides by "objects of worship" and a multiplicity of truths—even an "altar...TO AN UNKNOWN GOD"(Acts 17:23). But so long as you fail to see in this "unknown god" the singular Truth of Jesus Christ, you are merely wandering aimlessly on a hillside littered with stone idols.

Paul said to the Athenians, "Now what you worship as something unknown I am going to proclaim to you"(Acts 17:23). The Truth has been proclaimed! If we are still asking, "What is truth?" we are like Pilate standing in the presence of Christ and yet too blind to see the embodiment of our inquiry right before us.

Let us decide today that we will not spend one more day of our lives unearthing "stones" that are just stones. Jesus has come, and "The stone the builders rejected has become the capstone"(Ps 118:22)! May we claim this "capstone" as the one and only Truth. The sooner we realize that this Truth has "made known to [us] the path of life"(Ps 16:11), the sooner we will begin to enjoy the fellowship of the Spirit and the privilege of relationship with the living God.

The Truth says that there is a way out of the graveyard of inanimate stones into life. Let us believe that Jesus is that Truth!

---

[132] Albert Camus, *The Fall* (New York: Vintage International, 1991), 84.

July 4

Strength in Joy

Nehemiah 8:10—Do not grieve, for the joy of the Lord is your strength.

> Never let anything so fill you with sorrow as to make
> you forget the joy of Christ Risen.[133]
>
> —Mother Teresa

One of the great fallacies of contemporary Christian thinking is the notion that Christianity ought to be a life without pain or suffering. Nothing could be further from the truth. In fact, Jesus promises the exact opposite—"In this world you will have trouble"(John 16:33). The wonderful conundrum that follows is how this "trouble" can be parent to both grief and praise, sorrow and joy.

When tragedy strikes our lives, it is quite normal, even healthy, for the heart to grieve—for a time. But, it is equally unnatural, unhealthy, and sinful to wallow in that grief and so obstruct the resurrection of a joyful praise that glorifies God. When it comes to sorrow, "all sadness which is not either arising from the repentance of a concrete sin and hastening toward a concrete amendment...or else from pity and hastening to active assistance, is simply bad...."[134] As C.S. Lewis then goes on to say, "we all sin, by needlessly disobeying the apostolic injunction to rejoice...."[135]

Rejoicing is the end goal of all pain. But, if you find yourself in a time of great pain and sorrow on the heels of your transgression against God, then grieve. If affliction has overcome the life of someone you love, then mourn for him or her and the injustice that has come into his or her life. But let us not remain there. We must commit to move on to rejoicing in the forgiveness we have in Christ; or, similarly, to actively ameliorating the sorrow in the life of another through the love of Jesus.

Never allow yourself to grieve for grieving's sake or wallow in self-pity. Instead, commit to "Rejoice in the Lord always"(Phil 4:4) in spite of circumstances. You will then find, in the depths of your grief, the joy of the Lord—the only strength that will guide you through the pain. When you choose to praise the Lord in the pain, rest assured, you will find that the *joy of the Lord is your strength!*

---

[133] Malcolm Muggeridge, *Something Beautiful for God* (New York: HarperCollins, 1971), 68.
[134] C.S.Lewis, *The Problem of Pain* (New York: HarperCollins, 1996), 61.
[135] Ibid.

July 5

Anxiety

Philippians 4:6—Do not be anxious about anything....

> *...anxiety* is freedom's actuality as the possibility of possibility.[136]
> —Soren Kierkegaard

Anxiety is one of the chief symptoms of an unhealthy spiritual life. When we are anxious, our minds and hearts are plagued by doubt and worry. We are self-focused and self-consumed. But God wants our focus to be on Him and His love for us. He desires to fill us with joy and peace. Jesus says, "my peace I give you....Do not let your hearts be troubled..."(John 14:27). Why then do we so often choose to fret and wrestle with *anxiety* rather than embrace His peace? The answer is in Eden.

When Adam and Eve ate the forbidden fruit, "Knowledge brought with it doubt, which wrapped itself anxiously about their hearts...."[137] And doubt "is precisely the restlessness that destabilizes a life...in such a way that it can never find peace or enter into its rest...."[138] Are you struggling with doubt? Has *anxiety* wrapped itself around your heart?

Paul commands us: *Do not be anxious about anything....* But how do we twist free of *anxiety's* grip? In addition to embracing Paul's command to give thanks and pray (Phil 4:6), Jesus tells us to consider the "lilies of the field"(Matt 6:28). Though "They do not labor or spin....not even Solomon in all his splendor was dressed like one of these"(Matt 6:28-29).

The lilies are completely dependent upon God for their existence. In silent beauty, they drink the dew of heaven. They "dwell in the land and enjoy safe pasture"(Ps 37:3). They are content with what God has made them to be. The lilies teach us that "Dependence on God is the only independence...and... those who are entirely dependent on Him are light."[139] Dependence frees the lilies and "the birds of the air"(Matt 6:26) from the weights of doubt, worry, and comparison. Adam and Eve rejected dependence. Will you? Or, do you long to be as light as a bird?

While "Worldly *anxiety* always tries to lead a person...away from the sublime calm of simple thoughts,"[140] Jesus reminds us to consider the lilies. Like the flowers of the field, remember "how glorious it is to be clothed by God."[141] In this holy raiment, *anxiety* has no power over you!

---

[136] Soren Kierkegaard, *The Concept of Anxiety* (New York: W.W. Norton & Co, 2014), 51.
[137] Soren Kierkegaard, *Spiritual Writings* (New York: HarperPerennial, 2010), 25.
[138] Ibid, 34.
[139] Ibid, 111.
[140] Ibid, 120.
[141] Ibid, 120.

July 6

What I Thought, and What Truly Is

Acts 7:25—Moses thought that his own people would realize that God was using him to rescue them, but they did not.

When God reveals something to us and we act upon the conviction we have received, we must not assume that others will interpret our intentions and activities as divinely directed or inspired. While we may hope to glorify the Lord's name, it may be that God has intentionally "blinded their eyes and hardened their hearts, so they can neither see with their eyes, nor understand with their hearts…"(John 12:40). It may be that their time "is not yet here"(John 7:6). Perhaps their understanding, like Christ's public ministry and His ultimate glorification, has to wait for God's perfect timing before coming to fruition.

When, for instance, Moses struck the Egyptian who was beating an Israelite, he acted in a way one might assume would garner the understanding, support and favor of his own people. Instead, he was met with insubordination and derision—"'Who made you ruler and judge over us? Do you want to kill me as you killed the Egyptian yesterday?'"(Acts 7:27-28). In his surprise and fear of Pharaoh's potential response, Moses fled into the desert.

Have you found yourself similarly misinterpreted in the wake of words you spoke or things you did, thinking others would plainly recognize God using you in their lives? Perhaps it was a letter you sent in condolence, which, to your surprise, was read as insensitive. Maybe your gift of love was seen as manipulative. Did you sacrifice in ways that were interpreted as self-serving? If your intentions were good and your motives pure, maybe God's purposes or His timing in the lives of others is not yet aligned with what He has begun in you.

If, however, the Spirit convicts you with His peace, then persist in the work you have started—don't give up in the face of opposition or pressure. By the time Moses returned to deliver the people of Israel, he found them suddenly readied *by God* for exodus. Similarly, Jesus waited till the appropriate time to unfold a life ministry that changed the world forever.

Therefore, never assume God's revelation and truth to you will necessarily be understood or appreciated by the world around you in the moment. But never fail to be faithful to the calling you have received, till the Spirit checks or God's purpose comes to its timely fruition.

Marked Men

John 12:10-11—So the chief priests made plans to kill Lazarus as well, for on account of him many of the Jews were going over to Jesus and putting their faith in Him.

If you have ever felt hated by others because of some blessing in your life, then you might come close to knowing how the newly resurrected Lazarus felt at the hands of the Jewish authorities. Lazarus died and was buried. It was natural death; it was finished…until Jesus decided that it was not. Though Jesus was marked for death by the Jewish authorities, He raised Lazarus from the grave four days after he died. And why did Jesus do it? That God's name might be glorified.

It is easy to see why the Jewish authorities might have seen Christ as a threat after this display of power over the grave. But what did Lazarus do to mark him for death at the hands of the Jews? Nothing, but become the recipient of God's incredible blessing, a gift he never asked for.

When we are born again into new life with Christ, we, like Lazarus, are given a gift we don't deserve and never imagined possible. But this miracle of resurrection comes at a cost. Because Christ says to us, "Take off the grave clothes and let him go"(John 11:44), the power of God in us marks us as Satan's enemy. God's resurrecting miracle in us brings as much glory to His name as it did when Lazarus walked forth from the tomb. Nothing vexes the powers of darkness more than this life transformation.

If you have received this gift, do not be surprised to find yourself on the most wanted list—pursued, attacked, and hated for what God has done in you. You may not be Stephen, openly declaring your faith before the crowds, or Paul, imprisoned for preaching the Word of God. But simply being a man or woman reclaimed by Christ makes you like Lazarus, a man raised from the dead to new spiritual life. Your new life brings glory to Jesus, and that, to the legions of hell, is reason enough to pursue you.

But don't fear seeing your name written on the death list of darkness. Know that through the providential will of God, Jesus "shall lose none of all those [God] has given to [Him], but raise them up at the last day"(John 6:39). Death no longer has a hold on you. And though the powers of darkness pursue you, nothing will keep you from returning to the arms of the Father who created you.

July 8

Between His Shoulders

Deuteronomy 33:12—...and the one the Lord loves rests between His shoulders.

It is the loved and happy child who rides on the shoulders of his father. The little body is held secure by the father's strong hands, supported by his broad shoulders, and carried where his father's wisdom leads. This child is the chosen child, the beloved. And if you are in Christ, "all I want to say to you is that 'You are the Beloved,' and all I hope is that you can hear these words as spoken to you with all the tenderness and force that love can hold."[142] For the "beloved of the Lord rests secure in Him" and "rests between His shoulders"(Deut 33:12).

When Moses uttered these words concerning the tribe of Benjamin, he had specific connotations in mind. There was a physical specificity to the shoulders—the coming Temple, built on Mount Moriah, would sit in the land of Benjamin, between the shoulders of Israel's borders. But Benjamin was also the favored son of an aging father. He was the beloved boy whom Jacob (Israel) would not part with to the unknown perils of Egypt.

As children of God, we too have become this beloved child. We are promised the blessing of Benjamin. We will "rest secure in Him," supported by the Lord's broad shoulders, upheld by a Rock of strength that weathers all storms. As we trust in Him, "He will cover [us] with His feathers," hiding us in the protective shadow of His wings (Ps 91:4). And as we sit *between His shoulders*, we are carried by His wisdom and the love that says, "I have made you and I will carry you"(Is 46:4).

Do you feel these shoulders beneath you? Nouwen reminds us: "As children of God, we are God's chosen ones."[143] Are you convinced that you are this beloved child? If not, stop trying to invent yourself, to justify your purpose in life or fill your inner emptiness with anything other than Jesus. Cease to be dissipated on things that have no eternal significance. Recognize that "We are sent into this world for a short time to say—through the joys and pains of our clock-time—the great 'Yes' to the love that has been given to us and in so doing return to the One who sent us with that 'Yes' engraved on our hearts."[144]

Will you turn to your Father and be carried on the shoulders of the One who loves you and calls you His own? Say, "Yes!"

---

[142] Henri Nouwen, *Life of the Beloved* (New York: The Crossroad Publishing Company, 2002), 30.
[143] Ibid, 51.
[144] Ibid, 36.

July 9

The One Who Came Back

Luke 17:15—One of them, when he saw he was healed, came back, praising God in a loud voice.

The question is not whether you will receive goodness in your life, but rather what you will choose to do when you do receive it. Jesus gave to all ten lepers the same gift—healing and cleansing of their leprous disease. But only one man (and the Samaritan at that!) determined to turn around and thank the God who healed him and set him free from his physical bondage. The question is: why only one?

Will you be one of the nine healed lepers who ran away with their blessing and never returned to Jesus? Or will you decide to be the *one* in ten who *come back, praising God in a loud voice* (Luke 17:11-19)?

All too often we take our blessings for granted. We receive them gladly and run off with them, enjoying them and eventually even underappreciating them as our pride convinces us that we deserve them. This is perhaps most glaringly true with the greatest and most unappreciated gift of all—the salvation we have received in Christ and the spiritual healing He provides to our "leprous" souls.

Have you made it a point to regularly return to Jesus to thank Him for the healing in your life? C.S. Lewis reminds us, "praise almost seems to be inner health made audible."[145] Are you making it a point to praise Christ with a loud and unmistakable voice? Jesus asks, "'Were not all ten cleansed? Where are the other nine?'"(Luke 17:17). Have you allowed your life, healed and weighed down by blessing after blessing, to be a life counted among the "nine" who ran away?

Pray that you will not pass another day without turning to Jesus to thank Him for your healing. Choose to daily praise God in a loud voice for every blessing He brings into your cleansed life. When you do this, you will see that your "'faith has made you well'"(Luke 17:19). Let your heart say,

> I want to praise him
> loud as a trumpet
> in the vanguard of an army,
> I will run ahead and proclaim.[146]
> —Rainer Rilke

---

[145] C.S. Lewis, *Reflections on the Psalms* (New York: HarperCollins, 1986), 110.
[146] Rainer Rilke, *Book of Hours: Love Poems to God* (New York: Riverhead Books, 2005), 205.

July 10

Little by Little

Exodus 23:30—Little by little I will drive them out before you....

Many a mickle makes a muckle.[147]
—George Washington

We have increasingly come to expect instant gratification. The world is literally at our fingertips. With the push of a button we learn what we want and obtain what we desire. So the idea that the Promised Land must come *little by little* seems fine for the ancient Jews, but unacceptable in our contemporary lives. Yet the Lord does not change (Mal 3:6). His reasons for not giving the Israelites the land of Canaan all at once, may well be the same reasons He is delaying or slowly answering your heart's desire.

God said of Israel's enemies, "I will not drive them out in a single year, because the land would become desolate and the wild animals too numerous for you"(Ex 23:29). While the Israelites hungered for the promise, God knew they were not ready to obtain it. God was protecting the Israelites. They needed to grow in numbers and increase in strength and unity before they would be able to successfully "take possession of the land"(23:30). Too much, too fast, and the fledging nation would have been overwhelmed. Instead of tasting the fruits of the land, enjoying the blessing and moving into it, they would have been burdened by a responsibility too big for them to handle.

God knows what you are longing for, the "Promised Land" you are desiring. But He also knows that "Wealth gained hastily will dwindle, but whoever grows *little by little* will increase"(Prov 13:11 ESV). The reason the fulfillment of our blessings sometimes tarries is that we are not ready to possess them. We may still have to grow in our relationship with the Father, trusting Him one battle after the next. As we submit to His will and trust in His timing, He will give us the territory, *little by little,* until we are ready to possess it in its entirety.

Thank God today that He has not given you the "Promised Land" all at once. Thank Him for the restraint that holds back His blessing to manageable and incremental morsels of love that are both spiritually digestible and enjoyable. Thank Him that you can taste His goodness rather than becoming engorged or overcome by "wild animals." *Little by little*, He is working in your life to make you ready to possess the promise He has designed for you.

---

[147] Many small things add up to a large amount.

The Inconvenient Truth

Acts 24:25—As Paul discoursed on righteousness, self-control and the judgement to come, Felix was afraid and said, "That's enough for now! You may leave. When I find it convenient, I will send for you!"

As Paul, then in prison in Caesarea, stood before Governor Felix and "spoke about faith in Christ Jesus," he specifically "discoursed on righteousness, self-control and the judgement to come…"(Acts 24:25). Perhaps to his credit, Felix had enough spiritual integrity to listen and be "afraid." Paul's words, therefore, penetrated the Governor's conscience and forced him to see the *inconvenient truth* of who he really was in the eyes of God. Seeing the mess inside his heart, Felix decided it would be much more convenient to shut the door on it. While he might readdress it at a later time, Felix says to Paul, *"That's enough for now! You may leave. When I find it convenient, I will send for you."*

Have you, like Felix, made a habit of shutting the door on the message of Jesus when it forces you to face your *inconvenient truth*? Jesus may be just fine when He stays in His corner and leaves me alone. But when He steps forward and confronts me with who I really am, do I find myself saying, *"That's enough for now! You may leave"*?

For the skeptic like Felix, the problem with Christianity is often not some specific doctrine or teaching, or even the idea that there is someone or something greater "out there" to whom we are called to be in a relationship with or give thanks to. Some may say, "I can't believe in a God who would allow that kind of suffering." Or, "Who could honestly believe in a seven day creation story in the face of evolutionary evidence?" But these challenges are typically a smoke screen for a rejection that runs deeper. It is often rooted in the reality that Jesus forces us to face the *inconvenient truth* of who we are: sinners in need of a Savior.

We must be careful to not allow ourselves the liberty of Felix, believing we can simply disregard the truth when it is inconvenient or unpalatable. Just because we close the door on Christ's message does not mean that the mess inside our hearts isn't still there or that the gospel message is any less a reality. The *inconvenient truth* is still the truth whether we deal with it or not.

But there is hope! The mess of who we are apart from God can be transformed and made new. When we find the courage to be inconvenienced by the message of Jesus, and stop making excuses, then we are able to see the reality of who we are. In this honesty, Jesus will lead us to the life we have been running from. He will surround our *inconvenient truth* with His amazing love.

July 12

Room in the Inn of the Heart

2 Corinthians 7:2—Make room for us in your hearts.

> When the sun is vertically above a man he casts no shadow: similarly
> when we have come to the Divine meridian our spiritual shadow…will
> vanish. One will…be almost nothing: a *room* to be filled by God and our
> blessed fellow creatures, who in their turn are rooms we help to fill.[148]
> —C.S. Lewis

What you fill your heart with is entirely up to you. No one, not
even God Himself, will dictate its contents. You must decide who and
what things you welcome in. Only you can make room for them.

What have you made room for in your heart? Perhaps it is your
spouse or children, your friends or colleagues at work. Maybe it is your
hobbies, animals, or the men and women you serve at the shelter. But are
you continually making more room for God, His Son Jesus, and His Holy
Spirit? And, have you made space for God's people?

Paul commands the Corinthians to *make room for us in your hearts*.
He is not requesting or suggesting; he is giving a clear injunction. He is
stressing the importance of making space for God and His people in the
often overbooked and overcrowded lodgings of the heart.

Some of us appear to be, by God's design, more naturally "large-
hearted" than others. Some of us seem to be gifted with a warmth and
openness, a malleability of spirit which facilitates spreading wide the doors
of the heart to God, His people, and His purposes. But whether this
comes naturally or not, as the case might have been for the Corinthians,
does not matter. We are all called to make room in our hearts.

When we decide to do this, we notice something amazing happen
—the walls of our hearts, almost imperceptibly at first, start expanding. To
welcome God and His people into our hearts is to make our hearts grow.
God and His uncontainable Spirit begin to enlarge the capacity of our
hearts. How does this happen? Mother Teresa tells us: "Prayer enlarges
the heart until it is capable of containing God's gift of Himself. Ask and
seek, and your heart will grow big enough to receive Him and keep Him as
your own."[149] Are you praying this way?

Where God is, the walls of the heart are always expanding. Is God
expanding yours to make room for Him, His purposes, and His people?

---

[148] C.S. Lewis, *The Collected Letters of C.S. Lewis, Vol III* in *The Business of Heaven* (New York:
HarperCollins, 1984), 221-222.
[149] Malcolm Muggeridge, *Something Beautiful for God* (New York: HarperCollins, 1971), 66.

July 13

Making Joy Complete

1 John 1:3-4—And our fellowship is with the Father and with His Son, Jesus Christ. We write this to make our joy complete.

In a very real way, the completion of joy in our hearts necessitates a sharing with others. Whatever it is that brings us delight and elation of spirit is not half so exhilarating when it is kept to ourselves. We want to tell others about what we have seen and heard.

This is perhaps no more true than in our relationship with Jesus. When we encounter Him and have fellowship with Him and His Spirit, we are transformed. We are filled with a healing and joy that fills us with a love we want to express. We see this desire in the demon-possessed man who is exorcized by Jesus. This man "went away and began to tell in the Decapolis how much Jesus had done for him"(Mark 5:20). In another instance, the paralytic man encounters Christ and "Immediately he stood up in front of them, took what he had been lying on and went home praising God"(Luke 5:25).

One of the clearest tests of whether we are in love with the Lord and in fellowship with His Spirit is our need to talk about Him, frequently and favorably.[150] A lover extols his beloved, singing his or her praises in written and spoken word. The Song of Songs is an extended example of joy overflowing. Solomon's delight in his love is a joy that cannot be kept to himself. Through his "song" of praise, the beloved knows she is loved; the listeners are encouraged that such love exists; and the lover himself finds his joy complete in the sharing of his delight.

In the same way, when we love Jesus, we will emerge from our daily fellowship needing to tell others about him. Our joy will need completion in the praise we share with others. If you are asking, *"How can I keep from singing?"*[151] then you have likely seen Jesus, and the joy within you is searching for the wings of its completion. Keep singing!

---

[150] Thomas Watson, *All Things for Good* (Shawnee: Gideon House Books, 2015), 77-78.
[151] Chris Tomlin, 2006, "How Can I Keep From Singing," *See the Morning*.

211

July 14

Yet Will I Rejoice

Habakkuk 3:17-18—Though the fig tree does not bud and there are no grapes on the vines, though the olive crop fails and the fields produce no food, though there are no sheep in the pen and no cattle in the stalls, yet I will rejoice in the Lord. I will be joyful in God my Savior.

Life offers us all moments of feeling impoverished in some way. Maybe it's financial downturns, health problems or lack of relationship. Lost your job or your spouse? Perhaps your children have wandered away and are living prodigal lives. Whatever it is, will you choose to rejoice in the Lord in the midst of your poverty?

Habakkuk makes the decision that he *will rejoice in the Lord* and he *will be joyful in God*. Despite the destitution all around him and every reason to despair and be angry at God, Habakkuk chooses praise. How is this possible? How can he sing on an empty stomach and worship in a land of troubles? Habakkuk understands that the "Sovereign Lord is [his] strength…"(3:19). Though his fields produce no food, he has "food to eat that you know nothing about"(John 4:32). Though his trees are not budding with the hope of a coming spring, his hope is in the Lord.

For this reason, he does not worry. He understands the spirit of the Lord's command—"do not worry about your life, what you will eat or drink; or about your body, what you will wear. Is not life more important than food…? Look at the birds of the air; they do not sow or reap or store away in barns, and yet your heavenly Father feeds them. Are you not much more valuable than they?"(Matt 6:25-26).

In the midst of your poverty, you can choose to worry or give up and curse the Lord. You can attempt to claw yourself up out of the grave through your own efforts or decide instead to rejoice in the Lord and find your strength in Him. When you decide to be *joyful in God [your] Savior* you will be amazed at how provisions come. You may not be raised out of the pit in a day, but you will be sustained. In the midst of a desert, you will be fed as the birds of the air.

When poverty knocks on your door, will you trust that God loves you as deeply as He loved His servant Job who, stripped of everything, said, "Though He slay me, yet I will hope in Him"(Job 13:15)? In the midst of barrenness, will you say with the Psalmist, "I will praise the Lord all my life; I will sing praise to my God as long as I live"(Ps 146:2)? With commitment like this, your poverty cannot help but be filled by the abundance of God.

Disheartening

Deuteronomy 1:28—Where can we go? Our brothers have made us lose heart.

Many a jilted lover walks away disheartened. Because breakups happen so often, we will sometimes glibly respond, "You will love again." But is that always true? For the disheartened, is it that simple? And what of those who become disheartened in faith? There may be more lovers, but there is only one God. What happens when someone becomes disheartened in their spiritual journey?

How little attention we appear to give to our *disheartening* effect on the spiritual lives of others! We are called to be the "light of the world"(Matt 5:14) and yet, many of us too frequently darken the world of those around us with our negativity and dower perspectives. Instead of drawing others to Christ, we cause them to run away.

Such was the case of the scouts of Israel returning from their mission to the Promised Land. Instead of following the lead of Caleb and Joshua and filling the people's hearts with confidence and hope in the Lord, ten of the men decidedly discouraged the hearts of the entire nation. These men said, "The people are stronger and taller than we are. The cities are large, with walls up to the sky"(Deut 1:28). And because of the report, the people trembled in fear and were "unwilling to go up"(Deut 1:26) and take possession of the land. When the Israelites realized their error, the disheartened nation went up into the land *without* the Lord's blessing, only to find themselves defeated and chased "like a swarm of bees"(Deut 1:44). Ten men made a nation lose heart and an entire generation never entered the promise of God.

Is your life one in which the encouragement of Caleb and Joshua shines into the hearts of those around you? Or, do you more often affect others like one of the remaining ten scouts—by *disheartening* them? While we might never know the full effect of our words and actions on the faith of others, when we cause them to *lose heart* and turn away from the Lord because of the sickness of our own hearts, we sadden our Father. Further, our spiritual sickness can negatively affect the spiritual health of others.

Pray today that the Lord helps you to never dishearten the faith of another. Struggle as you must to claim your own spiritual maturity in the grace of the Lord, but ask God's mercy in preventing you from impeding Christ's work in the hearts of others.

July 16

Overtaken

Psalm 40:12—...my sins have overtaken me, and I cannot see. They are more than the hairs of my head, and my heart fails within me.

If we are honest, most of us have little to no conception of either the multitude or magnitude of our sins. Some go so far as to deny the idea of sin altogether or drown it in a self-perceived goodness. When David says, *"my sins have overtaken me and I cannot see. They are more than the hairs of my head,"* we might be tempted to see this as some righteous hyperbole given by a zealous man. But is it this? Or is it, perhaps, the most accurate description of our hearts that anyone could ever give?

Have we felt the all-encompassing nature of our sin? Can we say with David, "My guilt has overwhelmed me like a burden too heavy to bear"(Ps 38:4)? Do we have the spiritual clarity to see that "my sin is always before me," "my iniquity...great within me"(Ps 51:3; 25:11)?

To know Jesus and to understand what it is that He has done for me, I must first acknowledge my sin, in its most hideous depth and breadth. I must continually admit that I "have sinned and fall[en] short of the glory of God"(Rom 3:23) and that "I am poor and needy"(Ps 40:17). I require a Savior as much today as any day before.

When I first come to salvation, I understand that I have been cleansed of my unrighteousness and my transgressions have been removed "as far as the east is from the west"(Ps 103:12). But as I move on from this sentinel moment, I must never take the spiritual liberty to assume that I am *without* the capacity for sin. To use salvation as a mental "free pass" to live how I want to live is to place me in a spiritually more perilous position than I was before I "accepted" Christ's grace. Clothing my darkness with a white robe makes me no less dark. It simply hides the truth.

True faith begins with an inner transformation which awakens a spiritual awareness of my unrighteousness. Like David, I continually discern my sin in the on-going spiritual battle against a terminally defeated enemy (Satan). But, if I can recognize my sin and regularly confess it, "[Christ] is faithful and just and will forgive us our sins and purify us from all unrighteousness"(1 John 1:9)!

Are you numbering your sins on the fingers of your hands or the hairs of your head? Every day, commit to recognize the multitude and magnitude of ways in which you separate yourself from God. Give those ways to Jesus. And when you are feeling *overtaken*, rejoice in the One whose grace can present you spotless before the Lord!

A Little Yeast Goes a Long Way

1 Corinthians 5:6—Don't you know that a little yeast works through the whole batch of dough?

The nature of yeast is that it is invisible to the naked eye and goes unnoticed until it begins to change the substance it has been mingled with. This transformation is not instantaneous, but gradual and almost imperceptibly progressive until, before we know it, it has completely changed the dough we began with. While this bread yeast makes the dough rise, spiritual "yeast" can be an agent of change in our hearts. So it is with "the old yeast, the yeast of malice and wickedness…"(1 Cor 5:8). Paul exhorts the Corinthians to "get rid of the old yeast that you may be a new batch without yeast….the bread of sincerity and truth"(1 Cor 5:7-8).

What is the yeast in your life right now? Perhaps it is the occasional acquaintance of questionable moral character who causes you to think and do things in ways uncommon to who you are and counter to the gospel. Maybe it is the momentary glances you have recently been giving to pornography or the increasing liberty you have allowed yourself to gossip among your friends. Whatever it may be, it is likely so small as to seem insignificant and completely innocuous. What does a couple minutes here or there have to do with my eternal destiny? The answer: potentially everything.

Is the dough of your life, the substance of who you are, progressively becoming the *bread of sincerity and truth*? Or is there some yeast of wickedness, some unhealthy habit or way of thinking, that is slowly transforming you, puffing you up and inflating you and your thinking into a bread unfit for the service of the Lord? If you don't see it now, others may begin to notice the change. To avoid this inner corruption, the challenge is to first recognize the imperceptible power of spiritual yeast in our lives. Then, we must have the courage to root it out, or, where necessary, to start completely over by being cleansed and renewed by the blood of Christ.

If I am committed to a life with Jesus, I must be determined to be an "uncontaminated," unleavened bread for Christ and His Kingdom purposes. When I notice the effects of the "old yeast" in my life, however subtle, I must repent and get rid of it before it "works through the whole batch of dough"(1 Cor 5:6). Failure on my part to do this threatens to completely and unalterably ruin me.

Beware of the unseen yeast in your life.

God Amidst "gods"

Psalm 82:6—"I said, 'You are "gods"; you are all sons of the Most High.' But you will die like mere men; you will fall like every other ruler."

The world is full of "gods." In every direction you will see the face of a "divinity," some contrived by men, others by Satan. We allow the "god" complex to extend to athletes, actresses, politicians and businessmen. All of us at times think ourselves self-sufficient and above reproach. But is this divinity thinking all bad? Is it contemptible hubris? Or is it, like most things, a once beautiful thing fatally corrupted by Satan?

Since we were created by God, in the image of God (Gen 1:27), He has beautifully clothed us in divinity for His delight. The Lord says to us, *"You are 'gods'; you are all sons of the Most High"* (Ps 82:6). Jesus later quotes this same Psalm to explain His Sonship: "Is it not written in your Law, 'I have said you are gods'? If he called them 'gods' to whom the Word of God came—and the Scripture cannot be broken—what about the One the Father has set apart as His very own…?"(John 10:34-35).

The trouble then, is not that we have a divine nature in us, the semblance of God Himself, but rather that we have allowed our thinking to exclude the Lord as the God of all "gods." We quickly forget that "the Lord [our] God is God of gods and Lord of lords, the great God, mighty and awesome…"(Deut 10:17). We would much rather live in an equitable pantheon, where each of us is a god unto him or herself, coexisting and commingling, but bowing to no one else. We would just as soon forget that the God who created the gods, who formed the hands that built the very "pantheon" in which we exist, is Lord of our lives. For as soon as we acknowledge a supreme power, we are no longer "Lord" of our lives.

This reality might cause us to say: "You mean to tell me, I must bow down? But I'm a god! We must admit that we *will die like mere men* and *fall like every other ruler?"*

Yes! There is only one God with a capital "G." But He has clothed us in divinity and given us the rights of a son or daughter of the Most High. Rejoice in the richness and beauty of God's pantheon, of which you are part! But do not, for a moment, allow yourself the liberty to believe the pervasive lie that you are *God* of your own life. Rebuke the voice that urges you to substitute "G" for "g" in your heart and soul. In your royal robes, choose to bow down before the King of kings and the Lord of lords. Then, like Queen Esther, your King will extend His scepter toward you and give you life (Est 5:2), eternal life—the true right of the divinity for which you were created.

Live by Faith

2 Corinthians 5:7—We live by faith, not by sight.

To live by anything, whether a physical something or a principle, is to depend upon it so thoroughly that our existence is defined by and dependent upon it. For instance, it would be very true to say of my physical body, "I live by breathing." If I stop breathing, I understand that my body will die.

But when it comes to the spirit, by what does it live? Is it so thoroughly bound to the body as to be defined by mere physical processes only? Does your soul exist merely upon what it sees and empirically knows to be true? Or does it transcend the visible world, living by a set of principles, perhaps, even living by faith?

The prophet Habakkuk says, "the righteous shall live by his faith"(Hab 2:4). This means trusting and hoping in the Lord at all times, in all things, irrespective of circumstances and whether or not we can see what lies ahead. "Now faith is being sure of what we hope for and certain of what we do not see"(Heb 11:1). It is understanding "that the universe was formed at God's command..."(Heb 11:3). It is Noah believing in the "foolishness" of building an ark under halcyon skies. It is Abraham leaving his home to go to a foreign country and then trusting that Sarah's barren womb will bring forth the seed of a future nation (Heb 11:7-12).

When we live by faith, we are not bound by what we do or do not see, hedged in by the borders of reason, or constrained by the finite limits of the here and now. With eternal perspective, we recognize that we are "aliens and strangers on earth"(Heb 11:13). Our heavenly lenses were not meant to see some things, or, at least, not now. Living by faith means we go beyond the visible into the uncharted, unseen.

Have you ever ventured there? Not once, but as a way of living? Are you hoping, trusting, and walking forward by the Spirit's leading into unseen things? Perhaps you have tested this in the physical world by closing your eyes while walking, only to find, to your surprise, that you can continue to walk. Have you noticed in this "darkness" that your ears suddenly become aware of a symphony of sounds, unappreciated before— a listening that helps lead you on?

To live by faith does not mean we completely abandon sight. God gave it to us for a reason. But we are not bound by what we see. Whether our eyes are open or closed, whether there is light or darkness, we walk on, led by the Spirit. It means life is defined not exclusively by the world around us, but rather by the Spirit who lives within us.

Are you living by this faith?

July 20

Never Stop

Acts 5:42—Day after day…they never stopped teaching and proclaiming the good news that Jesus is the Christ.

When Peter and the Apostles are brought before the Jewish Sanhedrin, they are flogged and ordered "not to speak in the name of Jesus," and then let go (Acts 5:40). After such a beating and verbal threatening, it might seem entirely reasonable and downright rational to refrain from the activity that provoked such a punishing response. But the Apostles do nothing of the sort. They do not quietly go away. Rather, "*Day after day, in the Temple courts and from house to house, they never stopped teaching and proclaiming the good news…*"(Acts 5:42). They were held as in a vise, constrained by the love of Christ, and like the converted Apostle Paul, "compelled to preach": "Woe to me if I do not preach the gospel!"(1 Cor 9:16).

Is your life guided by this kind of spiritual fervor? Day after day, I must ask myself: does the time I spend, the activities I do, and the words I say, *teach and proclaim the good news that Jesus is the Christ?* The Apostles could not stop their ministry because they understood that a call to "following Jesus…is proclaiming a discipleship which will liberate mankind from all man-made dogmas, from every burden and oppression, from every anxiety and torture which afflicts the conscience."[152] In the depths of their hearts, they grasped that "Discipleship means joy,"[153] and nothing, and no one, could keep them from sharing that joy with others!

If my life is not persistently *teaching and proclaiming* the gospel message, it might be because I do not truly understand the grace I have been given. Once I begin to fathom the costliness of the grace that has been bestowed upon me ("costly because it cost God the life of His Son"),[154] I will not be able to stop telling the world who I have found, what He has given me, and who I now am because He lives in me. As Bonhoeffer reminds us, "Happy are the simple followers of Jesus Christ who have been overcome by His grace, and are able to sing the praises of the all-sufficient grace of Christ with humbleness of heart."[155]

When you begin to grasp what Christ has done in your life, your ministry, like that of the Apostles, will *never stop!*

---

[152] Dietrich Bonhoeffer, *The Cost of Discipleship* (New York: Touchstone, 1995), 37.
[153] Ibid, 38.
[154] Ibid, 55.
[155] Ibid, 55-56.

July 21

Lonely Places, II.

Luke 5:16—But Jesus often withdrew to lonely places and prayed.

> A life without a lonely place, that is, a life without a quiet center, easily becomes destructive.[156]
>
> —Henri Nouwen

Lonely places are a necessity in the Christian life. We cannot hope to know God without them. Jesus repeatedly, and often, *withdrew to lonely places and prayed.* Why should we expect and allow our lives to be any different?

Satan knows better than anyone that the solitude of *lonely places* facilitates our best communication with God. It should not be surprising then that Satan contrives to clutter our lives with activity and noise. He will try his best to preoccupy you with everything but quiet time to spend with your Father, because Satan knows that in relationships "solitude sometimes is best society,/ And short retirement urges sweet return."[157] Unless sought for and fought for, *lonely places* are hard to come by and, for some, harder still to justify. But we must have them if we are to know our Lord.

Are you making *lonely places* a priority in your life? It might be a special room in your house, a closet that shuts the rest of the world out, a woodland walk or a chair all alone on the beach. Whatever it is, wherever it is, it must allow you to leave the rest of the world behind you. It must permit your soul, like that of Christ's, to join in an unobstructed, undisturbed oneness with the Father who is calling your name.

If you do not feel spiritually close to your Father, it is most likely because your life lacks *lonely places.* Solitude is unlikely to force itself upon you. For this reason, you must make the solitude of *lonely places* a regular part of your life. Ask the Lord to help you organize your time and convict your heart to do this. No matter how cluttered your life may be with good things vying for your time, energy and attentions, commit to close the door on all of them, every day, for a few moments alone with your Father.

But if these *lonely places* are already a part of your life, pray that the Spirit helps you "find that your loneliness is linked to your call to live completely for God."[158] See the privilege of living in "undivided devotion to the Lord"(1 Cor 7:35). In the *lonely places* you will know a fuller meaning of your life's daily calling—*more of Him and less of you.*

---

[156] Henri Nouwen, *Out of Solitude* in *The Only Necessary Thing*, ed. Wendy Wilson Greer (New York: The Crossroad Publishing Company, 2015), 42.

[157] John Milton, *Paradise Lost* (London: Arcturus, 2014), 262.

[158] Henri Nouwen, *The Inner Voice of Love* (New York: Image Books, 1998), 36.

July 22

Welling Up

John 4:14—Indeed, the water I give him will become in him a spring of water welling up to eternal life.

Do you find that your soul is still thirsting for something more? Have you come to the endless wells of the world, only to find them incapable of quenching your deepest thirst? When it comes to my spiritual life, I must evaluate myself in regards to my "welling up." If I am intimately related to my Father because I have drunk deeply from the living water of Jesus, my soul will not thirst again. It will be marked by a *welling up to eternal life*, an ever-increasing effervescence that cannot be contained.

If our spiritual lives are not *welling up to eternal life*, it is likely because we have not asked Jesus to fill us with His water. Instead, we are racing around, desperately trying to slake our spiritual thirst the same way we slake physical thirst—with the things of this life. Like the Israelites, we "have forsaken...the spring of living water, and have dug [our] own cisterns, broken cisterns that cannot hold water"(Jer 2:13). But the soul's deepest thirst can never be quenched with anything this world has to offer. Like the Samaritan woman who finds herself standing at the well with Jesus, we find that though we have attempted to satiate our unsatisfied souls, we are still thirsty.

When there is a persistence of thirst or the absence of *welling up* in my life, I am to blame, not God. If only I "would have asked Him...He would have given"(John 4:10) the water to slake my thirst. I do not have, because I have not asked. Perhaps I haven't asked because, like the Samaritan woman at the well, I truly don't know "the gift of God" (John 4:10) in Jesus Christ. Or maybe, I do know of Him, but I still haven't asked because, frankly, I don't want to stop drinking the water of all the other wells of the world.

The disciple of Christ is the man or woman who has decided to never thirst again. This only happens when we drink deeply of the Spirit and allow a "*welling up*" with all that God's Spirit intends. Are you drinking from Jesus' well? If not, ask our Lord to fill you with the water that *wells up to eternal life.*

Living Letters

2 Corinthians 3:2—You yourselves are our letter, written on our hearts, known and read by everyone.

> …And my lament
> Is cries countless, cries like dead letters sent
> To dearest him that lives alas! away.[159]
> —G.M. Hopkins

It is unlikely that we have ever thought of ourselves as *living letters*. And yet, we are just that. Who I am and how I live reflects not only on me, but also on all those who have written into my life, not the least of whom is the Lord who made me. My life may be the finest letter of commendation for Christ or its truest adversary. The work I do, the way I parent my children, or the manner in which I pursue my relationship with the Lord, may be written on the hearts of my parents, pastors, friends and mentors in a way which no *curriculum vitae* ever could. Whether my life is the letter that brings to them a smile of joy or the tears of sorrow, is largely up to me. It depends on how I use the "pen" of my actions, talents, and affections.

What letter are you writing with your life? Are you demonstrating, as the Corinthians did to Paul, "that you are a letter from Christ"(2 Cor 3:3), written not with ink but with the Spirit of the living God; not on tablets of stone, but on the substance of the heart? Every letter has an author(s) and a recipient(s). Are you writing your own letter or are you allowing the Spirit of the living God to author it?

The degree to which you will be a letter of commendation or blessing in the lives of others depends directly upon the authorship. Write your own letter, and your life is more likely than not to be *"cries countless, cries like dead letters sent,"* lost in the archives of time. Or, perhaps it will be filled with a selfishness that brings sorrow to God and to all those who "read" what you have written into your life. If, however, you allow the Spirit of God to control the pen and compose the language of your letter, you will likely honor the Lord and bless those who love and know you best.

Commit to be a *living letter* written on the hearts of others and read by everyone for the glory of God, the "Author and Perfecter of faith…"(Heb 12:2). *Living letters* can be God's greatest gifts in the lives of others. Be that gift by allowing Christ to write into your life.

---

[159] Gerard Manley Hopkins, "I wake and feel the fell of dark, not day," in *The Poems of Gerard Manley Hopkins,* ed. W.H. Gardner and MacKenzie (Oxford: Oxford University Press, 1970),101.

July 24

The Expert Builder

1 Corinthians 3:10—But each one should be careful how he builds.

Each one of us is a builder, day by day constructing his or her eternal destiny. And the edifice that remains at the end of my life-long labors determines my eternity. To say that our building process matters would be an understatement. *Each one should be careful how he builds.* How are you building?

Paul tells us that there is only one foundation that will support the weight of eternity—Jesus Christ (1 Cor 3:11). Spiritual houses may go up all around mine, more quickly and easily, seemingly beautiful in appearance. But will they stand the test of time? Will the shoddy materials and apparently sloppy craftsmanship survive the constant beating of life's elements? Will attention to details in my spiritual life matter? The Apostle Paul says, "If any man builds on this foundation using gold, silver, costly stones, wood, hay or straw, his work will be shown for what it is, because the Day will bring it to light. It will be revealed with fire, and the fire will test the quality of each man's work"(1 Cor 3:12-13).

Are you building a life that will withstand the fire? People may spend fortunes on dream houses, fussing about the finishing touches in every room, while completely neglecting the construction of their souls. While there is nothing inherently sinful in appreciating the physical world we build, the efforts we spend there must pale in comparison to the labors we commit to our interior lives. If we are not more concerned about the craftsmanship of our own souls in the eyes of Christ than we are about our houses, careers, or families, we have it all wrong. Our spiritual houses won't stand in the flames of eternity.

You are in the building process right now, today, tomorrow and every day until the end. Are you building carefully as an *expert builder*? Have you determined that the details of your spiritual house matter more than any of the other details in your daily life?

Be a man or woman who chooses to build on the foundation of Christ with eternity in mind. If you build with only the things of the world, your efforts will be consumed by the flames. If you build with the things of God, for God, on God's foundation, you will receive your reward (1 Cor 3:14).

Consider

Jeremiah 2:19—Consider then and realize how evil and bitter it is for you when you forsake the Lord your God and have no awe of me....

When was the last time you approached the Lord with absolute awe of who He is? We live in a world so oversaturated with information and stimuli that our sense of wonder has been dulled to a dangerous degree. We have tragically lost the "eternal appetite of infancy,"[160] the spirit of wonder and awe that rings in the halls of heaven! But Jeremiah reminds us that it is both *evil and bitter* to forget how awesome the Lord truly is. The Psalmist attests to this, saying, "How awesome is the Lord most High, the great King over all the earth!"(Ps 47:2).

This kind of exclamatory praise is the sort we are meant to begin each day with. It is no mistake that the prayer Jesus taught us to pray begins with a statement of God's great and awesome holiness—"hallowed be thy name..."(Matt 6:9). If I truly consider who God is and what He has done, how can I not say, "O Lord God Almighty, who is like you?"(Ps 89:8)! For who else has "set all the boundaries of the earth," and "established the sun and the moon"(Ps 74:17, 16)? How awesome it is that you have "knit me together in my mother's womb," and that you know "when I sit and when I rise...and perceive my thoughts from afar"(Ps 139:13; 2)! How awe-inspiring are "all your wonders," for "What is man that you are mindful of him?"(Ps 9:1; Ps 8:4)! Even more, who am I that you sent your one and only Son to die for me?

If this kind of enthusiastic praise does not permeate our every day, then we have allowed our spiritual senses to become dangerously dimmed. To counteract this tendency, we must commit each day to "walk the world like a wonderful surprise...."[161] Let us, with the child-like wonder of our heavenly Father, "exult in monotony," and see in the "repetition of Nature...not a mere recurrence," but a "theatrical encore" for God.[162] When we *consider* the world around us in this way, we will stand in awe of who God is and what He has done! We will find that we "delight to praise what we enjoy because the praise not merely expresses but completes the enjoyment, it is its appointed consummation." [163] We will learn to love the Love that never leaves us or forsakes us. Does your love for Jesus engender an awe that brings you to praise?

---

[160] G.K. Chesterton, *Orthodoxy* (Peabody: Hendrickson Publishers, 2006), 55.

[161] G.K. Chesterton, *Manalive* (Mineola: Dover Publications, 2000), 73.

[162] G.K. Chesterton, *Orthodoxy* (Peabody: Hendrickson Publishers, 2006), 55.

[163] C.S. Lewis, *Reflections on the Psalms* (New York: HarperCollins, 1986), 111.

July 26

Who Are You?

Acts 19:15—One day the evil spirit answered them, "Jesus I know, and I know about Paul, but who are you?"

Do the demons of hell know your name because you live for Christ? Are they looking for the best way to bring about your spiritual demise as the fictionalized demons (Uncle Screwtape and Wormwood) are in C.S. Lewis' *The Screwtape Letters*?[164] Or are you, like the Seven Sons of Sceva, an unknown entity in the realm of darkness—*Jesus I know, and I know about Paul, but who are you?*

To be disciples of Jesus means that our pictures hang in the halls of hell with the caption, WANTED. The greater the reward by our names, the greater our fidelity to Christ and His Kingdom. Jesus told His disciples, "rejoice that your names are written in heaven"(Luke 10:20). But if they are written in heaven, they are also posted on the walls of hell. If the spirits of darkness do not know our names, if they are not in constant dialogue about how best to destroy us, unravel us, or frustrate our progress, we can be sure that our lives are not Spirit-filled. We are not disciples of Christ unless we are targeted by the powers of darkness.

Let us not be deceived. The legions of hell will not be fooled by our superficial righteousness anymore than God will be. We might use the name of Jesus. We might dress ourselves in acts of apparent righteousness. But if it is not the righteousness of Christ, the demons of hell will see right through it. They will say, "*Who are you?*" before they pounce on us and give us "such a beating that [we] run out of the house naked and bleeding"(Acts 19:16), just as the imposters before Paul were scourged by the demonic whip.

Who are you? Are you a disciple of Christ and an enemy of the darkness, or are you a fool playing a part that fools no one but yourself? Is your picture hanging on the walls of hell or are you just another member of the unidentifiable crowd? Satan attacked Job because his name was on the on the tip of God's tongue. God says to Satan, "Have you considered my servant Job? There is no one on earth like him; he is blameless and upright, a man who fears God and shuns evil"(Job 1:8). Can the same be said of you?

Is the Lord commending your faithfulness and condoning your righteous acts before an inquiring Satan? Let us pray that we will live our lives in such a way that the powers of hell know our names because they are on the lips of our Father.

---

[164] C.S. Lewis, *The Screwtape Letters* (New York: HarperCollins, 2013).

July 27

From a Distance

Hebrews 11:13—They did not receive the things promised; they only saw them and welcomed them from a distance.

In the beginning of our spiritual journeys, when faith is little more than a youthful and fanciful enthusiasm, it is not uncommon to think that we somehow deserve to see the fulfillment of God's promises directly on the heels of our obedience to Him. Sometimes God does decide to act with immediacy and clarity. In these moments we, like King David, find ourselves blessed enough to say, "The Lord has dealt with me according to my righteousness; according to the cleanness of my hands He has rewarded me"(Ps 18:20).

However, it is equally true that the lives of many of God's most beloved saints did not see actual possession of the Lord's promises on this side of the grave. They only saw them *from a distance*. Moses was such a man. His life was entwined with God. The Lord spoke to Moses in the burning bush, worked through Moses in the plagues of Egypt and the parting of the Red Sea, and honored him with sending manna from heaven as an answer to his prayer. Yet Moses was also a servant whose leg of leadership was destined to be forty years of wilderness wandering. In the end, Moses was told to "'Go up...to Mount Nebo...and view Canaan, the land I am giving the Israelites as their own possession....[for] you will see the land only from a *distance*, you will not enter the land I am giving the people of Israel"(Deut 32:48-49, 52).

This life of Moses is a wonderful reminder to us all of the relay race we are running in God's storyline. From the time the universe was formed at God's command (Heb 11:3), till the day when "He is coming with the clouds"(Rev 1:7), God's storyline marches on. And His saints, from Abel to Noah, Moses to Daniel, and from Paul straight down to you and me, are running different legs of that race. If you are feeling as if your part of the story, your leg of the race, has been one in which you have not received the things promised, either you have a false idea of how God fulfills His promises or He is honoring you with something special to come.

Some of us are best fit for the first lap, others for the last, and some for those in between. But whatever leg of the race God has given you in His storyline, the immutable promises of God remain unchanged. Whether you see His promises fulfilled in this life or only see them *from a distance*, God alone decides. But if it is the latter, take heart in knowing you have been highly favored. You are in the company of some of God's greatest saints. Your coming reward will be wonderful!

July 28

For Me—The *Pro Me*

1 Peter 3:18—For Christ died for sins once for all, the righteous for the unrighteous, to bring you to God.

I will never understand the person of Jesus Christ and what He came to do until I grasp Him as *pro me*—for "Christ is Christ, not just for Himself, but in relation to me. His being Christ is His being for me, *pro me*."[165] As long as I see the incarnation as a depersonalized story about a cute baby representing a god who comes down from heaven and takes on flesh, it will remain mere whimsical nonsense. It will be as meaningless as the Greeks' philandering Zeus taking on the flesh of Alcmene's husband only to seduce her.[166] And if the ministry and teachings of Jesus are not *pro me*, then they will be the mere moralistic babbling of a delusional fool. But if they are *pro me*, then they strike to the heart of who I am. They spiritually arrest, challenge, and transform me!

The same is true of the cross. Is it simply the death of a man who claimed, as the Jews said, to be the Son of God? Who cares, unless, He died *for me*—unless I was meant to be hanging there, and He took my place, *the righteous for the unrighteous*? Bonhoeffer says, "Where does [Christ] stand? He stands *pro me*. He stands there in my place, where I should stand, but cannot. He stands on the boundary of my existence, yet for me."[167]

Let there be no mistake—the Son of God has existed since the beginning, for He was "with God in the beginning"(John 1:2). But the present Christ, the Christ who fulfilled Scripture by becoming a man, the Jesus who walked on earth, healed the sick and loved the marginalized, who died on the cross, and rose again with the promise to return—this Christ is *pro me*! He is who He is now because of me and because of you—because He chose to be. Christ is the "centre of human existence,"[168] the center of my existence and yours alike.

Far too many of us miss this person of Jesus because we see Christ and Christianity as *"anti me."* We see a threat to who we are, without seeing the hope of what we're being called to be. This inversion is the skillful distortion of Satan and could not be further from the truth. Christ came *for me* and He came *for you*. Jesus Christ, the risen Lord, is *pro me* and *pro you* or He is not Christ at all. Does your heart cry out, "Thank you Jesus Christ, Son of God, for being for me, the *pro me*"?

---

[165] Dietrich Bonhoeffer, *Christ the Center* (New York: HarperCollins, 1978), 47.

[166] Edward Tripp, *The Meridian Handbook of Classical Mythology* (New York: Meridian, 1974), 35.

[167] Dietrich Bonhoeffer, *Christ the Center* (New York: HarperCollins, 1978), 60.

[168] Ibid.

Eternal Life

John 17:3—Now this is eternal life: that they may know you, the only true God, and Jesus Christ, whom you have sent.

What is eternal life? Is it simply the continuance of existence beyond the grave? Or is it something infinitely more, rooted in the here and now? Jesus clearly tells us that eternal life is *knowing* God the Father and Jesus Christ the Son. If you desire eternal life, you must *know* God.

The question then becomes, "What does it mean to *know* God?" What Jesus refers to here is not what the world now holds it be: A familiarity or intellectual understanding of Christ, what the philosophers call a "knowledge of acquaintance." Rather, "knowing" means deep intimacy. The Greek word used is *ginosko* and has the meaning of "knowing," as in the intimacy of sex. What is more intimate in the human experience—the union of two lives into one flesh and one combined existence?

It is this very "know" to which Jesus alludes when He speaks about eternal life. To have life everlasting is to be in relationship with the Father, Son, and the Holy Spirit in such an intimate way that we are "united" with the Trinity in a personal manner of existence. In this relationship, we find eternal life because Christ lives in us and Jesus Himself is "the life"(John 14:6). Eternal life, therefore, begins the moment we trust in Christ as our Savior.

We do ourselves a grave injustice to consider eternal life something relegated only to the existence beyond the grave. If we are in Christ, our eternal existence has already begun! Our relationship with the Lord links us, in this very moment, to the "life everlasting." This eternal life is Spirit-filled, brimming with "love, joy, peace, patience, kindness, goodness, faithfulness, gentleness and self-control"(Gal 5:22-23). And when it comes to the eternal life beyond the grave, we will not reach this "third heaven" (2 Cor 12:2) unless we first take hold of the eternity rooted in the here and now—our relationship with the Lord.

Eternal life begins with truly knowing God. Do you know about Him, or do you truly know Him? Are you intimately united with the Father, Son and Holy Ghost? The answer to this question has eternal implications. If you have grasped this "knowing," your eternal existence is present tense.

On the Backs of Others

1 Chronicles 22:5—"Therefore, I will make preparations for it." So David made extensive preparations before his death.

When was the last time you considered the contributions of others to your life? Or, do you believe the degree you earned, the company you helped build or the family you now have is the result of your efforts? Yes, you've made choices and perhaps worked hard. But do you understand that you are the sum of everything and everyone that God has poured into your life?

King Solomon was no exception to this reality. He is remembered as the wise king who amassed great wealth and splendor. He had rest from his enemies on every side and built the Temple of the Lord (1 Chron 22:9). But, these achievements first rested upon the goodness of God; and then, on the work of his father, King David.

David spent his life fighting the enemies of Israel. He had blood on his hands, and lots of it. And though he had it on his heart to "build a house for the Name of the Lord"(1 Chron 22:7), the very work God did through David's hands to bring peace to Israel made David unfit for the Temple building project (1 Chron 22:8). The political peace Solomon enjoyed was earned by the work of God through David.

Likewise, it was also David's preparatory work that made the building process possible for Solomon. David had "taken great pains to provide for the Temple of the Lord..."(1 Chron 22:14). He had collected workers and craftsman and even brought the Ark of the Lord back to Jerusalem. David gave Solomon "the plans of all that the Spirit had put in his mind for the courts of the Temple" and "gave him instructions for the divisions of the priests and Levites, and for all the work of serving in the Temple of the Lord..."(1 Chron 28:12-13). God's work through David made Solomon's work possible.

Who do you need to thank today for their contributions to your life? Whose wisdom, painful preparations, or loving care, administered through God's grace and providential planning, have enabled you to be who you are today? On whose backs do your achievements stand?

Thank God for what He has done and continues to do in you. Thank Him for all those people, great and small, near and far, who have helped you do the work God has called you to do.

July 31

Training in Godliness

1 Timothy 4:7-8—...train yourself to be godly. For physical training is of some value but godliness has value for all things....

The Apostle Paul calls us to train ourselves to be godly. But is godliness something we can train for? None of us are born godly. David says, "Surely I was sinful from birth..."(Ps 51:5). Similarly, we do not naturally mature into godly men and women—"For I know my transgressions, and my sin is always before me"(Ps 51:3). So can we train ourselves to become more like Christ? If so, how?

The answer is twofold: First, we rest in the grace of Jesus. This side of the grave, we will never be the "perfect" Christ calls us to (Matt 5:48). But one day we shall be raised to perfection: "For by one sacrifice He has made *perfect* forever those who are being made holy"(Heb 10:14).

Second, we recognize that we must be *made holy*. No Olympian has reached the Games without a life of sacrifice, discipline, and persistent training. Neither will the disciple reach the finish line without a disciplined life committed to God's training. God will not do this for us—we must do it. We must decide to be spiritual athletes!

As athletes, we "run with perseverance the race marked out for us"; but to do so, we must "throw off everything that hinders..."(Heb 12:1). From his own efforts to throw off all hindrances, Saint Ignatius created *The Spiritual Exercises.* He says of them, "For just as...walking and running are exercises for the body, so 'spiritual exercises' is the name given to every way of preparing and disposing one's soul to rid herself of all disordered attachments, so that one might seek and find the divine will...."[169] Ignatius did his spiritual exercises. Are you doing yours?

God, our spiritual trainer, has called us to a rigorous exercise program. We are told to pray continually, meditate on Scripture all day long, meet together in Christian community, and love one another (1 Thes 5:17; Ps 119:97; Heb 10:25; John 13:34). Are you making these disciplines part of your routine? If so, you are ready to "Run in such a way as to get the prize"(1 Cor 9:24). If not, make a spiritual "training schedule" and stick to it.

Whether training the body or the soul, it is exhausting work. But don't grow weary, for your fitness is not in vain (Gal 6:9). In the sweat and grit of your every day exercises, you will increasingly find that your prize is already within you—"Christ in you, the hope of glory"(Col 1:27).

---

[169] Saint Ignatius of Loyola, *The Spiritual Exercises* in *Saint Ignatius of Loyola: Personal Writings* (London: Penguin Books, 1996), 283.

AUGUST

Whip or Winsome

1 Corinthians 4:21—What do you prefer? Shall I come to you with a whip, or in love and with a gentle spirit?

To a great degree, we determine for ourselves the manner in which God comes to us. Will it be *with a whip, or in love and with a gentle spirit?* When I decide to become more like Christ, "gentle and humble in heart"(Matt 11:29), God is pleased to come to me in kind—gently and in love. As my Father, His love desires my best and has no pleasure in watching me suffer or bringing me down to size. If He did, He would not be loving me as a father should. For if we, "though [we] are evil, know how to give good gifts to [our] children, how much more will our Father in heaven give good gifts"(Matt 7:11) to the children He loves?

But when I assume a proud and defiant stance against God, on any topic, at any time, I take on the heart of Satan, and God is left with little choice but to send the "whip" against me. Because this arrogance sets itself up against God and challenges the very essence of who He is, it cannot be tolerated. When our children demonstrate a willful defiance that bucks our authority, they threaten to undermine our roles as parents and adults. We meet such resistance with discipline, and understand this as an act of love. Why should we expect the Lord of the universe to be held to any lesser standard when it comes to our eternal lives?

If God is sending the "spiritual whip" into my life, it may very well be that I have forgotten how to be a humble and obedient child in His arms. I may have traded the winning and winsome spirit of the child for a willful and defiant one that challenges my Father's providential love in my life. In this arrogance, God may choose to spiritually upbraid me, even "destroy" me as He did the Israelites, time and time again, "because the Lord disciplines the one He loves, and He chastens everyone He accepts as His son"(Heb 12:6).

But how much better to be the child who does not need chastisement—the daughter or son who knows their Father's will and delights in doing it rather than thinking they are in charge. Jesus was never confused on this point. He was, and is, God, but knew He was the Son and not the Father. Because Christ prays, "not my will, but yours be done"(Luke 22:42), His Father says, "This is my Son, whom I love; with Him I am well pleased"(Matt 3:17).

What do you prefer? How shall God come to you? If you desire a gentleness and love from God rather than the scourge of the whip, then you will need *more of Jesus and less of you.*

Everything He Desires

Acts 13:22—I have found David son of Jesse a man after my own heart; he will do everything I want him to do.

Do you ever reflect on your life and wonder if it is what God intended? Perhaps a series of poor choices has led you astray and caused you to question your life's place or worth in the purposes of God. When you find yourself in these moments of painful introspection, remember the life of King David.

David was chosen by God as a man after the Lord's heart. His life was marked by the favor of God's protection in countless battles. His intimacy of relationship with the Lord produced some of the world's most beloved spiritual poetry. But this same man's life was filled with terrible sin and heinous crimes: the murder of Uriah, adultery with Bathsheba, and a son, named Absalom, who murders his brother Amnon and publicly fornicates with David's own concubines after usurping David's throne (2 Sam 16). While David was praised by many, he was cursed by others, like Shimei: "'Get out, get out, you murderer, you scoundrel!'"(2 Sam 16:7). Through it all, however, David appears to have understood what many of us fail to: "The Lord will fulfill His purpose for me"(Ps 138:8 ESV).

Are you confident today that your life, composed as David's was of shining moments and shameful ones, will fulfill the purposes of God? If your heart is seeking after God, your life will accomplish *everything He desires*. This does not mean that you will live flawlessly; it does not imply that your way will be without detour, obstacle or persecution. You may fail miserably and sin shamefully just as David did. You may spend years of your life in a lonely place, misunderstood and mistreated like Joseph in the land of Egypt. But if you seek after God, He will fulfill His purpose for you. All that you live through will be used by God for His glory, even your worst moments—perhaps especially those moments.

We should not doubt that God's purposes will be fulfilled in us and through us. Rather, we should pray that the Spirit blesses us with an understanding and appreciation of just how wonderfully our lives fit into His providential plans. We may then be equipped, as David was, to be a man or woman with *a heart after God*.

August 3

The Uncommon Common

1 Corinthians 10:13—No temptation has seized you except what is common to man.

Sometimes temptation comes so subtly into our lives that we are, at first, unaware of its presence. At other times, however, it seems quite obvious; and we find ourselves overwhelmed by its immensity. We are simultaneously compelled by its enticements and, yet, somehow frightened by how well it appears to know us. Indeed, the tempter knows each one of us (perhaps better than we know ourselves). As a result, our temptation(s) will have a personal twist. But its underlying power is not unique: *no temptation has seized you except what is common to man.*

Satan would have us think the exact opposite. One of his best tactics is to convince us that we are all alone in our temptation. He wants us to forget that the uncommon is, in fact, common. Satan would have us think that our temptation is so personal, no one would understand it. This creates a vulnerable isolation. And if Satan can convince us of the singularity of our temptation and persuade us that we are without an escape, then we are much more likely to succumb to the temptation.

In reality, however, this isolated thinking is entirely perceptual. Satan does observe our "temperament and constitution: he lays suitable baits of temptation. Like a farmer, he knows what grain is best for the soil."[170] But, while our temptation will have these specific details pertaining to our individual lives, it is not otherwise unusual. It is not something "new under the sun"(Ecc 1:9).

When I remember that others may have been tempted similarly, then I open the door for them to be a source of encouragement and assistance to me in my time of temptation. In this way, "Temptations work for the good, as God makes those who are tempted, fit to comfort others in the same distress."[171] Most importantly, I must never forget that no temptation is greater than the God who made me and loves me.

Never allow the enemy to convince you that your temptation is so singular and so overwhelming that you are without a way out—that you *must* acquiesce. This is a dangerous lie. You always have the choice to follow the light out of the darkness, for "God is faithful; He will not let you be tempted beyond what you can bear. But when you are tempted, He will provide a way out so that you can stand up under it"(1 Cor 10:13). Fix your eyes on Christ and, though temptations will come, you will never be overcome by them.

---

[170] Thomas Watson, *All Things for Good* (Shawnee: Gideon House Books, 2015), 26.
[171] Ibid, 29.

August 4

The Plainclothes Priest

Revelation 1:5-6—...Jesus Christ....has made us to be...priests to serve His God and Father....

Do you realize that you are part of a priesthood? You may not be dressed in a robe, offering animal sacrifices or living in a monastery. But if Jesus is your Lord, you are a *plainclothes priest*. We are part of a "holy priesthood, offering spiritual sacrifices acceptable to God through Jesus Christ"(1 Peter 2:5).

In this priesthood, Christ's work on the cross has blessed us with direct access to God. The power of His death shook the earth and tore the Temple curtain in two (Matt 27:51). In this rending of fabric, the exclusive barrier to the Father was abolished. Have you considered the enormity of this act? What once was restricted as the "Most Holy Place behind the curtain"(Lev 16:2), is now freely open to us. And yet, in our busy lives, we rarely choose to enter His presence. Why?

Is this because we recognize there are duties and responsibilities in the priesthood? While we might see these as a burden, when God gave them to the Levites, He saw them as a gift (Num 18:7). These duties gave the Levites holy purpose and proximity to God. Through Christ, this gift is now ours. Do you see service to God as a gift?

Among our duties is the opportunity to care for God's temple, both in our physical bodies as well as in the body of Christ's Church (1 Cor 6:19; 1 Cor 12:27). Are you caring for His temple—your body and soul? We have further been called to live holy lives, "For God has not called us to be impure, but to live a holy life"(1 Thes 4:7). Have you committed to a purity of conduct and thinking washed by the blood of Jesus?

Beyond the call for holiness, the priests were also called to make regular sacrifices. Likewise, as priests we are called to worship the Lord and offer our lives as "living sacrifices"(Rom 12:1). Further, we are encouraged to offer the sacrifice of intercessory prayer on behalf of others —"And pray in the Spirit on all occasions with all kinds of prayers and requests....and always keep on praying for all the saints"(Eph 6:18).

If you are a follower of Christ, you are a *plainclothes priest*, set apart and devoted to God (Ps 4:3). You have been chosen to serve Him in an intimate holiness. In this privileged proximity, you must live differently! You must be a living sacrifice, committed to the service of your Lord.

August 5

Delight

Psalm 37:4—Delight yourself in the Lord and He will give you the desires of your heart.

> There are great *delights* hidden in the uneventful, still and placid stream of life....[172]
>
> —Ivan Turgenev

When I *delight* in someone or certain things, I pleasure in them. I know a full-bodied, deep-seated enjoyment in them. As I think about them, I smile; on the heels of my experience, I yearn for it again. *Delight* is the gift God gives to us to remind us of His extravagant love for us. And the tasting of this *delight* was designed to draw our hearts toward Him.

The unfortunate reality is, however, that the *delight* God places in our lives is often so good, so intoxicating, that the sin within us causes us to crave the *delight* itself rather than the One who gives it. We desire to have the *delight* repeatedly: "This itch to have things over and over again, as if life were a film that could be unrolled twice or even made to play backwards...was it possibly the root of all evil?"[173] Can something God created so good be twisted into something so terribly destructive and wrong? Is it possible that the very gift God gave us to focus our eyes on Him is being misused by us to draw our hearts away?

If I find myself wondering why God appears not to be giving me the desires of my heart, it may very well be that I have decided to *delight* in His *gifts* rather than *delight* in the Lord Himself. God is no fool, though I sometimes make Him out to be one. He knows full well when He is the object of my deepest love and fullest affections. When I take for granted the extravagant gifts He has placed in my life, I have redirected my desire from the Giver to the gift. Such diversion effectively ensures that I will never receive what I desire; or, if I do, that it will become a curse.

When I choose to *delight* in the Lord, however, irrespective of the presence or absence of the sweetness that He so often brings into my life, I begin to see my desires fulfilled. I begin to understand that the true desire of my heart is actually Christ Himself. And as I choose to *delight* in Jesus, everything else I once thought important, suddenly pales in comparison. Now, the desire my heart has always longed for is the very object of my *delight*—Jesus Christ. Is Jesus your *delight*?

---

[172] Ivan Turgenev, "Spring Torrents" in *First Love and Other Stories* (London: Everyman's Library, 1994),108.

[173] C.S. Lewis, *Perelandra* in *The Space Trilogy* (London: HarperCollins, 2013),187.

Changed

Daniel 8:27—I, Daniel, was exhausted and lay ill for several days.

Because God is who He is—immortal, invincible, omnipotent—there is an unfathomable distance between God and man. When God decides to bridge that gap and come close, we should not expect to leave our meeting with Him unchanged. What this transformation looks like depends entirely upon how God intends to manifest His glory in us.

Daniel was a man *changed* by his meetings with God. He loved the Lord and obeyed Him without wavering. But despite Daniel's intimacy with the Lord and familiarity with His power, he felt physically exhausted after the vision of the ram and goat. He is so affected by what God has shown him, so "appalled" by what was "beyond understanding"(Dan 8:27), that Daniel is emotionally and physically overwhelmed for several days. He cannot get up and go about his business for the king.

While Daniel's encounter with God left him momentarily "paralyzed," God's meeting with the prophet Elijah reveals the opposite way God may transform us—by strengthening us. When Elijah is visited by God's messenger in the shade of a tree, the angel tells Elijah to eat and drink in preparation for a journey. Strengthened by God, Elijah travels forty days and nights to Mount Horeb (1 Kings 19:8). Daniel's encounter with God drained him; Elijah's meeting with God empowered him.

Moses' life exhibits another response to encounters with God. After meeting the Lord on the mountain, Moses "was radiant," aglow with the glory of God (Ex 34:30). Conversely, Saul, the persecutor of the early Church, meets Jesus on the road to Damascus and is blinded by this same radiance of God (Acts 9). On the island of Patmos, the Apostle John, upon seeing Jesus, "fell at His feet as though dead"(Rev 1:17).

Have you encountered God in a way that has left you *changed*—emotionally, spiritually, perhaps even physically? If God has created you with a sensitive heart, your response may look something like Daniel's divine "illness." Like Elijah, God may strengthen you for a great journey. You may glow with His radiance or fall down before His power. But whatever your response, it is part of God's plan, not only for your transformation, taking you from Saul to Paul but, more importantly, for His glory and the spread of His gospel.

Do not be surprised, therefore, that you emerge *changed* every time you encounter the Spirit of God. Whether that leaves you with the limp of Jacob (Gen 32:31) or strengthens you for the race of a lifetime, depends on God's purposes for your life. Pray to understand what it is the Lord has for you.

August 7

Preparing a Way

Titus 1:5—...that you might straighten out what was left unfinished....

Some of the most beautiful roads are those that traverse the mountains. When we drive them, we are often so captivated by the surrounding scenery that we give little thought to how difficult those roads must have been to construct. Do we pause to consider the sweat and tears of the laborers who were given the job of making "the rough ways smooth"(Luke 3:5)?

If you are a disciple of Christ traveling on a rough, unfinished road, perhaps doing the business of "roadwork" or even finishing the work others have started, don't be surprised. God often uses His people to finish the unfinished business of the heart and to prepare a way for others to come to Him on the mountain tops. Titus was one of those men who was called to *straighten out what was left unfinished.* He was called to make passable the impassible road, that others might find their way to Jesus. John the Baptist was another road worker whose entire life was to "'Prepare the way for the Lord'" and to "'make straight paths for Him,'" bringing the mountains low and ensuring that "The crooked roads shall become straight..."(Luke 3:5).

The work of road building for the Kingdom is backbreaking and dangerous. It may cost your life, as it did for John the Baptist; it will certainly exhaust you and, at times, leave you frustrated and discouraged. But as you prepare the way of the Lord, "lean not on your own understanding"(Prov 3:5). Rather, "in all your ways acknowledge Him, and He will make your paths straight"(Prov 3:6). God will prepare the way for you. Like the Lord's servant Cyrus, the emperor of Persia, the Lord will say, "I will go before you and will level the mountains..."(Is 45:2). Your job is to show up and allow the Lord to do His divine work through you.

God is the One who will work in and through you to "'make straight in the wilderness a highway for our God'"(Is 40:3). When you are tired in your work, rest in Him (Matt 11:28). When you are discouraged, lift up your eyes and be refreshed with the knowledge that "His compassions never fail; they are new every morning"(Lam 3:22-23). When you are disillusioned, remember that the road you are working on prepares God's way for the glorious day when "the glory of the Lord will be revealed, and all mankind together will see it"(Is 40:5). In the words of the gospel song, sing: "Oh happy day, Oh happy day!"

Picking Your Battles

Matthew 17:26-27—"...the sons are exempt," Jesus said to him. "But so that you may not offend them...."

> ...knowing when to fight and when not to, brings victory....[174]
> —Sun Tzu

When Jesus was approached by the collectors of the Temple tax, He asks Peter: "What do you think Simon?...From whom do the kings of the earth collect duty and taxes—from their own sons or from others?"(Matt 17:25). Rather than claim an exemption because of His divine Sonship or chastise the tax collectors for the audacity that demands God pay a tax on His own house like a common man, Jesus chooses to pay. He elects not to offend. He decides that this is not a battle worth fighting.

Too many of us dissipate our life energies and injure the Kingdom's work fighting battles that have no eternal significance. Instead of humbly choosing deference over the "drachma taxes" of our lives, we bristle, snarl, and protest at every turn. We behave as if we are sons and daughters above the denigration of such banalities.

And yet Jesus, the only legitimate Son, shows us time and again, how to stoop down. There is nothing too small for Him—washing feet or paying taxes. He places His rights as the Son of God aside, and chooses, in this instance of taxation, not to offend. Jesus knows the tax, in and of itself, is a triviality—a coin worthy to come out of the mouth of a fish. He also knows it is not His time to fully reveal and glorify Himself in the eyes of men. Since timing is everything, He humbles Himself, "taking the very nature of a servant..."(Phil 2:7). He pays the tax.

The next time you find yourself offended over an issue of no eternal significance, will you respond in kind? When you are asked, as Jesus was, to give what you do not owe or do what you need not do, will you demur? Or will you recognize the petty skirmish for what it is and decide not to offend? Will you choose instead to fix your eyes on the greater war for Christ's Kingdom? For who knows, in "paying your tax," you may be opening the door to God's work in another life.

When we fight battles that have no eternal significance, we become a stumbling block to the work of Jesus in the lives of others. More often than not, the minor skirmishes push others away, while the winsome humility of Jesus draws them near. The seasoned saint has learned when to "pay the tax" and when to stand and fight. *Pick your battles* wisely!

---

[174] Sun Tzu, *The Art of War* (New York: Chartwell Books, 2012), 21.

August 9

Because

Leviticus 20:26—You are to be holy to me because I, the Lord, am holy, and I have set you apart...to be my own.

When confronted with the need for obedience, our children are notorious for asking, "Why?" It seems very clear to them why they should do what they want to do. But it makes little sense, and is frankly irritating, that someone else should say, "No," and demand something else entirely. "But why?" the child says. "*Because....*"

Is it really any different in our spiritual lives? Have we not cried out to our Father and asked: "Why must I do this? What is the point? It makes no sense"? And the Lord replies, "*because* I, the Lord, am holy, and I have set you apart...." We may not understand now why we must obey in some particular thing. But we will later. And even if we do not, it is irrelevant, *because* God is God and we are not. We are not in a position to bargain or demand justification any more than our petulant children. We are to be holy because He is holy. It is as simple as that.

But though the command is simple, holiness is costly, both to God and us. It cost the blood of Jesus to bridge the gap and make the impossible, possible—"we have been made holy through the sacrifice of the body of Jesus Christ once for all"(Heb 10:10). Justified by His blood, we can stand in the presence of our Father. But let us not pass a single day in the illusion that holiness will then require nothing of us. It will cost a great deal: perhaps personal pleasure, the freedom to do what we want when we want, or the control of our bodies or finances. We are "being made holy"(Heb 10:14), day by day, through the sanctifying work of God. And this will happen one costly decision at a time.

On any given day, we might come up with innumerable excuses for why we don't want to obey in some area of our lives. But God is a Father who does not care for our excuses. He loves us enough to know they are an impediment to our ultimate perfection.

God knows your circumstances, has designed your strengths, and allowed your weaknesses. You are His creation, and He knows you inside and out. When you are tempted to say, "Why should I obey in this?" remember God's great, *Because!* You must decide to be holy *because* our Father is holy. Christ tore down the curtain, but we must walk through. We must make the daily choices. We must remember: "Every man is as holy as he really wants to be. But the want must be all-compelling."[175] Be holy *because* your God is holy.

---

[175] A.W. Tozer, *Man, The Dwelling Place of God* (Public Domain), 105.

Worthless or Priceless?

2 Kings 17:15—They followed worthless idols and themselves became worthless.

In the "financial" valuation of the soul, three possible realities loom: increasing net worth, persistent devaluation, or stagnation. The direction this spiritual value takes in our lives depends entirely upon our choices. Will we decide to become increasingly *worthless or priceless*?

When Israel decided to reject God's decrees and the covenant He made with their forefathers, they *followed worthless idols and themselves became worthless*. They took the inestimable value they had as God's chosen people and threw it away, prostituting their spiritual lives on worthless idols that had no power to save them. As a result, they themselves became as worthless and powerless as the idols they chose to serve. They were destroyed, exiled, and replaced.

Like the Israelites, we too become what we allow ourselves to become. When we eat poorly and choose not to exercise, we grow heavy and become sickly. When we surround ourselves with men and women of questionable moral character, we too become corrupt.

So the question is: do you wish your spiritual life to grow in value? Is it your desire for your "life account" to be of greater value tomorrow than it is today? Do you long to hear God say to you, "you are precious and honored in my sight, and…I love you…"(Is 43:4)? If so, then you must invest wisely. You must follow hard after God, "forsaking all others." When you determine that your treasure is in heaven, you will move toward it, day by day, growing in grace, and storing up value in the only place where "moth and rust do not destroy, and where thieves do not break in and steal"(Matt 6:20). Instead of working your whole life for a "treasure" of no eternal value, choose the priceless "inheritance that can never perish, spoil or fade…"(1 Peter 1:4).

Worthless or priceless, never forget that the valuation of your life is for eternity, not just the here and now. It is the long game that matters. Everything you do in the present comes at a cost—a penny in or out of your eternal account.

If you decide to follow Jesus, your eternal value grows day by day.

August 11

Unchained

2 Timothy 2:9—But God's Word is not chained.

Thousands of years have been incapable of chaining the Word of God. Despite raging emperors, despotic kings, religious sects and hedonistic, pluralistic societies, the Word of God remains unshackled, alive and well. It is *unchained,* and it is always working. God has said, "my Word that goes out from my mouth: It will not return to me empty, but will accomplish what I desire and achieve the purpose for which I sent it"(Is 55:11). And why can't God's Word be chained? Why hasn't history repressed it? Because His Word is Jesus Christ, the conquering King.

Though "Heaven and earth will pass away," His "words will never pass away," because Christ is the Word (Matt 24:35; John 1:1). When we come into relationship with the Word through Christ's saving grace, we find that we too cannot be chained. We may find our physical bodies shackled by disease or political persecution and our lives, like the Apostle Paul, "suffering even to the point to being chained like a criminal"(2 Tim 2:9). But in Christ, our spirits remain free! Nothing can shackle them. For Christ came to "proclaim freedom for the prisoners and...to set the oppressed free..."(Luke 4:18). When your spiritual chains are unlocked and the Word dwells richly in you (Col 3:16), then you will know the truth of Christ's words—"So if the Son sets you free, you will be free indeed"(John 8:36).

How will you know that your spirit is unchained? You will know when the Word within you cries out with indomitable strength, "In God, whose Word I praise, in God I trust; I will not be afraid. What can mortal man do to me?"(Ps 56:4). Though you may be thrown in prison, "in chains for Christ," the Word within you will not only survive, but you will preach it (Phil 1:13,18). The Spirit will make it plain to you that chains only have power over those who have rebelled against God. The angels who abandoned their heavenly home and those souls who have determined to walk away from God shall be "bound in everlasting chains..."(Jude 1:6). The dragon himself will be chained by the "angel coming down from heaven..."(Rev 20:1). But for the disciple of Christ, chains are meaningless. We are free in Christ!

Thank God today that the unfettered Word of God is "living and active"(Heb 4:12). It has freed you to live in His power and do mighty things for His glory!

August 12

Loving Through to Trust

Psalm 52:8—I trust in God's unfailing love for ever and ever.

Where love is at its purest, it engenders trust. King David was called "a man after God's own heart…"(1 Sam 13:14). He loved the Lord. For this reason, the Psalms are littered with declarations of trust in God —"I trust in your unfailing love…"(Ps 13:5). Later David says, "But I trust in you, Lord; I say, 'You are my God'"(Ps 31:14). And, "When I am afraid, I put my trust in you"(Ps 56:3).

Where have I placed my trust? Do I rely on my finances, the strength of my spouse's love, my physical health, or my position of influence in the world? Or, like David, though a king in this world, do I love God to the point of absolute trust like a child in the arms of the Father?

Jeremiah says, "Cursed is the one who trusts in man, who depends on flesh for his strength, and whose heart turns away from the Lord"(Jer 17:5). King Solomon declared: "Whoever trusts in his riches will fall," and the one "who trusts in himself is a fool"(Prov 11:28; 28:26). Have you put your trust in power or position? Then you are like those who "trust in chariots and…horses….They are brought to their knees and fall"(Ps 20:7-8).

The strength of what you trust in will be revealed when you are thrown into fire or a den of lions. When "Daniel was lifted from the den, no wound was found on him because he trusted in the Lord"(Dan 6:23). The one who trusts in the Lord will find deliverance and blessing —"blessed is the one who trusts in you"(Ps 84:12).

As you trust in the Lord, do not worry when you fail to understand the way He takes you or the methods He uses in your life. Rather, "Trust in the Lord with all your heart and lean not on your own understanding; in all your ways submit to Him, and He will make your paths straight"(Prov 3:5-6). When you place your trust completely in Jesus, the "God of hope [will] fill you with all joy and peace as you trust in Him…"(Rom 15:13).

Are you feeling too broken in spirit and exhausted to reach out to trust? God knows. He will come to you as you look to Him. But perhaps you are not filled with God's joy and peace because you have chosen not to love Jesus completely. Are you holding on to some piece of yourself? If so, leave it at the altar. Choose the seemingly reckless and abandoned love of Jesus that engenders absolute trust. "Choose this day whom you will serve…"(Josh 24:15) Choose this day whom you will love. Choose this day to *love Jesus through to absolute trust.*

August 13

I, I, I

Galatians 2:20—I have been crucified with Christ and I no longer live, but Christ lives in me.

> The victorious Christian neither exalts himself nor downgrades himself. His interests have shifted from self to Christ. What he is or is not no longer concerns him.[176]
> —A.W. Tozer

The true disciple of Christ understands: "There are only two ways possible of encountering Jesus: man must die or he must put Jesus to death."[177] I cannot live for myself and, at the same time, claim that Christ lives in me. Either, "The life I live in the body, I live by faith in the Son of God…"(Gal 2:20), or I am merely a deluded hypocrite claiming to be something I am not. Have you been crucified with Christ? The life you live, is it Christ living in you?

One of the surest signs that Christ lives in me is the absence of "me" in all I do, say and think. Some Christians interpret this to mean that their lives must be full of a giving of themselves to others. While there is some truth to this, the problem is the propensity to think, "Look how selfless I am! I give of myself all the time." Good works can flow from a "good" heart, but they can also be a source of pride—an identity to hide behind.

The person who bases his or her Christian identity upon selfless living is like Camus' Clamence, the self-impressed and deluded lawyer who helps a blind man across the street and then tips his hat to him. But to whom is he tipping his hat? To the blind man who can't see him? Or to the crowd of observers and, ultimately, to himself? [178] Where is Christ in this "selfless" act?

When I am still living for myself, if I have any self-awareness at all, I will, like Clamence, "have to admit it humbly…I was always bursting with vanity. I, I, I is the refrain of my whole life, which could be heard in everything I said."[179] Is your life repeating, "I, I, I," or is it "Christ, Christ, Christ"? When I have been crucified with Christ, "I" no longer live, but Christ in me. So long as I am tipping my hat to the world, I have not died to myself. Let the refrain of your life be, *"More of Him and less of me."*

---

[176] A.W. Tozer, *Man, The Dwelling Place of God* (Public Domain), 131.
[177] Dietrich Bonhoeffer, *Christ the Center* (New York: HarperCollins, 1978), 35.
[178] Albert Camus, *The Fall* (New York: Vintage International, 1991), 47.
[179] Ibid, 48.

August 14

In the Book

Esther 2:23—All this was recorded in the book of the annals in the presence of the king.

Into the life of every disciple come moments when it appears that faithfulness goes unrecognized or unnoticed. Such was the case with Mordecai. Having become aware of a plot by two officials against King Xerxes, Mordecai informed Queen Esther. Later, "when the report was investigated and found to be true, the two officials were hanged on a gallows"(Esther 2:23). While Esther gives credit to Mordecai for discovering the plot, his faithfulness to the king is not recognized—at least, not yet. It was, however, *recorded in the book.*

As you serve the Lord, never permit yourself the illusion that your faithfulness goes unnoticed or will not, in God's perfect time, be recognized for what it is. If it has not been recognized yet, it may be that God is waiting for His purposes to unfold before He will honor you. Mordecai was not recognized until King Xerxes had a sleepless night and ordered the "book of the chronicles, the record of his reign, to be brought in and read to him"(Esther 6:1). In this reading, the faithfulness of Mordecai was revealed, and God honored him. Simultaneously, Mordecai's enemy, Haman, was humiliated and God's providential power over and through His people was declared: "you cannot stand against him [Mordecai]…"(Esther 6:13).

Perhaps your recognition won't come as quickly as Mordecai's. Perhaps, in God's wisdom, your faithfulness will only truly be recognized when you stand before Him in glory. But it will be recognized! Everything is *recorded in the book* and will be evaluated in God's time. For as John says, "I saw the dead, great and small, standing before the throne, and books were opened. Another book was opened, which is the book of life. The dead were judged according to what they had done as recorded in the books"(Rev 20:12).

What is being recorded about you *in the book* of life? Good or bad, it will be read in the presence of the King. Whether or not you are placed on His horse, covered in one of His robes and honored as a faithful servant, depends entirely upon what you do this very day.

Persist in faithfulness even when it appears to go unrecognized, knowing that everything is recorded *in the book.* The King reads every page and will honor your service to Him!

August 15

Testing

Psalm 66:10—For you, O God, tested us....

We should never for one moment imagine a God who does not at times test us. While we have little difficulty accepting the idea of a loving and merciful Father, when it comes to a God who allows His people to be thrown in prison, captured by enemy armies, or victimized by droughts or famine, we bristle. We snarl at a God who permits illness, broken relationships, or financial stress to enter our lives. But why? Must love and mercy exclude unthinkable pain? Is it possible that the very tests our lives endure are the evidence that we are loved?

This reality is resoundingly clear in the history of the nation of Israel. God led them through the desert for forty years "to humble...and to test [them] in order to know what was in [their] heart..."(Deut 8:2). The Psalmist says, "you refined us like silver. You brought us into prison and laid burdens on our backs. You had men ride over our heads; we went through fire and water..."(Ps 66:10-12). In short, God scourged the nation of Israel because He loved them.

Is your life being tested right now? Maybe you have enemies at work that are actively attacking you and your integrity. Perhaps you have just lost someone very dear to you. Whatever it is, do not allow the lie to enter your heart that God does not care. The trial you are facing today is happening under the direct supervision of your Father.

In the midst of the fire, it is understandable to question God's ways: David did. Even Jesus questioned on the eve of His crucifixion. But don't doubt God's love for you. Rather, like the Apostles leaving the Sanhedrin, dare to rejoice because you have been "counted worthy of suffering...for the Name"(Act 5:41). Know that in your testing the "Lord disciplines the one He loves, and He chastens everyone He accepts as His son"(Heb 12:6). We accept discipline from our mentors and coaches. Why should we expect anything different from our God? When we have stood the test, however, we will find that the Lord brings us to "a place of abundance"(Ps 66:12).

If you are a disciple of Christ, you can be certain that the Lord will allow tests to come into your life. They may be pain or excessive comfort. Whatever comes, however, never forget that only a God who did not love you would fail to refine you. Your test is evidence that you are loved.

247

August 16

Carpe Diem

2 Chronicles 29:36—Hezekiah and all the people rejoiced at what God had brought about for his people, because it was done so quickly.

Seize on to-day—nor trust the uncertain morrow....[180]

—Horace

Much of God's work in our lives involves periods of seemingly interminable waiting. In many ways, this waiting is the greatest of gifts, as it brings us closer to God Himself. But every now and then, God decides to surprise us with His spontaneity. And where we might be anticipating a long wait, He brings His purposes around more quickly than we imagined.

Hezekiah and the people of Israel experienced this spontaneity of God when they decided to reinstitute the Lord's services in the Temple (2 Chron 29:35). The speed with which the reconstructive work was accomplished surprised and delighted the people who *rejoiced at what God had brought about...so quickly.*

Have you ever been absolutely amazed at how quickly and easily things fell together in some category of your life? Perhaps you have prayed for years concerning a spouse and found nothing but frustrated efforts. Then, as if out of the blue, God brings him or her along, and in a veritable moment, the pieces fall together. Maybe your career has centered for years on a specific project, the culmination of which has eluded you. And then, it happens—the breakthrough you've been waiting for. It happens *so quickly* you can hardly believe it. Sometimes God brings the missing link much faster than we ever dreamed possible.

When it comes to our spiritual lives, we must be patient, willing and ready to wait upon God. Waiting is one of God's greatest teachers. But at the same time, we must also be prepared for the *carpe diem* spirit of a God who sometimes seizes the moment to surprise us with His spontaneity. And when He does, if we are not prepared, we might miss it altogether or, at least, forgo the pleasure of basking in the moment.

If God brings it all about quickly, be ready to rejoice. May your feet never be so set in the concrete of your expectations that you are not free to run with all that God brings about in the spontaneity of His pleasure. Are you ready to seize the day?

---

[180] Horace, "Ode XI," in *The Odes of Horace* (London: William Pickering, 1843), 22.

248

The Unforgivable

Mark 3:29—But whoever blasphemes against the Holy Spirit will never be forgiven; he is guilty of an eternal sin.

As disciples of Christ, our confidence is that "all sins and blasphemes will be forgiven"(Mark 3:28) save one: blaspheming against the Holy Spirit. Though the blood of Jesus can heal every wound, right every wrong against God and forgive every errant action or word, it will not remove the sin of blaspheming against the Spirit. Christ says this sin is an unpardonable one, the "sin that leads to death"(1 John 5:16).

If I find myself wondering if I have been guilty of this unpardonable sin, I can be sure, that in the very act of asking the question, I demonstrate that I am not. For such self-inspection exposes the sensitivity of the Spirit within us, the moral conscience of the heavenly realms that dwell in us. Those who are guilty of the eternal sin do not ask this question. Rather, they live in open defiance of God's love and truth. They make a clear and conscious rejection of God and persistently and willfully speak and live against God's truths. They abjure the spiritual conscience as infantile and impotent, and choose instead to exalt self-evaluation. Not once, but repeatedly, they decide that they do not need God. In their defiance, they blaspheme "the Lord, and…must be cut off from [their] people"(Num 15:30). Their "guilt remains"(Num 15:31).

When we come across such a man or woman, we should *not* pray for them (1 John 5:16). Like a rotting carcass, we must recognize the stench of spiritual death and steer clear, saving our prayers of intercession and our spiritual stamina for those whose sin does not lead to irredeemable death.

We must learn to recognize the face of Satan in the life of the man or woman who blasphemes against the Spirit, and then walk away. We must never permit our sense of spiritual heroics to draw us into their lives. They are, in a spiritual sense, a lost cause. Only God is capable of dealing with their eternal sin and your efforts to redeem them, however well-intentioned or noble in sentiment, may lead to disastrous consequences in your own spiritual life.

Let blaspheming against the Holy Spirit be your single "Stop" sign in your intercessory efforts in the lives of others. Pray for others unceasingly, but never for the life marked for eternal death.

August 18

The Love That is Known

1 Corinthians 8:3—But the man who loves God is known by God.

> ...Love is not love
> Which alters when it alteration finds....
> O no! it is an ever-fixed mark....[181]
> —William Shakespeare

Although we may be fooled for a time by dalliance, when we are truly loved for who we are, we know it. In the same way, God knows whether I love Him. He is not fooled by romantic gestures or public overtures of devotion. He sees straight through to the heart. And the heart that loves Him is known by Him.

Do you wish to be known by God, not as an infamous, spiritual rebel, but as a devoted child? If so, you must love the Lord. But how will you know you love Him? How can you be sure that your "love" is real?

To know if I love God, I can examine my heart with Thomas Watson's "tests of love." The Puritan preacher encourages us to ask the following questions: Does my mind muse upon the Lord and who He is? Do I desire to be with Him, spending time getting to know Him better? Does my heart grieve over the sins I have committed against Him or do I rationalize and explain? Is there a warm generosity to my love and a gallantry to my affection? Is my life marked with a sensitivity for God's honor and Kingdom purposes? Do I hate sin or do I tolerate it or even enjoy it in my life? Have I been crucified with Christ and made dead to the world and its enticements? Do I fear the Lord and the prospect of displeasing Him as a child would a parent he loves? Does my heart love what God loves, delighting in what delights Him? Does my mind think well of God, or do I find myself criticizing or complaining about Him? Is my life marked by obedience, knowing that Christ Himself said, "Whoever has my commands and keeps them is the one who loves me"(John 14:21)? Penultimately, is my heart's desire to see God glorified in the presence of others? Finally, do I hunger for the Lord's return and the prospect of being reunited with my Savior?[182]

If you wish to know whether your love for God is true, you need only apply to your heart the tests of love. Does your love for the Lord *admit impediments* or is it an *ever-fixed mark* known by God?

---

[181] William Shakespeare, *Sonnet 116* in in*The Complete Works,* ed. Stanley Wells and Taylor (Oxford: Clarendon Press, 1988), 765.
[182] Thomas Watson, *All Things for Good* (Shawnee: Gideon House Books, 2015), 67-79.

August 19

Living Sacrifices

Romans 12:1—...offer your bodies as living sacrifices, holy and pleasing to God—this is your spiritual act of worship.

Sacrifice is not something that most of us enjoy or look forward to. Whether it is the time and hard work we must put into our careers and the parenting of our children, or the possession we must part with to pay for some necessity, we know very well that sacrifice entails personal cost. While we may understand the value of such a transaction, it often does not make the sacrifice easier. This reality especially applies to the one thing we hold most closely and know the best—our bodies.

The "bodies" ancient Jews sacrificed to the Lord were not their own, but something they still valued highly: livestock, such as lambs, goats, pigeons or oxen. The Jews understood the importance of this act of worship as the gift of something valuable to God. But in the shadow of the work of Christ on the cross, the Apostle Paul calls us to something even more personal. While we are still called to worship the Lord, it is not with a physical death, but a life lived out!

Because Jesus conquered death, the sacrifices of worship must now be living. We are called to give Him our bodies as ongoing examples of His mercy, grace and power. Nothing could be more valuable to us, or more integral to who we are. And that is precisely why Jesus desires them. When we present our bodies, minds and souls as *living sacrifices* to Christ, we surrender the keys to who we are. The "Christian" who has not sacrificed his or her body to the Lord and given it over to God is not a committed disciple of Christ. The "Believer" who still thinks that they can hold on to the body to do with it what they want is deluded. The Spirit of God cannot dwell in them.

Have you decided that your life will be a *living sacrifice* to God? Are you determined to daily worship the Lord through the very body He has given you on loan? To be in Christ is to lay who you are, flesh and soul, mind and heart, on the altar before Him. Have you given your body to God in this way? You will never really be His disciple until you do.

August 20

Identity

2 Samuel 17:23—When Ahithophel saw that his advice had not been followed, he saddled his donkey and set out for his house in his hometown.

What will you do when the very thing you have built your life and reputation upon suddenly comes to an end? Will you, like the king's counselor Ahithophel, be forced to put your house in order and quit on life because what you built your identity on no longer appears to matter?

The way we construct our *identity* has eternal consequences. The reality is that some of us have fatally built entire lives upon a foundation that will not remain. When our company no longer needs us, our children have grown and left the house, our bodies become sickly or our money has disappeared, will the life we have constructed come crashing down? Or will it remain, secure on the foundation of Christ?

A personal *identity* which is built upon anything other than Jesus Christ has the potential to wash away when the rains fall. Jesus says, "the wise man...built his house on the rock. The rain came down, the streams rose...yet it did not fall, because it had its foundation on the rock"(Matt 7:24-25). Have you built your foundation on the Rock? Or have you, like Ahithophel, constructed your *identity* on something more like sand?

It may be that God has given you great talent, the power of influence or even the gift of loving others. But no matter how good your gift is, if you build your sense of worth and *identity* upon it, it will come crashing down. Ahithophel was a gifted advisor of kings— "Now in those days the advice Ahitophel gave was like that of one who inquires of God"(2 Sam 16:23). However, when his advice was not taken, he lost his sense of meaning and went home to die.

In the death of Ahithophel we see the imperative to construct our identities not upon who we are in the world, but upon who we are in the eyes of God. Ahithophel's advice was not bad, but he failed to see God's hand in frustrating that advice for a greater purpose and His glory. Ahithophel teaches us that we must hold loosely to our *identity* in the world and tenaciously to our place as a child of God who understands that his Father loves him and is in control of every detail.

Am I convinced that I belong to Jesus and it is for Him to build me up or tear me down so that His purposes might be fulfilled? Am I confident that no matter what storms come, what winds beat against me, and what waters rise, my *identity* will hold because it is built on the rock of Jesus Christ my Lord?

Be a child of God and hold loosely to every other *identity*.

August 21

Mindset

Romans 8:5—Those who live according to the sinful nature have their minds set on what that nature desires; but those who live in accordance with the Spirit have their minds set on what the Spirit desires.

To what channel is your mind set? Is it fixed on the success of your career? Perhaps it is dialed into the futures of your children, the finances you are juggling or the illicit hobby you hide from the eyes of those you love. But is your mind set upon Christ? Does it desire what the Spirit desires? Is it thinking about what Jesus thinks about?

I will know what my mind is set on by the proportion of time it dominates in my thinking. When I am living *according to the sinful nature,* my mind is set upon anything, or everything, but Christ. It is, however, a subtle deception to believe that the sinful nature must necessarily be composed of the *peccata mortalia,* or "mortal sins"—adultery, fornication, murder, idolatry, and the like. All things that do not honor Jesus, even if not intrinsically sinful, can, through our very focus upon them, become sin in our hearts.

Do you love your children? Then make sure your mind is set upon Christ and His presence in their lives, not simply on their achievements and their happiness. Is it your desire to see your career flourish? Then make sure your mind is set to the Spirit's voice in all that you do at work. Spend time with Christ first, focusing your spirit on God's Spirit within you. When you "set your mind to gain understanding and to humble yourself before your God, your words [will be] heard…"(Dan 10:12). The details of your life will fall into place. Didn't Christ say, "But seek first the Kingdom of God and His righteousness, and all these things will be added to you"(Matt 6:33)?

When my mind is set upon someone or something, then all of me —my will, body, time and energies—will soon follow. If I desire to follow Jesus, I must resolve to have my mind set upon Him and what His Spirit desires. This will not happen apart from a persistent, conscious effort on my part. I must be constantly corralled by the disciplines of faith, encouraged by the support of my fellow believers, and empowered by the grace of God. But as I set my mind upon Christ, my life will be infused with His Spirit and redeemed for His purposes. What once had the potential to lead me astray has now been redeemed by the work of Christ. Is your mind fixed upon Jesus?

August 22

Holding Fast

1 Kings 11:2—Nevertheless, Solomon held fast to them in love.

When we hear the words "holding fast in love" we usually have a positive connotation. We think of a steadfast and faithful love. But this assumes the love is a positive one. What or who we hold fast to makes all the difference. This is particularly true in our relationship with the Lord.

What is it that you are *holding fast* to despite God's clear commands? Is it your money or your reputation? Perhaps it is your gambling or alcohol. Maybe it is your incessant need to please others or simply your delight in good gossip. For Solomon, it was his multitude of foreign lovers.

The Lord clearly commanded the Israelites, "You must not intermarry with them, because they will surely turn your hearts after their gods"(1 Kings 11:2). And yet Solomon, anointed King of Israel and famed pillar of wisdom, allowed himself to become one of the most prodigious polygamists the world has ever known. He had 700 wives and 300 concubines from nations all around the known world. Either he deliberately chose to defy the Lord's command or, in the confused thinking of his day, his moral conscience terribly lost its place, so caught up was he in the pleasure of his sin. Either way, his *holding fast* indicates a willful and purposeful love, an addiction of sorts—sadly, not a love for the Lord.

Have you decided that Christ is first in your life, or are you still secretly *holding fast* to some other loves? Whether our loves have the open panache of Solomon's or are cloaked in subtle stealth like David and Bathsheba, they will, sooner or later, turn our hearts away from God's commands. God has given us His commands to keep our hearts focused on Him. The Lord says to us: "'Either *me*…either you *hold fast* to me unconditionally, in everything, or you—despise me.'"[183] Rather than rebel against these commands and hold fast to other loves, may we see the Lord's commands as love offerings—gifts that help draw us closer to Him.

Pray that the Spirit will empower you to *hold fast* in love to God and God alone, at the cost of all others. When you do, you will reap the bounty of His pleasure instead of setting the stage for the domino effect of downfall that Solomon brought on the nation of Israel.

---

[183] Soren Kierkegaard, *The Lily of the Field and the Bird of the Air* (Princeton: Princeton University Press, 2016), 44.

August 23

Not Just Idle Words

Deuteronomy 32:47—They are not just idle words for you—they are your life.

There was a time when reverence for God's Word had a much more hallowed meaning than it now does. The way in which the Word was physically handled, the austerity with which it was read aloud, and the manner in which it was spoken about carried a holy gravity of honor and worship that is now largely lost. The manuscript itself—beautifully scripted and often illuminated with ornate artwork—was honored as a sacred text with the power to save and destroy.

Does God's Word still have this ancient power in your life? Do you recognize that its passages *are not just idle words for you—they are your life*? The Bible may be on your shelf, but do you read it daily? Do you love it and revere it? Do you stand in awe of it and its power?

The Word of God no longer belongs only to the priests and temples. It is now mine and yours as well. But with this common distribution, a gift beyond measure, must also come the ancient responsibility. We cannot allow the pervasive nonchalance of modernity towards God's Word to affect our hearts and minds. While "Those who live in the modern age no longer believe in anything that is always and everywhere true and valid,"[184] we must daily remember that God's words are *not idle words:* they are the words of truth we are meant to live and die by! When I allow the Bible to collect dust, I treat God's Word with a dangerous indifference. That which we love and value, like life itself, we must consistently interact with and care for. God's Word is "living and active"(Heb 4:12) and must be treated as nothing less in our lives.

We must never forget that Jesus, our Lord, is the Word—"the Word was God"(John 1:1). Christ "moves out of the pages of this Book [Bible] and meets us with the impact of His person on our persons."[185] For this reason, the degree to which we ignore God's Word reflects our lackluster love and casual nonchalance for Christ Himself. We cannot call ourselves disciples of Jesus and not be living in His Word, day by day, moment by moment. We need to soak ourselves in it, reading, memorizing, and meditating on it.

Are you living with reverence for God's Word? Do you recognize that it is literally your life?

---

[184] Henri Nouwen, *The Wounded Healer* (New York: Image Doubleday, 2010), 15.

[185] E. Stanley Jones, *Conversation* in *Devotional Classics,* ed. Richard Foster and Smith (New York: HarperCollins, 2005), 282.

August 24

The Things They Carried

Numbers 4:32—Assign to each man the specific things he is to carry.

In the Exodus from Egypt, the Levites carried the Lord's dwelling place. Each clan had specific things to tote. The Kohathites were assigned the holy articles. To the Gershonites went the task of fabrics—"the curtains of the tabernacle, the Tent of Meeting…"(Num 4:25-26). And to the Merarites the duty of structural things—"the frames of the tabernacle, its crossbars, posts and bases…"(Num 4:31). Together, 8,580 men were assigned to carry and serve the Lord's presence among the people. If the Kohathites did not carry the holy things properly or the Gershonites failed to bring the curtains or the Merarites the frame, God's house would not stand among the people. Each and every one of the things the people carried mattered.

No less today. God's "temple" continues to travel with His people all over the world. Each one of us holds an essential component of His presence. The Lord lives in us through the indwelling of the Spirit. But when we come together as a community of believers on earth, we begin to appreciate the fullness of God's presence on a whole other level. The full "temple" is assembled. We see an even greater, complex and nuanced magnificence than we ever imagined. It is akin to seeing a rainbow in the distance. At first glance, it looks manageable and understandable. But closer examination allows us to see that all that color is composed of uncountable, dancing particles, doing their job of *"carrying their things"*—glorifying God in a magnificent, collective spectrum of color.

What you have been assigned to carry in your life, your piece of God's presence, handle faithfully and carefully, as unto the Lord. Don't give space to the lie that your assignment isn't important. Whether you're raising children to know the Lord, leading a Fortune 500 company, or mopping gymnasium floors, you are carrying some part of God's presence for the people. One role is not more important than the other. All are needed for completion of God's intended purposes. Your life's activities as much as the burdens you carry and the songs you sing, matter to your Lord. Whether you have been assigned a tent peg, curtain, or one of the holy articles, they are all essential for God's presence among the people.

The things you carry matter. Carry the Lord in them, among His people, all the way to the Promised Land. Pray for the grace to be faithful to the task you have been assigned, remembering that what you do, you do unto the Lord (Eph 6:7).

August 25

The Small Things

Zechariah 4:10—Who despises the day of small things?

It is easy to fall into the trap of expecting God to do big things in big ways. We look for Him in the wind, earthquake and the fire, but fail to consider that He might very well prefer the smallest whisper (1 Kings 19:9-12). God does do mighty things, sometimes in unbelievably grandiose ways. He created the universe and put the stars in their place (Ps 8:3). He "created my inmost being, and knit me together in my mother's womb"(Ps 139:13). And yet, when this Lord of Creation moves in my life and in yours, it is, more often than not, in the almost imperceivable and *small things*.

For this reason, we must be careful not to *despise the day of small things*. In these details God is quietly unfolding His plan in our lives. To de*spise the small things* is to reject the God who has chosen to work through them. Though God created the elephant and is capable of shaking the ground with each of his steps, He also created the miniature ant. Though they are small, they are extremely wise creatures that store up their food in summer (Prov 30:24-25). Like the silent industry of these small workers, the work of God continues in your life even when you fail to notice it.

Don't stop praying for great things—for the sick to be healed, for the lame to walk, for your spouse to come back to saving grace. Jesus promises that, as you abide in Him, "the Father will give you whatever you ask in [His] name" (John 15:16). God can, and does, do mighty things to glorify His name on earth.

But at the same time, remember that God's work often manifests itself in the *small things*. The Temple was rebuilt from the cornerstone to the capstone—one stone at a time. Will you, like the men of Israel, "rejoice when [you] see see the plumb line in the hand of Zerubbabel"(Zech 4:10), knowing that the temple of your soul will not be built in a day?

Do you despise the *small things*—those individual stones carried through seemingly endless days of tedious labor? There will be leveling and correcting, days in which stones might have to be replaced or repositioned. There will be days of discouragement and weariness, days of little vision and disillusionment. But the work will continue. Through the *small things* God will build His temple in you as He unfolds His greater Kingdom purposes. It may be that only in retrospect, looking upon the temple He has constructed, that you will truly appreciate the value of each individual stone. Even though you cannot see it now, pray that the Spirit gives you the vision and the courage to rejoice in the *day of small things*.

August 26

From Your Own Number

Acts 20:30-31—Even from your own number men will arise and distort the truth in order to draw away disciples after them. So be on your guard!

If I make the mistake of believing the body of Christ is immune from the wiles of Satan, then I can be sure that this is very place where the attack of the enemy will come to my life. Just because I surround myself with Christians, attend church regularly, and participate in Christian service, does not mean that this very spiritual environment cannot house a wolf in sheep's clothing. It may be the very place that wolf is hiding.

Paul says, *"be on your guard!"* When we become spiritually comfortable in the "church bubble," walled off in a perceptual security, the demons smile and plot how best to corrupt us. C.S. Lewis imagines the discourse amongst them:

> For a long time it will be quite impossible to remove spirituality from his life. Very well then; we must *corrupt* it. No doubt you have often practiced transforming yourself into an angel of light on a parade ground exercise. Now is the time to do it....A spoiled saint, a Pharisee, an inquisitor, or a magician, makes better sport in Hell than a mere common tyrant or debauchee.[186]

While the members of the Church should not live in suspicion of one another and so be a "house....divided against itself"(Mark 3:25), neither are they encouraged to be unwary sheep. We must never forget, that apart from God's grace, all people are capable of all things. We must recognize this truth: "The whole world has been booby-trapped by the devil, and the deadliest trap of all is the religious one. Error never looks so innocent as when it is found in the sanctuary."[187]

Are you on your guard against the infiltration of corruption into the very spiritual community you have come to trust? No one and nothing is immune—not even you. To expect otherwise is spiritually naive and makes one unnecessarily vulnerable.

Resist the temptation to follow anyone or any teaching, outside the Church or within its walls, that is not Christ and Christ alone. The subtle corruption from within is often Satan's most effective play. Pray for the Spirit's assistance to never be caught off guard! Follow Jesus Christ alone.

---

[186] C.S. Lewis, *The Screwtape Letters* (New York: HarperCollins, 2013),135.
[187] A.W. Tozer, *Man, The Dwelling Place of God* (Public Domain), 142.

The Deserving Undeserving

Luke 7:6—...I do not deserve....

Perhaps the most inveterate sin to which we are prone is the conviction that "I deserve." Satan fell from his heavenly beginnings for nothing more. Paradise was lost because man and woman thought they deserved the fruit of the forbidden tree. And our lives are no different. We face constant battles against lies about what we deserve.

Jesus publicly praised the centurion in part because the Roman refused to believe this lie. The centurion desperately wanted to see his sick servant healed. But despite the commander's position of power in an occupying army, he knew he was undeserving to have Christ under his roof: "I did not even consider myself worthy to come to you"(Luke 7:7). Though the Jews said of the centurion, "This man *deserves* to have you do this because he loves our nation and has built our synagogue"(Luke 7:4-5), the Roman himself said no such thing. He impressed Jesus with his humility and his unquestioning faith.

So long as we think we deserve blessings or an absence of pain or difficulty, we are far from the faith that Jesus desires for us. We deserve nothing and yet have been given everything we need. We might have lives recognized by good fruit (Luke 6:45). We may perceive our hearts to be in the right place. We might even be serving the Lord with diligence and propriety in the work He has called us to. But in the end, none of it entitles us to the grace and goodness of Jesus.

If there is a particular blessing we do not yet have and think we deserve, we will never receive it until the centurion's humility becomes our own. And if we do happen to receive it while we are still entrenched in our entitled thinking, we can be sure that it is more likely to be a plague to us, or a source of emptiness, rather than the blessing we imagine. The people of Israel saw this very thing happen to them when they thought they deserved to eat meat in the desert of Sinai. God gives them what they desire because they rejected the Lord. It arrives in such abundance that it comes out of their nostrils and they loathe it (Num 11:20).

In contrast, the centurion shows us that it is better to be the *deserving undeserving* than the one who feels he deserves and yet, does not. If we humble ourselves before the Lord, He will honor us. Seek to believe with the centurion this truth—"I do not deserve," and position yourself to see the mighty hand of God work in your life.

August 28

The "Go" of God

Deuteronomy 1:26—But you were unwilling to go up....

> Never object to the intense sensitivity of the Spirit of God in you when
> He is instructing you down to the smallest detail.[188]
>
> —Oswald Chambers

When the *"Go!"* of God comes to your life, it is at your own
spiritual peril to ignore or delay in responding. This is perhaps most clearly
demonstrated in the lives of the backsliding Israelites. God said to them
—*"Go* in and take possession of the land that the Lord swore He would
give to your Fathers..."(Deut 1:8). Thinking they knew better, the Israelites
cautiously delayed. They sent scouts who returned with disheartening
reports. Instead of obeying God's clear command, the people *were unwilling
to go up,* frozen in fear rather than emboldened in the strength of
obedience. Only after chastisement did they see the error of their ways and
decide to proceed. In their disobedience, they met defeat.

The *"Go!" of God* to pick up and leave for another place or another
life calling may come only once to a life, perhaps not at all. But many of
God's leaders have been given a *"Go!"* Abraham was told to *"go* to the land
I will show you"(Gen 12:1). Moses heard the words, *"go,* lead the people to
the place I spoke of..."(Ex 32:34). Elijah was instructed to *"Go* out and
stand on the mountain in the presence of the Lord..."(1 Kings 19:11). In
each case, the "called" decided to obey—to *go* where God commanded. In
each case, God met them at every step along the way.

But even if we are not called to *go* to another country or to
minister to a great people, the *"go"* of Jesus applies to us all, every day.
Christ says, *"Go* now and leave your life of sin"(John 8:11). *Go* live a life of
obedience. *Go* love your brothers and *"go* and be reconciled" with them;
"go and make disciples...."(Matt 5:24; 28:19).

There is no life to which the *"Go!" of God* does not come, whether
the movement is monumental or minuscule. As it comes to you, will you
be willing to *"go"*? Or will you, like the Israelites, find reason to object? If
we are *unwilling to go up,* our hearts are not likely devoted to the God we say
we love. But when we are filled with the Spirit, nothing delights us more
than to *"go" with God,* wherever He is leading, despite the difficulties and
because of the sacrifices. We know that where the *"Go!" of God* is, He will
also be.

---

[188] Oswald Chambers, *My Utmost for His Highest* (Grand Rapids: Discovery House Publishers,
1992), September 26.

August 29

Longanimity[189]

Jeremiah 15:15—You are long-suffering....

If you are a careful student of your own life, much less the lives of others as well, you cannot begin to fathom the amazing forbearance of God. In the Old Testament, it was referred to as *'erekh 'appayim*—"long of nose," to refer to a God who was slow to anger, despite the stench of His people's lives. As the Psalmist says, "The Lord is compassionate and gracious, slow to anger and abounding in love"(Ps 103:8). When we consider these words in the context of the people of Israel and their repeated stubbornness of heart and sinfulness, we must remember that we are one of their number. There is nothing odious that happened in the desert of Sinai that has not happened in our souls. God's wrath is long-suffering for all of us—and thank God that it is!

But more than being slow to anger, God is also long-suffering of soul. In the New Testament it is *makrothumia*—long of mind or soul. As Peter reminds us, "He is patient with you"(2 Peter 3:9), a patience compelled by the love of Christ. We are commanded to "[bear] with one another in love"(Eph 4:2), because God has set the example for us in this *longanimity*. Even though we are undeserving of His patient kindness and love, He is rich in His administration of it—"The Lord is gracious and compassionate, slow to anger and rich in love"(Ps 145:8).

But if Israel is our example, the *longanimity* of God has its limits, that His glory might not suffer. God declares, "For the sake of my name I delay my wrath, and for my praise, I restrain it for you...."(Is 48:9). Paul later says, "What if God, although willing to demonstrate His wrath and to make His power known, endured with much patience vessels of wrath prepared for destruction? And He did so to make known the riches of His glory upon vessels of mercy..."(Rom 9:22-24 NAS). The *longanimity* of God eventually bows to His justice. When Israel's actions defamed God's name, Israel was chastened by persecution, exile, and enslavement.

Is your life pushing the borders of God's *longanimity*? His long-suffering is a deep ocean that swallows the insolent stones we toss into it, so long as His name is glorified. But remember that God's justice is always around the corner, a powerful storm that can rise up, "ready to burst out in wrath, a driving wind swirling down..."(Jer 30:23).

Thank God today for the *longanimity* of His love in your life and never take it for granted. Do not provoke the Lord to anger (Jer 7:18-19).

---

[189] patient endurance of hardship

August 30

For His Ends

Proverbs 16:4—The Lord works out everything for His own ends....

As he stood on the brink of battle with the Ammonites and the Arameans, the Israelite commander Joab said to his brother, "The Lord will do what is good in His sight"(2 Sam 10:12). In this moment, Joab articulated an understanding of what many of us so often forget when we face danger or difficulty: *God is in control.*

In these moments, we can choose to approach the day with apprehension and fear. We can decide that the battle lines drawn out before us are insurmountable, even if they are not. Or, like David we can declare, "Though an army besiege me, my heart will not fear; though war break out against me, even then will I be confident"(Ps 27:3). The confidence David asserts is not based upon a guaranteed outcome, but rather a very certain truth: *God is in control* and will work out everything for His glory and His purposes.

When I live my life with this conviction, I become an indomitable warrior of faith. Though I may still know moments of fear and doubt, perhaps apprehension at the sight of overwhelming odds, these "enemies" will have no lasting hold on me. As I, "Keep deepening [my] conviction that God's love for [me] is enough, that [I am] in safe hands," though the attacks of Satan increase, "as [I] face them without fear, [I] will discover that they are powerless."[190] I will find confidence that God will work out the details according to His plan. He will provide the resources I need to do what I am called to do. And while God's plan may very well include my physical sickness, emotional isolation or spiritual exhaustion, I will proceed in the knowledge that my eternal good is tied to His glory, wherever that may take me. I am not guaranteed safety or success. But I am assured that no matter how complicated, bloody or costly the road I travel, *the Lord works out everything for His own ends,* and those ends are glorious!

Are you certain that God is working out His own ends in your life? Or, are you still captive to simple self-determinism or capricious chance? When you see your destiny in the hands of your Father, there is no battle that will keep you from the victory you have in Jesus. You may bleed. You may even die on the battlefield in this assault or the next. But in Christ, you will rise again, and then forever, joined in the glory of God.

Pray today that the Spirit convicts you that the *Lord works out everything for His own ends,* and that those ends are ultimately beautiful!

---

[190] Henri Nouwen, *The Inner Voice of Love* (New York: Doubleday, 1998), 93.

August 31

Just Do It

Ruth 3:13—...as surely as the Lord lives, I will do it.

If the contemporary body of Christ had half the determination of Boaz, it might be an unstoppable force for social change in our world. Boaz was a man of honor, conviction, and devotion played out among real people under the watching eyes of God. Boaz understood what few now do—that duty to the Lord is an honor and a privilege to be grasped.

Ruth sought the shelter of her kinsman-redeemer, and Boaz gladly accepted the responsibility. Unlike the nearest kin, he did not say, "I cannot redeem it because I might endanger my own estate"(Ruth 4:6). Rather, trusting in the living Lord of Israel, Boaz committed to do the honorable thing by Ruth and the Lord.

When it comes to my duty to God, am I closer to the response of Boaz or the kinsman-redeemer? Am I simply worried about my "own estate," or have I committed to do God's will? The world would convince us that God is dead and obsolete. And if He is dead, then duty to Him is a superfluous triviality. Satan's deception, therefore, is that our chief duty is to our own "estate." Anything, or anyone, that endangers that estate, must be rigorously avoided. This is particularly true of God. But Boaz was not fooled. He knew "the Lord is the true God; He is the living God, the eternal King"(Jer 10:10). And Boaz chose to do his duty to his King.

What is God asking you to do? What is your duty to your King? While the world tells you to reject duty-bound thinking, you must decide, like Boaz, to embrace it. The disciple sees duty as an opportunity for the expression of love to his living King. The man of duty prays,

> ...dear Lord—
> Help me put what is right before my own interest;
> Help me put others before myself...
> Help me put the attainment of what is true and just
>   and honorable above the enjoyment of present pleasures;
> Help me put principle above reputation;
> Help me put you above all else.[191]

If we choose today to believe that the Lord lives, let us do whatever it is He is calling us to do, great or small. Like Boaz, let's say—*I will do it!*

---

[191] John Baillie, *A Diary of Private Prayer* (New York: Scribner, 2014), 55.

SEPTEMBER

September 1

God of All Comfort

2 Corinthians 1:3-4—Praise be to the God and Father of our Lord Jesus Christ, the Father of compassion and the God of all comfort, who comforts us in all our troubles, so that we can comfort those in any trouble with the comfort we ourselves have received from God.

Comfort is something we all crave. Whether physical or emotional, psychological or spiritual, we long for the warm embrace of comfort rather than the cold shoulder of indifference, austerity, or rejection. But if comfort is so desirable, why is it often so difficult to obtain? Are we seeking it in all the wrong places? Have we misconstrued its primary purpose in our lives?

One of the reasons true comfort often eludes us is that we look for it in all the wrong places. We may be spiritually exhausted or emotionally worn out. We may have been cheated on, lied to, persecuted or forgotten. But instead of seeking comfort in the arms of the Father who created us and loves us more than we can imagine, we often pursue comfort in the embrace of a lover, a bottle, or our own self-pity. To these feeble efforts, God says, "I, even I, am He who comforts you"(Is 50:12).

God is *the Father of compassion and the God of all comfort.* His boundless love desperately desires to *comfort us in all our troubles.* He cries out, "Comfort, comfort my people…"(Is 40:1). Therefore, we pray most effectively when we say to our Father: "May your unfailing love be my comfort"(Ps 119:76). God will not likely ignore such a cry for love.

But while seeking comfort from our Father is the prerequisite to obtaining lasting consolation, the fullness of God's comfort will still elude us if we do not also recognize the greater trajectory of the comfort He provides us. Paul reminds us that we are comforted, not only for ourselves, but more importantly, that we may then *comfort those in any trouble with the comfort we ourselves have received.* We are recipients of God's comfort to be vehicles of His comfort in the lives of others. Paul says, "if we are comforted, it is for your comfort…"(2 Cor 1:6).

Understanding this overarching plan of God's comfort is essential to our full appreciation and enjoyment of divine consolation. True comfort often eludes us because our focus is fatally on ourselves. While we must seek comfort in God, we must also recognize that the comfort we receive is ultimately about Christ in the lives of others. When we see our personal consolation in this way and we seek to be instruments of God's comfort in the lives of others, our lives will become *more of Him and less of us.*

Never Outnumbered

2 Kings 6:16—"Don't be afraid," the prophet answered. "Those who are with us are more than those who are with them."

When you follow hard after God you will know times of persecution and spiritual siege when it seems the darkness is all around you. As the enemies surround you, what you see with your eyes may induce you to believe that there is no hope of rescue or deliverance. That is exactly what the prince of darkness wants you to believe. In that moment, you are like the servant of the man of God, who looked out around the city to see "an army with horses and chariots" encircling the city—"'Oh, my lord, what shall we do?'"(2 Kings 6:15). These soldiers of the King of Aram had come to capture Elisha because his prophetic vision was frustrating Aram's attacks against Israel. Elisha's servant feared for his life.

Into this fear, God speaks—*Don't be afraid...those who are with us are more than those who are with them.* When the darkness seems oppressive and all-pervasive, when Satan tries to convince you that all hope is lost, you, like Elisha, must refuse to fear. Never forget the perceptual tactics of your enemy. Satan knows better than anyone that perception is reality. As a result, he also knows how he can cast a shadow into your life to redirect your heart away from your Lord.

If Satan can convince us that we are woefully outnumbered, that all is lost and there is no hope, then the battle belongs to him before it has even started. For Satan is no different than any adversary in this respect: His "ultimate achievement is to defeat the enemy without even coming to battle."[192] But when we say to the Lord, "My hope is in you"(Ps 39:7), suddenly, like the servant of Elisha, our eyes will be opened, and we will see "the hills full of horses and chariots of fire all around..."(2 Kings 6:17).

Remember that in Christ Jesus you are *never outnumbered*. When the darkness presses in and lays siege to your life, pray that God will open your eyes to see the hills around you filled with His army. Refuse to be partner to the perceptual games of Satan that seek to distract your hope in the Lord. Trust that God is always greater! While "The horse is made ready for the day of battle...victory rests with the Lord"(Prov 21:31).

Are you looking to the hills to see the army of the Lord surrounding you? Open the eyes of your heart and God will show you that you are *never outnumbered* as you trust in Him.

---

[192] Sun Tzu, *The Art of War* (New York: Chartwell Books, 2012), 17.

September 3

In Prosperity

Deuteronomy 28:47-48—Because you did not serve the Lord your God joyfully and gladly in the time of prosperity, therefore in hunger and thirst, in nakedness and dire poverty, you will serve the enemies the Lord sends against you.

> …comparison is perhaps one of the most ruinous types of contagion.[193]
> —Soren Kierkegaard

Whether we recognize it or not, we may well be living right now in the time of our *prosperity*. Our constant comparisons to those around us may lead us to believe that we have little and that we are relatively deprived. But comparative thinking hides the truth of the richness of our lives, the "better" than we deserve. For even if we think what we now have is paltry, it might be gone tomorrow. Then, in its absence, today suddenly becomes immensely rich. In this place of present blessing, are we choosing to *serve the Lord God joyfully and gladly*?

God warns the Israelites that disobedience amidst blessing will result in "curses, confusion and rebuke in everything…"(Deut 28:20). The secret to avoiding these punishments and remaining in God's blessing is grateful and enthusiastic service in the time of present *prosperity*. From God's abundant grace "we have all received one blessing after another"(John 1:16). The tragedy of today is that so many miss the blessings all around them while they focus on other blessings they think they deserve.

Sometimes what we think we deserve might simply be peace in the midst of painful circumstances. This peace is possible only if we "give thanks in all circumstances; for this is God's will for you in Christ Jesus"(1 Thes 5:18). When we choose to serve the Lord joyfully and gladly in the time of our *prosperity*, He will lead us to further blessing. But if we choose to focus on comparison, we will, in "hunger and thirst, in nakedness and dire poverty…serve the enemies"(Deut 28:48) all around us.

This comparative thinking robs us of the joy and gladness of heart in the here and now. Ironically, however, it also steals from us the very ingredients we need to garner further blessings from the hand of our Father. He says, "all these blessings will come upon you and accompany you if you obey the Lord your God"(Deut 28:2). Are you giving thanks right now for the blessing all around you?

Serve the Lord joyfully and gladly in the *prosperity* of the present and watch as He leads to you to the blessings of the future.

---

[193] Soren Kierkegaard, *Spiritual Writings* (New York: HarperPerennial, 2010), 109.

September 4

His Open Hands

Psalm 145:16—You open your hand and satisfy the desires of every living thing.

All too often we portray God as a miserly Father who clings tightly to the blessings we hope for and believe we deserve. We blame God for the things we do not have, imagining His clenched fists, instead of seeing our part in the unfulfilled desires we experience before the open hands of God. We forget that giving is a two way relationship. Giving requires a receiver, and we cannot receive unless our hands are also open.

Jesus says to us, "Ask and it will be given to you..."(Matt 7:7). I may ask of my Lord, but are my hands open to receive? I may not be getting what I'm asking for because my hands are not free. It is worth asking, "What am I holding tightly in my clenched fist?"[194] Until I can humbly pray, "Dear God, I am so afraid to open my clenched fists! Who will I be when I have nothing left to hold on to? Who will I be when I stand before you with empty hands?"[195] I will never be able to see the open hands of the God who loves me and wants to *satisfy the desires of every living thing*.

God longs to grant our hearts' desires. But, we often do not receive them because we are asking with hands that are still clinging to something He wants us to release. Whatever it is, it is rooted in our sense of independence. As we desperately hold on to it, however, we miss the ironic truth: "To be dependent on God, utterly dependent, is to be independent."[196] We are only free when we depend on *His open hands*.

Do you want to see the open hands of God in your life? Then you must open your hands as well. You must release your grip on everything and everyone, recognizing that it is all God's anyway. When you have the courage to let go, to stand unencumbered, vulnerable and naked before your God, completely dependent upon what you receive, then you will finally be able to see the bounty of God's open hands. If you have the temerity to stand with open hands, you will receive the greatest gift imaginable—God's open hand in yours.

God's hands are giving hands; they are open hands. Are your hands open to receive the hands of God?

---

[194] Henri Nouwen, *With Open Hands* (Notre Dame: Ave Maria Press, 2006), 27.
[195] Ibid.
[196] Soren Kierkegaard, *Spiritual Writings* (New York: HarperPerennial, 2010), 111.

September 5

The Sun-Scorched Land

Isaiah 58:11—The Lord will guide you always; He will satisfy your needs in a sun-scorched land and will strengthen your frame.

There are stretches of life's journey that take us across *sun-scorched land*. There is no alternative route. And how I respond in these places determines my arrival into the arms of the Father. When faced with this barren country, will I decide to push on or reroute? Will I determine to follow the Guide who has led me, or resolve to make my own way?

In times such as these, there will be no absence of rabbit trails leading away from *the sun-scorched land*. When we choose to take one or more of them, "We...desert God first" and "therefore we have none to blame but ourselves"[197] for the troubles we find ourselves in during our wanderings. Fortunately, however, God can redeem even these temporary desertions and use them to refine our souls for His purposes in our lives and the lives of others. But how much sweeter to follow where He leads from the beginning!

Do you find yourself standing on the edge of what appears to be a *sun-scorched land?* Are you in a difficult place of financial stress or relationship trauma where you feel as if you are just holding on? If God has led you to this place, then trust that "He will make your paths straight"(Prov 3:6). Know that He will not abandon you. He promises to *guide you always* and *satisfy your needs* as He *will strengthen your frame.* As you trust in Him, He will refresh your soul and guide you along the path of righteousness for His name's sake (Ps 23:3).

It may be that He is leading you into a "dry and weary land where there is no water," so that your soul remembers to thirst for Him (Ps 63:1). If you follow where He leads, even across the desert places, He will take you to the other side. He will comfort you with the assurances of His faithfulness and provide the oasis you need, when you need it (Is 43:19). But, you must trust Him. If you go about it your own way, if you try to reroute and rejoin in another place, you reject your Guide. You may not find your way back to the "straight path"(Ps 27:11). And you risk forfeiting your opportunity to find "streams in the wasteland"(Is 43:19).

Ask of the Lord, "Show me the right path, O Lord; point out the road for me to follow"(Ps 25:4). And if He directs you through the *sun-scorched land*, go that way! Know that He will lead you safely through.

---

[197] Thomas Watson, *All Things for Good* (Shawnee: Gideon House Books, 2015), 33.

September 6

The Personal Court of Opinion

Romans 14:22—So whatever you believe about these things keep between yourself and God.

> Were men everywhere to ignore the things that matter little or not at all and give serious attention to the few really important things, most of the walls that divide men would be thrown down at once....[198]
> —A.W. Tozer

Christians all too often confuse personal opinion with gospel truth or, at a minimum, drown the truth of Christ in a sea of trivialities. What we eat, how we dress, whether we drink wine or how sacred we consider one day versus another have some individual meaning, but no universal, eternal significance. When we elevate the nonessential topics to eternal significance, we sin against God and become enemies of the cross.

Have you allowed your opinions about some topic to become a "stumbling block or obstacle in your brother's way"(Rom 14:13)? It is one thing to formulate opinions: we all have them. But it is quite another to permit them to affect the things we say and the interactions we have with others. When we succumb to this temptation, we prove that we serve our opinions and personal preferences rather than God: "For the Kingdom of God is not a matter of eating and drinking, but of righteousness, peace, and joy in the Holy Spirit..."(Rom 14:17).

If we find ourselves forming opinions about someone or something, we must discipline ourselves to ask the simple question —"Does this have eternal significance in Christ's Kingdom?" Should the answer be anything but a resounding "Yes!" we must strive to keep our opinions between ourselves and the Lord. However, if the Spirit gives us a persistent sense of the "rightness" of a thing and the need to speak, then we may proceed with judicious grace to present our constructive ideas to another. Without this Spirit-led tact, we may become a stumbling block to the purposes of God.

When you find yourself disagreeing with something in the life of another, take your concerns to God first to discern if the issues are of eternal significance and, therefore, worth airing. We must hold loosely to our opinions and tightly to Christ. We must focus on the main things, which are the plain things[199]—Christ crucified, Christ risen, Christ in all things!

---

[198] A.W. Tozer, *Man, The Dwelling Place of God* (Public Domain), 167.
[199] Alistair Begg, *Truth for Life Ministries.*

September 7

God's Fellow Workers

1 Corinthians 3:5—What, after all, is Apollos? And what is Paul? Only servants, through whom you came to believe as the Lord has assigned to each his task.

> Our activity is apostolic only in so far as we permit Him to work in us
> and through us, with His power, with His desire, with His love.[200]
> —Mother Teresa

Everyone has a special, assigned task in the Kingdom's work. We are, as Paul reminds us, members of one body (1 Cor 12:12-31). Every part is integral to the whole, and each contributes vitally to its proper functionality. To faithfully carry out my assigned task for the glory of God and His Kingdom is the very reason I have been created—my *raison d'être*.

When I fail to glorify God in some category of my life, should I grow discouraged and worried about what others will think of me? *What of Apollos? What of Paul?* What of me? No! Rather, I must determine to cling to the knowledge that God's providence has allowed for my failure that it may bring Him glory in some yet unseen, unpredicted way. Instead of mourning myself, I ought to rejoice in God, knowing that His greater purposes are at work.

And when I seem to succeed, I must not grow proud and self-satisfied. For what if "I planted the seed" and "Apollos watered it…"(1 Cor 3:6). Did not God make it grow? Whether God works through me or someone else, we "have one purpose, and each will be rewarded according to his own labor"(1 Cor 3:8). One task is not more important than the other and one life not more valuable than the next. God is the motive power in all things, and whether He works through me or others matters not all. What matters is that His work is done.

We are *God's fellow workers*. He is working and so are we, as He works in and through us. The sooner we recognize that the work we do and the lives we live have nothing to do with us, and everything to do with Christ and His Kingdom work in us, the more readily we will fill the shoes we were designed to fit. Too often we allow ourselves to get hung up on our part of the labor, forgetting the bigger picture and completely missing God's purposes.

Whether you are planting or watering, weeding or fertilizing, rejoice in the fact that you are part of one purpose—God's purpose. It is God who makes it grow and, as His fellow workers, everything you do is to nurture and support that growth.

---

[200] Malcolm Muggeridge, *Something Beautiful for God* (New York: HarperCollins, 1971), 65.

September 8

Always With You

Psalm 73:23-24—Yet I am always with you; you hold me by my right hand. You guide me with your counsel, and afterward you will take me into glory.

When Jesus said, "I am with you always, to the very end of the age," He gave us perhaps our greatest daily comfort—the assurance that we are never alone (Matt 28:20). Since the exodus from Egypt, the Lord has been telling His people that He will "never leave nor forsake" them (Deut 31:6). The Psalmist was convinced of this truth and said, "*I am always with you.*" But with the coming of Christ, this promise becomes all the more real to those who choose to believe. The Lord is no longer merely on the mountain, in the cloud, or behind the curtain. He now walks among us, shares bread with us, and lives within us through His Holy Spirit.

Has your life left you saying like the Psalmist, "my heart [is] grieved and my spirit embittered"(Ps 73:21)? Are you so saddened and exhausted that you feel almost numb at heart, "senseless and ignorant…[as] a brute beast…"(Ps 73:22)? If so, know that Jesus is right beside you and promises to be with you always. Though your tears blind your vision and you cannot see straight, know that He will guide you with counsel and afterward take you into glory (Ps 73:24). Even if your "flesh and heart may fail," He will be "the strength of [your] heart and [your] portion forever"(Ps 73:26).

Is your heart lonely? It needn't be. If you are looking for completion in someone else, you are destined for disappointment. No one but Jesus can satisfy your deepest loneliness. And He is right there—*with you always!* "The certainty that God is always near us, present in all parts of His world, closer to us than our thoughts, should maintain us in a state of high moral happiness most of the time."[201] But even in those moments when suffering brings us to tears in the "conscious presence of God," those "tears have their therapeutic effects," and fall on the embracing arms of a Father who loves us.[202]

Ask the Lord to open your eyes to see the One who has been standing beside you, longing to embrace you in His love (Ps 145:17-18). When you have truly looked upon the risen Lord, your heart will be satisfied. The disciple who looks steadily at Jesus can say with confidence and sincerity, "earth has nothing I desire besides you"(Ps 73:25). Say this and believe it: The God who made me, loves me, and is *always with me!*

---

[201] A.W. Tozer, *The Knowledge of the Holy* (New York: HarperCollins, 1961), 76.
[202] Ibid.

September 9

The Task Before Me

Acts 20:24—However, I consider my life worth nothing to me, if only I may finish the race and complete the task the Lord Jesus has given me—the task of testifying to the gospel of God's grace.

> There is much talk today about discovering an identity, as though it were something to be looked for, like a winning number in a lottery; then, once found, to be hoarded and treasured. Actually…the more it is spent the richer it becomes.[203]
>
> —Malcolm Muggeridge

So many of us spend huge chunks of our lives trying to figure out who we are, why we are here, and what we are to be doing with our lives. Not all of us articulate it, but we are still doing it—fumbling through life. We might bounce between various jobs and several relationships as we stab in the dark to find a personal identity, yet we may still not acquire the soul satisfaction that says, "This is me—this is what I am here to do!"

This wandering often comes at great costs, both to ourselves and to all those who share our lives with us. And the worst part of it all is that it is so unnecessary—not because it is inherently bad for us to try our hands at different professions or grow interpersonally in various relationships. God can and will use it all for His glory. But rather because we are missing the point entirely. We are not focused on the right question.

Until I, like Paul, reach the personal epiphany that acknowledges that my life is *nothing* but the *task of testifying to the gospel of God's grace*, I am still helplessly lost, wandering aimlessly through my spiritual identity. It does not matter what my job is. Whether I preach to God's people, clean houses, raise the children He has given me or treat the patients He has entrusted to my care, the goal is the same. What matters is that I have placed my life in Christ's hands to be used by Him in the task He has designed me for—*testifying to the gospel of God's grace*.

The question for our lives is not, "What job?" or "What person?" Rather, "Have I determined to do the task Christ has called me to do?" When I decide to lose my life for the sake of Christ (Luke 9:24), the specifics become increasingly irrelevant. I begin to understand that I can accomplish the *task* God calls me to in any occupation and activity and in every place. God will work out the details. Because of this hope, let us bring our struggles over issues of identity and fulfillment to an end by doing the *task* He has called us to: *testifying to the gospel of God's grace*.

---

[203] Malcolm Muggeridge, *Something Beautiful for God* (New York: HarperCollins, 1986), 16.

September 10

Stumbling Blocks

2 Corinthians 6:3—We put no stumbling block in anyone's path, so that our ministry will not be discredited.

The reason given for why many non-Christians are not Christians is "Christians" themselves. Becoming a *stumbling block* in the spiritual journey of another is dangerously easy to do. For this reason, we must consistently evaluate whether the "garbage" of our lives is littering the road to Calvary in the spiritual journey of those around us.

God may place into your life a person whose entire picture of Jesus, right or wrong, may be formulated upon the example of your life. To this person, you are "Christ's ambassador"(2 Cor 5:20). The words of your mouth, the choices you make, and the tenor of the Spirit within you can be the very tools that God uses to bring another life to Himself. Your life may be God's "chosen instrument" to carry His name into the heart of someone who does not yet know Him, just as Ananias was used by God to help open the eyes of Saul; and Paul was later used by the Lord to carry His gospel to the Gentiles (Acts 9:15-19).

Yet, too often, men and women who call themselves "Christians" allow their spiritual lives to fall into a disrepair that can become a *stumbling block* in the lives of others. Despite an appearance of spirituality, the rubble of their disintegrated relationship with Jesus can become the very block over which others trip. Jesus said, "Woe to you teachers of the law and Pharisees, you hypocrites! You give a tenth of your spices….But you have neglected the more important matters of the law—justice, mercy and faithfulness. You should have practiced the latter without neglecting the former"(Matt 23:23).

Have I become a hypocrite, a "blind guide"(Matt 23:24) in the eyes of those who bump up against my life? We must beware of allowing our relationship with Jesus to fall into such a state of disrepair that it becomes not only injurious to our spiritual destiny, but also a *stumbling block* in that of another.

Pray each day that the Spirit enables you to live a life "worthy of the gospel of Christ"(Phil 1:27), so that you may be an instrument in the hand of God rather than a *stumbling block* in the lives of others. Pray to be used by God for His purposes, rather than kicked aside as a hypocritical impediment.

September 11

Zealous

Romans 12:11—Never be lacking in zeal, but keep your spiritual fervor, serving the Lord.

When it comes to your relationship with Christ, are you *zealous*? Do you find yourself filled with a passion, enthusiasm, love, fervor and devotion to Jesus? For many Christians, zeal has no place in their spiritual lives. Where there might be an ardor for Christ, there remains a lifeless faith. Do I find myself among this crowd of the spiritually listless? Have I lost my fervor for Jesus?

Paul exhorts the Christians in Rome to *never be lacking in zeal, but keep…spiritual fervor, serving the Lord.* To be *zealous* for Christ requires, on my part, both an active passivity and a fervent activity. An active passivity begins when I decide to allow the Spirit to live within me. I must actively lay down my defenses, open the door when the Spirit knocks, and then passively allow Him to step in and take over my life. God chooses me, but I must permit Him to dwell within me. I will never be *zealous* for the Lord so long as I keep His Spirit outside. The Christian who has decided to give residence to God's Spirit cannot help but be exposed to His zealous urges for the things of God.

But where an active passivity is required to give residence to the Spirit, a fervent activity is necessary to live a *zealous* life for God. I might go so far as to passively allow the Spirit to come in and to feel His inner leadings, urging me on in righteousness, but I can still decide to be stiff-necked and hardhearted like the stubborn Israelites (2 Chron 36:13). I can rebuff Him. I can say, "No, I don't think so." But the heart that is *zealous* for God moves forward in a fervent activity.

When I decide to be *zealous* for God, I choose to work out my love for Him. I decide to focus my time, my thoughts, my relationships, my work and my way of life around Christ—*serving the Lord!* God will not do these things for me—I must do it, and do it with zeal! If I am lacking spiritual fervor, it is either because I have refused to let the Spirit into my heart, or I am consistently choosing not to devote myself in loving obedience to the urges of the Spirit within me.

Are you blocking the Spirit at the door? Do you find yourself resisting Him in the everyday choices? Pray that your life with Christ will be a *zealous* one, filled with the love of devotion. For a heart that has no zeal for Jesus does not truly love Him.

Self-Mastery

1 Corinthians 6:12—...I will not be mastered by anything.

> One can have no smaller or greater mastery than mastery of oneself.
> —Leonardo da Vinci

Every life must endure the constant assaults for mastery of the soul. The attacks may be so subtle that they are not recognized for the takeovers that they are; and yet, they are hijackings, nonetheless. Perhaps it is our sexual freedom, our obsession with our children, exercise or diets. Maybe it is a career that consumes our thinking day and night or a contemporary heresy that appeals to our progressive ideas of justice and equality. Anything, intrinsically good or bad, can master us in a manner that diverts our attentions from Jesus. The degree to which we are mastered is the measure of our defeat.

Perhaps the most insidious mastery, however, is a distortion of the mastery Christ calls us to—*self-mastery*. Paul says, "*I will not be mastered by anything.*" In this declaration, he commits to a freedom and disentanglement for Christ. Paul does not do this for himself. Because Paul knows that he is not his own—he was bought at a price (1 Cor 6:19-20)—he does it for Jesus. *Self-mastery* for Jesus means that I am constantly, tirelessly refocusing on Christ. I am reining in my sinful nature and committing to the disciplines of faith. It is a life-long work of perseverance and love.

The knavery of Satan, however, is to take this biblically significant principle of *self-mastery* and twist it into a dead end of spiritual destruction. Satan does not make us abdicate the idea of *self-mastery*. Rather he applauds it, albeit with a different object and purpose: the self for the self. Instead of *self-mastery* representing the deepest commitment of our love for Christ, suddenly it becomes an infatuation of self that drives us away from Jesus. If Satan can make us believe *self-mastery* is about us and our improvement, then he has shifted the focus away from Christ. He has dealt the subtle blow and mastered us in his deception.

Are you committed to *self-mastery* for Jesus? To be a disciple of Christ is to commit to master every faculty of heart, soul, body and mind for Jesus. Ask the Spirit to give you the grace and power to be mastered by nothing, not even yourself for yourself, but only yourself for Christ.

September 13

Right There With Me

Romans 7:21—When I want to do good, evil is right there with me.

The closer we come to Christ and the more replete we are with His Spirit, the more acutely we become aware that *evil is right there with me.* Before salvation, "evil" is much more of an exceptional thing, found in fairy tales and those rare, monomaniacal figures of history who terrorized the helpless masses. But to become acutely aware of the fact that evil lives in me right now, right here, in this place, and at this time—that is a revelation that only the Spirit can bring.

Are you aware of your capacity for evil? Do you feel the constant warring of light against darkness taking place on the very turf of your soul? If you cannot sense this struggle within, question how the Spirit has been "quenched" in your life. Since that fateful day in the Garden, the presence of sin and the capacity for evil is in us all. However, there is only war if God's Spirit is within us as well—for darkness will not war against itself. Paul reminds us: The "struggle is not against flesh and blood, but against…the powers of this dark world and against the spiritual forces of evil in the heavenly realms"(Eph 6:12). This battle rages in the fallen interior of each one of us.

Before Christ comes to shed His light on this dark interior, the midnight of the soul does not seem half so dark. But, with the contrast of the Spirit's illumination, the presence of evil around me, next to me, and within me becomes exceedingly clear. And though I may *want to do good*, the presence of evil within me is constantly there, "waging war against the law of my mind and making me a prisoner of the law of sin…"(Rom 7:23).

Am I then an innocent prisoner taken against my will? Hardly. My will is always mine to control. And, as Saint Augustine emphasizes, sin follows on the heels of a passive will. He says, "That there lay the cause of my sin….I saw that when I acted against my wishes, I was passive rather than active; and this condition I judged to be not guilt but a punishment."[204]

Have you been rescued from this punishment by the blood of Jesus? Though the war of evil against your good intentions will always rage within you, you need not be a prisoner of it. Recognize the evil within you rather than deny or live in fear of it. And then, set your will against it and the passive tendency to allow your good intentions to become hijacked by its persuasive power over you. Christ will empower you to do it!

----

[204] Saint Augustine, *Confessions* (Oxford: Oxford University Press, 1992),114.

September 14

Gates

Matthew 7:13-14—Enter through the narrow gate. For wide is the gate and broad the road that leads to destruction, and many enter through it. But small is the gate and narrow is the road that leads to life, and only a few find it.

> So the truth is that the difficulty of all the creeds of the
> earth is not as alleged in this cheap maxim: that they agree
> in meaning, but differ in machinery. It is exactly the opposite.
> They agree in machinery....They agree in the mode of teaching;
> what they differ about is the thing to be taught.[205]
> —G.K. Chesterton

Near the end of His Sermon on the Mount, Jesus clearly said that there are *two* gates—the narrow gate and the wide one. What He did not say, is exactly what the culture now preaches: there are many gates and innumerable roads that all lead to the same place.

This belief in inclusivity is destructive because it is not true. It attracts us to itself by its sense of fairness, equality, and open-minded liberality. We want to believe in a merciful God who allows many ways to Him. The idea that all religions, all ways of living and seeking "truth" and purpose *agree in meaning, but differ in machinery*, offends few and satisfies many. Yet, nothing could be further from the truth Jesus teaches.

As unpalatable as it sometimes may be, God's truth, as expressed and embodied by Jesus Himself, is that there is only one choice to be made —the narrow gate or the wide one. Speaking of the narrow gate, Jesus said, "I am the gate; whoever enters through me will be saved"(John 10:9). When I choose to be a disciple of Christ, I decide to enter through that narrow gate. I accept every charge of narrow-minded thinking, singularity and exclusivity, understanding that it is Christ Himself who has created the choice, not me. I resolve not to be duped by the world into thinking there is anything less than two possible destinations—heaven and hell—and any more than one gate that leads to either one.

What gate have you chosen to walk through? If you are standing on the road, surrounded by the multitudes, question the caliber of the gate you have ventured through; for "*small is the gate and narrow is the road that leads to life, and few find it.*" Pray that the Spirit helps you find it and proclaim it!

---

[205] G.K. Chesterton, *Orthodoxy* (Peabody: Hendrickson Publishers, 2006),126.

September 15

Filled to Full

Luke 4:1—Jesus, full of the Holy Spirit....

The degree to which we find ourselves filled with the Holy Spirit is the measure of our likeness to our Lord. When Jesus emerged from His baptism in the Jordan River, He was completely filled with God's Spirit and ready for the desert of Satan's temptations. There was no part of Christ, His body, soul or mind, in which the Spirit did not have complete and total occupancy. Do you aspire to be filled as Christ was?

As followers of Jesus we are commanded to "be filled with the Spirit"(Eph 5:18). We cannot expect to go half empty into Satan's arena of war and emerge spiritually alive. We must be "full of the Spirit and of wisdom," "filled with power, with the Spirit of the Lord…"(Acts 6:3, Micah 3:8). When we are filled in this way, we become instruments of God, ready for the battle. We join the great company of the "Spirit-filled' who have gone before us.

Perhaps, like John the Baptist, you will be called to proclaim the "baptism of repentance for the forgiveness of sins"(Luke 1:5, 3:3). Or, your fullness might lead you to embody the encouragement of Barnabas, the missionary spirit of Paul, or the heartfelt devotion of Peter (Acts 11:24; 9:17; 4:18-21, 31). You may be required to demonstrate the uncompromising strength of Stephen in the midst of persecution (Acts 6:8-15). Your fullness might even have a concrete, artistic objective for God, like the gifted hands of Bezalel. The Lord "filled [him]…with the Spirit of God, with skill, ability and knowledge, in all kinds of crafts"(Ex 31:3), so that he could produce artistic designs for the tabernacle of God.

When we are truly filled with the Spirit, there is no room for anything else. The Spirit's presence within us excludes every other competing "god" in our lives. So long as we have a room in our inner house for worldly "idols," we are not *filled to full* with God's Spirit.

What is the fuel in your spiritual tank? Is it God's Spirit and His fruit? Are you heading into today on "empty"? Nothing but FULL will do for the work of God. Remember that "the man that has the most of God is the man who is seeking the most ardently for more of God."[206] Are you ardently seeking to be filled? If you are not full to brimming, open wide the doors of your heart and let the Spirit fill you. Pray to become, like Jesus and the saints who have preceded us, *full of the Holy Spirit.*

---

[206] A.W. Tozer, *Man, The Dwelling Place of God* (Public Domain), 159.

Mouth to Mouth, Eyes to Eyes, Hands to Hands

2 Kings 4:34—Then he got on the bed and lay upon the boy, mouth to mouth, eyes to eyes, hands to hands.

There will come a time when someone you care deeply for will be in desperate need. Because of your affection for him or her, your heart will sympathize; it may ache for them, and with them. But how will you respond? If they are not nearby, will you pick up the phone and call them? Will you write a letter or commit yourself to intercessory prayer? Or will you go to be with them and invest in them?

Elisha found himself faced with these very questions when he learned of the death of the Shunammite's son. His heart went out to the woman and his desire was to immediately help her. At first, he does so from a distance, by telling his servant to go and lay his staff on the boy's face. But the servant returns to Elisha and says, "'The boy has not awakened'"(2 Kings 4:31).

What does Elisha do next? He goes to be with the boy. He begins with prayer, and then physically and spiritually, *got on the bed and lay upon the boy, mouth to mouth, eyes to eyes, hands to hands.* And, "As he stretched himself out upon him, the boy's body grew warm"(2 Kings 4:34). It took this intimate investment in the life of the dead child to overcome the grip of death.

Is there someone in your life right now who is on the brink of spiritual death, waiting to be awakened, like the boy in Elisha's upper room? How are you responding? Have you bathed his or her life in prayer? Have you gone to be with and invest in the life of him or her?

It may not be enough to simply send the "staff" of your blessing. God may need you to take your life to the hurting so that He can breathe His Spirit into them through you. God may want to manifest His power in the proximity of your personal presence. But if you go, don't be surprised if the healing God works through you comes slowly as it did for Elisha. Be prepared for it. Though the boy's body grew warm, he did not awaken immediately. Elisha had to stretch out "upon him once more"(2 Kings 4:35).

When it comes to the work of salvation in others, we must be ready to go and meet them *mouth to mouth, eyes to eyes, hands to hands.* God often works through us in the most personal and intimate of ways. Are you prepared to be used by God in this way?

September 17

Transforming Tears

Luke 22:62—And he went outside and wept bitterly.

> ...no God can save us except a suffering God, and...no one can lead
> others except the one who is crushed by their sins.[207]
> —Henri Nouwen

In a very real sense, we are not effective disciples for Christ until we have gone *outside and wept bitterly.* We may have listened to every sermon our Lord preached, broken bread with Him, and even walked by His side as He performed countless miracles; but until we have wept over the gap between who we are and who Jesus is, we are not prepared to go and do His Kingdom work.

The Apostle Peter loved Jesus with a heartfelt enthusiasm. But until Peter failed by denying his Lord, it was just that—enthusiasm. It took terrible failure for Peter to be transformed from a man who heard the message of Christ into an Apostle whose heart understood that message well enough to go out and reach the world with it. Jesus said to Peter, "And when you have turned back, strengthen your brothers"(Luke 22:32). It was Peter's turning away, going outside and weeping, that prepared him to return in a way in which he could strengthen his brothers.

Have you gone *outside and wept bitterly*? Has the face of Jesus stared at you and caused you to cry over your failure to Him? If so, be ready for ministry. The heart that has failed enough to weep over that failure, is the very one that understands the forgiveness of the cross and the power it has, not only for its personal brokenness, but for the brokenness of the world at large. Until my failure brings me to tears at the feet of Jesus, the gospel is just another story. But when I have wept bitterly over who I am and what I have done to my Lord, then the Spirit can heal and transform my life into a vehicle for His Kingdom's work.

If you have never joined Peter in the predawn darkness of weeping over your failure, you may not be prepared to faithfully stand for Jesus and declare the message of the cross. Once you have shed those tears, however, your life will never be the same. *Transforming tears* will make you an instrument in the hands of Jesus as He uses you to help change the world.

---

[207] Henri Nouwen, *The Wounded Healer* (New York: Image Doubleday, 2010), 78.

September 18

Turned to Joy

John 16:20—You will grieve, but your grief will turn to joy.

If we belong to Christ, the great trajectory of our lives is towards unending joy! Because of Christ's work, we move from crucifixion to resurrection and, ultimately, to ascension. We will know pain, and we will be acquainted with sorrow: "In this world you will have trouble"(John 16:33). But no matter how dark the night, His mercies are new every morning (Lam 3:22-23). Our grief will be *turned to joy* as we trust in Him.

Do you see dark skies and pouring rains watering the fields? Know that "Those who sow with tears will reap with songs of joy"(Ps 126:5). The sorrows of our hearts are the water for our growth. God can, and will, transform our grief into joy as we trust in Him.

The desire of Jesus is that we "may have the full measure of [His] joy…"(John 17:13). He wants us to know His connection with the Father and the joy of doing His will. While I might not know that joy today, I will be incrementally filled with "the joy of Lord"(Neh 8:10) as I decide to walk with my Savior and obey His commands. For most of us, this filling up of joy is often not instantaneous or easy, but comes only as a result of a growing relationship with the Father. I will have days of doubt or despair. But in Christ, these days will not linger. They will not hold me.

Christ teaches us that true joy is irrespective of circumstance. It is rooted in knowing the Father and doing His will. As I walk with Christ, I come to understand that the joy my heart so desperately craves is the God who walks beside me. True joy will evade me until I find it in Christ: "Joy…is the gigantic secret of the Christian."[208]

Jesus creates this joy as He transforms the griefs of my heart, using them as instruments to lead me further into the arms of the Father who loves me. I will increasingly understand that "Melancholy should be an innocent interlude," but the joy of praise "the permanent pulsation of the soul."[209] Ultimately, I will know the completeness of joy when I am finally united with Christ (Rom 6:5).

Do you believe that your greatest joy is yet to come? As you walk with Jesus, "With joy you will draw water from the wells of salvation"(Is 12:3). Though "weeping may last through the night…joy comes with the morning"(Ps 30:5). With Jesus there is "an inexpressible and glorious joy"(1 Peter 1:8)—the unending joy of knowing and being known by our Father.

---

[208] G.K. Chesterton, *Orthodoxy* (Peabody: Hendrickson Publishers, 2006), 155.
[209] Ibid, 154.

September 19

The Wisdom of Foolishness

1 Corinthians 1:21—For since in the wisdom of God the world through its wisdom did not know Him, God was pleased through the foolishness of what was preached to save those who believe.

If we have the courage to look at Christianity from a distance, we are bound to see that the Christian faith simultaneously makes perfect sense and, at the same, may seem foolish. This sometimes confusing duality may cause us, like the young C.S. Lewis, to say, "Christianity itself [is] very sensible 'apart from its Christianity.'"[210]

Christianity is, however, the spiritual paradigm that best makes sense out of nonsense. If our hearts are closed and the "eyes" of the soul shut, we might find the story of Christianity too fantastic to be real, too restrictive to be appealing, or too riddled with common spiritual themes to be exclusively true. I might fixate on apparent inconsistencies. I could hover over the yet unproven "facts" and struggle with its singular claim on truth. Isn't Christianity, like all other religions, simply "a kind of endemic nonsense into which humanity tended to blunder"?[211]

But unlike other religions, this "nonsense" of Christianity is infused with God's wisdom. It runs counter to everything the world holds dear. The world tells you to cling to your life. Jesus tells you to lose it for His sake (John 12:25). The world preaches revenge. Christ tells you to turn the other cheek (Matt 5:39). If I cling to my own definitions of spiritual truth, I will never be able to understand this "foolishness" of Christ. I must be willing to sacrifice my own version of wisdom in favor of God's. This does not mean I stop thinking, but rather that I submit to God's superior wisdom in my life.

Are you still struggling to see sense in the pain, depravation, tragedy or inequity that has afflicted you? Do you still grapple with the undefinable and the yet unexplainable? So long as you resist the apparent "nonsense" of Christianity, you will never know how your wisdom can become captive to the Lord's. You will never be divinely illuminated.

If there is something within you that feels a necessity to make sense of what you can't explain, then believe the foolishness of God. In this choice, you will know the power that makes all things visible. You will know the *wisdom of the foolishness* of Christ.

---

[210] C.S. Lewis, *Surprised by Joy* (New York: Houghton Mifflin Harcourt, 2011), 193.
[211] Ibid, 60.

Humility

Matthew 11:29—…for I am gentle and humble in heart….

Humility is simply the disposition which prepares the soul for living on trust. [212]
—Andrew Murray

If you have decided that you want your life to be *more of Him and less of you*, then the first step in actualizing this is *humility*. "Humility, the place of entire dependence upon God, is…the first duty and the highest virtue…and the root of every virtue."[213] No one demonstrated this better than Christ. Although Jesus could have used a great many words to describe Himself—omnipotent, omniscient, or conquering King—what He chose to say was: *I am gentle and humble.*

Until I recognize that *humility* is the foundation of who Jesus is, I do not know Him, His ministry or His victory. I certainly cannot hope to become more of Him. I must fully understand that "In Jesus, the Holy One of God who makes us holy, a divine humility was the secret of His life and His death and His exaltation…."[214] Jesus did what He did because He was willing to humble Himself and live a life of humility among men.

But what does *humility* mean for us? Simply put, "humility is nothing but the disappearance of self in the vision that God is all. The holiest will be the humblest."[215] Humility is the absence of self. It requires "the giving up of self, and the taking of the place of perfect nothingness before God."[216] Jesus did this flawlessly. His time on earth, whether in His ministry to the "untouchables" of society or in His death upon a cross, was entirely defined by *humility*. If my life is to become *more of Him and less of me*, it must be marked by this giving up of self for Christ.

How the Lord goes about shaping this *humility* within us varies. But regardless of the methods or means, our response must be the same: to "accept with gratitude everything that God allows from within or without, from friend or enemy, in nature or in grace, to remind you of your need of humbling and to help you to it."[217]

Do you see *humility* as "your very first duty before God…"?[218] The *humility* that saved you must be the *humility* that defines you.

---

[212] Andrew Murray, *Humility* (Peabody: Hendrickson Publishers, 2005), 42.
[213] Ibid, 6.
[214] Ibid, 31.
[215] Ibid, 33.
[216] Ibid, 46.
[217] Ibid, 54.
[218] Ibid, 54.

September 21

To Be or Not To Be

1 Corinthians 15:31—I die every day....

> To be or not to be—that is the question...?
> Who would [burdens] bear,
> To grunt and sweat under a weary life,
> But that the dread of something after death
> The undiscovered country, from whose bourn
> No traveler returns—puzzles the will,
> And makes us rather bear the those ills we have
> Then fly to others that we know not of?[219]
> —William Shakespeare

When it comes to our spiritual lives, to live for Christ is to daily struggle with Hamlet's soliloquy: *To be or not to be—that is the question?* The dilemma, for most of us, is not one of physical existence, as it was for the Danish prince. Most of us are far too self-infatuated to struggle with this battle. Rather, the questions are: Who is in control and for how long? Will I live for myself? Or, will I daily die, that Christ might live in me?

Just as I cannot serve both God and money, I cannot live for both myself and Christ. "No one can serve two masters"(Matt 6:24). When I am saved, "I have been crucified with Christ and I no longer live, but Christ lives in me"(Gal 2:20). But the reality, however, is that this decision to live or die for Jesus must be made anew every day, in each moral choice I make. In Christ, the power of sin over my eternal destiny has been broken, but the daily struggle remains until He comes again. This means that I must *die every day* to every natural inclination that keeps me from living for Jesus. It means remembering that "Only a few years will pass before I go on the journey of no return"(Job 16:22) to the *undiscovered country from whose bourn no traveler returns*—be that heaven or hell.

Have you died to yourself today? If there is not one moment in this day in which I did not have to say "no" to my natural inclinations in favor of the "law" of Christ, I should question whether the Spirit lives within me. Maybe it is the satirical retort I prayerfully restrained, the lustful glance I averted, or the money I offered when part of me wanted to hold on to it. To live for Christ is to daily die to these self-inclinations. It is to choose Christ above self. *To be or not to be—that is the question?*

---

[219] William Shakespeare, *Hamlet* in *The Complete Works,* ed. Stanley Wells and Taylor (Oxford: Clarendon Press, 1988), 669-670.

Madmen

Mark 3:21—…they said, "He is out of His mind."

> Because your sins are so many
> and your hostility so great,
> the prophet is considered a fool,
> the inspired man a maniac.
> —Hosea 9:7

If we are following in the footsteps of Jesus, there will likely come a time when others think we are out of our mind. We may have a great business opportunity, but the Spirit leads us in a different direction. We may feel called to give up what we have to go to a place no one wants to go to minister to a people no one has ever heard of. Whatever it is, when the world sees us as mad for following the Spirit's voice, we are likely in our clearest, purest sense. We are in the company of Jesus.

Jesus was God incarnate, unparalleled in a wisdom and justice that knew no favorites. His wisdom, however, was "not the wisdom of this age…"(1 Cor 2:6). It was a purity of sanity and sense which was largely unrecognizable to a fallen world, as much then, as it is today. Because Christ was so widely misunderstood, some labeled Him as a *madman*. Even His own family could not always understand why He did what He did.

When Jesus had newly called His twelve disciples, He found Himself surrounded by a crowd hungry for His teachings and miracles. Seeing this mob and fearing the Pharisee's response, His family "went to take charge of Him…"(Mark 3:21). They thought He was *out of His mind*. Not understanding God's ways, they attempted to insert their own.

If every choice we make and everything we do makes sense to others, we must question whether the Spirit is our true compass. Most of the disciple's life will look rational. Jesus ate, drank, slept, walked among friends, worked as a carpenter and did a whole host of commonly held "rational" things. But Jesus also did the unexpected, what the world saw as nonsensical or unbelievable. So when God is in control of our lives, we too must expect the unexpected or unconventional. Not every time, not even often, but sometimes, as God sees fit, we may do surprising things.

When we obey and take the step of faith that risks following what may seem to be the *"madness"* of Jesus, we will see the perfect sense of God's intent, even in those things which initially make little sense. To tiptoe through life intent on living an existence of absolute "rationality" is to miss the possible miracle. Let us not be afraid of joining Jesus in the unexpected, which may sometimes appear irrational or unbelievable.

September 23

Lovers of Light

John 3:19—Light has come into the world, but men loved darkness instead of light because their deeds were evil.

One of the truest tests of spiritual health is our affinity for the Light. The person who hates the light of Christ does so "for fear that his deeds will be exposed"(John 3:20). But the one who keeps the law has no need to fear the law, and those who live by the grace of Christ need not run from the radiance of His presence. Rather, the disciple welcomes Christ's light. He prays, "Do not let any corner of my being be left in darkness, but illuminate every part of me by the light of your face. Do not leave anything within me that could darken the brightness of the day. Let the Spirit of Jesus, whose life was the light of all people, rule within my heart...."[220]

When we avoid the Light, we prove we have something we want to hide. Do you find yourself avoiding the presence of God or His people? Are you skipping your quiet time with the Lord and neglecting His Word? If so, the darkness may be becoming more and more your companion. If, however, that darkness drives you back to the Light, then it may be your truest companion yet. According to Thomas Kelly, a Christian "must above all be one who practices the perpetual return of the soul into the inner sanctuary, who brings the world into its Light and rejudges it, who brings the Light into the world...."[221] But if the darkness leads you deeper into night, then it may become your worst enemy.

To avoid being consumed by the darkness, we must hunger for the Light. We must also let go of the illusion that we are without fault. His radiance will expose every blemish and cover-up. But instead of inducing fear, this reality should cause us to rejoice! We can find confidence in knowing His radiance will bleach every blemish white as snow. This Light will cleanse us as it nourishes growth and produces fruit in our lives. For "whoever lives by the truth comes into the Light, so that it may be seen plainly that what he has done has been done through God"(John 3:21).

If you find yourself escaping into the shadows, choose today to bring your imperfect self into the Light. When you do, you will know a warmth of love that drives away all fear. The darkness will increasingly lose its hold on you. God wants His people to stand illuminated with the radiance of His presence. Be a *lover of the Light* who shines!

---

[220] John Baillie, *A Diary of Private Prayer* (New York: Scribner, 2014), 27.
[221] Thomas Kelly, *A Testament of Devotion* in *Devotional Classics*, ed. Richard Foster and Smith (New York: HarperCollins, 2005), 175.

September 24

Today—Between Yesterday and Tomorrow

Genesis 16:8—...where have you come from, and where are you going?

And let today embrace the past with remembrance and the future with longing. [222]

—Kahlil Gibran

When Hagar is mistreated at the hands of Sarah, she flees into the desert. God pursues her there. His angel asks her—*where have you come from, and where are you going?* God knew perfectly well Hagar's past, present and future, just as He knows yours and mine. But Hagar is questioned to force her to examine her present situation in light of past experiences and future prospects—to see the hand of God in both. When was the last time you paused to consider God's work in the bookends of your life?

Scripture clearly tells us that we are not to live in the past. God commands us to "Forget the former things; do not dwell on the past"(Is 43:18). This is not a command to amnesia, but to claim our victory and freedom from the past. In Christ we are no longer prisoners to the former things, good or bad. At the same time, God wants us to recognize where we have come from. Knowing our path to the present helps us better understand ourselves and the God who has guided our way.

But while the past informs us, we should live in the moment, knowing "Each day has enough trouble of its own"(Matt 6:34). Without the hope and perspective of the future, these troubles can sometimes be paralyzing. But God wants us to face today's challenges with the knowledge that He owns eternity. For, "What freedom can exist in the fullest sense without the assurance of eternity?"[223] And in that future, there is a heavenly home and a Father's warm welcome waiting for those who persist in faithfulness. Jesus has gone to "prepare a place for [us]..."(John 14:3)!

Like Hagar, standing in the desert with no destination in mind, your next step depends upon the goal of your future. It might be an aimless next step, but it doesn't have to be. You may be tired and disillusioned, so weary from your journey, so worn out from your past, that your future seems unclear and hopeless. If so, pause by the "spring in the desert"(Gen 16:7). Examine the past for the evidences of God's goodness. Consider the future for the direction of your next step. And live in the moment for the God who is standing beside you always. Then, like Hagar, you will say—"You are the God who sees me....I have now seen the One who sees me"(Gen 16:13).

---

[222] Kahlil Gibran, *The Prophet* (New York: Vintage Books, 2015), 67.

[223] Albert Camus, *The Myth of Sisyphus* (New York: Vintage International, 1991), 57.

September 25

Looking at the Hands of Grace

Ezra 8:22—The gracious hand of our God is on everyone who looks to Him, but His great anger is against all who forsake Him.

In a world which increasingly clamors for equality and fairness in all things, at all times, it is little wonder that the duality of God's grace and justice has become unpalatable. School children are being taught to expect an award for every effort, however modest it might be. This system of rewards is akin to hearing only the first few words out of Ezra's mouth—*The gracious hand of our God is on everyone...*—without listening to the rest of what he has to say.

But God's reality is revealed in the full statement. There is grace and grace abundant from the hands of God. He desperately desires to give it to us! But we have a part to play in the reception of that grace. And how we play that part affects what we receive.

The clarity of this personal responsibility was vivid to Ezra as he made his way back to Jerusalem to rebuild the city and Temple of his Lord. Ezra knew he was going about God's work. But the priest also knew that the grace of his Lord would only abide with him *as he looked* to God. If Ezra decided to do it in his own strength or go about it in his own way, the gracious hand of God might very well depart. In Israel's history, this misguided self-reliance had already happened many times before.

In a cycle of idolatrous recidivism, Israel "forsook the Lord, the God of their ancestors," and "aroused the Lord's anger..."(Judg 2:12-13). God disciplined them repeatedly. He proved that "The wrath of God is being revealed from heaven against all the godlessness and wickedness of people who suppress the truth by their wickedness..."(Rom 1:18).

Do I find myself today suppressing the truth by listening to only the first part of what Ezra has to say? Am I expecting God's gracious hand in my life while I go about forsaking Him, looking everywhere else but to Jesus? God may give grace to any and all He chooses, but I should never look for grace when I have turned my back on Him. I should not expect a trophy for my efforts because of some notion that God must be fair and equal in His treatment to all, irrespective of my focus on Him. This is fallacious and spiritually dangerous thinking that proves I have no conception of God's character.

The Lord does give grace to those whose eyes are on Him. But we must choose to set our gaze on God. He will not do it for us. Jesus constantly looked to the Father, and "the grace of God was on Him"(Luke 2:40). Why should we expect to be any different?

What are you looking at?

September 26

Salted with Fire

Mark 9:49—Everyone will be salted with fire.

No one is left untouched by the scorching temperatures of life. Sooner or later we are all charred by fire. But just as "Salt is good"(Mk 9:50), so also is fire. Salt brings out essential flavor. It preserves and is, as Spurgeon reminds us, the symbol of "an unchangeable, incorruptible covenant, which would endure as salt makes a thing endure, so that it is not liable to putrefy or corrupt."[224] Further, salt has a purifying effect, as it "eats into the meat; it drives away corruption...."[225] Likewise, fire also purifies. Indeed, both salt and fire bring out the best in what we eat and who we are as spiritual people. They unlock and protect the essence of what lies hidden inside.

But fire, like salt, is best in moderation. Too much salt makes the food inedible. Too little salt and it is bland. And if salt "loses it saltiness, how can you make it salty again?"(Mk 9:50). Likewise, if there is too little fire nothing cooks. If there is too much, all is consumed. God's love brings the essential balance. For, "Because of the Lord's great love we are not consumed..."(Lam 3:22). Our lives are "salted with fire," just the amount God thinks right, that the best of who we are might be drawn out. The essential flavors lie deep inside until fire reveals them.

Imagine a life of faith untested by the fires of pain, persecution and depravation. Without the trials and tribulations, those difficulties that char our memories, we are nothing more than permanent spiritual novitiates. *Salted with fire*, however, just the right amount, and our lives begin to become a panoply of complex flavors and aromas pleasing to the Lord and all those who interact with us. Others begin to take delightful notice. We have earned a "fired fragrance" desirable to the Lord.

We should, therefore, not be ashamed of our charred memories or embarrassed of our spiritually smoky fragrance. Rather, let us own it and rejoice in it as a testimony of the Lord's preparation of our lives. Similarly, we are called to carry our "saltiness" into the world around us (Matt 5:13). Without the fire or the salt, our lives are relatively tasteless, and certainly raw. Let us embrace the flames, past, present and future. Let us trust that God will deliver the best of who we are from the tongues of the Refiner's fire.

---

[224] C.H. Spurgeon, *Sermon No. 1942* in *The Complete Works of C.H. Spurgeon,* Vol. 33 (Delmarva Publications, 2013).
[225] Ibid.

September 27

The Currency of Grace

Acts 8:20—Peter answered: "May your money perish with you, because you thought you could buy the gift of God with money!"

Too many of us, like Simon the sorcerer, are still living our lives under the impression that we can purchase the gift of God. We have convinced ourselves that the fullness of life in the Spirit, even heaven itself, can be attained through the currency of moral living. This illusion appeals because it gives us control: a spiritual "power of the purse." But Peter's voice thunders into this false reality—*May your money perish with you, because you thought you could buy the gift of God with money!*

"It is by grace that you have been saved, through faith—and this not from yourselves, it is the gift of God…"(Eph 2:8-9). This gift of God is the grace that saves us in Jesus Christ and the Spirit who then dwells within us. No amount of moral living can purchase this gift. It is cost prohibitive, and intentionally so. But we are not wrong to think that this gift of God has a price, or that it was purchased. It had the ultimate price. It was purchased by "the precious blood of Christ…"(1 Peter 1:19).

The gift of God cost Jesus Christ the humiliation of "'taking… (the) manhood into God,'"[226] living amongst us and dying on a cross. The gift of God cost Christ everything. And it cost our Father the agony of watching His Son suffer, knowing He could stop it, yet withholding His hand. The gift of God to us is *"grace* because God did not reckon His Son too dear a price to pay for our life, but delivered Him up for us."[227]

Have you truly received this gift of God, or are you still trying to purchase it with money, moral living, or the intellectual lies that allow you to hold on to what you have, while grasping for what God offers? We will know we have truly received this gift when we recognize that it will cost us dearly as well. Till then, we are fatally deluded. To open up the gift of God, to put it on, and walk out into the world radiant in it, comes at a cost. It is "costly because it compels a man to submit to the yoke of Christ and follow Him…."[228] The cost is my old life and the keys to my new one. It is my control over who I am and who I will become. It is submission.

To be like Simon is to make the gift of God a cheap and trivial thing. Let us never forget what it cost Christ to redeem us and never be fooled as to what that ultimate purchase will also cost us. But in the *currency of grace* that personal cost is worth every penny!

---

[226] C.S. Lewis, *Reflections on the Psalms* (New York: HarperCollins, 1986), 135.
[227] Dietrich Bonhoeffer, *The Cost of Discipleship* (New York: Touchstone, 1995), 45.
[228] Ibid.

Circumcise your Hearts

Deuteronomy 10:16—Circumcise your hearts....

Circumcision was designed by God to set His people apart. It was an outward manifestation of an inward devotion to a holy God. But it was quite possible, then as well as now, to be circumcised in the flesh, but remain wayward in the heart. Such a disconnect between the body and the soul infuriates God. He says, "Circumcise yourselves to the Lord, circumcise your hearts, you men of Judah and Jerusalem, or my wrath will break out and burn like fire because of the evil you have done..."(Jer 4:4).

As Paul would later explain, circumcision of the body only had value if one maintained the law perfectly (Rom 2:25). As "all have sinned and fallen short of the glory of God," what God cares about is "circumcision of the heart..."(Rom 3:23; 2:29). A circumcised heart is one that has cut off the outer layer of self. The skin of self-sufficiency has been removed. Just as there is blood and personal pain in the cutting of the foreskin, there is a cost to obedience of the heart. Only in a circumcision of the heart can a life be capable of loving the Lord with all its heart and soul (Deut 30:6).

If your heart has not bled before the Lord, prayerfully consider whether it has been truly circumcised in His presence. Only a heart fully exposed to Jehovah is wholly devoted to Him. We do ourselves a great injustice imagining there are private parts to our lives which God needn't be involved in, either because they are too embarrassing or too personal. But it is these very parts, the most private and vulnerable ones, where circumcision to God matters the most.

Unless you can say with confidence that your heart is devoted to Jesus, set apart for the Lord, then it still needs to be circumcised. No matter your age or stage, your position or your sex, your heart must be purified just as surely as the male member was in the symbolic obedience of the flesh. Though painful, Abraham and his adult sons chose to make public and private identification with God through the act of circumcision. Blessing upon blessing followed. Until we too identify with God through the self-suffering of obedience, we will never be able to love the Lord as we were designed to do. We will not enter His blessing until we have obeyed.

September 29

Jars of Clay

2 Corinthians 4:7—But we have this treasure in jars of clay to show that this all surpassing power is from God and not from us.

The reason you are both beautiful and breakable, a work of art and a simple piece of the earth, has nothing to do with you, and everything to do with God. When God created us as vessels to be filled with His Spirit, He could have made us of shining gold or of the rigid toughness of iron. But He chose clay—the dust of the earth, the ground beneath our feet. He used the commonplace and the completely unremarkable. And yet, in the hands of the Potter, this ordinary substance can be made into a work of art for His glory and use, full of form and a functional beauty.

Had you or I been made of gold, we might have become objects of worship, like the golden calf at the foot of Mt. Sinai (Ex 32). Since we are prone to worship men and women in their flesh, imagine if God had made us of silver or gold and bedazzled us with jewels!

As jars of clay, whatever beauty God gives us is also a functional one, made to be filled with His Spirit. A vessel that does not serve to be filled by Him is a worthless one and destined for destruction. We were never intended to merely be put on a pedestal for display in a museum. Rather, God made us to be filled up and "poured out like a drink offering"(Phil 2:17) for the Lord. And just as any beauty we have reflects the creative power of the God who made us, so also our fragility as a jar of clay testifies to our transient mortality. We are the vessels, not the Potter. At any time, we might fall and be shattered to pieces. We're always one push away from fragmented selves. Do we need any further reminder that we are vessels of clay?

In the ordinariness of this substance, the power of God within me can be fully demonstrated. If I am ever in doubt as to who is the source of the glory in me, I need only look beneath my feet to see the clay I stand upon, the "self-same" substance I walk on. *We have this treasure in jars of clay to show that this all surpassing power is from God and not from us.*

I am beautiful because God has made me in His image, the artwork of His hands. I am breakable, because I am made of clay, to remind me that I am not God. I am a vessel, to be filled up and poured out in the service of my Lord.

You too are a *jar of clay*. Will you choose to be filled with the power of God, a vessel brimming with the fantastic purposes of the Lord?

September 30

Not Your Own

1 Corinthians 6:19-20—You are not your own; you were bought at a price. Therefore, honor God with your body.

So much of our unhappiness and inner turmoil results from battles of ownership. What the world will not tell you is that *you are not your own*. The contemporary culture screams the exact opposite. And so, we bite at the bit—we endlessly buck in the corral, kicking furiously, round and round in circles, when we might be galloping across the open country, if we would only accept the Lord's authority in our lives.

This fight for personal ownership is perhaps no more obvious than in the matter of our bodies. We are commanded, "Do not be like the horse or mule, which have no understanding, but must be controlled by bit and bridle or they will not come to you"(Ps 32:9). And yet, that is exactly the way we do behave. Rather than freely coming to the One who has purchased us, body and soul, we resist. We try to hold on to as much as we can, particularly when it comes to what we do with our bodies. The last thing we want to do is to honor God with our bodies because this requires us to admit that our bodies are not our own. We are not free to do with them whatever we please, whenever we want.

Have you considered that your body, your mind, and everything else you consider yourself to be is not your own? Has your "self" come to grips with the reality "that its claim to be or do *anything* may not for a moment be allowed," and that "It is in this, above and before everything, in which the conformity to Jesus consists, the being and doing nothing of ourselves, that God may be all"?[229]

Are you aware that you were bought at a price? The inner conflict we feel in any category of our lives likely stems from our inability to recognize Christ as the Author and Owner of what we think is ours. However, when we concede that we are not our own, we suddenly find a freedom and purpose we never thought possible. We begin running the race we were designed to run, rather than fighting endless battles we were never meant to fight.

Relinquish today any residual thought you might have that you are your own. Rejoice in the freedom of knowing that the One who owns you, loves you, and has filled you with the power of His Holy Spirit! What shall we fear?

---

[229] Andrew Murray, *Humility* (Peabody: Hendrickson Publishers, 2005),15.

OCTOBER

October 1

God's Place is My Place

1 Corinthians 7:17—Nevertheless, each one should retain the place in life that the Lord has assigned to him and to which God has called him.

When we find ourselves in an unexpected place in life, we can have one of two responses: We can embrace it and make it our own for God's work in our lives; or we can reject it, escaping into some vision of our own. In choosing to *retain the place in life that the Lord has assigned* to me, I make the decision for contentment. Even though I may not understand what has brought me to this place, I recognize that God is in control, and He knows best. He has me here, in this place, for a reason—*His* reason. And because of this, I determine to be "content with what [I] have, because God has said, 'Never will I leave you, never will I forsake you'"(Heb 13:5). God is with me and that is all that matters.

This does not mean my present position will last forever. God may call me somewhere else. He may assign me a new place in His providential plan. But I resolve to trust in the Lord. I choose to be content until He leads me onward. I determine to wait upon His call.

The opposite decision is the choice for discontent. It is the voice that says, "I know better; I deserve more; I will not waste my time trying to find the diamond in the rough of where I am." This choice mocks Paul's assertion, "I can do all things *through Him* who gives me strength"(Phil 4:13) by saying, "I can do all things through *my* strength, and I will make for myself a better place." This decision undermines my relationship with God by insulting His providence. It forfeits the peace I might have enjoyed had I rested in His control over my life. A restless discontent is the symptom of this rebellion. In the end, this heart is always unfulfilled, while "Godliness with contentment is great gain"(1 Tim 6:6).

Contentment in the place where God has you now can only come in Christ. When we find our fulfillment in Jesus, we find that nothing else matters. A profound, somehow inexplicable contentment, comes and fills us to the brim.

Have you been filled in this way? If not, you must seek to obey Jesus, for "Only through unconditional obedience can one unconditionally encounter 'the place' where one is to stand; and when one encounters it unconditionally, then one understands that it is unconditionally a matter of indifference even if 'the place' is a dunghill."[230] Does your heart know the unconditional contentment of making God's place for you your place?

---

[230] Soren Kierkegaard, *The Lily of the Field and the Bird of the Air* (Princeton: Princeton University Press, 2016), 53-54.

October 2

The Floodgates of Heaven

Malachi 3:10—...see if I will not throw open the floodgates of heaven and pour out so much blessing that you will not have room enough for it.

Are you robbing God of what is rightly His? Are you bringing only a portion of His tithe or no tithe at all? Do you find yourself, like Samuel's sons, pulling the choice meat from God's offering (1 Sam 2:12-16)? God tells us that the absence of "tithes and offerings" is proof positive that we have "turned away" and wandered into an avaricious country (Mal 3:7-8). The Lord says, "Return to me, and I will return to you"(Mal 3:7), not as thieves and robbers, but as men and women who bring the "whole tithe into the storehouse..."(Mal 3:10). It is the wicked who "borrow and do not repay, but the righteous [who] give generously"(Ps 37:21).

So long as we live in the illusion that what we have is ours, we deceive ourselves and steal from God. We live "under a curse"(Mal 3:9). As Paul reminds us, "What do you have that you did not receive?"(1 Cor 4:7). Even your body belongs to God—"You are not your own; you were bought at a price"(1 Cor 6:19-20). When I fail to bring the "whole tithe," I am not depriving God of some necessary sustenance. His Church and His Kingdom purposes will march on, with or without my precious pennies. In giving to God, however, I honor Him as Lord of my life, sustainer of my body and soul, and the source of every good thing (Jam 1:17).

In contrast, if I withhold from God, then I say to Him, in effect, I don't need you and you are not able to meet my needs. Therefore, I will hang on to this portion to safeguard against what is to come. This not only rejects God's loving provision and robs Him of what is rightfully His, but further shows what a fool I am, for "This very night [my] life [may] be demanded of [me]. Then who will get what [I] have prepared for [myself]?"(Luke 12:20).

Instead of hedging against God's goodness and love, we are called to trust in His promise: "I will bless my people....And in the proper season I will send the showers they need. There will be showers of blessing"(Ezk 34:26 NLT). May we give to God what is God's and see if He will not bless us as He *opens the floodgates of heaven* to provide all that we need and more!

October 3

Consistency

Daniel 6:10—Now when Daniel learned that the decree had been published, he went home....he got down on his knees and prayed, giving thanks to his God, just as he had done before.

Faithfulness is evidenced in *consistency.* Show me a man or woman of faith, and I will show you a disciple whose life is marked by *consistency* of thought and action. While no one's spiritual life is as constant as the rising sun, much less the God who created it, "God is faithful"(1 Cor 1:9), and the more He is within us, the more we will become like Him.

The spiritual critic will say, "What of those who are unfaithful? Does this unfaithfulness nullify the faithfulness of God?"(Rom 3:3). By no means! God's "faithfulness endures to all generations"(Ps 119:90). Indeed, "The steadfast love of the Lord never ceases..."(Lam 3:22). Ennobled by this *steadfast love*, we, like Daniel, can demonstrate God's faithfulness to the world around us. In the *consistency* of what we do and say, we can show "the Lord is faithful, and He will strengthen and protect you from the evil one"(2 Thes 3:3). Though Daniel knew there would be consequences to continuing daily prayers in defiance of the royal edict, *he went home* and honored God with his consistent faithfulness in prayer. In the face of persecution, Daniel persisted in faithful worship to God. He rested in the truth that "The Lord is our judge, the Lord is our lawgiver, the Lord is our King, it is He who will save us"(Is 33:22).

Too often we play the part of immature providences, deciding it wiser to give up on spiritual consistency and to proceed to make decisions which eclipse God out of the equation. When faced with a collision of our spiritual lives and the demands of the world, we often try to compartmentalize or compromise on faith to avoid the conflict or personal loss that might result from maintaining faithfulness. Daniel refused to do this. He remained spiritually consistent. He forged ahead with complete confidence that God was able to rescue him from the teeth of lions and the claws of men, trusting that God's name would be glorified.

Do you have the confidence of Daniel to persist in faithfulness? Are you *consistent* in your quiet time and constant in your prayer (Rom 12:12)? When trials and storms come to our lives, we have little hope of being faithful if we have not been *consistent* in the calm—"Whoever can be trusted with very little can also be trusted with much..."(Luke 16:10).

Pray that God gives you the strength and grace you need to be *consistent* in your faithfulness, first in the calm, and then in the storm.

October 4

Enriched

1 Corinthians 1:5—For in Him you have been enriched in every way....

A life with Christ is meant to be an *enriched* one. Coming to salvation is one thing: the acceptance of a gift, the opening of the door and letting Jesus into the foyer of the soul. But to live an *enriched* life, a life full of Christ, we must welcome Him into the center of our spiritual homes. We must give Him the seat of honor at our table, sit with Him, and listen and talk to Him. The degree to which our spiritual lives are *enriched* depends entirely upon our willingness and commitment to invite Christ in and get to know who He really is.

Have you determined to know Jesus deeply or have you been simply satisfied with the knowledge of salvation and the happy vibe of Christian culture? Do you feel that your life has *been enriched in every way* through your relationship with Christ? If not, why? We have no business complaining that our spiritual or physical lives feel impoverished or wanting if we have not resolved to know our Lord. He "gives good gifts to those who ask Him"(Matt 7:11), but we must be in His presence, getting to know Him, if we are to ask in the first place.

Enrichment in our lives is *in Him*. Fullness of life is *in* Christ, for He came that we might "have life, and have it to the full"(John 10:10). In Jesus, everything that is good is so much better. The beauty of the sunset takes on new magnificence; the laughter of our children has a deeper resonance in the soul; the meaning and purpose of our everyday lives takes on a dimension we never thought possible before getting to know Christ.

Where the Spirit of Christ is, there is abundance, wealth, fullness and spiritual meaning. If I want my life to be *enriched* in this way, I must make it happen. I must choose to spend time with Jesus, reading His Word, bowing my knees in prayer, and sitting with my Savior to listen to everything He has to say.

Don't settle for anything but the *enriched* life—the life full of Christ. Anything else is a spiritual specter, a shadow existence that only you have the power to step out of. If Jesus is still in your spiritual foyer, welcome Him in to the center of your "home" and decide that you will get to know everything there is to know about who He really is. The *enriched* life will follow.

October 5

The Unsettled and Unfulfilled

Deuteronomy 28:65-66—...the Lord will give you an anxious mind, eyes weary with longing, and a despairing heart. You will live in constant suspense, filled with dread both day and night, never sure of your life.

One of the signs that we are living in a world starved for the Spirit of God is the anxiety which grips its people. The Lord told the Israelites that an anxious mind, a weary spirit, and a despairing heart would follow on the heels of disobedience to Him (Deut 28:58-68). These inner plagues continue to punish those who have turned away from God. Many today use medication to attempt to treat psychological pain or drown it in addiction. While the pundits try to explain the need for what Chesterton calls "pills for pale people,"[231] God has already foretold it. The world has chosen not to listen.

The Lord clearly told Israel that willfully turning away from Him would lead to destruction: "He will put an iron yoke on your neck until He has destroyed you"(Deut 28:48). Disobedience will cause us to be uprooted and scattered with "no resting place for the sole of your foot"(Deut 28:65), much less the peace of our minds. In rejecting God, the world has thrown out the only peace (the peace of Christ) that heals the anxious mind. Jesus says, "Peace I leave with you; my peace I give you. Not as the world gives do I give to you. Let not your hearts be troubled..."(John 14:27).

Do you find yourself victimized by anxiety? Are you "never sure of your life"(Deut 28:65)? The answer to the curse that binds you is not in a pill, or some pleasure, a bigger bank account, or more enlightened thinking. The answer is Jesus! He is the One who calms the waves. When we take our eyes off of Jesus, like Peter, we go from walking amidst the waves to sinking in our fear and doubt (Matt 14:22-36).

If our minds are anxious, they have forgotten God's providential wisdom. If our hearts are despairing, they have neglected the Father's love. If our eyes are weary with longing, they have failed to see the manna right before them. If there is an absence of peace in our lives, we are largely to blame. The world screams, "'Peace, peace'...when there is no peace"(Jer 6:14) apart from Christ. The world needs Jesus. You and I need Him. Let our hearts be settled and fulfilled in the peace of Christ.

---

[231] G.K. Chesterton, *Manalive* (Mineola: Dover Publications, 2000), 73.

October 6

The First Step Starts with You

Proverbs 6:5—Free yourself, like a gazelle from the hand of the hunter, like a bird from the snare of the fowler.

> To be a Christian means to forgive the inexcusable, because
> God has forgiven the inexcusable in you.[232]
> —C.S. Lewis

There can be no forgiveness, much less reconciliation, without contrition. When the presence of a great hurt or error threatens to destroy our relationship with a friend, spouse, or our Father God, healing hinges on personal repentance. Are you estranged from others? Are you distanced or "trapped by what you said, ensnared by the words of your mouth"(Prov 6:2)? Then you must free yourself with the speed of a *gazelle from the hand of the hunter.* You must "Go and humble yourself; press your plea with your neighbor!"(Prov 6:3). So long as we cling to the idea that someone else must do it, there will likely be no forgiveness and no reconciliation.

The power to find yourself forgiven and the wounds of your heart healed in the embracing arms of reconciliation begins with you. You must initiate. You must *free yourself* by stepping forward and bowing down. Humble yourself before the one who holds you in his or her hands, regardless of who is guilty, and to what degree (Prov 6:3). Apologize with sincere contrition. It does not matter if forgiveness or reconciliation necessarily follows on the heels of your act of submission. Neither the extricating grace of forgiveness nor the balm of reconciliation are yours to fully dispense for yourself. But the ability and the power to set the stage for God's transforming work in your life *does* lie in your hands.

When it comes to the healing of wounds, we too often error in one of two directions: the belief that we must and can completely heal ourselves or, obversely, that we have little to no part to play, and someone else must do it. But the truth lies somewhere in between. There can be no healing unless we "go" and humbly confess our wrong, without a word of accusation or justification: a simple apology and plea for forgiveness will suffice. When we humble ourselves in this way, then the "someone else" has the capacity to finish the work we have initiated. God can help them to forgive and to reconcile. The Lord takes notice of our "go" and He who has "healing in [His] wings"(Mal 4:2) will "cover [us] with His feathers…"(Ps 91:4). Therefore, let us *free ourselves* by bending down. When we do, we will find God's hand of forgiveness reaching down to pick us up.

---

[232] C.S. Lewis, *The Weight of Glory* (New York: HarperCollins, 2001), 182.

October 7

Holy Hatred, II.

Psalm 97:10—Let those who love the Lord hate evil....

>...the Psalms serve as a reminder that there is in the world such a thing
>as wickedness and that it (if not its perpetrators) is hateful to God.[233]
>
>—C.S. Lewis

In our current efforts to create more equitable societies, we have
attacked *hatred* and intolerance and promoted acceptance and inclusion.
Such thinking has even crept into the Church, where the once
unimaginable compromises sometimes take place. But is *hatred* always
wrong? Is there a place for biblical loathing?

The Psalmist says, *"Let those who love the Lord hate evil...."* Love is
incongruous with *hate,* just as surely as good is with evil. When we love
Jesus and become filled with His Spirit, we must, by necessity, *hate* evil. It is
the antipode of good. And as God is good (Mark 10:18), evil cannot share
space in the affections of the disciple's heart.

Similarly, God *hates* wickedness (Ps 45:7). We must too: First in the
recesses of our own hearts and then in the world around us. John contends
that anyone who *"hates* a brother or sister is in the darkness and walks
around in the darkness..."(1 John 2:11). But David reminds us that those
who persist in defiantly rejecting God should be *hated*—"Do I not *hate*
those who *hate* you, O Lord, and abhor those who rise up against you? I
have nothing but *hatred* for them, I count them my enemies"(Ps 139:21-22).

Are feelings of *hatred* ever appropriate? Satan and everything he
represents must be *hated.* The Church has become increasingly guilty of
pandering to evil and extending tolerance where God has already clearly
spoken. Is this because no one wants to offend? Few desire to be seen as
partial or narrow-minded. Perhaps your life has been guilty of this. The
Psalms exhort us to biblical *hatred* for everything that willfully rejects God.

If I claim to love the Lord, I must determine to *hate* "the deeds of
faithless men," and decide that "they will not cling to me"(Ps 101:3), even
as I ask God's grace in loving those who defy Him. In every instance, I
must ask myself the following: Is this activity likely to glorify God's name?
Does this man have the opportunity to be redeemed by Christ, or has he
committed the unforgivable sin (Matt 12:31-32; Mark 3:28-29)? If the
answer is "No," then Satan's work must be *hated* with the vim and vigor of
a Holy God. Pray that the Lord gives you discernment in knowing what to
hate and when to do it, for His name's sake.

---

[233] C.S. Lewis, *Reflections on the Psalms* (New York: HarperCollins, 1986), 38.

October 8

Just One

Romans 5:18-19—Consequently, just as the result of one trespass was condemnation for all men, so also the result of one act of righteousness was justification that brings life for all men. For just as through the disobedience of the one man the many were made sinners, so also through the obedience of the one man the many will be made righteous.

You may never know what *just one* act of obedience has done to change your life or to alter the course of another for the better. It was because of *one* trespass, one simple act of willful disobedience, that sin entered the world and irreversibly changed the lives of every man and woman to come. So also, it was through the obedience of *one* man that salvation came to the world.

Do you find yourself at a point of inner turmoil, questioning God and yourself as to why you should be obedient in some particular category of your life? It may be honoring your parents, telling the truth, or forgiving a great wrong. Perhaps it is your sex life. Why shouldn't you live with your girlfriend? Is a quiet affair with this man really going to destroy my marriage? Don't I deserve to be happy? Maybe it is your finances. Does God really need ten percent? Doesn't He know how tight things are now?

The topic may seem trivial and the obedience God requires in it nonsensical—the forbidden fruit was no different. Wasn't it just a piece of fruit? What does it matter? Didn't God say, "'We may eat fruit from the trees in the garden...'"(Gen 3:2)? Why not the tree in the middle? Can it really make a difference? Turns out, it makes all the difference!

When you find yourself questioning the "utility" of obedience in your life, remember that *just one* act of disobedience or righteousness can forever change the course of your life (or that of another). There is no such thing as a trivial act of disobedience. It may start as a simple phone call or cup of coffee. Way leads on to way. Every decision, big or small, to disobey what God has clearly commanded, pushes God away, just as every act of righteousness affirms our love for our Father and draws us to Him.

Remember this: God "requires obedience, unconditional obedience; if you are not obedient in everything, unconditionally, then you do not love Him, and if you do not love Him, then—you hate Him."[234] If we love the Lord, we must make the decision to obey, *one* act of righteousness at a time, even when it appears to make no sense (*especially then!*). Let us pray for the grace and strength to obey, recognizing that just one decision can change our lives forever.

---

[234] Soren Kierkegaard, *The Lily of the Field and the Bird of the Air* (Princeton: Princeton University Press, 2016), 45.

October 9

Bound in the Bundle

1 Samuel 25:29—...the life of my master will be bound securely in the bundle of the living by the Lord your God.

Are you confident of the providential protection of God in your life? Do you believe that you are *bound securely in the bundle of the living by the Lord your God* and that nothing can separate you from Christ our Lord? Have you been "convinced that neither death nor life, neither angels nor demons, neither the present nor the future, nor any powers, neither height nor depth, nor anything else in all creation, will be able to separate us from the love of God that is in Christ Jesus our Lord"(Rom 8:38-39)?

When Abigail looked at David, she understood that he was a man who was convinced of this binding relationship with God. Abigail was the wife of the quarrelsome and indignant Nabal who refused to feed David's troops. She knew a hard heart when she saw it; she was married to it. But in David she saw a man after God's heart. Though pursued by King Saul and hunted in the desert like a wild animal, David learned to "take refuge in the shelter of [God's] wings"(Ps 61:4). David found protection from God alone, saying, "The Lord is my rock, my fortress and my deliverer; my God is my rock, in whom I take refuge. He is my shield and the horn of my salvation, my stronghold"(Ps 18:2). Because of God's love for David, David was bound up in the *bundle of the living,* as a precious possession held closely, where no one and no thing could steal him away.

If you cannot feel yourself *bound in the bundle,* as close to the bosom of Christ as a newborn baby in the arms of its mother, it may be that you still have one foot firmly fixed in the world. So long as your life is merely about self-protection and gratification, you will never know the confidence that defies every enemy, even death himself. But when you let this life go into the arms of Christ, everything changes. For, "whoever loses his life for [Christ's] sake will find it"(Matt 10:39). The man who does this will be *bound securely in the bundle of the living* and nothing will be able to separate him from the love of God in Christ Jesus!

Once you release your strangling grip on your life, you will begin to feel instead the binding of God's bundle around you. When you do, you will be filled with an indomitable confidence—the confidence of the victorious Christ—and surrounded by the loving arms of a Father who will never let you go!

October 10

Even Though

Psalm 44:17-18—All this happened to us, though we had not forgotten you or been false to your covenant. Our hearts had not turned back, our feet had not strayed from your path.

A great many have walked away from Jesus disillusioned by the pain that pierces their faulty perception of justice for the "faithful." They overestimate their own faithfulness to God and miscalculate His purposes in their lives. In the presence of pain, this combination can leave them disheartened and disillusioned.

Some of this alienated feeling results from our perception that pain strikes seemingly indiscriminately. In its wake, we find ourselves crying out—*"though we had not forgotten you or been false to your covenant,"* yet *"all this happened to us"*(44:17). Why God? Why?

Jesus tells us He "causes the sun to rise on the evil and the good, and sends the rain on the righteous and the unrighteous"(Matt 5:45). What is true of the physical world is also true of the spiritual one—God controls them both, whether we like it or not. When the rain falls indiscriminately, we intuitively understand and accept that the matter is out of our control. But when it comes to our spiritual lives, we expect different rules of the game. We suppose that if we live righteously and walk faithfully we must necessarily be blessed. Further, while we will not readily admit it, we imagine our faithfulness should also protect us from pain. But the storms come and the rain falls just where God wants it to. And where it does, things grow, beautiful and green.

Righteous living is the prerequisite for the blessing of God. But it is no guarantee against pain and suffering. And thank God that it is not. For if the storm's clouds never gathered, and the winds never blew, our lives would be barren deserts. It is through the rains that accompany the storms that God chooses to produce fruit in our lives.

Do you find yourself still being surprised and angered at the presence of pain amidst what you perceive to be faithful living? Are you saying to God, *"Even though* I have been faithful, yet this has come to me. Why?"* If so, choose to release your cares to the winds that assail you. Let the gusts carry those frustrations off. The sooner you do, the sooner you will be able to grab on to the life-giving water God brings on the heels of the storm's advance.

Capricious though they sometimes are, don't fear the storms in your life—they bring rain for you to dance in. Revel in the coming growth God is going to bring about in you—beautiful beyond your wildest imagination!

October 11

Faithful to Your Calling

1 Kings 13:21-22—…This is what the Lord says: "You have defied the word of the Lord and have not kept the command the Lord your God gave you. You came back and ate bread and drank water in the place where He told you not to eat or drink."

When the Lord speaks into your life or leads you in some particular direction, you must be careful to carry it through to completion —to be *faithful to the calling:* His calling to you. Sometimes we start out with a very clear sense of what it is God is leading us to do or say. And then we begin to second guess ourselves, doubting what the Lord has spoken into our lives. Rather than obtain confirmation from the Lord Himself, we start seeking counsel in the opinions and advice of others. Often, these are very good, godly people with sound advice—but not, necessarily, counsel consistent with what God has told us.

The "man of God" who confronted King Jeroboam was quite clear on what God required of him. He says, "I have been told by the word of the Lord: 'You must not eat bread or drink water there or return by the way you came'"(1 Kings 13:17). But when another prophet confronts him, the "man of God" second guesses his own vision. The prophet says to the "man of God," "I too am a prophet, as you are, and an angel said to me by the word of the Lord: 'Bring him back with you to your house so that he may eat bread and drink water'"(1 Kings 13:18). Instead of red flags waving in the face of completely contradictory counsel, the "man of God" allows the words of a man, even another godly man, to divert him from his calling. In this confused disobedience, the "man of God" meets an untimely death in the attack of a lion.

As this man's story demonstrates, never confuse the counsel of others with the voice of God in your life. When the Lord leads you in a particular way, be obedient to the calling He has given you to the very end. Refuse to be diverted by anything or anyone save the Lord Himself and His persistent voice of redirection. While there is a time, a place, and a true value in the counsel and advice of other godly men and women, these voices must always be subordinate to that of the Lord. When God speaks into your life, all other voices must fall away. To give credence to any other voice above that of God is to meet your lion on the road.

Be *faithful to your calling*—to the very end.

October 12

Sanctified

John 17:17—Sanctify them by the truth; your Word is truth.

Sanctification is the great ongoing work of our lives. To be *sanctified* is to be set apart or declared holy before and for God. It is to be readied for the intended divine use of the Lord whom created us. This process is a purifying one, sometimes arduous, and always specific to the individual and God's design for his or her life. No one person's sanctification will be like another's.

God does this sanctifying work in our lives in innumerable ways. He uses relationships and marriages, physical illness and financial challenges. There may be unspeakable pain and uncountable joys. But one component of the sanctifying process is universal—the Word of truth. No one can be set apart for God without it. Jesus prays for His disciples, "Sanctify them by the truth; your Word is the truth"(John 17:17). Elsewhere we are told, Jesus is the "Truth" and He is the "Word"(John 14:6; 1:1,14).

Do you desire to be set apart for God and employed by Him in the holy purposes for which you were created? If your heart is longing to fulfill the purpose of your life, it is longing to be *sanctified*, and this must be done through the "truth" of the Word. Without regular, consistent contact with the Word of God, you will never be *sanctified*—you will never be set apart unto God for the work He created you to do. It is foolish to imagine your life fulfilling its intended purpose without the Word. For God has "bound Himself to the Word that He might speak to men,"[235] and that He might reveal to us who He is, who we are, and what He wants to do through us.

For this reason, it remains for us to read the Word, to interact with it, pray through it, wrestle with it, and live in it. God will not do this for us. Our hearts will not be sanctified through a passive osmosis. We must take His Word and eat it (Matt 26:26). And as we do, we will find in the Word, Christ Himself, who is the Word made flesh. We will find our reason for being.

Sanctification has a volitional component. You will never be *sanctified* unless you decide to live in the Word and let it change you. Pray that the Word of truth will never again depart from your daily life. Without it, you will never be who you are meant to be.

---

[235] Dietrich Bonhoeffer, *Christ the Center* (New York: HarperCollins, 1978), 49.

October 13

Lion Taming

Genesis 4:7—...sin is crouching at your door; it desires to have you, but you must master it.

> Thus a great warrior takes control of others and does not
> let others control him.[236]
> —Sun Tzu

If you have died with Christ, you have been freed from the power of sin (Rom 6:7). But while sin no longer enslaves you to death, you probably need no reminding that it continues to plague you. Though Christ has conquered sin and its final destiny has been sealed, sin remains in the world until He comes again. It is the wounded lion, dying but dangerous, *crouching at your door*, wanting to bring you down to the grave with it.

For this reason, the victory that Jesus has won over sin must be reclaimed in your life every day. Though the gift of life has been given to you by Christ, the daily battles must still be fought. Sin must be *mastered!* Have you determined to master it in your life? Have you acknowledged it as an unrelenting, ever present enemy? What is *crouching at your door* even now? David had Bathsheba bathing next door (2 Sam 11). Who or what is outside your door?

There is no hope of *mastering* sin in your life until you acknowledge both its presence and its terrible power. So long as you treat sin in your life as either a nonentity or as some kind of domestic animal to be petted and toyed with and then shooed away when it becomes unwanted or noisome, you risk falling prey to the wild animal that seeks to destroy you.

You must recognize that you have a true adversary in sin, one that is capable of doing you great harm. Only when you acknowledge its power, do you have any hope of ruling over it in your life. You must *master* sin with the authority and power of Jesus Christ. This means reclaiming His victory in your life, every day, in all things. It means keeping constant vigilance, both within the recesses of your heart and mind, and in the world around you. It means being battle ready, shoes on and armor strapped to your body (Eph 6:10-17).

Christ has released you from the power of sin so that your hands and feet are ready for battle. In this unrelenting war, you have God's power in you to take control of sin and not be controlled by it. As you subjugate sin in your life, you reclaim Jesus' victory until He comes again. He is faithful and will empower you to fight the good fight.

---

[236] Sun Tzu, *The Art of War* (New York: Chartwell Books, 2012), 33.

October 14

Rejecting the Prophets

Amos 7:12-13—Then Amaziah said to Amos, "Get out, you seer! Go back to the land of Judah. Earn your bread there and do your prophesying there. Don't prophesy anymore at Bethel, because this is the king's sanctuary and the temple of the kingdom."

There is no shortage of pundits and prophets speaking into our lives. At nearly every turn, on nearly every topic, we are told how we should live our lives. The challenge for the believer is to decipher the Spirit of God amidst all the background noise. At times, this noise can be almost overwhelming, and the tendency is to shut out the voices speaking into our lives. This is particularly true of any voice speaking something personally unpalatable. But when we do this, we risk becoming Amaziah. We risk excluding the voice of the Spirit from our inner Bethel because we don't like what the Spirit speaks into our lives or the messenger He uses for His message.

Amos was the Spirit's messenger. He was not a career prophet or a priest of his people. He was a shepherd and "took care of sycamore-fig trees"(Amos 7:14). But without degree or title, he was God's chosen mouthpiece to the people of Israel. In rejecting Amos, Amaziah rejects the God who sent him.

Like Amaziah, the Spirit of God will be among the many voices speaking into your life. Be careful, however, not to repeat Amaziah's mistake and throw the Spirit out with the other voices. In humility, fully examine those voices and "do not believe every spirit, but test the spirits to see whether they are from God, because many false prophets have gone out into the world"(1 John 4:1). You will know that the spirit is from God if it "acknowledges that Jesus Christ has come in the flesh…"(1 John 4:2). Until you have tested the spirit, you must leave open the possibility that the voice speaking into your life is that of God. You must not prematurely rule out an unconventional manner or an unexpected person. Do not throw Amos out until you have tested the message for Christ in it.

The surest way for us to stumble in our spiritual lives is to close our sanctuary to the voice of the Spirit. Satan knows this truth better than anyone and so bombards us with voices—a cluster bomb technique. If we hide in our own inner temples in the midst of this incessant shelling and begin to worship false gods there, we will be all the more prone to reject Amos when he walks into our lives with the voice of the Spirit.

God may be speaking into your life right now, but His voice may be one of many. Are you in the process of throwing Him out or do you have the courage to test the spirits and see if Jesus is standing there? If you look for Him, you will find Him.

October 15

The Great Mediator

Job 9:33-34—If only there were someone to arbitrate between us…someone to remove God's rod from me, so that His terror would frighten me no more.

In the midst of his great suffering, Job longs for a mediator between God and man. He says, *"If only there were someone to arbitrate between us…someone to remove God's rod from me…."* Job longs for what we have received: Jesus Christ our Savior. By God's grace, we no longer live in Job's world of "ifs." For in Christ, "we have been justified by His blood, how much more shall we be saved from God's wrath through Him!"(Rom 5:9).

Job must have felt as if God's wrath was upon him. He appears to have felt alone, estranged from God and without a mediator, someone to bear "God's rod" of affliction. Understandably, Job was terrified. Do you find yourself in a similar scenario? Do you feel alone, without an advocate in life, much less in heaven, someone to bear the weight of who you are and what you have done? Are you longing for someone to bridge the gap, to bring God near, and drive away the terror of His wrath? If so, rejoice that God has heard Job's longing! You needn't feel Job's estrangement or fear anymore. The Mediator has come—"For there is one God and one mediator between God and men, the man Christ Jesus…"(1 Tim 2:5). Jesus came as the "mediator of a new covenant"(Heb 9:15), a covenant of grace and love that has delivered you from God's judgement upon your sin.

Christ, the Mediator between God and men, came down from heaven. He was rejected, crucified, and raised from the dead: that which "we have seen with our eyes, which we have looked at and our hands have touched…"(1 John 1:1). Having taken on our flesh, the very flesh of the suffering Job, and shouldered our iniquities, He conquered sin and death and forever removed God's wrath from all those who believe in Him. Sitting now at God's right hand, Jesus is the *Great Mediator*.

If you are still living in Job's world of "ifs," believe in Jesus and what He has done for you on the cross. We need not fear the wrath of God anymore, for the love of Christ has set us free and "now my witness is in heaven; my advocate is on high. My intercessor is my friend as my eyes pour out tears to God; on behalf of a man He pleads with God as a man pleads for his friend"(Job 16:19-21).

Job uttered the dream and we are living in it. We have been loved into freedom by the person and work of Jesus and "There is no fear in love"(1 John 4:18). Rejoice in what the *Great Mediator* has done for you!

October 16

Secrets

Romans 2:16—...God will judge men's secrets through Jesus Christ....

There is a common misconception to which many cling—the *secrets* of the heart are unknowable. While Solomon tells us the "hearts of kings are unsearchable"(Prov 25:3) to their subjects and many may hide their *secrets* from others for years, we go astray when we begin to see ourselves as "kings and queens" whose *secrets* are hidden from the Lord. We may have succeeded in a lifetime of carefully harboring an unknown reality from everyone we know, but we will never be able to conceal it from God. For the Lord "knows the *secrets* of the heart"(Ps 44:21). Our Father promises to "search the heart and examine the mind"(Jer 17:10) and leave no stone unturned in His evaluation of each one of us.

Have you convinced yourself that your *secrets* are hidden from God? No matter how well you have disguised them, how carefully you have covered your tracks, "there is nothing hidden that will not be disclosed, and nothing concealed that will not be known and brought into the open"(Luke 8:17).

What hidden reality is waiting to be revealed by God in your life? Perhaps it is a *secret* pain you believe is yours and yours alone. Your *secret* is no more yours than the money in your pocket. Though it may be in your pocket, and in no one else's, God still owns it, for "The *secret* things belong to the Lord our God..."(Deut 29:29). You may be the protagonist in your hidden reality, but it belongs to God. He alone has the capacity to heal it, redeem it, and rejoice over it!

The sooner we recognize that our *"secrets"* are not *secrets*, but known realities in the hands of God, the sooner we can be released from their pain or rejoice with others in their blessing. However, if we attempt to hide and hold on to them, these *secrets* will be judged through Jesus Christ. But when we recognize that God has searched us and that He knows us (Ps 139:1), we can choose to give Him control over everything we once thought hidden. Then despite these *secrets*, and perhaps because of these *secrets*, we can be redeemed.

However painful or shameful, delightful or desperately dark your hidden realities are, give them to God. You can be judged by your *secrets*, or redeemed in spite of them. The choice is yours.

October 17

You are the Man!

2 Samuel 12:7—Then Nathan said to David, "You are the man!"

> Whenever we find that our religious life is making us feel that we are
> good—above all, that we are better than someone else—I think we may
> be sure that we are being acted on, not by God but by the Devil.[237]
> —C.S. Lewis

When it comes to our own self-assessment, we are all too often like David before Nathan—quick to cry out, "As surely as the Lord lives, the man who did this deserves to die...because he did such a thing and had no pity"(2 Sam 12:5-6). Blinded by pride, we project our guilt upon everyone but ourselves. We hope to hide, or perhaps ignore, our own culpability. But Nathan says to David, what God says to us: *You are the man!*

Do you recognize that at some point, *"You are the man!"*? Are you convinced that you are the sinner who has "displeased the Lord"(2 Sam 11:27)? Or are you, like David, living under the illusion that your sin goes unnoticed, that you have so carefully covered your tracks that no one would ever notice or care, much less a God you have never seen? Jesus says to us, "You hypocrite, first take the plank out of your own eye, and then you will see clearly to remove the speck from your brother's eye"(Matt 7:5).

The only appropriate perspective of spiritual self-examination is to recognize we are both *"guilty"* and *"saved."* We are never innocent, but we are loved, forgiven and redeemed. This jurisprudence runs completely contrary to the "innocent until proven guilty" belief of our culture, where even "proof" is relative. As a follower of Jesus, I must first recognize myself in the story, no matter how vile, profane or embarrassing that role may be. Rather than compare myself to the world around me, justifying my own relative righteousness, or hiding behind the masks I have created, I must claim my part. I must have the courage and the honesty to see myself as the "man who did this," whatever "this" may be.

I will know I am walking with Christ when I say with my mouth, and believe in my heart, that there is no sin I am not either guilty of or capable of committing. *I am guilty.* Similarly, I am caught in the grip of Satan so long as I see myself as "good," or at least "better than" the very ones I would condemn. But thanks be to God, that though we are guilty, in Christ we are not condemned!

Recognize that yes, *you are the man, you are the woman,* but that Christ came for such a man as you and me. Rejoice in the love that redeems us!

---

[237] C.S. Lewis, *The Business of Heaven* (New York: HarperCollins, 1984), 103.

October 18

The Gentle South Winds

Acts 27:13—When a gentle south wind began to blow, they thought they had obtained what they wanted; so they weighed anchor and sailed along the shore of Crete.

Has the Spirit recently placed a warning in your life? Do you feel like the winds are against you and your progress is slow and difficult? Such was the case for Paul and his companions on their journey to Rome. They were sailing along the coast of Crete, but the winds were against them and made their progress ponderous. Aware of the inevitable, Paul says to the crew, "'Men, I can see that our voyage is going to be disastrous and bring great loss to ship and cargo, and to our own lives also'"(Acts 27:10). But wanting to reach a better harbor for winter, the crew ignores Paul and his Spirit-guided premonition.

When a *gentle south wind* begins to blow, they set sail against the warning of God. "Before very long, a wind of hurricane force...swept down from the island"(Acts 27:14). The ship was caught and driven towards the very end Paul foretold.

Sometimes our going is ponderous because we, like Paul, are doing the very work God wants us to do and the enemy is trying to frustrate it. But if the winds are against you *and* the Lord has spoken a warning into your life, be careful not to push recklessly on in your way. If the Spirit checks you, listen, and be ever so cautious in your interpretation of the *"gentle south winds"* that blow into your life in the presence of God's restraint. Things may look favorable, the winds may luff your sails with the hope you have been looking for. But if they blow in the face of God's word in your life, you can be sure that a "wind of hurricane force" will follow to drive you to disaster if you persist in the way you are going.

Never allow the "winds" to dictate your going against the word of the Lord in your life. No matter how good or favorable something appears, if God is not in it, it will likely shipwreck your soul. If you have already set sail and are finding your progress difficult, examine your heart to see if you are engaged in the work of God or if He is trying to tell you to stop or change directions. Do not allow the enticement of the *gentle south wind* to lure you into certain disaster.

The winds are changeable; God is not. Let the unchangeable One lead you onward.

October 19

The Choice For Prayer

Isaiah 37:21—...Because you have prayed to me....

I may never know what I have failed to see materialize in my life simply because I chose *not* to pray. When the army of Sennacherib was attacking Israel, King Hezekiah did not make that mistake: he prayed. And because of his prayer, a seemingly insurmountable enemy was decimated by the hand of God.

Are you feeling as if an "army" of difficulties surrounds you? Have you come to the end of your hope, wondering how you will make it till tomorrow? If so, seek the Lord as Hezekiah did. Choose to pray.

Jesus says, "If you believe, you will receive whatever you ask for in prayer"(Matt 21:22). It may not come when we think it should or in the form we believe it must. But it will come, in God's way, in God's time. If we ask in the name of Christ, He will give us what we need—*more of Him.* Everything else needed for the crisis at hand will then be provided, "so that the Son may bring glory to the Father"(John 14:13).

But if I choose not to pray, I choose not to put my trust in God. I limit what God does in my life by walking away from prayer. If I doubt this, I need only look at Scripture. It was prayer that empowered Elijah to resurrect the widow's dead child (1 Kings 17). It was prayer that gifted Solomon with wisdom and Abraham's prayer that saved Lot from the sulfurous rain of heaven (1 Kings 3; Gen 19). Prayer also brought Jesus through the agony of Gethsemane to surrender His will to the will of His Father. By this prayer alone, the destiny of the world changed. Can you imagine what your prayers might do in your life and the lives of others?

When I am tempted to think my prayers do not matter, I must remember that "The prayer of a righteous man is powerful and effective"(Jam 5:16). God will answer my prayers: "Before they call *I will answer*," and "He will call upon me, and *I will answer* him"(Is 65:24; Ps 91:15). But if I do not pray, I should not expect to receive God's promises.

Don't live a life of missed opportunity. Choose to pray at all times, in all things. Remember that "Discipleship does not mean to use God when we can no longer function ourselves. On the contrary, it means to recognize that we can do nothing at all, but that God can do everything through us. As disciples, we find not some but all of our strength, hope, courage and confidence in God. Therefore, prayer must be our first concern."[238] Hezekiah was a "disciple" who chose to pray. Will you?

---

[238] Henri Nouwen, *Compassion* in *The Only Necessary Thing,* ed. Wendy Wilson Greer (New York: The Crossroad Publishing Company, 1999), 93.

October 20

Running in Vain?

Galatians 2:2—...for fear that I was running or had run my race in vain.

> Never, never, never give up!
> —Winston Churchill

Have you ever felt as if your life was filled with wasted effort? Perhaps, that everything you've worked for has been for nothing. That you are *running or had run your race in vain?*

In the rearview mirror of history, few lives have been more influential in the hearts of others than the Apostle Paul. And yet, in his letter to the Galatians, even Paul, the great missionary for Jesus Christ, struggles with a moment of doubt. Paul, who through the power of the Holy Spirit was helping to win the known world for Jesus, wonders whether his life and efforts have been in vain!

As the life of Paul shows us, moments of doubt, second-guessing, and spiritual exhaustion bordering on disillusionment, are normative in the life of the disciple. If we've never questioned our spiritual race, we're probably not running. Because we are human and because we are sinners, we will have periods, perhaps hours, days, weeks or even months, when we fail to clearly see God's purpose in some particular area of our lives. We may even question the purpose and utility of our lives as a whole. At first, we may see a roadblock that disheartens us. But the Spirit then helps to turn it into an opportunity to glorify God's name. We may run up against criticism which discourages us. But then God graces our lives with the encouragement and love we need to press on in the race.

Do not fear the doubt and spiritual exhaustion of the race you are running. Remember that the race is long, but that it is God who "gives strength to the weary and increases the power of the weak"(Is 40:29). Ask the Spirit's help to give you the stamina to never give up, even when your body and soul desperately desire to do so. The disciple who trusts in God's provision "will not grow tired or weary"(Is 40:28).

October 21

Living Confirmations of Grace

Acts 14:3—So Paul and Barnabas spent considerable time there, speaking boldly for the Lord who confirmed the message of His grace by enabling him to do miraculous signs and wonders.

What are our lives but living confirmations of God's grace? The evidence that we understand this truth and have matured from spiritual milk to solid food is our recognition that every victory and success is nothing more than a confirmation of the message of God's grace in us.

Do we still believe that our success at work is the result of hard work? Are we under the impression that our kids have turned out well because we are stellar parents? While strong efforts do matter, if we don't see God as the source of all good, Paul says, "You are still worldly....acting like mere men..."(1 Cor 3:3). We have forgotten the primacy of grace.

When I become spiritually mature, I understand that the "Lord has assigned to each his task"(1 Cor 3:5). And while I might plant the seed and another might water it, God alone makes it grow (1 Cor 3:6). Any labors, "miracles or wonders" we are enabled to do are simply the evidences of God's grace intended to draw eyes to Jesus. The problem arises when we refuse to recognize or agree with this and decide to hijack the praise of men and women as our own. When we do this, we demonstrate our rejection of the reality that "neither he who plants nor he who waters is anything, but only God who makes things grow"(1 Cor 3:7).

Are you living your life with the conviction that you are a *confirmation of God's grace*? If not, you are a stumbling block to men and an enemy of the cross! But when we succeed, the world will either want to destroy us in jealousy or praise us in adoration. They will desire to torture us or make gods of us, just as they did Paul and Barnabas in Lystra: "'The gods have come down to us in human form!'"(Acts 14:11). In the presence of such persecution or idolatrous praise, we must redirect all eyes to the One who enables us to do all things.

Our lives are meant to be showcases of God's grace. We must recognize that we are "God's fellow workers"(1 Cor 3:9), but that it is God alone who makes things grow. We flourish or wither because of the Lord. We are enabled and empowered only to be a living confirmation of God's grace. Let us live in that grace!

October 22

Stand Up!

Joshua 7:10—The Lord said to Joshua, "Stand up! What are you doing down on your face?"

There is most certainly a time and need for bowing down before the Lord in contrition. Most of us rarely do it, yet it ought to be a regular part of our lives. But God does not want us to remain there. To have our faces forever down would be to miss the radiance of His glory. To be forever kneeling would be to forgo the privilege and calling of carrying His message and His work out into the world.

When Israel was routed by Ai, Joshua "tore his clothes and fell face down to the ground before...the Lord"(Josh 7:6), and he humbled himself. But instead of asking forgiveness for the yet unrecognized, unseen sin that led to the defeat, he lamented his personal plight. He questioned and doubted God's providence, the promise the Lord had given him and the power of the divine injunction he had received: "Do not be terrified...[or] discouraged..."(Josh 1:9). And not only did Joshua fail God in this, but he lingered in that place of weakness, "remaining there till evening"(Josh 7:6). So the Lord said to Joshua, "*Stand up! What are you doing down on your face?*"

Are you, like Joshua, lingering with your face down in the wake of some defeat in your life? Have you chosen to stay there "till evening" when God desires for you to *stand up,* root out the sin in your camp and do His work? Lying face down in a personal despondency would not rid Israel of the stolen, devoted things that angered God. Joshua had to *stand up* to do God's work.

What is God calling you to *stand up* and address in your life? If I am still lying flat on my face and choosing to wallow in my doubt, self-pity and spiritual blindness, I am more in the grip of the enemy than I am in the hands of God. Instead, I must bow down before the Lord in worshipful contrition, ask forgiveness for my sin, know that I am forgiven, and then *stand up* and do what God is calling me to do.

In the moment of your humiliation, be careful you do not miss what God is calling you to do. *More of Him, less of you.*

October 23

The Phalanx of Faith

Isaiah 7:9—If you do not stand firm in your faith, you will not stand at all.

The strength of the military phalanx formation lies in its collective unity—standing or marching firmly together in close proximity. Speaking to the nation of Israel, Isaiah demonstrates a deep understanding of the importance of standing steadfastly. As he reminds the Israelites, it profits no one to stand, unless one stands firmly. Fight with valor or be defeated.

Standing firm in the faith depends first upon an individual relationship with the Lord that is nurtured by our personal, spiritual disciplines and sustained by God's grace. But standing firm also depends upon collective unity—the phalanx of Christian community, Church tradition and, ultimately, the strength of the General leading the cause.

Every solider in the formation of faith must march into battle with the conviction that he is fighting in a cause that matters. God's solider has been freed by the blood of Jesus and must fight with a determination to never be enslaved again—"It is for freedom that Christ has set us free. Stand firm, then, and do not let yourselves be burdened again by a yoke of slavery"(Gal 5:1). How do we do this? By putting on the "full armor of God"(Eph 6:10) and readying ourselves in the Word—"Your Word, O Lord, is eternal; it stands firm in the heavens"(Ps 119:89).

Though personally prepared, the spiritual warrior also needs others to stand beside him in his fight. Together, they "stand firm in one spirit, contending as one man for the faith of the gospel, without being frightened in anyway by those who oppose [them]"(Phil 1:27-28). The soldier is encouraged, "standing firm in the faith, because [he knows his]... brothers throughout the world are undergoing the same kind of sufferings"(1 Peter 5:9). They are empowered by the example and teachings of those who have gone before them—"So then, brothers, stand firm and hold to the teachings we passed on to you..."(2 Thes 2:15). Most importantly, every disciple in the phalanx of faith must believe, without wavering, that their General, the God who created them and leads them, is the omnipotent God of their battle strength—"Now it is God who makes both us and you stand firm in Christ"(2 Cor 1:21).

Standing in the ranks of faith, do you believe that God is able to keep you from falling, even when the battle is fierce, and your companions are fearful or scattered (Jude 1:24)? Victory in Christ comes to those who stand firm under the banner of the Lord (Ex 17:15). With conviction, sing until your dying breath—"On Christ the solid rock I stand!"[239]

---

[239] Edward Mote, 1834, "My Hope is Built on Nothing Less," *The Lutheran Hymnal*, 370.

October 24

Words

Matthew 12:36—But I tell you that men will have to give account on the day of judgement for every careless word they have spoken.

...*words* which do not give the light of Christ increase the darkness.[240]
—Mother Teresa

When Winston Churchill said, "We are masters of the unsaid *words*, but slaves of those we let slip out," he stressed the tremendous power of *words,* both the unspoken and the spoken. Before a word is uttered, we still master it. We remain in control of its potential for good or evil. But once a word is spoken, it is no longer in our control. It is gone from us. Yet, as Christ reminds us, we are still responsible for it—"For by your *words* you will be acquitted, and by your *words* you will be condemned"(Matt 12:37). Like children that bear our name, these words belong to us still.

Too little emphasis is given to the *words* we speak. Our media-saturated culture spews *words* into the digital world in seconds. Social forums have allowed these *words* to become dangerously disembodied, creating an artificial distance that emboldens a recklessness and carelessness. In an offhanded manner, sometimes in intended jest, we speak poorly of our friends or we softly denigrate the very God who created us.

But these *careless words* are not just *words.* They carry eternal consequences. It is by our *words* and subsequent actions that we will be enslaved to eternal condemnation or freed to victorious life in Christ. There is no salvation apart from *words.* You must "confess with your mouth, 'Jesus is Lord...'"(Rom 10:9). Similarly, we must remember that our *words* have the power to condemn us. Jesus reminds us that we will *have to give account on the day of judgement for every careless word [we] have spoken.*

From the "overflow of the heart the mouth speaks"(Matt 12:34). Are you in the habit of examining your heart before you speak? Have you learned the discipline of pausing before you speak? Do you regularly pray, "May the *words* of my mouth...be pleasing in your sight, O Lord, my Rock and my Redeemer"(Ps 19:14)?

Seek to give the world only those *words* which glorify Christ. Pray for the grace to master the careless *words* and speak only those which come "out of the good things stored up"(Matt 12:35) in you. In this way you will glorify God and stand humbly before Him on the day of judgement.

---

[240] Malcolm Muggeridge, *Something Beautiful for God* (New York: HarperCollins, 1971), 66.

October 25

Battle of Wills

James 4:15—Instead, you ought to say, "If it is the Lord's will, we will live and do this or that."

> There are only two kinds of people in the end: those who say to God, "Thy will be done," and those to whom God says, in the end, "Thy will be done."[241]   —C.S. Lewis

Self-actualization is cheered by the world. If you will it, you can do it and get what you want. But while this self-empowered thinking appeals to the inner "god" in each one of us, the providential purpose of the human will and its interplay with the divine will is much more complex and mysterious. Created in God's image, we were each given a will. God wants us to use it, as He does His. The Lord could have created robots. He did not. God created us as men and women endowed with a will to plan, purpose, and pursue. The question then becomes—what is your will willing in your life? Is your will becoming more like your Father's?

God has "made known to us the mystery of His will according to His good pleasure, which He purposed in Christ..."(Eph 1:9). We are called to grow in our understanding of "His good, pleasing and perfect will" as we "test and approve it"(Rom 12:2) on the battlefields of our daily lives. Some come to an understanding of God's will relatively easily. Others may take a lifetime of spiritual wrestling, intellectual testing, or suffering "according to God's will"(1 Peter 4:19). Either way, the only certainty is that God's will will win. He is the One "who works out everything in conformity with the purpose of His will"(Eph 1:11).

To doubt this truth is like clinging to the idea that the sun orbits the earth. Despite ancient opinion, the astronomical truth has always been a "heliocentric one." And the solar system in which we live is no different than our spiritual lives: "Son"-centric. The sooner we come to accept this divine paradigm, the sooner we are freed to use our wills to plan, purpose, and pursue our lives without the need of being broken by God.

But when we submit to God's will, we find pleasure, power, and peace. If He leads us in an unfamiliar direction, we are filled with excitement and confidence! We understand that He knows best and something better must be ahead! We have learned the secret blessing of saying, *"If it is the Lord's will, we will live and do this or that."* Have you learned to say to God, "Thy will be done"? Pray that the Lord gives you the grace to submit your will to His and to use it to glorify Christ in your life.

---

[241] C.S. Lewis, *The Great Divorce* (New York: HarperCollins, 2001), 75.

October 26

"Yes" in Christ!

2 Corinthians 1:20—For no matter how many promises God has made, they are all "Yes" in Christ.

It is the ongoing genius of Satan that he is able to equate God in the hearts and minds of men and women with the omnipotent "NO!" Ever since the Garden, Satan has forced our attention on God's negation rather than His affirmation. "How unreasonable it is of God for Him to expect this of you!" Satan says emphatically. "Why should you do this? It makes no sense! You know better than that."

Such questioning is rooted in the scheming of the darkness. For the idea that God is just some omnipotent "killjoy" in the sky who doesn't understand us or want what is best for us, could not be further from the truth. Satan's desire is to hide the fact that in Christ we have been liberated into a life of "Yes!" We are no longer slaves to our sinful natures, but free to find the peace and blessing of living in God's promises.

When God says, "I will never leave you nor forsake you"(Josh 1:5), in Christ I know this is true. When the Lord says, "'I know the plans I have for you...to prosper you and not to harm you, plans to give you hope and a future'"(Jer 29:11), in Christ this is guaranteed—*"Yes" in Christ!* When Jesus says, "For God so loved the world that He gave His one and only Son, that whoever believes in Him shall not perish but have eternal life"(John 3:16), it is clear that God loves us more than we could ever imagine!

God's Word, applied to our lives and lived out in the person of Jesus Christ, is anything but a life fettered by "NO!" To those who come to Jesus and believe in Him, the promises of Scripture are fulfilled. Life becomes one glorious "Yes!" after the next. It is not always easy, but it is possible. We will still pass "through the valley of the shadow of death"(Ps 23:4), but we will say "Yes" to the knowledge that He is with us, and His rod and staff comfort us. We will be persecuted, and we will know pain and depravation; but we will rest in the conviction that He has overcome the world and that He will work all things for the good in the lives of those who love Him (John 16:33; Rom 8:28).

Do you doubt the promises of God? Then fix your eyes on Jesus, *for no matter how many promises God has made, they are all "Yes" in Christ.* In Christ, you will be able to say of your life what Joshua said to Israel: "Not one of all the Lord's good promises to the house of Israel failed; every one was fulfilled"(Josh 21:45). The Lord is longing to fill your life with "*YES!*"

October 27

Rend Your Heart

Joel 2:13—Rend your heart and not your garments.

In the marriage between human emotion and action, it does not always follow that the leadings of the heart are manifested in the work, or that the action necessarily represents the landscape of the interior. Public presence and private reality often differ. No one knows this sad truth better than the God who created us.

Speaking through the prophet Joel, God implores His people to *rend their hearts and not their garments*, reiterating His censor through the prophet Isaiah: "The multitude of your sacrifices—what are they to me?... Your hands are full of blood; wash and make yourselves clean....Stop doing wrong, learn to do right!"(Isa 1:11, 15). The outward show of contrition or praise in the presence of inward corruption is an abomination to God. He hates it!

To be sure, deep grief, like the shock of evil, or the joy of praise, has a "face." Before God, the face of each emotion has its place. David dances before the Lord's ark and, in another moment, mourns the death of his friend Abner (2 Sam 6:14; 3:31). Other spiritual actions are no exception. We can worship with or without our hearts, pray with or without inward devotion, or fast with or without a soul that hungers for God. In the end, what matters to the Lord is not the sacrifice, in and of itself, but the "acknowledgement of God" with the heart (Hos 6:6).

God wants a heart that is broken before Him, torn in two. Have you made an effort to *rend your heart*? David says to God, "You do not delight in sacrifices, or I would bring it; you do not take pleasure in burnt offerings. The sacrifices of God are a broken spirit, a broken and contrite heart, O God, you will not despise"(Ps 51:16-17). Are you offering up a *broken and contrite heart* before God? As Joel says, "Return to the Lord your God, for He is gracious and compassionate"; for, "Who knows? He may turn and have pity and leave behind a blessing"(Joel 2:13-14).

Let us seek to live with a spiritual integrity that works its way from the inside out. If we only rend our garments and not our hearts, we will miss the glorious opportunity of finding our hearts truly healed by a Father who loves us more than we can imagine!

October 28

Befriending Darkness

Psalm 88:18—...the darkness is my closet friend.

> But deep in the darkness is God....[242]
> —Rainer Rilke

The embrace of darkness is one of God's greatest gifts. At first, this might seem counterintuitive. But we can fear the darkness or we can choose to see it as a friend sent by God to lead us back to Him. Too often, Christians will demonize the dark. They simply understand it as a place where they cannot see, an emptiness that threatens to consume them, and a solitude that exposes their most intimate weaknesses.

The darkness is all of these things. And because it is, it is to be seen as one of our closest friends. We should never fear the dark, but rather the artificial light that masquerades as the true Light. For it is the darkness that helps to show us the Light more clearly. The dark reminds us that emptiness is meant to be filled and that solitude is meant to be embraced by the arms of God.

Like this embrace, astrophysicists understand dark energy and dark matter to be the unseen forces that literally hold the universe together. So also the love of God. In the darkest of our nights, it surrounds and contains us, holding us together even when we believe we will be consumed by the dark—"Because of the Lord's great love we are not consumed..."(Lam 3:22). Similarly, the solitude of the darkness is best seen "not as a wound but a gift—as God's gift—so that in our aloneness, we might discern how deeply we are loved by God."[243]

When we stop fearing the dark and begin to embrace it as God's gift to us, there is a total transformation of the heart. We begin to understand the words of David—"If I say, 'Surely the darkness will hide me, and the light become night around me, even the darkness will not be dark to you; the night will shine like the day, for darkness is as light to you'"(Ps 139:11-12). When we see the darkness as God's gift in our lives, we will begin to see the light of Love shining through it, transforming the darkness and us at the same time.

Because darkness is often God's tool to help bring the disciple home, do not fear the darkness. Embrace it, knowing that through it, and because of it, we will see God better than we ever have before.

---

[242] Rainer Rilke, *Book of Hours: Love Poems to God* (New York: Riverhead Books, 2005), 109.
[243] Henri Nouwen, "A Quality of Heart," in *The Only Necessary Thing*, ed. Wendy Wilson Greer (New York: The Crossroad Publishing Company, 2015),43.

October 29

Wholly Devoted

2 Kings 17:32—They worshipped the Lord, but they also….

In his final words of dedication to the Temple of God, Solomon says to the people of Israel, "Let your heart therefore be *wholly devoted* to the Lord our God…"(1 Kings 8:61 NASB). When you consider your own heart and its worship, are you *wholly devoted* to the Lord, or are you worshiping the Lord, *but also*…?

The tendency for us all is to complicate our spiritual lives, rather than simplify; to add to, rather than focus on, what we have and know to be true. Solomon was no exception this rule. Even after he clearly exhorted Israel to be "wholly devoted to the Lord," he went on to foolishly marry countless foreign women and allow the worship of their gods. This spiritual trend for admixture continued to plague Israel after Solomon's death. In the years following the Assyrian conquest, God's chosen people found themselves mixed with inhabitants from foreign lands who "worshipped the Lord, *but they also* appointed all sorts of their own people…as priests at the high places"(2 Kings 17:32). They "worshipped the Lord, *but they also* served their own gods…"(2 Kings 17:33). These foreigners were anything but singularly devoted to the Lord.

If God were to examine your heart and evaluate the practices of your life today, would He find a worshipper *wholly devoted* to Him? Is the time you spend, the things you do and the thoughts you linger on, suffused with the Holy Spirit? The spiritual life of the disciple demands absolute fidelity. Anything other than full devotion will be viewed by God as an adultery of the heart. Solomon started with good intentions, but finished as an adulterous hypocrite. Have we remained *wholly devoted* to the One we claim to love?

God will not share His worship with anyone or anything. It does not matter if it is your spouse or children, the congregation you serve or the company the Lord helped you build. A great many good and honorable things can become the object of idolatrous worship in our lives. As long as our lives are marked by a "*but also,*" they are not "*wholly devoted.*"

Commit today that the Lord will find in you a heart that is *wholly devoted* to Him. Resist the temptation to add a pinch of this or a sprinkle of that to your spiritual life, and trust God will empower you to do it. It must be Christ and Christ alone!

October 30

Inquiring

Joshua 9:14—The men of Israel sampled their provisions, but did not inquire of the Lord.

The life of faith grows with a slow and steady maturation. We are not born as spiritual adults. We must be children first because only as children can we come to know our Father. First we know Him as a child knows his parents: we are nursed and held. We are led by the hand as Israel was through the desert of Sinai. As children we are constantly learning from our Father, sometimes through a curious or necessitated *inquiring*. For to inquire is to reveal that we do not yet know. We do not fail because we ask too many questions, but rather because we hesitate to ask. All too frequently, we think we are ready for independence, and we leave our Father out of the equation.

The conquering Israelites were guilty of this youthful hubris. When God's people entered Canaan and encountered the Gibeonites pretending to be a people from a distant land, the Israelites thought they were ready to judge for themselves the truth of this claim. They empirically tested the strangers, sampling their provisions to verify their story. In these efforts, the Israelites relied on their own wisdom and did not inquire of God. As a result, they were duped.

King Saul would later commit a similar mistake. He "did not inquire of Lord"(1 Chron 10:14), but struck out on his own. He even consulted a "medium for guidance"(10:13). Ultimately, he prematurely "died because he was unfaithful to the Lord"(10:13).

Whether we are spiritually young or mature, when we are confronted with confusion, we must inquire of the Lord. When we fail in this, we do so to our own detriment. But as we mature in faith, our need to inquire becomes less often and less formal. It is not because we need God less, but because we become "so much in contact with God that [we] never need to ask Him to show [us] His will."[244] Our decisions will be part of His will.

Have you become so intimately related to Jesus that you know His will without asking? Are your thoughts and actions growing to be more instinctually those of Christ? As you continue to seek this perfect, divine oneness with Christ, never stop *inquiring*. He will be faithful to lead you to His best.

---

[244] Oswald Chambers, *My Utmost For His Highest* (Grand Rapids: Discovery House Publishers, 1992), March 20.

328

October 31

Blinding Traditions

Mark 7:8—You have let go of the commands of God and are holding on to the traditions of men.

Constant vigilance in our lives is necessary to keep the commands of God from becoming subordinate to the traditions of men. Jesus scolded the Pharisees' failure to do just this. They had become so wedded to their traditions and so scrupulous in keeping them that God's heartbeat for the world had become lost in a morass of moral rules of conduct.

Tradition has played an enormous role in history, secular and religious alike. Jesus knew this. He chastised the men who had deified the keeping of the traditions, not the traditions themselves. Jesus said, "Do not think that I have come to abolish the Law or the Prophets; I have not come to abolish them but to fulfill them"(Matt 5:17). In these words, Jesus stresses that He came to save and sanctify us by refocusing our attention on what truly matters to our Father: the transformed heart.

Our Father cares for this condition of the interior. His commands are simple: "Love the Lord your God with all your heart and with all your soul and with all your mind," and "Love your neighbor as yourself"(Matt 22:37, 39). Any spiritual tradition that fails in the execution of these two fundamental imperatives to love, misses the mark. It becomes a tool of a divisive devil rather than a loving God.

We must recognize that today's Church may be no less guilty than the Pharisees in this fundamental idolatry of tradition. In some sectors, much fuss is made of practices rooted in traditions: denominational differences, patterns of worship, styles of dress, or what we eat or drink. Jesus comes crashing through these nonessential, peripheral issues and says, "You have let go of the commands of God..."(Mark 7:8). He says, "Nothing outside a man can make him 'unclean' by going into him. Rather, it is what comes out of a man that makes him 'unclean'"(7:15). Rebuking all, Christ says, "on the outside you appear to people as righteous but on the inside you are full of hypocrisy and wickedness"(Matt 23:28).

If the traditions we cling to do not clearly present the sinfulness of men, the amazing love of God in Christ Jesus, the forgiveness of our sins through His blood, and the power of the resurrection, then they are not true to our Lord. They are enemies of the Kingdom's mission. When we hold to these traditions at the cost of God's essential truths, we stand as guilty as a whitewashed Pharisee. Let us be careful to hold loosely to our opinions, interpretations, and preferences, but steadfastly to the unconquerable truths and resolute commands of our Lord Jesus Christ —"For Christ's love compels us..."(2 Cor 5:14).

NOVEMBER

November 1

The Giver and the Given

Psalm 40:10—I do not hide your righteousness in my heart; I speak of your faithfulness and salvation. I do not conceal your love and truth from the great assembly.

When we come to Christ we become the recipients of abounding love and grace. We find a peace that passes understanding and God's unwavering faithfulness. In short, we are gifted beyond measure. We are free to respond to this blessing in one of two ways—we can become a *giver and the given* or we can become a spiritual "hoarder."

The heart that truly understands the gifts of God cannot keep from giving back out of the richness it has received. This giving begins with rejoicing and gratefulness. It is the life that chooses, like the healed invalid at the pool, to go out and "speak of [God's] faithfulness and salvation"(John 5:1-18; Ps 40:10). In this spirit of thanks, the transformed heart decides to become the *giver and the given* in concrete ways.

The follower of Jesus recognizes that "we are chosen, blessed and broken so as to be given."[245] Our lives become the sacrament given to others. We are the broken bread in the way we work, the money we give, the words we say, and the time we spend. When we commit to give back a portion of all that God has given to us, we begin to realize the pleasure God has in being the greatest of givers. We find, "True joy, happiness, and inner peace come from the giving of ourselves to others,"[246] as Christ has done for us.

The alternative to becoming a *giver and the given*—the broken bread of God's work in the world—is to hoard what we have so freely received. We can choose to stow it away and bury it deep in the ground. Such a response demonstrates both spiritual dry rot and lack of trust in the goodness of the Giver. It shows that we don't understand Christ's command—"Give, and it will be given to you"(Luke 6:38). To this "hoarder," God says, "You wicked, lazy servant!"(Matt 25:26).

If we find ourselves hoarding what God has given us, we can be sure that we don't understand the purpose and pleasure of God's giving. He gives that we might give in return, blessing us to the point of overflowing. When His gifts dead end in our lives, the Holy Spirit is not moving. In our blessings, we must decide to become *givers and the given*— the broken bread for Christ and His Kingdom.

---

[245] Henri Nouwen, *Life of the Beloved* (New York: The CrossRoad Publishing Company, 2002), 121.
[246] Ibid, 109.

November 2

Time

Psalm 90:12—Teach us to number our days aright, that we may gain a heart of wisdom.

Time is a matter of perspective. It is relative to the observer and the velocity and gravitational forces involved. But it does not stand still. Fast or slow, it marches on. While for God "a thousand years...are like a day that has just gone by or like a watch in the night"(Ps 90:4), for us, *time* can feel fleeting at one turn and interminable at the next. We often regret moments that go too quickly and tire of those that appear to drag on forever. How we experience these perceived fluctuations of *time* greatly affects our spiritual lives.

The Psalmist prays, *"Teach us to number our days aright, that we may gain a heart of wisdom."* The more spiritually mature we become, the more richly we understand the importance of *time*. We begin to recognize "There is a *time* for everything, and a season for every activity under heaven"(Ecc 3:1). Patience and endurance grow as we begin to see that God's work in us is often of the slow and steady type. At the same time, we see more clearly the sin of dissipating our days and life energies on things that have no eternal significance. Like our Lord Jesus, we do not rush God's work and timing—"The right *time* for me has not yet come"(John 7:6)—but neither do we stand still when the will of God directs us forward.

We will pray most effectively when we ask God to help us *number our days aright.* We must be good stewards of *time.* We must not waste or forget to enjoy the precious *time* God gives us and use it effectively for His Kingdom's glory. We must recognize that though "My life today will be lived in *time,*...it will involve eternal issues. The needs of my body will shout out, but it is for the needs of my soul that I must care the most."[247] As *time* marches on, "One should look after one's own soul at whatever cost...."[248] On the spiritual *time* clock, this is the true "heart of the matter."[249]

Have you asked the Spirit to give you wisdom in your understanding of *time*? Fast or slow, He gives it to us for His purposes and His glory. Let us pray to number our days aright, committing to live out the *time* we have been given for the glory of God. Though *time* marches on, we get the chance to harness our piece of it for God and His purposes!

---

[247] John Baillie, *A Diary of Private Prayer* (New York: Scribner, 2014), 47.
[248] Graham Greene, *The Heart of the Matter* (New York: Penguin Books, 1999), 161.
[249] Ibid, 107.

November 3

On Account of Christ

Matthew 11:6—Blessed is anyone who does not stumble on account of me.

From prison, John the Baptist sends his disciples to inquire of Jesus: "Are you the one who was to come, or should we expect someone else?"(Matt 11:3). John knew the answer to his own question. He baptized Jesus, saying, "I need to be baptized by you, and do you come to me now?"(Matt 3:14). But while John knew Jesus was the Christ, in the suffering of prison, in a moment of his own personal weariness, he *stumbles* on account of who Jesus is. John's idea of a Redeemer did not fit the needs of his current circumstances.

Maybe you have *stumbled* over Jesus once, twice or many times. If so, you are not alone. In His coming, Jesus became a *"stumbling* block to the Jews and foolishness to the Gentiles..."(1 Cor 1:23). Christ had, and still has, no interest in being a protean god, fitting into all the preconceived expectations and whimsical fancies of the men and women He created. His behavior often disappointed expectations. His coming was offensive to Jews—a humble birth, the son of a woman betrothed to a carpenter from an obscure place. Jesus did not come as the robed and gallant, conquering king. His ministry defied all expectations and conventions. He healed on the Sabbath, ate with prostitutes and tax collectors, and spoke in parables that seemed inscrutable. His death, to many, appeared meaningless in the moment, and His resurrection an inexplicable mystery or hoax.

But Jesus did not come to satisfy the Pharisees or to fulfill the political agendas of the Israelites. Nor did He leave heaven to simply please our personal opinions and desires. He came to shock us as He overturns our tables and transforms us completely. He came to change the world. He came to change you and me, once and for all.

If you are finding that you are *stumbling* over Jesus, it is because your expectations are bumping into His divine reality. You can either be offended and fall away, as many Jews did, looking for someone else to fulfill your idea of the Messiah King. Or, you can persist through the apparent "foolishness" of Christ to find yourself forever changed—*Blessed is anyone who does not stumble on account of me.*

Pray today that the Spirit of God helps you to embrace Jesus just as He is—the unconventional King who is both willing and able to transform us from the inside out.

November 4

Morning and Evening

1 Chronicles 23:30—They were also to stand every morning to thank and praise the Lord. They were to do the same in the evening.

The Psalmist writes, "It is good to praise the Lord and make music to your name, O Most High, to proclaim your love in the morning and your faithfulness at night..."(Ps 92:1). So convinced was King David of this truth that he assigned the Levites to *stand every morning to thank and praise the Lord* and *to do the same thing in the evening.* Does this pattern of regular praise and thanks reflect your spiritual life? Are the bookends of your day, as well as everything in between, dedicated to the Lord?

Devotionals have often sought to frame the soul's daily focus as David did with the Levites—*morning and evening.*[250] [251] [252] But even with a specific reading or ceremony, we must first decide to incline our attention to the Lord at the beginning and end of each day. When we determine to praise and thank God amidst the morning's uncertainty of what lies ahead, we find the proper focus and perspective for the rest of the day. If we say to God, "I will sing of your strength, in the morning I will sing of your love..."(Ps 59:16), we affirm in the infancy of the day (before we are tested, tried, wearied or blessed), that our Father loves us and that His strength is with us. We declare that He is worthy to be praised, no matter what the day brings.

Having greeted the Lord in this morning worship and walked with Him through the day, it is time to return to Him with praise in the evening. As the Levites demonstrated, while the morning devotion is praise in anticipation and uncertainty, the evening is thanks in light of the faithfulness observed. What did the Lord teach me today about myself and about Him? Can I thank Him for the blessings of today as well as the discouragements, difficulties and chastisements I might have received? Will I close this day knowing my Father better than when I started?

Let us commit, *morning* and *evening*, to praise and thank the Lord for who He is and what He has done and will do in our lives. If we cannot give God the bookends of our days, we are unlikely to give Him the chapters in between. However, if we dedicate the "bookends" of our days to God, and God alone, we will find ourselves willingly, lovingly, giving Him every chapter in between. God wants the whole story, every page of who we are!

---

[250] Charles Spurgeon, *Morning and Evening* (Geanies House, Fearn: Christian Focus Publications, 1994).
[251] John Baillie, *A Diary of Private Prayer* (New York: Scribner, 2014).
[252] David Jeremiah, *Morning & Evening Devotions* (Nashville: Thomas Nelson, 2005).

November 5

Portent to Many

Psalm 71:7—I have become like a portent to many....

One of the surest signs that we are living a Spirit-filled life is the sense of wonder our lives bring to everyone we encounter. Are we are a *portent*—an inspirational and exceptional marvel of God? Do we elicit a God-honoring admiration and curiosity in the hearts of others? When the Spirit fills us, we are amazing and unusual in the way we live, the things we say, and the beliefs we hold tightly to. As Chambers says, "We always know when Jesus is at work because He produces in the commonplace something that is inspiring."[253] If we are not an anomaly among men and women, we are not likely living full of the Spirit, for the Spirit is nothing but a marvel.

Isaiah says, "Here am I, and the children the Lord has given me. We are signs and symbols...for the Lord Almighty..."(Is 8:18). My life is meant to be a portentous one, a sign and a symbol for the Lord among the men and women He has planted me among. If I am no different in the hope of my heart, the words of my mouth or the conduct of my body, then I am most certainly not a light shining brightly in the darkness. If I am not set apart, then I am likely not wholly God's, because the Lord is unlike any other.

It takes nothing to go with the current—a fallen leaf does that. But many a so-called "Christian" has also decided to simply follow the cultural trends. Increasingly, Yeats' words appear prophetic: "The best lack all conviction, while the worst/ Are full of a passionate intensity."[254] Instead of living lives that either inspire holy wonderment or incite the spite and animus of the ungodly, many "Christians" have decided it is more comfortable to drift along, impeding no one, offending few, and inspiring little. Such ineffectual living is not God's desire, however. He wants His name "known among the nations"(Ps 105:1). And that proclamation starts with our lives, a *portent to many* in the places where we have been planted.

Where God resides, the world cannot help but wonder! Perhaps there will be praise, perhaps persecution and hate. But not indifference! The current indifference of our world towards God may in part be because His people are not living Spirit-filled lives. When we decide that we will live for Jesus, our lives suddenly take on a radiance that the world cannot ignore. Are you ready to be a *portent to many*?

---

[253] Oswald Chambers, *My Utmost for His Highest* (Grand Rapids: Discovery House Publishers, 1992), August 21.

[254] W.B. Yeats, "The Second Coming," in *Modern British Literature,* ed. Frank Kermode and Hollander (New York: Oxford University Press, 1973), 192.

November 6

Set Purpose

Acts 2:23—This man was handed over to you by God's set purpose and foreknowledge....

What amazing freedom and peace come when we finally understand the *set purpose and foreknowledge* of God in our lives. Your life right now might be filled with unimaginable, inexplicable pain—death, betrayal, persecution or a surprising medical diagnosis. There may seem to be no sense to the pain. Or perhaps your ache is none of these afflictions, but involves questions of life purpose: *Who am I? What am I here to do?*

Into the midst of all these uncertainties God declares, "My purpose will stand, and I will do all that I please....What I have said, that will I bring about; what I have planned, that will I do"(Is 46:10-11). If I am struggling with a sense of purpose in my life, it is likely because I have divorced my personal experience from God's overarching, providential plan. The mistake in this is mine. The deposed King Nebuchadnezzar learned to say of God's purpose: "All the peoples of the earth are regarded as nothing. He does as He pleases with the powers of heaven and the peoples of the earth. No one can hold back His hand or say to Him: 'What have you done?'"(Dan 4:35).

Are we still asking God, "What have you done?" Or, are we resting in the truth that God's purposes have been established since the dawn of creation? Jesus remained resolute and peaceful in the Garden of Gethsemane because "He was with God in the beginning"(John 1:2) and knew His Father's *set purpose* in all things.

No matter the vicissitudes of your life, the pain that tears at your heart or the joy that causes you to sing and dance, know that "God has put it into [men's] hearts to accomplish His purpose..."(Rev 17:17)—the glorification of His name and the reclamation of His people. Jesus Christ was and is the full embodiment of this purpose. Your life and mine exist only to further play out this divine purpose. Indeed, "Man's chief end is to glorify God, and to enjoy Him forever."[255] We will only fulfill this purpose when, in the freedom and peace of Christ, we understand that God is in control, for "The Lord Almighty has sworn, 'Surely, as I have planned, so it will be, and as I have purposed, so it will stand'"(Is 14:24).

Can you affirm God has *set purposes* in your life? Do you believe they are for your good? Rest in the arms of the divine foreknowledge that laid the foundations of the world and knit the sinews of your body.

---

[255] Thomas Watson, *A Body of Divinity* (East Peoria: Versa Press, 2015), 6.

November 7

Grumbling

James 5:9—Don't grumble against each other, brothers, or you will be judged. The Judge is standing at the door!

How many of us have the courage to admit we are often ungrateful grumblers, must less that our grumblings are sin? And yet, God, the "Judge standing at the door," sees our *grumbling* as nothing less. We live in a world that grumbles incessantly, almost always about matters of no eternal significance. *Grumbling* has become so endemic in our conversations with others, and even with ourselves, that we are often totally unaware that we are *grumbling*. We may even enjoy a good grumble—a well-articulated complaint that serves as a catharsis. Misery loves company.

But whether our complaints are voiced to the multitudes or simply whispered in the quiet of our own hearts, Jesus is conscious of our *grumbling* (John 6:61). Our constant complaining tires the patience of God —"How long will this wicked community grumble against me? I have heard the complaints of these *grumbling* Israelites"(Num 14:27).

Why does this bother God? Because the effrontery of *grumbling* undermines the very lavish generosity He has bestowed on each of us. God knows that our grumbling comes from a spirit of ingratitude. We are a people fed manna and quail from the heavens, but unhappy that these gifts did not come in a variety of flavors or preparations. When we grumble, we are not giving thanks. When we complain, our focus is on the muck before us, not the heavens above us. For this reason, God hates *grumbling*.

It should come as no surprise, therefore, that we are commanded not to grumble—"Don't grumble...." In this command, James echoes Jesus before him—"Stop *grumbling* among yourselves"(John 6:43). When you spot the slightest trace of *grumbling* in your heart, stop immediately. Do not go further until you have ruthlessly destroyed the source of your *grumbling*. Failure to do so will ensure that it not only festers and spreads within you like a cancer, but that it will also continue to grieve the Spirit who indwells in you. Complaint by complaint, the Spirit is inched out of the temple of your soul.

The Spirit of God cannot, and will not, coexist with *grumbling* in a temple of ingratitude. Temples are places of worship and praise. Our souls must be nothing less. The measure to which you choose to grumble is the degree to which you will grieve the Spirit of the living God in your soul. Commit yourself, therefore, to gratitude. Reject *grumbling*, absolutely. Be filled with the Spirit in increasing measure.

November 8

Examine Yourself

2 Corinthians 13:5—Examine yourselves to see whether you are in the faith; test yourselves. Do you not realize that Christ Jesus is in you—unless, of course, you fail the test?

Self-examination is an essential component of the spiritually healthy and mature disciple of Christ. Perhaps not surprisingly, it is also one of the hardest disciplines of faith to actually *do* because of the humility it requires. And so, very few believers do it regularly—some not at all. Whether this reluctance or refusal to "look to thyself" comes from a spiritual laziness or a conscious fear of what we will or will not find, the fact remains, that God wants us to do it—and to do it routinely.

This is the very message the Apostle Paul tells the Corinthians. He exhorts them to examine their hearts to see if they are in the faith. Such an examination, in the Corinthian heart or yours, should elicit no fear, if the Spirit is living in us. The disciple who is *in the faith* will find, upon self-examination, the filthy rags of a sinful life, the complete absence of the perfection that we are called to (2 Cor 13:11). But this very same disciple will also find the overwhelming grace of Jesus Christ, which covers every corner of the tarnished soul. This disciple will find that, though he or she is imperfect, he walks with the Spirit, and he has an irrepressible love for the Father, welling up within him. There will be, within the depths of his heart, a confident recognition, that despite being more flawed than he would like to admit, he is loved by Christ more than he could ever imagine.

When was the last time you examined your heart in this way? Are you testing yourself regularly to ascertain whether the Spirit is alive and well in your heart? Have you found that the love of Christ Jesus is in you? If you are finding yourself avoiding or neglecting self-examination, it is likely because you know very well, on some subconscious level, what you will find—*more of YOU and less of HIM.*

As disciples of Christ, however, we must be willing to honestly face what we see within our hearts and to deal with it according to the grace of Jesus. The more we heed the voice of the Spirit in our lives, the more we will become aware of just how sinful we are (1 Tim 1:15), but also, that the blood of Jesus covers it all!

Ask the Lord today to give you the courage and grace you need to test yourself. Only you can do it, and you must do it, if you are to grow to have *more of Him and less of you.*

November 9

Kicking Against the Goads

Acts 26:14—It is hard for you to kick against the goads.

When Jesus encounters Saul of Tarsus on the road to Damascus, Jesus says to him, "'Saul, Saul, why do you persecute me? It is hard for you to kick against the goads'"(Acts 26:14). In these two sentences, Christ sees right through the proud Pharisee. Our Lord then invokes a common farming practice to both empathetically and emphatically convict the conscience of Saul. Since the ox goad, or cattle prod, was used to *goad* or spur on the ox, the stronger the resistance, the deeper the prod went into the animal. Jesus is asking Saul why he is resisting the advances of the Holy Spirit. Our Lord gently pleads with Paul to stop the self-inflicted injury of *kicking against the goads*.

The question Christ asks of Saul could just as easily be posed to you and me. I might not be persecuting Christians like Saul was, but I am likely *kicking against the goads* of God in some category of my life. Which of God's prods am I resisting today? Is it His authority over my finances, my use of time, or my sex life? Perhaps it is Christ's call to be with Him on a daily basis. Whatever it is, the more I resist, the more injury I do to myself.

Like Paul, the Lord goads us because He loves us. Often this prodding is persistent and protracted over years. If God were not goading us, it would be because He didn't care for us. The absence of His prodding would indicate His recognition that I have rejected Him and left Him no choice but to leave me alone as He shakes the dust off His feet in His departure (Matt 10:14).

Have you thanked God today for the goading of the Holy Spirit in your life? If He is bothering to persistently prick your conscience, it is because He loves you. Let the prodding of Jesus lead you closer to Him as you refuse to inflict any more self-injury upon yourself.

Ask the Spirit for the grace and personal restraint to stop *kicking against the goads* of God in your life. Embrace the prodding as the love of a Father who cares enough to pursue you and guide you.

November 10

Comfort in Weakness

1 Kings 19:3—Elijah was afraid and ran for his life.

Have you ever been disappointed with yourself for your fear, worry or inability to trust in God, despite evidence in your life of His power and grace? If so, the character of Elijah should be a great comfort to you. Elijah stands as one of the biblical greats: A man whose faith raised the dead, divided the Jordan River, and allowed him to ascend into heaven in a chariot of fire (1 Kings 17; 2 Kings 2). He is one of two men who meet with Christ in the transfiguration, and his prophetic prowess is so well known in Israel that it is his name which is assumed when Christ says, "*Eli, Eli, lama sabachthani*"(Matt 17; 27:46).

In perhaps his most memorable moment, Elijah has just emerged from an epic spiritual battle against over 800 pagan priests. He has harnessed the power of God to bring fire down from heaven and to draw rain clouds out of a sky barren for three long years. He has recently experienced the omnipotence of God up close and personal. At such a moment, Elijah might seem unlikely to fear or worry. And yet, this pillar of faith was *afraid and ran for his life* at the threats of Jezebel the queen.

At this juncture, Elijah offers us the example of a life of faith momentarily broken by human weakness and cowardice. No matter how stalwart we think our faith, we too have moments like this. And what do we do then? If we look to the example of Elijah, we see a God who does not chastise. Rather, He pursues His faithful servant into the desert and sends His angels to feed and attend to him.

The story of Elijah offers us the courage to forgive ourselves our own weaknesses because God forgave Elijah. And where we find grace to forgive our own fallibility, we must also extend this grace to those around us—friends, family members, spiritual leaders, even our pastors—who sometimes fail regardless of their faith. No one is immune from "Elijah moments," and we should never expect that of ourselves or others.

We may take comfort today in the example of Elijah. We have a God who loves us, just as we are—even when we run on the heels of His great victories in our lives. This is a source of praise!

November 11

Bringing the Stones Back to Life

Nehemiah 4:2—What are these feeble Jews doing? Will they restore their wall? Will they offer sacrifices? Will they finish in a day? Can they bring the stones back to life from those heaps of rubble—burned as they are?

When we are employed in the work of the Lord we will likely be ridiculed and attacked. If we are never the object of such hostility, we must question whether we are truly doing God's work at all. The intent of such animosity against us is always the same—to frustrate and discourage the progress of the Kingdom. Satan, in his subtly, knows very well that one of the best ways to slow down God's work is to attack the weakest links—you, me and every other worker employed in the Lord's labor.

This was the very tactic used against the Israelites rebuilding the wall around Jerusalem. The enemies of Israel came to ridicule and discourage the work—*will they restore their wall?...Can they bring the stones back to life from those heaps of rubble—burned as they are?* Amidst such animosity, the temptation of the tired laborers would have been to say, "there is so much rubble that we cannot rebuild the wall"(Neh 4:10). But strengthened by God, and encouraged by the leadership of Nehemiah, "the people worked with all their heart"(Neh 4:6), as the wall slowly, but steadily, was rebuilt.

In the face of the discouraging efforts of the enemies around us, we must always remember that the words of men have no power over the God within us. I cannot rebuild the wall only in a day, but with the strength of God within me, I can work with all my heart to finish it in His time. Similarly, although I cannot bring the stones back to life, the God within me can! He can make the dry bones live again (Ezek 37)!

The degree to which I am defeated in heart and head by the enemies around me is the degree to which I allow myself to be blinded from the power of God within me. The enemy screams distractions. I can choose to listen to them or not, but the God living in me can overcome the assaults!

Let the words of your enemy fall as they may, for "If God is for us, who can be against us?"(Rom 8:31). We shall only be defeated if we forget who is fighting for us: Christ in us! Pray today that the Lord helps you cling to the promises of the God who dwells in you and fights for you.

November 12

The Compelling

2 Corinthians 5:14—For Christ's love compels us, because we are convinced that one died for all....

One of the fundamental laws of God's universe is that all motion depends upon an acting force. Nothing moves without a push or pull. There must be a compelling or a repulsing. What is it that compels me? Am I driven through each day by the need for financial security, the approval of others, or the simple satiation of my gut? Is my life nothing more than a pinball machine in which I am bounced from the push of one event or pull of another appetite?

We were made for more. We were designed, as the Apostle Paul reminds us, to be *compelled by the love* of Christ. When, and if, I surrender my life to Jesus, I crucify myself and all my compelling appetites, and "I no longer live, but Christ lives in me"(Gal 2:20). The Spirit opens my eyes to see that "all things that are done under the sun...are meaningless, a chasing after the wind"(Ecc 1:14), unless the love of Christ compels me in my efforts.

And how will I know that I am compelled by Christ and not by some personal motive force? I will know when my life convincingly demonstrates that "one died for all, and therefore all died....That those who live should no longer live for themselves but for Him who died for them and was raised again"(2 Cor 5:14-15). I will know when I begin to love like Jesus loves, when the fruit of the Spirit begins to pervade the corners of my every activity and relationship. I will be assured when my life bears the signature of obedience: "If you love me, you will obey what I command"(John 14:15). I will be without a doubt when I "hunger and thirst for righteousness," and when I can say, without hesitation, "I desire to do your will, O my God"(Matt 5:6; Ps 40:8).

If you are unsure today whether or not you are *compelled by the love* of Christ, pause. Be convinced that the love of Jesus guides the trajectory of your life just as surely as His power perfectly hurtles the planets through space. Without this assurance of the Spirit, you are simply headed into an eternal and consuming night. Without this confidence, this day and all you do in it, will not radiate with His glory.

Let Christ's love compel you with His Kingdom purposes.

November 13

Choosing Carefully

1 Kings 21:25—There was never a man like Ahab, who sold himself to do evil in the eyes of the Lord, urged on by Jezebel his wife.

When it comes to our spiritual lives, who we choose as our companions matters immensely. If I spend my time cavorting with men and women who love to satisfy their sinful natures, eventually, I will too. In the end, my resolve will not be strong enough to resist the persistent negative influences in my life. But if I choose the company of godly people, I am much more likely to remain faithful to my calling.

This importance of relationship is, perhaps, no more crucial than in marriage. When we join our lives with another man or woman, we inevitably become more like them. Our spouses end up having tremendous influence on us as proximity and the protracted time of interaction allow them to know us, inside and out. For this reason, spouses have the power to help heal and lovingly instruct one another. But, they can also tear us down and fuel negativity or sinful ways of thinking and acting.

Such was the case with King Ahab of Israel. The king was wicked in his own right and had departed from the ways of the Lord. But when he married Jezebel, the Phoenician princess, he had little to no hope of pursing righteousness. Like Solomon's foreign wives, Jezebel turned the heart of Ahab away from God and toward Baal; she encouraged, *urged on*, his *evil in the eyes of the Lord*. Jezebel persecuted the prophets of the Lord and murdered Naboth over a vineyard that Ahab coveted (1 Kings 21).

You may not have an Ahab or a Jezebel in your life, but if you are married, humbly recognize before God the incredible position of influence you have been given in the life of your spouse. Seek God's grace in helping you to bring your spouse closer to Jesus. If he or she is not following hard after Christ, remain in your marriage and persist in godly love so that your spouse may be sanctified through you (1 Cor 7:14).

If you are single, you too can influence and be influenced by your friends and those you share your heart with. Take care in selecting all close companions. Do not settle for anyone who does not help you love Jesus and His people more. Remember, "As soon as a love-relationship does not lead me to God, and as soon as I in a love-relationship do not lead another person to God, this love, even if…it were the highest good in the lover's earthly life, nevertheless is not true love."[256]

Pray that God helps you to choose your intimate companions with true love in mind, so that you love and are loved in a Christ-like way.

---

[256] Soren Kierkegaard, *Works of Love* (New York: HarperPerennial, 2009), 124.

November 14

Lifting up Holy Hands

Exodus 17:11—As long as Moses held up his hands, the Israelites were winning....

Likely you will not, like Moses, have the privilege of watching your winning prayers for an epic "battle" played out before your uplifted hands. Perhaps you have prayed for years over someone or something, obeying the injunction to "pray without ceasing"(1 Thes 5:17 ESV). But you have seen nothing of substance: no fruit, no advancement against the "enemy" in your life. And, to be truthful, your arms and your heart have grown tired.

Ask God for strength not to give up. Dare to be "faithful in prayer"(Rom 12:12), remembering that you are doing God's work. You are supporting His army. But you are also opening the door for Him to work through you. God wants "men everywhere to lift up holy hands in prayer"(1 Tim 2:8) so that they might come to know Him and marvel at His power in supplication satisfied.

When you grow weary in your prayer, it is okay to admit so to God and your fellow believers. There is no weakness in saying, "I'm tired," as Moses did before the Amalekites. God knows your exhaustion and will provide a stone for you to sit on and an Aaron and a Hur to help you keep your arms lifted. When we "lift up [our] hands toward [His] Most Holy Place"(Ps 28:2), He hears our cries and fights in our battles, even when we do not see it.

As you raise your hands in prayer, remember that the Joshua you are praying for needs your uplifted arms more than you can imagine. If you cease in your prayer, the enemy will advance like the encroaching Amalekites. You may never know the battles won in your own life because someone decided to keep his or her arms raised to heaven in constant prayer. God has willed that victory should be dependent upon prayer. It is not that He needs our prayers to win the battle, but He wants us to find Him and know His power in prayer.

God will not likely decide to defeat the enemy unless we commit to keep our arms lifted towards heaven. Whatever it takes, determine that you will not lower your arms until the battle is won. If you will this, God will make it happen. You decide; He will provide. There will be a stone to sit on and friends to help uphold your hands. As you resolve today to keep your arms lifted to heaven, look with anticipation for the strength and support He will bring to actualize His victory in your life.

November 15

The Standstill

Ezra 4:24—Thus the work on the house of God in Jerusalem came to a standstill....

When we are engaged in what we believe to be God's work, we like to think that it will be smooth sailing—steady winds, gentle waves, and forward progress. But in reality, even God's work in our lives must endure the gale winds of the storms, the moments of complete stillness, and every variation in between. There will be times when the winds of God's favor blow forcibly and our lives move along so quickly that we may feel the desire to lower the sail or, at least, let it out. At other times, however, the providence of God may cause the winds to stop altogether. We are brought to a complete *standstill*. God appears to be doing nothing at all. Are we "dead" in the water or simply waiting for God's moment?

When the Israelites were engaged in the rebuilding of the house of God, there can be little doubt that these men believed they were employed in work of the Lord. What could be more God's work than the rebuilding of His house and place of worship? And then opposition comes. Political forces bring the construction process to a complete *standstill*. The murmuring among God's people might have been, "Why God?" But then, at just the right time, God's time, the winds of favor pick up again, and the work moves forward to its final completion.

Has God brought your life to a *standstill*? Is the wind still and the water like glass all around you? Instead of asking "why" or bemoaning the lack of progress, see this time as a gift from God. Something important is happening in this *standstill* that is essential to God's overall plan. Perhaps He is teaching you patience. Maybe He is softening someone's heart to make it more favorably disposed to you. Whatever it is, when it has been completed, then your work, if it is God's work, will begin again. He will cause the winds of favor to rise and power His forward progress in you.

Recognize the *standstill* times as "working" in a different way: invisibly, behind the scenes, and perhaps in alternate places. And while you may not understand the purpose or utility of sitting motionless on the water, know that God is in control. Use the *standstill* times to grow in your trust of His providence. His purposes never fail and His work never ceases. If your work is God's work, it will begin again.

November 16

The Dissipated Heart

Luke 21:34—Be careful, or your hearts will be weighed down by dissipation....

The heart of the world is dissipated—devoted to pleasures of all kinds. A lonely traveler, it goes from place to place looking for a home. It is found in the unfaithful lover who hops from one bed to another. It is in the greedy hands that spend to accumulate. It is always searching, but never remaining, always having but never holding, always looking but never seeing. The *dissipated heart* is unfulfilled and unsatisfied. It clings "to the good it had first thought of and turned the good which was given it into no good."[257] It is never content.

Jesus says to this life, *"Be careful, or your hearts will be weighed down with dissipation...."* Instead of stopping to give thanks and drink in the richness of the moment, we all too often race off to the next thing. We are driven by our anxieties and whipped by a self-imposed sense of necessity. Instead of embracing the love that we have been given, we squander our energies and affections on pleasures we imagine to be better. We are plagued with a perpetual illusion that the "grass is greener" somewhere else. Our lives are fragmented and our hearts dissipated. And we are to blame for our unfulfilled hungers.

Jesus wants your heart to know the one love that never fails, the marriage that will "have and hold" forever. If you are feeling exhausted or weary, unfulfilled or unsatisfied, downcast or discouraged, you may have allowed your heart to be dissipated. In your confusion, you have needlessly raced about. Stop! Cease going in every direction but the one you were created for: "But seek first His Kingdom and His righteousness, and all these things will be given to you as well"(Matt 6:33). Remember, "We were made for God."[258] We were created "that God may love us, that we may become objects in which the Divine love may rest 'well pleased'."[259] Until we rest in this Love, our hearts will be forever dissipated.

The power to prevent this dissipation of the heart on false loves is yours. Jesus's desire is that "your joy may be complete"(John 15:11) *in Him.* Ask God for the grace to rest in His love and to spend yourself on your love for Him above all else.

---

[257] C.S. Lewis, *Perelandra* in *The Space Trilogy* (London: HarperCollins, 2013), 205.
[258] C.S. Lewis, *The Four Loves* (New York: Houghton Mifflin Harcourt, 1988), 331.
[259] C.S. Lewis, *The Problem of Pain* (New York: HarperCollins, 2001), 41.

November 17

Who Was I?

Acts 11:17—…who was I to think I could oppose God?

When was the last time you witnessed something that completely transformed your way of thinking about a particular topic? Some may call it an epiphany; some a revelation; others, a miracle. By whatever name, it is transformative.

The Apostle Peter had such a moment when he watched the Holy Spirit come upon the Gentile believers in Joppa (Acts 11:15). In the hours preceding this event, Peter was given a dream of a sheet filled with all kinds of "unkosher" animals descending from heaven. It was accompanied by the command, "'Get up, Peter, kill and eat'"(Acts 11:7). Because Peter was firmly fixed in the idea that salvation was intended for the Jews, he couldn't have been more surprised by this injunction.

But when Peter goes to be with the Gentiles and witnesses the gift of the Spirit extended to them, his understanding radically changes. Instead of resisting this revelation, shaking his fists at heaven, and clinging to his personal convictions and opinions, Peter has the wisdom to say, *"who was I to think that I could oppose God?"*

Is there some firmly fixed belief or opinion in your heart that you are clinging to in opposition to a God who has revealed something new, perhaps even surprising or troubling, to you? If so, have the wisdom to release it before God chooses to break you of it. Sometimes the most important directions in our lives are the ones that are the most surprising or unexpected. It is not at all uncharacteristic of God to ask us to do the very thing we said we would never do or go to the place we swore we would never visit. This happened for Peter and his life changed when he witnessed the Holy Spirit fall upon the Gentiles. He realized that salvation was truly for all men, and all people, everywhere. The gospel was now poised to go global—and Peter was called to usher it in. Saul, the man who once persecuted Christians, would be transformed into Paul the great missionary: the next surprising twist!

The next time God surprises you with something you never expected, perhaps something you even disagree with or dislike in the moment, have the wisdom to say, *"Who am I to oppose God?"* Rejoice in the present mystery of what you have seen, recognizing that God knows best, especially when you don't understand.

November 18

Cleaning House

Matthew 21:13—"'My house will be called a house of prayer,' but you are making it a 'den of robbers.'"

In His ministry of love and forgiveness, Jesus referred to Himself as "gentle and humble in heart"(Matt 11:29). But there was one anomalous example of Christ's vehement anger: the temple rampage. Right after Jesus is praised as "He who comes in the name of the Lord," "gentle and riding on a donkey"(Matt 21:9,5), He enters the Temple in a righteous rage. His love for His Father's house drives out the merchants and overturns the tables of the money changers. Christ is outraged to find God's Temple turned into a place of robbers, cheats and thieves.

Do we share the outrage of Jesus at the desecration of His Father's house? In our worship, have we allowed ourselves to become so accustomed to the absence of the holy that we are no longer bothered by the infiltration of the world's thinking into God's house? This can be flagrant—a doctrinal fallacy accepted as true—or subtle, such as a well-intentioned outreach where presentation appears more important than the truth of God's Word. The cluttering of the Temple courts can drown out the voice of the Father.

What is true of the physical Temple is no less true of our hearts— God's temple within each of us (1 Cor 6:19). Are we ready to admit that the desecration of God's house is happening within us as well? Have I given Jesus cause today to rampage through the courts of my interior? Must He overthrow in me the tables of lust, greed, slander or hypocrisy? Instead of preserving our temples as places of worship and prayer, dedicated to God's Spirit, we often fill our spiritual houses with the cares of a secular world. Nothing short of constant, vigilant housecleaning can keep them out. And even then, we need God's grace to make it happen. Fortunately, He is delighted to provide it!

Jesus is zealous for holiness in His Father's house. He will not tolerate a "den of robbers" who steal His holy glory by focusing on worldly cares. If we claim to belong to Jesus, and if the Spirit lives in us, we must daily overturn the tables of our hearts. We must leave no sin to clutter God's house. We must decide that our temple will be a holy place, cleansed by the blood of Jesus and dedicated to God and nothing else —"for zeal for your house consumes me…"(Ps 69:9).

Pray for the grace to keep a clean spiritual house.

November 19

Persistence

Romans 2:7—To those who by persistence in doing good seek glory, honor, and immortality, He will give eternal life.

If I am under the impression that discipleship in Christ means living a perfectly moral life, I have missed the gospel message completely. I am still living under the law, and Christ died for nothing. Such distorted thinking is a tool of Satan to frustrate our relationships with the Lord and poison our interactions with all His children.

As a disciple of Jesus, I have a perfect righteousness "which is through faith in Christ—the righteousness that comes from God and is by faith"(Phil 3:9). But though I am viewed by God as righteous because of the work of Jesus, I remain a sinner until my Lord returns to call me home. I will fail my God daily and regularly. If I am set upon living a "perfect" life in the eyes of God, I will become disillusioned and downcast. What matters is not perfect living. Rather, it is the willful *persistence in doing good* as I seek the *glory, honor and immortality* of Christ in my life.

Is your heart discouraged by your imperfections? Do you struggle with the weakness of your faith? Have you allowed the failings of those you love to poison your thinking about the God they claim to serve? Each day, this very day, I must own my imperfections and allow for these and other imperfections in everyone else around me. Can I say with David, "For I know my transgressions, and my sin is always before me"(Ps 51:3)? In this self-awareness, can I commit to persist in doing good?

The disciple of Jesus is not perfect, or even good—he or she is the sinner who fails. But saved through the blood of Jesus, he commits to persist in doing good. Peter denied Jesus, but persisted to build the Church. Paul persecuted Christ, but saved by grace, persisted to give the gospel to the world. Will you, in your commitment to persist, be a disciple who helps change the world for Christ and His Kingdom?

If you are spending your time focused on your imperfections or the failings in others, you will make little to no progress in your spiritual life. *Persistence* is what matters. *Persistence* is a choice—your choice. With eyes focused on Christ and your imperfections covered in His blood, decide each day to walk forward in the *persistence* of faith.

November 20

You Have Been Given

Isaiah 26:12—...all that we have accomplished you have done for us.

The pervading tendency of the mind is to drift into the illusion that we are the creators of our lives and all that they bear. The world teaches, and we may begin to believe, that what we have, we have because we have earned it. But this could not be further from the truth—*all that we have accomplished you [God] have done for us.*

We may argue that we have worked hard. Perhaps so. But do we fail to remember that even our capacity for hard work was given to us? "What do you have that you did not receive? And if you did receive it, why do you boast as though you did not?"(1 Cor 4:7). We were "knit together in [our] mother's womb"(Ps 139:13), by no work of our own. Our very breath is a gift from God—"The Spirit of God has made me; the breath of the Almighty gives me life"(Job 33:4). The greatest gift, eternal life (1 John 5:11), has also been given to us apart from anything we have done. James reminds us, "Every good and perfect gift is from above, coming down from the Father..."(Jam 1:17).

Ironically, those who have been most gifted often struggle most to remember where those gifts come from. Satan plays to our natural tendency for self-aggrandizement. He nurtures in us the gospel of self-sufficiency. The more deeply he can entrench our thinking in the idea that we are what we accomplish and we accomplish what we set our minds and hands to, the more completely he removes truth from the picture. Satan has no higher goal than the obsolescence of God in our hearts.

The best defense against the progressive drift into this idolatrous thinking is to give thanks in all things at all times—"Give thanks to the Lord, for He is good..."(Ps 107:1). When we make gratitude to God the daily discipline and pleasure of our lives, we steady the course. We mitigate the drift into Satan's perversity. We find a growing, inviolable peace—the peace of God, giver of all good things. If we choose, instead, to cling to the gospel of self-sufficiency, God will deal with us. For, "The creature's illusion of self-sufficiency must, for the creature's sake, be shattered; and... God shatters it 'unmindful of His glory's diminution.'"[260]

Do not be deceived—all that you have accomplished God has done for you. Begin the discipline of gratitude today as you remember that all that you are, and ever will be, has been given to you.

---

[260] C.S. Lewis, *The Problem of Pain* (New York: HarperCollins, 2001), 96.

November 21

The Neutral Nothing

Matthew 12:30—He who is not with me is against me, and he who does not gather with me scatters.

> If God has condescended to be the one who can be chosen, then human beings ought to choose—for God is not mocked. Thus it is true that if a person desists from choosing it is the same as…choosing for the world.[261]
> —Soren Kierkegaard

Spiritual neutrality is not possible. Jesus does not give us that choice. He says, *"He who is not with me is against me."* It appeals to the modern moral conscience to consider the spiritual realm akin to that of the political, in which neutrality is not only an option but, perhaps, a preference. But while one nation may have the nexus of evil at its doorstep with the battle for good at every border, and say amidst this turmoil, "I want no part of this," the powers of heaven and hell do not abide by these political niceties. Human diplomacy is impotent in the battle for eternity.

You cannot be a *neutral nothing* in any realm other than that of your own imagination. Jesus clearly says, "I am the way and the truth and the life"(John 14:6). If you are not marching under the banner of heaven, you are an enemy of the cross, whether you have pitched your tent in the enemy's camp or not. Do you find yourself "gathering" for Jesus, doing the work of the Kingdom? If not, you are "scattering," and your life is an obstruction to the cause of Christ. Ironically, in your will to do nothing, you are doing Satan's work—frustrating the Kingdom's progression.

Do not permit yourself the comfortable illusion that neutrality between Jesus and the world or Jesus and the "Kingdom of You" is a permissible idea. The doctrine of today will insist, with diplomatic sense and inclusive kindness, that the neutral position, the way of goodness and "do no harm," is not only reasonable, but right. Yet our Lord could not disagree more! He did not come to bring some diplomatic equanimity. He said, "I did not come to bring peace, but a sword"(Matt 10:34).

Make no mistake—the battle is raging all around you. To close your eyes and pretend that the war does not involve you is a terrible mistake. Spiritual neutrality, irrespective of the degree of intentionality, simply clothes you in the uniform of the enemy. You are either all in with Jesus or you are not in at all! To pretend that you are a "neutral nation," sovereign and uninterested in the matters of eternity, is a spiritual death wish. There is no *neutral nothing!*

---

[261] Soren Kierkegaard, *Spiritual Writings* (New York: HarperPerennial, 2010), 141.

November 22

Invictus[262]

Exodus 9:16—But I have raised you up for this very purpose, that I might show you my power and that my name might be proclaimed in all the earth.

> ...a great man knows he is not God, and the greater
> he is the better he knows it.[263]
>
> —G.K. Chesterton

Today's world is full of shouting and protesting for personal freedoms. Some desire the elimination of perceived inequalities. Others want an unrestrained autonomy. The air is charged with a fierce individualism, an *invictus* attitude that screams, "I am the master of my fate, I am the captain of my soul."[264]

While there are causes worth fighting for, the protesters must remember that every life and every cause is subordinate to the cause of Christ. In the end, Pharaoh and every other *captain of the soul* bows down to the purposes of God, whether they like it or not. Regardless of our "power," or lack thereof, we have been raised up *that God might show us His power and that His name might be proclaimed in all the earth.*

Do you doubt that the chief purpose of your life is to demonstrate the power of God to the world? Both the worst and the best of who we are and what we are capable of doing are reconciled by God into one overarching, providential purpose—that God's name *might be proclaimed in all the earth.* I may not agree with some persistent inequality I observe in the world. I might not understand how a God of goodness could allow the horrific human sacrifice of war and genocide. But this does not mean that God is not in control. It does not mean His name will not be glorified. Any attempt to squeeze God into the scope of my limited understanding is an act of tragic arrogance. God is God, and I am not. His plans and His purposes march on whether I agree with them or like them.

We have been raised up for a single purpose: God's purpose. We can go where we want and fight for the causes we believe in. But let us not be so naive as to think we are our own: We "were bought at a price"(1 Cor 6:20). Our lives exist and persist that God's name might be glorified. We can submit to this will and rejoice in the unfolding of God's pleasure in it, or we can resist and be broken, like a Pharaoh under the plagues of God.

---

262 Latin adjective, "unconquered, unsubdued, invincible"

263 G.K. Chesterton *The Everlasting Man* (Oxford: Oxford City Press, 2011), 159.

264 W.E. Henley, "To R.T.H.B. (Invictus)," in *A Book of Verses* (New York: Scribner & Welford, 1891), 56-57.

November 23

Driven

Proverbs 16:26—The laborer's appetite works for him; his hunger drives him on.

Are you *driven* in your pursuit of God and His purposes in your life? Is your soul craving God and working for Him as a hungry worker labors to fill his stomach? The Lord has given us hunger as a gift to drive us on. As Tozer says, "The impulse to pursue God originates with God, but the outworking of that impulse is our following hard after Him...."[265] Do you find yourself following hard after God? Do you have the spiritual hunger of David that says, "my soul pants for you, O God"(Ps 42:1)?

Too many of us have either given up on God in favor of something else, or allowed our spiritual lives to take on a "stiff and wooden quality...[as] a result of our lack of holy desire."[266] We have lost the hunger that drives us on because we have filled our lives with innumerable distractions and spiritual appetizers. We are too full to hunger after the main course: God Himself! The result is a spiritual complacency, and "Complacency is a deadly foe of all spiritual growth. Acute desire must be present or there will be no manifestation of Christ to His people. He wants to be wanted."[267]

Is your life acutely desirous of Jesus? Or, are you "panting" after other desires? If my hunger is always placated with other things, I have no hope of growing spiritually—I will become spiritually unfit and complacent. If I want to grow spiritually, I must desire God as acutely as my body desires its next meal and pursue after Him with the same regularity and disciplined obedience that I apply to feeding my physical body. If I am not growing spiritually, it is because I am not *driven*—I am not following hard after Him.

Let us thank God today for the pangs of spiritual hunger that drive us to Jesus. But if we are not feeling hungry for God, if we don't miss our time with Him more than we miss our last meal, we are lost in a complacency that will be our slow demise.

Be grateful for a hunger that leads you into the arms of your Father.

---

[265] A.W. Tozer, *The Pursuit of God* in *The Classic Works of A. W. Tozer* (Public Domain), 8.
[266] Ibid.
[267] Ibid.

November 24

On the Heels of Singing

2 Chronicles 20:22—As they began to sing and praise, the Lord set ambushes against the men of Ammon…and they were defeated.

> The world does not bid you sing, but God does. Song is the sign
> of an unburdened heart….[268]   —Oswald Chambers

Finding themselves faced with a vast, multi-national army ready to destroy them, King Jehoshaphat and "the men of Judah, with their wives and children and little ones, stood there before the Lord"(2 Chron 20:13), paralyzed with fear and indecision. Into this weakness, God speaks through Jahaziel, saying, "Do not be afraid or discouraged because of this vast army. For the battle is not yours, but God's. Tomorrow march down against them…"(2 Chron 20:15-16). In obedience, the king and the people set out. And not only did they obey, but they did so with singing. *As they began to sing and praise, the Lord set ambushes against the men of Amnon….*

Have you, like the besieged Israelites, decided to obey the Lord's leading in your life? Are you determined to set out for God singing and praising or are you dragging your spiritual feet, grudgingly going, perhaps complaining all the way? For the people of Israel, the Lord's promise was fulfilled on the heels of a singing obedience: "Jehoshaphat appointed men to sing to the Lord and to praise Him for the splendor of His holiness as they went out at the lead of the army…"(2 Chron 20:21).

Are you resolved to proceed the marching footsteps of your obedience with praise? There may be times when your discouragement of heart inhibits a spirit of thanks and worship. In these moments, all you can do is muster the strength to walk forward in the direction of obedience. But more often than not, the choice to obey with singing and praise is well within my capabilities. Indeed, God may not move in my life until I decide to couple my obedience with a heart of worship; for the Lord has little affection for the consistently grudging heart. The spirit that drags its feet and complains each step of the way brings Him no delight. He desires a grateful child who trusts in the words He has spoken. Wouldn't you desire the same from the child you love?

My decision to walk forward in an obedience that sings and praises attests to the measure of my trust in my Father. The singing heart is the trusting heart. My praise is my affirmation of who God is and what He says He will do. On the heels of singing, the battle belongs to God!

---

[268] Oswald Chambers, *The Love of God* in *The Complete Works of Oswald Chambers* (Grand Rapids: Discovery House Publishers, 2000), 656.

November 25

Penumbra[269]

Job 26:14—And these are but the outer fringe of His works....

No matter how well we think we know God the Father, we have no true conception of the fullness of who He is. As the Apostle John asserts, Jesus is the Son whom "we have seen and testify...to be the Savior of the world"(1 John 4:14). Because Christ is "the exact representation of [God's] being"(Heb 1:3), we know the Father through what we know of Jesus. We know the Holy Spirit because He has been placed within us as God's "seal of ownership on us, and...as a deposit guaranteeing what is to come"(2 Cor 1:22).

But because we are finite and our triune God is not, we don't know the full extent of Christ or the Holy Spirit. Similarly, we don't fully know the individual person of God the Father either. And what we do know of Him, the evidences we have before us, are *but the outer fringe of His works* and His person—the *penumbra* of a divine colossus so terribly awesome that we cannot in our finite selves ever truly envision Him.

It is as if we are living our entire lives in an eclipse, seeing only the outer edge, glorious in its own right, capable of blinding us, but only a sliver of the power that lies behind. And then, when the celestial, blocking body moves, we are bathed in a light so immensely glorious that our whole existence is illuminated. What we once thought we knew, looks completely different—beautifully so! What a day that will be!

In the midst of his agony, Job understood how far he was from this full revelation of God's glorious immensity. Job noted the *outer fringe* of God's works, how "He spreads out the northern skies over empty space," and "suspends the earth over nothing"(Job 26:7). God "marks out the horizon on the face of the waters for a boundary between light and darkness," and "wraps up the water in His clouds..."(Job 26:10, 8). But despite these marvelous evidences, "how faint the whisper we hear of Him! Who then can understand the thunder of His power?"(Job 26:14).

We would do well to consider, as Job did, that all we really know about God the Father is the *outer fringe*. And if this *penumbra* is as glorious as it is, can we imagine what lies behind? The thought of it ought to bring us to our knees in a fearful, awe-inspiring praise!

---

[269] In astronomy (as in an eclipse), the space of partial illumination between the shadow of the celestial body and the full radiance behind it

November 26

The Distribution of Grace

Ephesians 4:7—But to each one of us grace has been given as Christ apportioned it.

How much of our life energies have been squandered in fruitless comparison. Consider the moments when we wondered at another's blessing. How could such a man possess so much in so many categories? At other times we might have seen a suffering friend and questioned the "justice" that rewards his comparative goodness with such difficulty. How could it be so? Why should it be so?

All this mental musing misses the point, however. Paul says, "Oh the depth of the riches of the wisdom and knowledge of God! How unsearchable His judgments, and His paths beyond tracing out!"(Rom 11:33). God's ways are not our ways—His ways are unsearchable, unknowable, and incredible!

When we look at the world around us to make comparisons and judgments, we allow our reason to become the plumb line of holy justice. This is an exercise in futility and injurious to our souls. God alone is the source of "all grace"(1 Peter 5:10). It is His prerogative to distribute or withhold it as He pleases. Jesus illustrates this point in the parable of the workers in the vineyard. When some complain over unequal wages, the owner replies, "Don't I have the right to do what I want with my own money? Or are you envious because I am generous?"(Matt 20:15).

When I am tempted to think that someone has been too amply blessed or too severely treated, I must remember that God's economy is beyond my understanding (Matt 20:1-16). What we all deserve is the calling of our debt—the absence of grace. What we have received, instead, is abounding grace (2 Cor 9:8). Therefore, we must make it our business to examine only ourselves. As Paul says, "Each should test his own actions. Then he can take pride in himself, without comparing himself to somebody else..."(Gal 6:4-5). The rest belongs to the grace of Christ.

In His wisdom, Jesus richly distributes His grace in various forms and to differing degrees. His purpose is clear: "that the body of Christ may be built up..."(Eph 4:12). Therefore, when I see God's blessing thrown out like paint across the canvas, some spots falling full and heavy with color, others thin and anemic, I must work to see a picture—God's work of art. I may not, yet, understand the distribution of color, but I can choose to marvel at the creative genius that stands behind it all. I am called to "adore...where [I] cannot see reason of it,"[270] knowing that one day all will be made clear. Will you adore God's *distribution of grace?*

---

[270] Thomas Watson, *A Body of Divinity* (East Peoria: Versa Press, 2015), 88.

Freely and Wholeheartedly

1 Chronicles 29:9—The people rejoiced at the willing response of their leaders, for they had given freely and wholeheartedly to the Lord.

How we give of our lives for the Lord can have enormous implications in the hearts of others. Whether it is our time and energy for service, our financial resources, mercy for the wounded and weary, or the simple worship with our voices, the response we give to God can move mountains in the irresolution of others.

In the final preparations for the building of the Temple of God and the succession of his throne, King David asks the people, "'Now, who is willing to consecrate himself today to the Lord?'"(1 Chron 29:5). To this call, many of the leaders "gave willingly"; and, as a result, "The people rejoiced at the...response"(1 Chron 29:6, 9). As they gave *freely and wholeheartedly,* the leaders encouraged the faith of all those around them.

Are you in a position today to potentially bless others with your willing response to God? Can you, with David say, "'But who am I, and who are my people, that we should be able to give as generously as this?'"(1 Chron 29:14). If God has positioned you in a place of blessing (and there is no one who does not have some blessing that can be shared!), it is because He wants you to honor Him and bless others as you give back to the Lord what comes from His hand (1 Chron 29:14). You might be only the poor widow giving a penny, but your example may survive 2,000 years of history to bless and encourage others along the way (Mark 12:41-44).

While some will give money, others will give time teaching children to love the Lord or giving consistent words of encouragement to a colleague at work. Or, like Mother Teresa, they may give the mercy of "someone who has merged herself in the common face of mankind, and identified herself with human suffering and privation."[271] What counts to God is that you give back to Him with a cheerful heart (2 Cor 9:7), for it is the *mode, not the matter* of your giving, that will most likely inspire the hearts of others to look to Christ. When we give back to God *freely and wholeheartedly* we demonstrate a love that encourages and enriches the lives of all those around us.

Are you grudgingly consecrating your life to the Lord or are you giving it with open hands and a happy heart? Remember that *how* you give may be the very gift that God uses to draw someone else into His presence.

---

[271] Malcolm Muggeridge, *Something Beautiful for God* (New York: HarperCollins, 1986), 16.

The Tears That Make Men Stumble

Acts 21:13—Then Paul answered, "Why are you weeping and breaking my heart?"

There will likely come a time in your life when someone you love deeply will be called by God to go somewhere you don't want them to go or to do something you fear will be hurtful to them. From a human perspective, your apprehensions may be very well-founded, your fears completely justified, and your counsel, sound and proper. But that is just it —from a *human perspective.* God's perspective may be completely contrary to yours. This disparity may be true in your own life or the lives of others, regardless of how well you think you know them or how deeply you care for them.

Such a scenario played out in the life of the Apostle Paul when he felt led by the Spirit to return to Jerusalem. His companions had just heard a prophetic warning from a man called Agabus telling that Paul would be bound and handed over to the Gentiles. Fearing, perhaps, their loss more than the interests of God's Kingdom, Paul's friends "pleaded with Paul not to go…"(Acts 21:12). In their love for Paul, the disciples tried to dissuade him, even to the point of weeping tears of sorrow. So Paul replies, "Why are you weeping and breaking my heart?"

Has God led someone you love, like Paul, into a difficult place? Perhaps you are weeping over what he or she is planning to do. If so, be careful that your tears do not become a stumbling block to the work of God in the life of the one you love. Because God has given you the capacity to love and the emotions with which to express that love, it is not wrong to be concerned and not sinful to weep. But you must never remain there. Do not break the heart of the one you love or, worse yet, allow the course God has given him or her to be altered by your vision of how you believe things should go. On the heels of your tears, be ready to say, "The Lord's will be done"(Acts 21:14). Trust that God knows best and will care for your beloved better than you ever could.

Can you trust the Lord with the life of the one you love, even when you see the storm clouds rising? Do you have the courage to admit that your tears may be breaking the heart of God in your beloved? Weep with God for the things of God, but never allow your tears to interfere with His calling in the life of another.

November 29

Only By Prayer

Mark 9:28-29—"Why couldn't we drive it out?" He replied, "This kind can come out only by prayer."

Some Christians find themselves deeply attracted to the character of Jesus. They are amazed at His power and drawn by His love. These same people, however, may remain ignorant of, or resistant to, what it means to become a follower of the Lord. They may be, like the early disciples, well-intentioned in their devotion. They may believe they are living for Jesus and doing the work of God. But when they hit a wall of opposition, they are left wondering: Why does sheer strength of will and enthusiasm not make it happen? Are we not doing good work—God's work? Why couldn't we drive out the demons?

Jesus softly answers, *"This kind can come out only by prayer."* In other words, personal effort must be directed to the work of supplication. Prayer harnesses the power of God to make the labor successful. When we set out to do the work of the Lord, we often do so with excited energy and personal strength. But sooner than later, a work beyond our abilities comes. Our frustrated efforts teach us that God's work can only be accomplished with preparatory prayer.

Or perhaps we are among those who have no intention of devotion to Jesus but are, nonetheless, amazed at what is done in His name. We are induced to think we can simply apply the name of Jesus to some miraculous effect. Why not, like the seven sons of Sceva, invoke the name of Christ in our personal efforts (Acts 19:11-20)? Will His name not bless my work? Will it not empower me to do great things?

When we attempt to harness the power of Christ for our own personal agendas, we prove that we don't really know or love Him. We demonstrate we are not bowed before Him. We mistake ourselves into thinking Jesus is some kind of genie in a lamp. But even the powers of darkness recognize real power in their midst. They say, "Jesus I know, and Paul I know about, but who are you?"(Acts 19:15). Neither Satan nor God can be fooled by our disingenuous attempts to graft the power of Christ into our uncommitted lives. Such buffoonery will only give us a beating that leaves us "naked and bleeding" like the Jews who attempted to drive out demons by simply invoking the name of Jesus (Acts 19:16).

If you are trying to will your efforts without the work of prayer, the demons are laughing. Are you prepared for a scourging? If your desire is to do the work of the Lord, you must do it in His strength and His way. You must do it in prayer and then proceed in Christ's power.

November 30

The Prayer of Jabez

1 Chronicles 4:10—Jabez cried out to the God of Israel, "Oh, that you would bless me and enlarge my territory! Let your hand be with me, and keep me from harm so that I will be free from pain."

Doubtless we all spend too much care in the avoidance of our own pain....[272]

—C.S. Lewis

Tucked in the list of names of ancient Israel is the character of Jabez and his prayer for blessing. In a few short sentences, Jabez instructs us in several spiritual lessons: The need to cry out to God and engage Him in our lives, to seek His blessing, and to desire the enlargement of His ministry in our lives. Finally, Jabez asks God to be with him and to keep him from harm. The prayer of Jabez encourages us to seek God's favor.

But Jabez's prayer must be carefully interpreted by the disciple who wishes to truly know God. We are told that God "granted his request"(1 Chron 4:10). Yet, did Jabez's blessed life cause him to know and love God more? Perhaps there is a reason why Jabez is not remembered like Joseph, Moses, David, or Paul—all men who suffered and knew great pain.

Jabez was "more honorable than his brothers"(1 Chron 4:9). But was he, like David, a man after God's heart? Could it be said of him, like Josiah, that he loved the Lord with all his heart, soul and strength (2 Kings 23:25)? Did he, like Paul, "want to know Christ...and the fellowship of sharing in His sufferings..."(Phil 3:10)?

A life that is *more of Him and less of me* does not simply desire physical blessing and an absence of pain. It longs to know God better and to love Him more. While these choices are not mutually exclusive, and to know God is to be blessed with His relationship, a life "free from pain" is a limited one. Without pain, we cannot *know* God the same way. The snag for us in Jabez's prayer is the temptation to live our lives simply avoiding pain rather than seeing it as one of God's greatest tools to bless us.

Without the "blessing" of pain, we may know *about* God, but we can never *know* Him intimately. For this reason, Christ's disciples determine to know and love Him more, irrespective of bumps, bruises, cuts or breaks. If my life is free from pain, yet I don't know Christ, I have nothing!

Let the prayer of Jabez inspire you to seek God's blessing. But set your heart on knowing God! When you do, you will be blessed, your territory enlarged, and your soul kept from harm in the arms of the Lord who loves you—even in the pain.

---

[272] C.S. Lewis, *The Problem of Pain* (New York: HarperCollins, 2001), 114.

DECEMBER

December 1

For it is Written….

Matthew 4:4—Jesus answered, "It is written…."

When Jesus is forty days weary and hungry from His desert fasting and prayer, He finds Himself tempted by Satan along the lines of His current vulnerabilities and the very Word of God He came to fulfill. Satan knows all too well that one enemy of sound, spiritual decision-making is exhaustion. It takes a certain fortitude of body, mind, and soul to hold to truth even in our most spiritually fit of times. But when we are tired, particularly tired of soul, we can get turned around and confused. The result: dangerous compromises can be made.

Expect, like Jesus, to be tempted in the times of your exhaustion. If you have recently emerged from some crowning spiritual moment and now you find yourself in the "desert," alone and tired, do not be surprised if Satan seizes upon this opportunity to tempt you. He did it to the newly baptized Jesus. And Satan will do it to you as well.

When your temptation comes, as it did for Jesus, it will often share the very appearance of truth. It may seem quite reasonable and, "When reason fails, the devil helps!"[273]   Paul reminds us that "Satan himself masquerades as an angel of light"(2 Cor 11:14). Satan knows the Word of God. He "is a better theologian than any of us and is a devil still,"[274] who will twist God's Word to fit his scheming in your life. How should you respond? Just as Jesus did. Speak the Word of God. Because Christ knows Satan is "a liar and the father of lies"(John 8:44), Jesus speaks God's truth into the moment of temptation.

When we are tempted, we must be able to respond the same way. If Satan attempts to twist the meaning of God's Word in your life, you must know Scripture well enough to rebuke Satan just as Jesus did (Matt 4:1-11). The demonic "truth" will often appear plausible, maybe even pleasing in the fugue of your exhaustion. If you do not know God's Word, you are likely to be fooled by a reasonable alternative. For Satan's "wiles are worse than his darts."[275]

Know that when the tempter comes, your salvation and victory are in Jesus. He will rescue you. But like Jesus, you must know Scripture as well as Satan and cling to God's truths even in weariness. God's Word must dwell richly in us (Col 3:16), so that when Satan comes, we will be ready to respond, "It is written…," and "Away from me, Satan!"(Matt 4:4,10).

---

[273] Fyodor Dostoevsky, *Crime and Punishment* (New York: Bantam Books, 1987), 65.

[274] A.W. Tozer, *Man, The Dwelling Place of God* (Public Domain), 125.

[275] Thomas Watson, *A Body of Divinity* (East Peoria: Versa Press, 2015),139.

December 2

All in?

Mark 8:34—If anyone would come after me, he must deny himself....

> When I go toward you
> it is with my whole life.[276]
> —Rainer Rilke

Many so-called "Christians" live their entire lives without the remotest understanding of what it means to *deny self*. They may go to church, stay faithful to spouses, and withhold their desire to cheat their colleagues at work. They may even turn the other cheek. In short, they are moral people who have repeatedly denied many natural urges. In comparison to the world around them, they have done quite well.

But what these "Christians" do not understand is that Jesus doesn't want a percentage. Jesus wants the whole thing—the undivided life, *en totale*. Though He gives us the choice to follow Him— "*If* anyone would come after me...."—He wants the full "self" of His followers. We can elect to hold on to what we have. But we cannot hold on and follow at the same time.

A danger lies in thinking that giving a portion of ourselves is better than no offering at all. Look what happened to Ananias who dropped dead after Peter said to him, "how is it that Satan has so filled your heart that you have lied to the Holy Spirit and kept for yourself some of the money you received for the land? Didn't it belong to you...? And...wasn't the money at your disposal?"(Acts 5:3-4). The "piecemeal me" is a wicked illusion that produces a smug spirituality. It keeps me from following Christ.

We fool ourselves when we think we can follow Jesus while holding on to something or someone. We have to let go. Jesus may not take it all. He may not take a thing we truly value. But we must be willing to give it. We must be an Abraham placing Isaac on the altar. It will not do to say, "I am going to maintain control of my finances," or "My sex life is mine and no one can tell me what I can do with my body." Or, perhaps, "I have a right to my hopes and dreams." No we don't—not with Jesus!

If we want absolute control of our lives, we must walk the other way. Jesus gives us this choice. But if we want to follow Christ to the fullest life, there is no bargaining. We must give Him all before we will find everything. For the fully committed, Christ is "able to do immeasurably more than all we ask or imagine..."(Eph 3:20). Are you *all in*?

---

[276] Rainer Rilke, *Book of Hours: Love Poems to God* (New York: Riverhead Books, 2005), 111.

December 3

The Singularity

Exodus 8:19—The magicians said to Pharaoh, "This is the finger of God."

The controlling question for your life and mine is: How many plagues must we endure before we acknowledge the *finger of God?* The magicians of Pharaoh matched the first two plagues of God. Using their magic arts, they turned water into blood and raised up a pestilence of frogs from the waters of Egypt. Their efforts challenged God's demonstration of power through Moses. They emboldened the obstinance of Pharaoh.

While it might be tempting to view those magicians as arcane sorcerers irrelevant to today, nothing could be further from the truth. The black magic of these conjurers was an attempt to explain away God. It was an effort to divest the Lord of His power.

Is our world not guilty of similar efforts today? Science has largely displaced black magic as the tool to "debunk" the purported myths of God's story. Moral relativism and inclusive thinking attempt to steal goodness and spiritual truth from God and place them in the hands of men, like some Prometheus absconding with fire from the heavens. The modern "magicians" continue to practice their trade against God, but they are now dressed in scientific reason.

Sooner or later, however, their explanations become impotent. Science can only explain the universe down to an indivisible point, the "primeval atom,"[277] the *singularity*.[278] In physics, it is the point of infinite density, the origin of the universe. Science has no idea where it came from. No amount of conjuring can take the indivisible God, the "*Singularity*," out of the equation. Pharaoh's magicians could not produce the gnats of the third plague and said, "This is the *finger of God*." They realized they had reached the border of their power and what lay beyond was the *finger of God*. But Pharaoh still would not listen. Our world today is no less deaf.

Is your life suffering under the plagues of a heart hardened like Pharaoh's? The longer we persist in our delusion that God is not the *Singularity* of our lives, the more plagues we will have to endure. And if our lives have not been tested by pestilence but only graced by comfort, we must be all the more careful to examine our hearts to know that God reigns there. Perhaps our comfort is a plague sent to test our obedience. If we have not recognized where we end and only God remains, we must surrender our hearts and praise Him who is the beginning, end and master of all things. We must say, *"This is the finger of God!"*

---

[277] Stephen Hawking, *The Universe in a Nutshell* (New York: Bantam Dell, 2001), 22.
[278] Ibid, 36.

December 4

Standing Firm

1 Corinthians 10:12—So if you think you are standing firm, be careful that you don't fall.

Ironically, we are most prone to fall when we think we are *standing firm*. And we are most vulnerable to defeat, just when we believe ourselves least susceptible. There is an Achilles' heel in every man and woman. Often, it is the very point of his or her strength. The real tragedy lies when that strength is his "faith."

When we stand in faith, if we are standing at all, sooner or later we feel the quiver of exhaustion in our spiritual legs. At times, if our strength is not in the Lord, these legs will even threaten to give out—they may even collapse beneath the weight of what we are attempting to carry on our own. And though I may deceive myself into thinking I can stand on my own two feet, I quickly find that God's "delight is not in the legs of a man; the Lord delights in those who fear Him, who put their hope in His unfailing love"(Ps 147:10). In my own strength, I will fall.

Do you feel as if you are *standing firm* in your faith right now? On what do you base this confidence? Is it your disciplines of faith, your church community, your accountability partners, or the sheer strength of your spiritual willpower? Or, is it the grace of Jesus Christ and the power of the Spirit within you? When you choose to fear the Lord, to delight in His strength rather than your own, and to hope in His unfailing love, God promises not to "tempt you beyond what you can bear"(1 Cor 10:13). He will give you a way to stand up under the load you are carrying. And He promises to keep you from falling, as you seek His face—"If the Lord delights in a man's ways, He will make his steps firm; though he stumble, he will not fall; for the Lord will uphold him with His hand"(Ps 37:23-24).

God alone can steady the shaking spiritual legs. Only the strength of the Holy Spirit keeps us from falling. When we feel as if we are *standing firm* in our faith, we must ask ourselves, "Where does our strength come from?" If we cannot answer, "My strength comes from the Lord..."(Ps 121:2), then we must be careful that we don't fall. Are you *standing firm* in God's strength?

December 5

Irrepressible Words

Acts 2:40—With many other words he warned them; he pleaded with them, "Save yourselves from this corrupt generation."

We will know whether or not the Holy Spirit is living in us by our willingness to actively participate with Christ in the salvation of others from the *corrupt generation* surrounding us. When the Spirit of God fills us, God's heart of love becomes ours. We can no longer look at the world and not weep for where it is. At the same time, we desire to reach out in love to bring it to where it should be—in the arms of the Father. Filled with God's love, "we can never observe the other person with detachment, for he is always and at every moment a living claim to our love and service."[279]

In the very first moments of the Church, the Spirit entered and filled the early disciples with this energetic and emphatic passion to save the lost. Peter spiritedly *warned* and *pleaded* with the unbelievers to come to salvation in Christ. With words he attempted to redirect the hearts of the lost, for "we cannot help speaking about what we have seen and heard"(Act 4:20). The Spirit filled the Apostles with *irrepressible words*.

You may say, "My gift is not words. How can I win the lost to Christ?" God has not created everyone to be a preacher. But words, however imperfect, must accompany the work of salvation in the lives of others. Decide you will speak in truth what you know. Deliver it in the impassioned love of Christ. And as you do, trust that the Spirit will fill in the gaps as He uses your words and your life of faithfulness to His effect in the lives of all those who are listening. God wins the souls of the lost; you must simply stand in the place and decide to open your mouth for Christ.

But remember, your words must also be accompanied by actions of righteousness. The early disciples "devoted themselves to the Apostles' teaching and to the fellowship, to the breaking of bread and to prayer"(Acts 2:42). They "gave to anyone as he had need," and "ate together with glad and sincere heart, praising God…"(Acts 2:45,47). The result of this Spirit-infused outreach—"the Lord added to their number daily those who were being saved"(Acts 2:47).

If you are your Father's child, you cannot stand idly by in the midst of a *corrupt generation* that is unsaved and wash your hands of them as Pilate did of Christ. The Spirit within you will compel you to speak the Truth in love, to reach out in kindness, and to live with a purity that draws others to the light of Christ within you. You are in this generation because God has placed you here. Let the Spirit's *irrepressible words* speak through you.

---

[279] Dietrich Bonhoeffer, *The Cost of Discipleship* (New York: Touchstone, 1995), 184.

December 6

The Stranger

1 Peter 1:17—...live your lives as strangers here....

Do you sometimes feel like an outsider? Have you, at times, struggled with a deep sense of alienation from your contemporaries? Can you identify with the Psalmist—"I am a *stranger* on earth..."(Ps 119:19)?

The degree to which you appreciate your sense of nonconformity to the world around you is a good barometer of your intimacy with the Lord. The Apostle Peter implores us to *live...as strangers here,* not because he wants us to feel separate and lonely, but because being *"strangers* in the world"(1 Peter 1:17; 2:11) is a necessity for holy living.

The disciple of Christ who is walking in step with the Spirit cannot simultaneously walk in step with the world. He or she is in the world, walking through it, interacting with its people, and enjoying its pleasures or enduring its pain. But if he belongs to Christ, he is an alien here. His "citizenship is in heaven"(Phil 3:20). The disciple's soul is filled with God's Spirit, who, as Jonathan Edwards reminds us, "operates in the minds of the godly by uniting Himself to them, and living in them, and exerting His own nature [holiness] in the exercise of their faculties."[280]

Because of this indwelling of God, the disciple's life may appear strange to the world. But should this nonconformity cause us to fear or grieve? Never! We should rejoice in it! It indicates that our home is in heaven and emphasizes the Lord's special provision for us. *Strangers*, like orphans and widows, fall under God's special protection: "Cursed is he who distorts the justice due an alien, orphan, and widow"(Deut 27:19). Again the Lord says, "Do not oppress...the *stranger*..."(Zech 7:10 NAS), for "The Lord protects the *strangers*..."(Ps 146:9 NAS).

Ultimately, the mystery of being a *stranger* for Christ is how it affects our relationships with nonbelievers. The closer we come to Christ, the more a *stranger* we become to the world. But as this distance increases, our love for its people grows because of the love of Christ in us. The *stranger* is elevated to the position of ambassador of God's love.

The next time you feel as if you are a *stranger* in the world, rejoice in your growing oneness with Christ. In that increasing intimacy, pray for the world around you, a world increasingly unlike you, but in dire need of the Savior within you.

---

[280] Jonathan Edwards, *Selected Sermons of Jonathan Edwards* (Public Domain),15.

December 7

The Heart that Goes Out

Luke 7:13—…His heart went out to her.…

When tragedy or deep sadness strikes in the lives of others, does your heart go out to them? Are you able to step into their shoes and taste the pain that brings their tears? The heart of Jesus teaches us that we must be capable and willing to demonstrate this deepest empathy.

When our Lord saw the weeping widow of Nain following along in the funeral procession of her only son, *His heart went out to her.* Christ's love compelled Him to go up and touch the coffin, to participate in her deep grieving and bring healing to her bitter sadness. Jesus could have uttered some sympathetic words and walked on. But instead, He stopped. He allowed His heart to get involved. He participated in the woman's pain. In the end, not only did healing come, but God was glorified: "They were all filled with awe and praised God"(Luke 7:16).

If we are to be followers of Jesus, we must have a *heart that goes out* into the suffering around us. Sweet soliloquies of sympathy will not bring the gospel into the lives of the hurting. Sympathy simply articulates pity or sorrow on behalf of another. But empathy requires us to walk in their shoes and to understand and participate in their sorrow.

Christian living must be this empathic living. Whether it is in our relationship with our spouse, children, friends or work colleagues, or even the casual acquaintance who sits beside us on the plane or train, we must allow the Spirit to sensitize our souls to the pain of others. We must permit the movement of our hearts to respond to the wounded and help lead them to Jesus. For, "the deeper we are willing to enter into the painful condition…the more likely it is we can become successful leaders, leading people out of the desert and into the Promised Land."[281]

This does not mean that we are called to be "bleeding hearts" that recklessly wander into every sad story. But, as disciples, neither can we keep our hearts shut up against the world. Tempered by reason and the Spirit's timing, we must open the gates of our hearts and allow them to gallop out and meet the needs of the suffering.

Does your heart go out to the suffering around you? Are you more often empathizing or critiquing, listening or trying to "fix" things? While there is a place for practical measures and loving instruction, the heart of Jesus teaches us to let our hearts "go out" to the hurting with a consoling empathy. When we do this, we just might have the privilege of participating in the resurrecting work of God in the life of another.

---

[281] Henri Nouwen, *The Wounded Healer* (New York: Image Doubleday, 2010), 67.

December 8

Going My Way

Deuteronomy 29:19—When such a person hears the words of this oath, he invokes a blessing on himself and therefore thinks, "I will be safe, even though I persist in going my way."

When it comes to our souls, the one thing more dangerous than ignorance of God's truth is a selective familiarity with it. While ignorance can be enlightened, altered truth cannot. Sometimes the man or woman who is vaguely familiar with a piece of God's story may focus on it to the exclusion of the whole. They may say, "Oh yes, I know that," or "I'm familiar with this," but in reality have no conception of God's true meaning. They miss the essence of the message—they miss God Himself.

God warned the Israelites against the folly of a "man or woman... whose heart turns away from the Lord...to go worship the gods of [other] nations," while trying to live in the blessing of the Lord's covenantal oath (Deut 29:18). This selective allegiance and narrow thinking is no less relevant today. For instance, it would be very correct to say that God is a God of love. But to say that He is only a God of love, and that love does not also include justice, or power, or wisdom, would be to miss the meaning of the cross and the resurrection: the crux of God's storyline and the essence of Christianity. God's redemptive narrative for us is not uni-faceted.

The religious familiarity which becomes selective allows us to fit God into our lives rather than mold our lives around God. For example, we can choose to focus on the blessings of God, invoking them upon ourselves as the unfaithful Israelites did, and believing that everything that follows will then be sanctioned, or at least passed over. Or, we can attempt to say, "God's love is greater than my sin," therefore, "What does it matter how I live my life?" But this kind of thinking is of the devil—a wicked lie that does not fit with the whole of God's person or His story for mankind. We delude ourselves if we think we can use fragments of God's truth and character as a kind of talisman to bless the way we have decided to go. Either we go the way of the cross or we go our own way. God will not suffer to be used to our advantage!

I must not allow myself to believe that I can *persist in going my own way* and have God's blessing as well. The "Lord will never be willing to forgive" this kind of thinking and "His wrath and zeal will burn against" the one who lives by it (Deut 29:20).

Have you decided to go God's way, whatever the cost? Or are you still trying to have God's blessing on your own way? You cannot have them both. Choose today to go God's way!

December 9

Naked

Genesis 2:25—The man and the woman were both naked, and they felt no shame.

The only way to be intimately known is in your nakedness. Whether in the body, soul, or mind, you cannot experience the fullness of intimacy unless you have exposed yourself and allowed the "uncovered you" to be shared and enjoyed. This is true in our marriages, our friendships, and even more so in our relationship with our divine lover, the God who created us. He formed us, like Adam and Eve, "in His own image"(Gen 1:27)—*naked*. As Job says, "*Naked* I came from my mother's womb and *naked* I will depart"(Job 1:21).

But when was the last time your heart and soul were *naked* before God? Since the Garden, we have spent so much of our time and life energy in efforts of self-coverage. Like the first couple, we try to hide "from the Lord God among the trees of the garden"(Gen 3:8). We stand quivering in shame and embarrassment over our failures or perceived imperfections, trying to mask our "nakedness" with rationalizing. Since sin has entered into the equation, we have forgotten the beauty of our creation, the image of God Himself in us.

Though I cannot return to the Garden and claim the innocence of the dawn of creation, I can, and must, have the courage to be *naked* before my God. I must say with conviction, "I am fearfully and wonderfully made"(Ps 139:14). In my relationship with my Father, I must take comfort in the truth that He has searched me and knows me. He perceives my very thoughts, anticipates my every word, and guides my every step (Ps 139:1-3). There is no corner of the Garden or the created universe where I can flee His presence. He knows me, inside and out, better than I know myself. And He loves me, nonetheless!

So why all the fruitless efforts at concealment? Why all the desperate need to dress up my heart and soul, to adorn it for others with their opinions that have no eternal significance? You are loved by God as you are. Your ability to be vulnerable before Him, to be held in His loving arms, is the degree to which you will know the ecstasy of divine intimacy. There is only one who will understand and love your complete nakedness, its blemishes and its imperfections—Jesus, your Lord, the bridegroom for whom you were created. Be spiritually *naked* before Him and know the love of God!

December 10

The Soul Neglected

Mark 8:36—What good is it for a man to gain the whole world, yet forfeit his soul?

Apart from God nothing matters.[282]
—A.W. Tozer

One of the prevailing doctrines of today is that of acquisition. What can I gain? The culture teaches the lie that the more I have, the happier I will be. It may be the acquisition of material things, power, or the praise of others. It may be a career or a family. Increasingly, it appears to be the acquisition of experiences: travels, adventures, lovers—one more check on the "bucket list." It may be a great many things, none of which are inherently bad in and of themselves, for "The world is only evil when you become its slave."[283] But when acquisition neglects and subordinates the destiny of the soul, death follows.

Death is a certainty for the body. Immortality, however, is the destiny of every soul. As C.S. Lewis says, "You have never talked to a mere mortal."[284] Whether we live on in new life or in eternal torment in the unquenchable flames depends on what we choose now. We can spend our lives in constant acquisition, building bigger homes and chasing one more exhilarating experience after the other. But even if we *gain the whole world*, if it comes at the cost of our souls, we end with nothing but torment and tragedy. Jesus says to such an acquiring life, "You fool!...who will get what you have prepared for yourself?"(Luke 12:20).

We should not be so naive as to think we can sideline the matter of our soul's destiny. We are worse still to pretend our souls do not exist and that they will not live on eternally. The greatest tragedy is the *soul neglected*. It is the rich man groaning in hell compared to the poor Lazarus safe in the arms of heaven. Lazarus trusted in Jesus and found rest in heaven. The rich man, however, survived his death only to find the torment of Hades—"agony in this fire"(Luke 16:24).

Jesus calls us to life, and life in its fullest. He wants us to enjoy all that He has provided. But in each acquisition, we must tend to the soul. If what we acquire does not lift our hearts to heaven or, if we cannot at any moment give it back to God, then these acquisitions are not gains. We risk becoming the rich man in Hades. Acquire with eternity in mind!

---

[282] A.W. Tozer, *Man, The Dwelling Place of God* (Public Domain), 168.

[283] Henri Nouwen, *Life of the Beloved* (New York: The CrossRoad Publishing Company, 2002), 130.

[284] C.S. Lewis, *The Weight of Glory* (New York: HarperCollins, 2001), 46.

December 11

Unashamed

Romans 1:16—I am not ashamed of the gospel....

There is a very good reason why some interviewers may ask, "What are you proud of in your life?" The answer to this question strikes right to the heart of who we are and what we value. It might be our children, the portfolios we've amassed or the church or business we have helped to build. But would we dare to say that we're proud of the gospel of Christ? And if not, do we find ourselves making excuses for it or covering it in our lives, as if it were something of which we are ashamed?

Defensive posturing can arise because we live in a world that has come to marginalize and, in some cases, openly malign the gospel. Some critics view it as a quaint relic of the past, to be acknowledged for its historical contributions, but certainly not taken seriously in these more modern, "enlightened" times. For others, it is the object of frank hostility and invective. Such venom spews forth from the mouths of men who say, "you will lead a better, fuller life if you bet on his [God] not existing, than if you bet on his existing and therefore squander your precious time on worshiping him, sacrificing to him, fighting and dying for him, etc."[285]

Amidst such open critique and misguided thinking, how will I respond to the gospel message within me? Is my tendency towards retreat and apology? Do I put up a defensive justification or public disavowal? Or do I, like Paul, openly declare, "I am not ashamed of the gospel, because it is the power of God for the salvation of everyone who believes"?

There is no denying that to be a disciple of Christ has nearly always meant risking being a deviant in the eyes of the world. I can either respond to this ostracized treatment with inner shame, stifling the power of God within me, and giving the victory to Satan; or, I can choose to take pride in what I know to be true: Jesus Christ has the power to save me and all those who call upon His name.

If I allow myself to be ashamed of the gospel, Jesus says to me, "Whoever is ashamed of me and my words, the Son of Man will be ashamed of them when He comes in His glory..."(Luke 9:26). Am I prepared to be shamed before my Father? But if I have the courage to claim the gospel as truth, to be unashamed of Christ, Jesus will acknowledge me before His Father in heaven (Matt 10:32).

The next time you are tempted to feel ashamed of the gospel, wholeheartedly refuse. Why should you make excuses for "good news"? Own it in your own life and proclaim it in the lives of others.

---

[285] Richard Dawkins, *The God Delusion* (New York: Mariner Books, 2008), 131-132.

December 12

Wash Your Hands

Isaiah 1:15-16—…even if you offer many prayers, I will not listen. Your hands are full of blood; wash and make yourselves clean. Take your deeds out of my sight! Stop doing wrong.…

When we feel as if God is not listening to our prayers, as individuals or as a society, the first thing we must do is look at our hands. If they are covered in the "blood" of our willful disobedience, God *will not listen* to a word we have to say. Even though we offer many prayers in a show of tearful devotion and righteousness, God's ears only hear our persistent spiritual rebellion.

Such was the case with the Israel of Isaiah's time. An endemic hypocrisy plagued the nation. People trampled the courts of God by bringing "meaningless offerings" before Him (Is 1:12-13). There was a multitude of sacrifices, but no rending of the heart, no inner transformation (Is 1:11). There was "the blood of bulls and lambs and goats"(Is 1:11), but a simultaneous willful persistence of evil deeds in the sight of God (Is 2:16).

Are you offering prayers to God with "blood" on your hands? While God may not appear to answer our prayers for a variety of reasons in the time frame we anticipate or in the manner we hope for, the only reason that He does not *listen* to our prayers is when our *hands are full of blood.* If I have not decided to rid myself of my willful disobedience against God, I have no business expecting God to listen to what I have to say. Though I spread out my hands in prayer, He will hide His eyes from me (Is 1:15)—He cannot do otherwise, because the sin I refuse to part with is incompatible with who He is as a holy God.

If my expectation is for God to listen to my prayers, I must wash myself and make myself clean by bringing my bloody hands to Jesus. And "'Though [my] sins be like scarlet, they shall be as white as snow; though they are as red as crimson, they shall be like wool"(Is 1:18). God is all ears to the life that decides to take its evil deeds and place them at the foot of the cross!

Wash your hands, therefore, before you raise them in prayer.

December 13

My Eyes Have Seen

Deuteronomy 4:9—Only be careful, and watch yourselves closely so that you do not forget the things your eyes have seen or let them slip from your heart as long as you live.

The trouble with most of our lives is not that they fail to witness the evidences of God's mercy and justice, or even that we fail to recognize these things as from the Lord. Rather, we too often forget what we have seen. With time we allow these memories to *slip from the heart*. They become crowded out by a constant deluge of new blessings and seemingly more pressing challenges—the here and now. But to forget the things our eyes have seen is to do a grave injustice to the present as well as risk a potentially unnecessary folly in the future. The past is meant to inform them both.

God has ordained every detail of our pasts. What *our eyes have seen* has not been by chance. The Israelites also saw the mercies and the justice of God firsthand in seemingly unforgettable ways. They saw the Red Sea part before them and fire come down on the mountain. They witnessed manna drop from heaven on a daily basis. As for justice, not only did they see the Egyptian army destroyed, but with their "own eyes" they saw "what the Lord did at Baal Peor," as He "destroyed...everyone who followed Baal of Peor..."(Deut 4:3). Why then did they forget? Indeed, why might we? What have we forgotten of God's mercy and justice in our lives?

Whether it is in the grace that has sustained us or the justice that has chastened us, *our eyes have seen* the Lord's hand in our lives. Have we been careful to resist forgetting? Because life moves us on to new territories, just as the Israelites did before us, we must be intentional in our commitment to remember. Perhaps it means writing down what we have seen and returning to it periodically. Or it may mean telling God's story in my life to another. Whatever the method, it must be done.

Are you making a practice of examining your life and praising God for *what your eyes have seen?* The unexamined life is the vulnerable life, and praise best protects the disciple's heart. The heart that clings to what it has learned, watching closely to not forget, will be prepared to "live and...go in and take possession of...[what]...the Lord, the God of your Fathers, is giving you"(Deut 4:1). *What your eyes have seen* is God's gift to help you find your way home. Work to hold on to your memories of God's mercy and justice in your life.

December 14

Temple Resonance

1 Samuel 3:3-4—…and Samuel was lying down in the house of the Lord, where the ark of God was. Then the Lord called Samuel.

> To each of us you reveal yourself differently:
> to the ship as a coastline, to the shore as a ship.[286]
> —Rainer Rilke

God speaks in His house just as surely as we do in ours. When the Lord chose Samuel to be the future leader of His people, His voice reached the listening ears of the boy resting in the Lord's house. And though Eli, the Lord's priest and the more likely recipient of a divine communication, was nearby, only Samuel heard the Lord's voice calling out in the night. Why this exclusivity?

When God speaks, His voice has a specific target. It might be a group. But often it is an individual, like the young Samuel. The particular resonance of that voice is slightly different to every listening ear. Just as every seat in the concert hall experiences the music slightly differently, no two positions in the house of God will hear His voice the same way.

With the coming of Jesus and the indwelling of the Spirit in each of us, this has become all the more pronounced. For, "Don't you know that you yourselves are God's temple and that God's Spirit dwells in your midst?"(1 Cor 3:16). Christ's work put the Temple into our hearts. God's voice now echoes with innumerable variations in that temple of the heart.

Because of this incredible variation, we must be careful in the application of our personal *temple's resonance* upon others. While God's eternal truths never change, how the Lord speaks to us, and through us, will vary. All we can ever know for sure is the voice in our own temple. And even that takes years of training to decipher well. The inconceivable variations of His voice makes it possible to reach into the recesses of the most stubborn and inaccessible places in you and me.

So the next time you become aware of God speaking in a voice you cannot hear or do not recognize, remember Eli. He did not doubt the voice Samuel heard, even though he could not hear it. Rather, he believed: "He is the Lord; let Him do what is good in His eyes"(1 Sam 3:18). Have you been this gracious in your interactions with others? If God has spoken into the temple of another person in your life, have you listened as Eli did? Instead of resisting the nonconformity of God's voice, embrace its variegated beauty. His Spirit will do what is "good in His eyes."

---

[286] Rainer Rilke, *Book of Hours: Love Poems to God* (New York: Riverhead Books, 2005), 177.

December 15

Wholly, Holy His

Exodus 4:24—At a lodging place on the way, the Lord met Moses and was about to kill him.

Nothing would appear more nonsensical than the Lord's killing of the very man He had just so intentionally chosen to deliver His people from the Egyptians. And yet, this is exactly what the Lord intended to do when He came to Moses on the way to Egypt. Only the circumcision of Zipporah's son and the foreskin of obedience upon the feet of Moses was enough to stop the hand of the Lord's anger—"Surely you are a bridegroom of blood to me..."(Ex 4:25).

God had raised Moses up for this very moment of return to Egypt. The Lord trained him in Egypt, refined him in the desert, and blessed him with the staff of God's almighty power. But though chosen to do God's work, Moses, like us, was still a sinner. He was about to return to Egypt as God's chosen instrument of redemption, yet there was blatant disobedience in his life—an uncircumcised son. God would not tolerate it.

We might not have the calling of Moses. But, if we belong to Christ, we are His chosen people. We, like Moses, are His emissaries to a nation in spiritual slavery. For this reason, God will not tolerate willful disobedience in our lives any more than He did in the life of Moses. To do God's work, whether in the delivering of an entire nation from slavery or to daily witness to our co-workers, we must live lives of obedience. Had Moses arrived in Egypt with an uncircumcised son, he would have lost the respect of the elders. Circumcision was a sign of covenantal relationship with the Lord. Without circumcision in his very own son, Moses's credibility as God's chosen leader would have been compromised by an obvious lack of obedience.

As God's representative in your world of influence, is your life hiding some secret disobedience that discredits God in the eyes of others? Do you recognize that God's perceived credibility in the eyes of unbelievers is, rightly or wrongly, largely dependent upon His manifestation in your life and the lives of other believers? We are called to "shine like stars in the universe..."(Phil 2:15). But we will not glow with His radiance unless our lives are "blameless and pure...without fault in a crooked and depraved generation"(Phil 2:15). Let us examine our lives today and circumcise them before God must meet us at some resting place in our journeys of faith. He wants us to be *wholly, holy His.*

December 16

Weeping at His Feet

Luke 7:38—...and as she stood behind Him at His feet weeping, she began to wet His feet with her tears.

Have you dared to approach Jesus with your tears? Have you stood before Him and wet His feet with your pain and shame? The woman who "had lived a sinful life in that town" courageously brought her alabaster jar of perfume and her heavy heart before Jesus (Luke 7:37). She didn't know if she would be received in the Pharisee's house with overtures of grace or rejected as "a sinner." And yet, she chose to come just as she was to worship at the feet of Jesus. She "loved much"(Luke 7:47). To the Pharisees she was a pariah. To Jesus she was an exemplar of humility.

All too often we sit down at the table with the Pharisees believing we are good, or at least better than most, and certainly not a "sinner" like her. But the truth is that we have no right to sit at the table with Jesus until we come to Him as the woman came—wetting His feet with our tears. As long as we are comparing ourselves to others and evaluating our lives against the "sinners" around us, we are blind to who we are. The "sinful woman" was the only person in the presence of Jesus who understood His goodness and her own sinfulness well enough to weep.

Without our tears that wet the feet of Jesus we likely have no conception of the sin within us. Before a holy God, none of our lives, if honestly scrutinized, can do anything but induce weeping.

Have you wept at the feet of Jesus? Until we have the courage to see ourselves with the clarity of the sinful woman, we will never truly know the power that says, "Your faith has healed you; go in peace"(Luke 7:50). As Henri Nouwen says, "The invitation of Christ is the invitation to move out of the house of fear and into the house of love: to move away out of that place of imprisonment into a place of freedom."[287] To grab hold of this freedom, we must not stifle our tears. We must look deeply and honestly into our hearts. If we have never wept at the feet of Jesus, we've never really seen ourselves accurately.

Pray that the Spirit gives you the courage to come before Jesus, just as you are, to wet His feet with your tears. Until you are *weeping at his feet*, you will never find the healing you so desperately desire.

---

[287] Henri Nouwen, *The Road to Peace* in *The Only Necessary Thing*, ed. Wendy Wilson Greer (New York: The Crossroad Publishing Company, 2015), 75.

December 17

Personal Ascendency

Judges 17:6—In those days Israel had no king; everyone did as he saw fit.

After the death of Joshua, there arose in Israel a time of spiritual lawlessness. With the exception of periodic judges whom God raised up to deliver the people from their oppressors, there was no central leadership, and *everyone did as he saw fit*. This personal interpretation even crept into the practice of worship. The idolatry of the surrounding nations infiltrated the people's syncretic thinking—"I solemnly consecrate my silver to the Lord for my son to make a carved image and a cast idol"(Judg 17:3). Moral relativism reigned—*Israel had no king*.

Do you find yourself living now in a similar "time of judges"? Does it seem to be an age governed more by moral lawlessness and vigilantes wielding a personal relativism rather than a unified and codified ethic? Is your life lived under the rule of a King?

The prevailing doctrine of today is little different than the time of the judges—complete and total personal autonomy is celebrated and vigorously defended. Who are you to tell me how to live my life? Rather than living by the standards of the law of God, the contemporary world has championed individual morality. It increasingly eschews absolutes.

So it was in the days of the judges. Though God said to His people, "You shall not make for yourself an idol in the form of anything"(Ex 20:4), a man named Micah creates an idol in the name of God. He even hires a priest to serve in the shadow of this graven image and seemingly convinces himself "that the Lord will be good to me since this Levite has become my priest"(Judg 17:13).

Have I been guilty of a similar spiritual blindness and deluded syncretism in my own life? Does Micah's folly of idol worship continue to be my own? Am I simply trying to incorporate God into my personalized "religion," placing Him on the shelf with all the other idols of my life?

Because the world has largely rejected God as King, as disciples we must rebuke the temptation to allow the spiritual creep of *personal ascendency* in our hearts. While the world preaches "do what is right for you," we must decide to do what God says is right for Him, regardless of what it means for us. Although we are living in a lawless time of "judges," a time where personal kingship is the reigning delusion, we must decide to remember His Word: "God is the King of all the earth"(Ps 47:7).

Ask the Father's forgiveness today for any effort you have made to be king of your own life. Pray that the Spirit helps you to resist the temptation to create your own gods.

December 18

Overcomers

Luke 10:19—I have given you authority…to overcome all the power of the enemy; nothing will harm you.

> …those who see God have *overcome* the world.[288]
> —Soren Kierkegaard

As a disciple of Jesus, confrontation with the enemy is inevitable. If he is not actively warring against us, it may reveal our lack of true discipleship. We might question what side of the war we are on. At first, this war will be personal—the exorcism of our inner demons like pride, anxiety, doubt and other personal weaknesses. Then, freed by Christ to do the work of the Spirit, the war will become more global. We will be called to move into the lives of others through the battles of intercessory prayer. In both cases, we "*overcome* the world" because we are "born of God" and believe "that Jesus is the Son of God"(1 John 5:4-5).

The early disciples returned to Jesus from their initial skirmishes against the enemy filled with joy. They said, "Lord, even the demons submit to us in your name"(Luke 10:17). Jesus replied, *"I have given you authority to trample on snakes and scorpions and to overcome all the power of the enemy; nothing will harm you"*(Luke 10:19). Because Christ has "overcome the world"(John 16:33), as His disciples we take on the mantle of His power. Paul reminds us, "If God is for us, who can be against us?"(Rom 8:31). As a result, we are not called to quiver in fear before the enemy, but to know that "we are more than conquerors through Him who loves us"(Rom 8:37). When we are attacked, we stand in the name of Jesus. Rebuking the devil in Christ's name, we will force the enemy to flee from us (James 4:7).

Perhaps you would rather not believe in the reality of an enemy. But be careful not to be deceived into thinking he does not exist or is not interested in your life. Such thinking merely proves that you are in the deceiver's hands already. His most potent weapon against you is agnostic thinking. In the name of Jesus, you must cast it out into the darkness.

But the disciple is not called to live a defensive existence only. In Jesus Christ, we have been sent out into the world, albeit "like lambs among wolves"(Luke 10:3). We are, however, not without a shepherd. The invocation of His name alone scatters the pack of snarling wolves and allows us to *overcome* the enemy. In our ongoing battles against him, let us never forget that Christ *has given us authority…to overcome all the power of the enemy!* We are *overcomers!*

---

[288] Soren Kierkegaard, *Spiritual Writings* (New York: HarperPerennial, 2010), 77.

December 19

Nothing Undone

Joshua 11:15—…he left nothing undone of all the Lord commanded….

Trouble can arise when we leave things undone. Relationships can be broken, business deals can fall through, and lives can be lost or mangled beyond recognition. Follow-through and completion are, perhaps, more nebulous, but no less important, when it comes to our spiritual lives. In the realm of the unseen, the work of God is often left undone due to our casual indifference or willful neglect. Loose ends remain. We may twist ourselves into spiritual pretzels trying to explain why we haven't finished the work, rather than just doing what God has commanded.

Joshua was a servant of the Lord who refused to leave God's work undone. What God commanded through Moses, Joshua executed with precision and finality. Joshua had witnessed Israel's disobedience on the edge of the Promised Land. When the Lord commanded Israel to go forward and conquer, Israel hesitated. In fear and doubt incited by reports of walled cities populated by giants, Israel decided to leave the work of God undone—a decision that led to their undoing. God's anger burned against this disobedient generation, and they were driven into the desert to die. Not one of those who left the work of God undone lived to see the blessings of the Lord. Only Caleb and Joshua entered the Promised Land.

What has God commanded of you? Is there a Kingdom work you have neglected that has loose ends waiting to trip you up? You may not be a Joshua, standing on the edge of a national conquest God has commanded. But God does command you, like Joshua, to be strong and courageous, without terror or discouragement in the work He has called you to (Josh 1:9). More often than not, "the best results are obtained by people who work quietly away at limited objectives…[as the]…art of life consists in tackling each immediate evil as well as we can."[289] In God's work, you are to be a spiritual warrior who wins one battle at a time, a weaver who incorporates every single thread, and a cook who misses no ingredient, until the work is finished.

What God commands you to do, do with completion. Choose not to allow fear and doubt, discouragement and exhaustion to turn you back from your Kingdom assignment. Rather, look to God and "Cast all your anxiety on Him because He cares for you"(1 Peter 5:7). Decide to persist and God will provide. Leave *nothing undone!*

---

[289] C.S. Lewis, *The Weight of Glory* (New York: HarperCollins, 2001), 79.

December 20

Walls

Psalm 89:40—You have broken through all his walls and reduced his strongholds to ruins.

There is an inherent danger in the blessings and promises of God in our lives. It has, of course, nothing to do with God, and everything to do with us. But the danger is this: God's goodness can be so good that we feel freed and empowered to erect *walls* of personal and false security.

David was the victim of such thinking. He began his race well. He started with a clear understanding of his place in the service of a God who said, "'I have exalted a young man from among the people. I have found David my servant; with sacred oil I have anointed him'"(Ps 89:19-20).

But the blessings of God, the triumphs in war and the promises of dynastic perpetuity, would soon lead David to a reckless sense of personal invincibility and moral blindness. What was once the shepherd boy who approached Goliath in the strength of the Lord, became a man plagued with a dangerous, exceptional thinking. He was God's anointed and knew it. He was the favored son of Israel, the conquering king. Why shouldn't he have the beautiful Bathsheba? What is the life of one Uriah in the pleasure of a king? Why not take a census of his army's strength?

David allowed the blessings of God to give room for building *walls* against the prodding of the Spirit in his life. But God loved David so much that the Lord repeatedly chastened him. Having *broken through his walls, and reduced his strongholds to ruins,* God refused to let David perish in his sin.

Have you allowed your position as a child of God to permit the construction of *walls* around your moral consciousness? Have you forgotten: "God is no acceptor of persons..."?[290] We might be the anointed of God, or leading as priests, CEO's, presidents or generals. But underneath it all, we will always remain the simple shepherd boy that God called to be a *servant.* If we allow ourselves to think differently, we build *walls* of exclusive thinking. We become like the Pharisees: blind and dangerous to the Kingdom. Behind these *walls*, the best we can hope for is an act of destruction in our lives—God's smashing of our fortifications in hopes of redeeming us for His purposes.

Never allow the blessings of God to give you liberty to build *walls*. Don't require God to make a choice between reducing your "strongholds to ruins" or letting you perish within the prison you have constructed for yourself.

---

[290] C.S. Lewis, *The Weight of Glory* (New York: HarperCollins, 2001), 167.

December 21

Pain that Deafens

Exodus 6:9—…but they did not listen to him because of their discouragement and cruel bondage.

Unless your life has been graced with some incredible hardship or deep pain that has educated you in empathy, you may find it difficult to understand the apparent deafness with which others respond to your overtures of hope and kindness in the midst of their pain. It is easy to think they are not listening. But can any of us really know the depth of another's bondage or the expanse of their discouragement?

The people of Israel who suffered in the back-breaking slavery of Egypt had hearts deafened by pain. When God called Moses to speak to these weary hearts, they *did not listen to him because of their discouragement and cruel bondage.* Though pain was "God's megaphone"[291] in their lives, they were not listening. The depth of their hurt was too great and the exhaustion of their bodies and minds too profound for the words of God's servant to touch them. Still, Moses did not give up. And most importantly, God did not abandon His hurting and disillusioned people.

When you, or someone you love, find yourself deafened to the promises of God by the pain of life, remember how much God loves you. His love "always protects, always trusts, always hopes, always perseveres"(1 Cor 13:7). He will never give up on you! If you are enslaved to the hardships of your life, know that He will "free you from being slaves to them…and will redeem you with an outstretched arm and mighty acts…"(Ex 6:6). He will be your strength as He leads you to the fulfillment of His promises.

If you are ministering to someone who has withdrawn into their hardened shell, persist in love, just as Christ has always persisted in His love of you. Love the discouraged as God loves you, always hoping, always persevering. Be gentle in your understanding of the pain that isolates and deafens them to your overtures, but forceful in your execution of grace, love and mercy upon the darkness that binds them. Always remember that there is no discouragement God cannot redeem and no bondage He cannot extricate us from. Let God be the God of deliverance in your life and all those hurting hearts He brings before you, even when the *pain deafens.*

---

[291] C.S. Lewis, *The Problem of Pain* (New York: HarperCollins, 2001), 93.

December 22

Redefining Me

Malachi 2:17—You have wearied the Lord with your words....By saying, "All who do evil are good in the eyes of the Lord, and He is pleased with them"....

Parents know all too well the exhaustion of dealing with children who don't like the rules and try, sometimes desperately, to modify them according to some particular objective. They childishly attempt to redefine reality for personal pleasure or gain. But are we, in our dealings with our Father in heaven, really any different than our sometimes willful children? Malachi would say, "No," for *we have wearied the Lord with [our] words.* I may talk circles around reality, hoping that the more words I use to explain myself will, in some way, help to redefine the truths inherent in who I am. But in the end, the only person fooled is me. Micah reminds us: "He has showed you, O man, what is good"(Micah 6:8). Jesus says, "No one is good—except God alone"(Mark 10:18).

And yet, we don't like this truth. We no more want to subject ourselves to God's definitions and terms of engagement than the children we raise always want to obey us and live under our definitions of reality. So we spend our lives in sometimes subtle, but persistent, efforts to redefine ourselves. When will we understand that these efforts push us away from the very Father who wants to draw us near?

We have been warned—"Woe to those who call evil good and good evil, who put darkness for light and light for darkness, who put bitter for sweet and sweet for bitter"(Is 5:20). As surely as our eyes know the difference between light and dark and our tongues between bitter and sweet, our hearts know good from evil. But we allow ourselves to mix the flavors of the soul and blend the distinctions of the spiritual tongue. I may like the taste of what I create, but it doesn't mean God does. And God's palate is the only palate that matters.

I must be aware of my daily propensity to redefine the reality of my soul, for "the reality...is found in Christ"(Col 2:17). I should not weary God with my efforts to mask my bitter with a pinch of sweet. Rather, I am better off owning my bitterness, claiming the pungent flavor for what it is, and giving it to Him. Just as He knows bitter, He knows evil, and He is able to transform it and make it delightfully new. When I stop trying to redefine me, I cease being a petulant child and become a redeemed man or woman able to say, "How sweet are your words to my taste, sweeter than honey to my mouth"(Ps 119:103).

December 23

The Constant Dripping

Genesis 45:24—Then he sent his brothers away, and as they were leaving he said, "Don't quarrel on the way!"

The sons of Jacob have just been reunited with their long lost brother, Joseph. They have been forgiven for selling him into slavery; they have even had their bellies filled and been given the promise of a future filled with provision. And yet, as Joseph sends them back to his father Jacob, the words they are given are not those of happiness or praise. Rather, they are an exhortation against the baser nature—*don't quarrel on the way!*

Israel's sons had every reason to be filled with joy. The reception of Joseph and the blessing of God through Joseph's hands ought to have filled them with exuberant thanks. The journey back to Canaan should have been decorated with a recounting of God's goodness and mercies, His triumphs in the life of Joseph, and His shepherding of the future. Why then does Joseph warn his brothers not to quarrel?

The answer is in you and me. Despite lives filled with a richness and abundance that even Joseph could never have imagined, we all too often fill the air around us with complaining, quarreling, and bickering. We are told that "It is to a man's honor to avoid strife, but every fool is quick to quarrel"(Prov 20:3). Still we, like Joseph's brothers, play the fool. We point fingers and say, "Didn't I tell you…(Gen 42:22)? We need no reminding that a quarrelsome spirit is "like a *constant dripping*," and makes others prefer to "live in a desert" alone or "on a corner of a roof," rather than to share our company (Prov 19:13, 21:19, 25:24). But because of the sin in us and, in Joseph's case, the selfishness and jealousy that led his brothers to sell him into slavery, we fall into quarreling when we should be giving thanks.

Is your life guilty of a *constant dripping*? In the balance of things, are you more prone to complain, quarrel, and bicker than you are to give thanks and rejoice in the Lord? The next time you are tempted to quarrel with God or another man or woman in your life, remember the exhortation of Joseph. You have been commanded—"Don't have anything to do with foolish and stupid arguments, because you know they produce quarrels"(2 Tim 2:23). For the "Lord's servant must not quarrel; instead he must be kind to everyone, able to teach, not resentful"(2 Tim 2:24). Though it is sometimes difficult, we must make our heavenward journey one of thanks, not quarreling. Let us remember the goodness of God!

The Not So Improbable Victory

1 Samuel 17:39—David fastened on his sword over the tunic and tried walking around, because he was not used to them. "I can't go in these," he said to Saul, "because I am not used to them."

> ...the phrase "David and Goliath" has come to be embedded in our language—as a metaphor for improbable victory. And the problem... is that almost everything about it is wrong.[292] —Malcolm Gladwell

When the Philistine hero, Goliath, steps forward before the ranks of Israel, the Israelites were "dismayed and terrified"(1 Sam 17:11). What they saw was an enemy giant. What they did not see was the truth: There is no enemy greater than Almighty God.

But, David saw clearly. As a result, he says, "Let no one lose heart on account of this Philistine; your servant will go and fight him"(17:32). David's confidence was not in his strength, speed, or accuracy as a "projectile warrior."[293] While his training as a shepherd had endowed him with all these things, David understood that the battle belonged to God. When Saul dresses David in armor and equips him with his sword, David has the wisdom of the Spirit to be true to who God made him to be: a shepherd warrior, a "servant" of God. David steps forward in his pastural clothes, armed with smooth stones, a sling, and the power of the Lord.

In light of this divine strength, framing David's advance against Goliath as an underdog before a superior force misconstrues God's story. David's victory over the Philistine was anything but improbable. It was a certainty—God was fighting for him. David says, "I come against you [Goliath] in the name of the Lord Almighty, the God of the armies of Israel....This day the Lord will hand you over to me...(17:45-46).

Have you approached the "giants" in your life with the confidence of David? As disciples, we too often respond like the Israelites. Instead of viewing our enemies as David did, we quickly forget that "Giants are not what we think they are. The same qualities that appear to give them strength are often the source of great weakness."[294] The arrogant self-confidence that stands against God is the very "strength" that will give God's enemies into our hands. In Christ, you are never an underdog! Instead of walking into battle in clothes that don't fit, advance against the enemy in the power of the God within you. Victory is the Lord's (17:47)!

---

[292] Malcolm Gladwell, *David and Goliath* (New York: Little, Brown and Company, 2013), 8-9.
[293] Ibid, 11.
[294] Ibid, 6.

December 25

He Took on Flesh

Matthew 1:1—A record of the genealogy of Jesus Christ, son of David, the son of Abraham....

If you were ever in doubt as to God's ability to redeem the historical threads of your life, you need look no further than the genealogy of Jesus of Nazareth. When Jesus decided to leave His heavenly throne for the salvation of humanity, He chose to condescend into the womb of a woman. He could have chosen any woman, betrothed or not to any man. But He chose Mary. He chose Joseph. He chose a family in the Davidic line of kings. Knowing His plan from the beginning, Jesus could have neatly arranged a genealogy fitting for a heavenly king, one packed with holy and "respectable" lives. But He didn't; and He didn't for a reason.

When we read Matthew's genealogy of Jesus, we see the coalescence of golden palaces with the gutters of the red light district. We see the faith of a man that helped found a nation (Abraham) and the idolatry of another (Ahaz) that helped to exile it. There is Perez, the son of incest and Rahab the prostitute of the street. David is the conflicted king whose honor was tarnished by adultery and murder. There is the profligate Solomon and his hundreds of foreign wives. And then Manasseh, the ruler who "sacrificed his sons in the fire" and "practiced sorcery, divination, and witchcraft..."(2 Chron 33:6).

Perhaps your family tree is as diverse as Jesus's. But more likely, it is not. More likely, it is composed of everyday sinners who didn't make the history books. God not only decided to have His Son born into a family of relative infamy, but He orchestrated a genealogy filled with some of the most heinous acts known to man. Christ took on the flesh of kings and carpenters alike—the flesh of sinners. When He did, He did so with the full intention that this lineage of sin might be broken in His body.

Christ broke the bread of His body and gave it to us to eat as a New Covenant and a sign that our bondage to the generations of sin within us has been broken, once and for all. Jesus said, "It is not the healthy who need a doctor, but the sick"(Luke 5:31). When Jesus took on flesh, He took on the "sickness" of the heredity of sin in its most subtle and atrocious forms. He nailed it to the cross; He broke it in His body; He conquered it when He rose from the grave.

There is no story too terrible for Jesus to redeem, no familial sin too heinous to forgive in the body and blood of Christ. Your lineage of sin has been broken if you "believe in your heart that God raised Him from the dead" and "declare with your mouth that Jesus is Lord"(Rom 10:9). This hope is the true gift of Christ's birth!

December 26

Four Seasons

2 Timothy 4:2—Preach the word; be prepared in season and out of season....

Do you love Jesus? If the answer is "Yes!" then do you talk about Him? One of the ways we will know we love Christ is how often we talk about Him. This exuberant love is evident in one of the Apostle Peter's first public addresses. He says, "we cannot help speaking about what we have seen and heard"(Act 4:20). This same Peter, who denied Jesus three times, is the man who Jesus reinstated with the question—"do you truly love me...?"(John 21:15). Peter responds three times: "'Yes, Lord, you know that I love you'"(21:16). And it is this love that couldn't keep from preaching.

Are you, like Peter, preaching the gospel of Christ in your life? God may not have placed you in a pulpit, but He wants you to be a preacher, nonetheless. If Jesus was sent to "preach good news to the poor"(Is 61:1), then, as His disciples, we must do the same, *in season and out of season.* We must be "prepared to give an answer to everyone who asks [us] to give the reason for the hope that [we] have"(1 Peter 3:15).

As in most communication, the difference between effective and ineffective "preaching" often comes down to the delivery. The message speaks for itself, but we can do a great deal of damage to that message by delivering it poorly or hypocritically. When we preach, we are to do it with "gentleness and respect" and with "great patience and careful instruction," not with a "high and mighty," "holier than thou" tone (1 Peter 3:15; 2 Tim 4:2). As followers of Christ, our lives must "preach the gospel"(Mark 16:15). And if our lives do not testify in this way, we shall be shamed as the very "stones will cry out" around us (Luke 19:40). God's gospel must be preached either way, for "How, then, can they call on the One they have not believed in? And how can they believe in the One of whom they have not heard?"(Rom 10:14).

If you are not preaching the good news with your life, consider whether you really love the Lord. Jesus asked Peter three times—"Do you love me?" How many times must He ask you? When you are in love with Christ, nothing will please you more than to speak about Him. And, as you tell of the One you love, you will know just how "'beautiful are the feet of those who bring good news'" in the eyes of the Lord (Rom 10:15).

Be a lover of Christ who preaches the gospel *in season and out of season,* in all things, at all times, with the grace and love of the Spirit.

Preach the Word!

December 27

Your Price

Numbers 22:18—Even if Balak gave me his palace filled with silver and gold, I could not do anything great or small to go beyond the command of the Lord my God.

> Everyone has a price, the important thing is to find out what it is.
> —Pablo Escobar

When Satan looks at your life he is constantly calculating *"your price."* What will it take to buy your soul? How far will he have to go before he gets you to say, "Know that your words have won me at last... Yet not your words alone, but mine own fantasy..."?[295] Have you considered your price? For what would you be tempted to *"go beyond the command of the Lord..."*? Or has Christ's blood made your soul priceless?

King Balak of Moab tried to buy Balaam's favor for divination. He wanted Balaam to call down curses on the Israelites. But Balaam told the messengers of Balak that even a palace filled with silver and gold would not entice him to deviate from what the Lord revealed to him. Balaam knew God well enough to know that disobedience to the Lord had consequences. Like Balaam, Satan knows your life and mine, backwards and forwards. He knows that "no fool ever made a bargain for his soul with the devil: the fool is too much of a fool, or the devil too much of a devil...."[296] So he studies each us to know our tastes and preferences, our likes and dislikes, our Achilles' heel. He may come at us with wealth like Balak's, a position of power, the beauty of a woman, or something much more subtle—our reputation or the exposure of our fears. Whatever it is, he will search it out. And when he comes, he will say, as the king to Balaam, "Am I really not able to reward you?"(Num 22:37).

You must know yourself well enough to recognize your "even if" when it is offered. Know your price, and ask the Spirit to help you to resist succumbing to it. For, "if you know yourself and know your enemy," then by God's grace, "you will gain victory a hundred times out of a hundred."[297] When Satan comes to entice you with his glittering offer, you will be ready to say, as Balaam did to the messengers of the king, *"I could not do anything great or small to go beyond the command of the Lord...."*

Be bound in obedience and sustained by God's grace. Be priceless in Christ.

---

[295] Christopher Marlowe, *The Tragical History of Doctor Faustus* in *The Norton Anthology of English Literature,* ed. M.H. Abrams (New York: W.W. Norton & Company, 1993), 772.

[296] Joseph Conrad, *The Heart of Darkness* in *Modern British Literature,* ed. Frank Kermode and Hollander (New York: Oxford University Press, 1973), 148.

[297] Sun Tzu, *The Art of War* (New York: Chartwell Books, 2012), 21.

December 28

For the Joy of Obeying

John 14:15—If you love me, you will obey what I command.

Love is as multi-faceted and richly complex as the God who created it and embodies it, for "God is love"(1 John 4:8). But, how do we hope to love a God who is Love itself? We begin with a fixed understanding that "We love because He first loved us"(1 John 4:19). Because His love reaches to us and through us, we can love Him and others in return. How will this love manifest itself in us? Jesus says, *"If you love me, you will obey what I command."*

Obedience demonstrates love because it necessitates submission. It requires a capitulation of self. Often, this act of obeying will not be a difficult task. It might very well meet our perceived needs and make sense in every possible way. But obedience of this sort is not the test of love.

True obedience evidences itself when love requires us to do something that seems nonsensical, unduly difficult, or frankly ridiculous. When this call to obedience comes, then, and only then, do we begin to remotely understand the Christ who knelt in the Garden of Gethsemane. We cannot know the power of love that led Him to say, "not my will, but yours be done"(Luke 22:42), until we too have to decide to *obey* at great personal cost.

C.S. Lewis made this point exceedingly clear in his temptation scene in *Perelandra*. He reminds us that if obedience in our lives is always reasonable and pleasing, "What you call obeying Him [God] is but doing what seems good in your own eyes also." Lewis continues: "Is love content with that? You do them…because they are His will, but not only because they are His will. Where can you taste the joy of obeying unless He bids you do something for which His bidding is the only reason?"[298]

If I claim to love God and live for Christ, I must ask myself, "When was the last time I obeyed Jesus simply to *obey*?" Do I love Christ enough to *obey* even when it seems ridiculous to do so? In love, Jesus obeyed His Father to the death. Will I do the same?

Do you hunger for the joy of obedience that lies beyond the realm of the reasonable? That is the land of love. That is the obedience that brings a smile to our Father's face. Pray that the Spirit helps you find the *joy of obeying*.

---

[298] C.S. Lewis, *Perelandra* in *The Space Trilogy* (London: HarperCollins, 2013), 249.

Greater than Jonah

Matthew 12:41—The men of Nineveh will stand up at the judgement with this generation and condemn it; for they repented at the preaching of Jonah, and now one greater than Jonah is here.

Have you found yourself demanding signs from God, evidences of His power and purpose in your life? Have you said, along with the Pharisees, "Teacher, we want to see a miraculous sign from you"(Matt 12:38)? Every time we demand a sign from Jesus, we demonstrate our disbelief. We prove to God what He already knows—just how weak our faith is. And, in doing so, we sadden the heart of our Father.

It is true that sometimes God does humor our questioning incredulity. He altered the dew on Gideon's fleece and He reversed the shadow's progression for a doubting Hezekiah (Judg 6; Is 38:8). Perhaps God has graced your disbelief with such a sign. But if He has, He did not do so with joy. Such demonstrations bring the Father no pleasure. He would rather we never asked for a sign. His delight is in "those who have not seen and yet have believed"(John 20:29).

It is the weakness of our faith that demands demonstrations of God's power. Instead of taking Him at His word, instead of saying, "I will trust and not be afraid"(Is 12:2), we demand proofs to bolster our disbelief. When we do so, Jesus tells us to remember the men of Nineveh, the 120,000 strong, who repented and believed without a sign and only on the word of one of God's most reluctant prophets. Jesus reminds us that the Ninevites will *stand up in judgement* against those who do not believe in Christ; for the preaching of Jonah was enough to turn their hearts, but this generation fails to believe despite the preaching of God Himself.

We are, today, without excuse. The script has been revealed and the protagonist has walked among us, done His work, left His Spirit, and promised to return. To ask for a sign amidst such evidence is to reject God. And while He may answer a specific request for a sign in our lives as He did for Gideon and Hezekiah before us, it may grieve Him to do so.

The next time you find yourself asking God for a sign, remember the men of Nineveh. Consider all those who have gone before you who chose to believe God's word with far less proofs and no single "miracle." Think about the multitudes who can, and will, stand up in judgement and condemn all those who have failed to believe the insurmountable evidence. Though we cannot see them, we are surrounded by witnesses. They testify to the truth that someone greater than Jonah has come and walked among us. Let us stop demanding signs and start believing what has already been revealed.

December 30

Fan the Fire

2 Timothy 1:6—...fan into flame the gift of God....

Fire must breathe. If you suffocate it, it will die. If you fan it, it will flame. If you pump the bellows, it will burn white hot. There is a fire in each of us because we were created in God's image, and God is a "consuming fire"(Heb 12:29). The question becomes: what is the temperature of your fire?

Paul exhorts Timothy to *fan into flame the gift of God* within him. Paul wants Timothy's spiritual life to burn with intensity and power, the "spirit of power"(Tim 1:7) that comes from God Himself. Your spiritual fire is no different than any physical fire—it requires a *fuel*, a *spark*, a continued *breath*, and *careful tending*. The result—combustion and unparalleled power.

The *fuel* is the gift of God within you, however God, in His providence, has chosen to bestow that gift from the dawn of creation. It might be a gift of healing power, prophecy, wisdom or knowledge, faith or service (1 Cor 12:5-10). Whatever the gift, it must be maintained by the reading of His Word and by a constant communion with the Giver Himself through the discipline of prayer. The *spark* is the moment of rebirth, a God-given gift of ignition bestowed upon you in His grace (John 3:7). You cannot ignite it. Only God can make it begin. The *breath* is the Spirit of God Himself which must blow across your flame to keep it hot and burning brightly, for the "breath of the Almighty gives me life"(Job 33:4). Without the Spirit, the fire is lifeless.

When we become spiritually lazy and do not *carefully tend* our fire with the disciplines of faith, it will slowly die. An untended flame will dwindle. If we cover it, close our windows and vents, and keep it hidden from the *breath* of God, it will cool to the temperature of death. Therefore, let our hearts be open to the Spirit, that there might be a constant influx of His life-giving air. Nothing would please the Spirit more than to invigorate our fire as we carefully tend to it.

Pray for a flame that speaks His Word (Jer 23:29). Ask for a light that leads His people (Ex 13:21) and illumines the night (Ps 105:39). Plead for an inferno that leaves men in awe of His marvelous power (Ex 3:3). Seek a holy fire that reminds you, and everyone who comes across your life, that one day the Ancient of Days will take His seat on a throne "flaming with fire...it's wheels all ablaze. A river of fire...flowing, coming out before Him"(Dan 7:9-10). Fan your flame into the eternal fire—for this very purpose you were made.

December 31

The Power of Faith

Matthew 9:29—Then He touched their eyes and said, "According to your faith it will be done to you."

When we truly have an encounter with Jesus, when we meet Him "face to face," we are asked the very question posed to the blind men seeking sight: "Do you believe that I am able to do this?"(Matt 9:28). Whether we are healed or not as a result of our encounter with Christ depends not upon the ability of Jesus, but upon the faith we place in Him —*according to your faith it will be done.*

Have you, like the blind men, decided in your heart that Jesus is able to heal you? We are called to "live by faith, not by sight"(2 Cor 5:7). Are you doing so? "Now faith is being sure of what we hope for and certain of what we do not see"(Heb 11:1). Is your spiritual life marked by a sureness of hope and a certainty of the unseen? Or are you still doubting? Are you allowing your skeptical incredulity to hinder the work of God in your life? The blind men could not see Jesus standing before them in the flesh, but they saw Him with the eyes of faith. They were sure of what they hoped for and certain of the One they could not see. *According to their faith,* they were healed.

Jesus tells us that if we "have faith as small as a mustard seed" we can move mountains (Matt 17:20)—nothing will be impossible for us. With this promise in mind, will you choose to have the confident hope of the bleeding woman who pushes through the crowd saying, "If only I touch His cloak, I will be healed"(Matt 9:21)? When Jesus approaches you and asks, "Do you believe that I am able to do this?"(Matt 9:28), will you say with conviction and enthusiasm, "Yes, Lord!"?

There is no infirmity of the body, no illness of the heart or sickness of the soul that Jesus cannot heal with a simple word or a gentle touch. Whether you are healed or not depends *not* upon the ability of Christ, but rather the providential plans of God and your faith in Him. According to His glory and the measure of trust you put in Him, will it be done to you.

Commit to be a "believer"—a blind man who chooses to see or a mother who watches her daughter be healed (Mark 10:52; Matt 15:28). If you long to hear Jesus say to you, "your faith has healed you"(Matt 9:22), resolve that your thinking will be *more of Him and less of you,* and you will see His power working in your life.

ABOUT THE AUTHOR

Dr. Eubanks is blessed to be a child of God who has become a disciple of Christ. His mission field is currently medicine, where he is an Associate Professor of Orthopaedic Surgery at Case Western Reserve University School of Medicine and the Chief of Spine Surgery at University Hospitals Ahuja Medical Center. He is the author of *Rotations: A Medical Student's Clinical Experience*, over 20 peer-reviewed scientific publications, multiple textbook chapters and editorials, and poetry appearing in journals such as *JAMA*, *The Annals of Internal Medicine*, *Tar River Poetry*, and more. He lives outside of Cleveland, Ohio.

Made in United States
North Haven, CT
05 August 2024